Strategic Management of Technological Innovation

Strategic Management of Technological Innovation

Melissa A. Schilling
New York University

McGraw-Hill
Irwin

Boston   Burr Ridge, IL   Dubuque, IA   Madison, WI   New York   San Francisco   St. Louis Bangkok
Bogotá   Caracas   Kuala Lumpur   Lisbon   London   Madrid   Mexico City   Milan   Montreal
New Delhi   Santiago   Seoul   Singapore   Sydney   Taipei   Toronto

**McGraw-Hill
Irwin**

STRATEGIC MANAGEMENT OF TECHNOLOGICAL INNOVATION

Published by McGraw-Hill/Irwin, a business unit of The McGraw-Hill Companies, Inc., 1221 Avenue of the Americas, New York, NY 10020. Copyright © 2005 by The McGraw-Hill Companies, Inc.

Some ancillaries, including electronic and print components, may not be available to customers outside the United States.

This book is printed on acid-free paper.

1 2 3 4 5 6 7 8 9 0 DOC/DOC 0 9 8 7 6 5 4

ISBN   0-07-111195-6

About the Author

Melissa A. Schilling, Ph.D.

Melissa A. Schilling is an associate professor of management at the Stern School of Business, New York University. Professor Schilling earned a B.S. in business from the University of Colorado in 1990 and a Ph.D. in strategic management from the University of Washington in 1997. She worked as an assistant professor for Boston University for four years before joining Stern. She recently won a National Science Foundation Early CAREER award that includes a grant to support her research for the next five years. She also won the Broderick prize for research while working at Boston University.

Professor Schilling's research focuses on technological innovation and knowledge creation. She has studied how firm's fight technology standards battles, and how they utilize collaboration, protection, and timing of entry strategies. She also studies how product designs and organizational structures migrate toward or away from increasing modularity. Her most recent work focuses on knowledge creation, including how variation (rather than specialization) can accelerate the learning curve, and how the structure of knowledge networks affects their overall capacity for knowledge creation.

Professor Schilling has published articles in a wide range of journals, including *Academy of Management Journal, Academy of Management Review, Management Science,* and *Organization Science.* She teaches Strategic Management and Technological Innovation Management in the undergraduate and MBA programs at the Stern School.

Preface

Innovation is a beautiful thing. It is a force with both aesthetic and pragmatic appeal: It unleashes our creative spirit, opening our minds to hitherto undreamed of possibilities, while simultaneously accelerating economic growth and providing advances in such crucial human endeavors as medicine, agriculture, and education. For industrial organizations, the primary engines of innovation in the Western world, innovation provides both exceptional opportunities and steep challenges. While innovation is a powerful means of competitive differentiation, enabling firms to penetrate new markets and achieve higher margins, it is also a competitive race that must be run with speed, skill, and precision. It is not enough for a firm to be innovative—to be successful it must innovate better than its competitors.

As scholars and managers have raced to better understand innovation, a wide range of work on the topic has emerged and flourished in disciplines such as strategic management, organization theory, economics, marketing, engineering, and sociology. This work has generated many insights about how innovation affects the competitive dynamics of markets, how firms can strategically manage innovation, and how firms can implement their innovation strategies to maximize their likelihood of success. A great benefit of the dispersion of this literature across such diverse domains of study is that many innovation topics have been examined from different angles. However, this diversity also can pose integration challenges to both instructors and students. This book seeks to integrate this wide body of work into a single coherent strategic framework, attempting to provide coverage that is rigorous, inclusive, and accessible.

The subject of innovation management is approached here as a strategic process. The outline of the book is designed to mirror the strategic management process used in most strategy textbooks, progressing from assessing the competitive dynamics of the situation, to strategy formulation, and then to strategy implementation. The first part of the book covers the foundations and implications of the dynamics of innovation, helping managers and future managers better interpret their technological environments and identify meaningful trends. The second part of the book begins the process of crafting the firm's strategic direction and formulating its innovation strategy, including project selection, collaboration strategies, and strategies for protecting the firm's property rights. The third part of the book covers the process of implementing innovation, including the implications of organization structure on innovation, the management of new product development processes, the construction and management of new product development teams, and crafting the firm's deployment strategy. While the book emphasizes practical applications and examples, it also provides systematic coverage of the existing research and footnotes to guide further reading.

This book is designed to be a primary text for courses in the strategic management of innovation and new product development. Such courses are frequently taught in both business and engineering programs; thus, this book has been written with the needs of business and engineering students in mind. For example, Chapter Six

(Defining the Organization's Strategic Direction) provides basic strategic analysis tools with which business students may already be familiar, but which may be unfamiliar to engineering students. Similarly, some of the material in Chapter 10 (Managing the New Product Development Process) on computer-aided design or quality function deployment may be review material for information system students or engineering students, while being new to management students. Though the chapters are designed to have an intuitive order to them, they are also designed to be self-standing so instructors can pick and choose from them "buffet style" if they prefer.

This book arose out of my research and teaching on technological innovation and new product development over the last decade; however, it has been anything but a lone endeavor. I owe much of the original inspiration of the book to Charles Hill, who helped to ignite my initial interest in innovation, guided me in my research agenda, and ultimately encouraged me to write this book. I am also very grateful to colleagues such as Juan Alcacer, William Baumol, Gary Dushnitsky, Tammy Madsen, Goncalo Pacheco D'Almeida, Raghu Garud, Bill Starbuck, and Christopher Tucci for their suggestions, insights, and encouragement. I am also thankful to my editors, Ryan Blankenship and Lindsay Harmon, who have been so supportive and made this book possible, and to the many reviewers whose suggestions have dramatically improved the book:

David Berkowitz
University of Alabama in Huntsville

John Bers
Vanderbilt University

Paul Bierly
James Madison University

Paul Cheney
University of Central Florida

Cheryl Gaimon
Georgia Institute of Technology

Elie Geisler
Illinois Institute of Technology

Andrew Hargadon
University of California, Davis

Glenn Hoetker
University of Illinois at Urbana-Champaign

Sanjay Jain
University of Wisconsin—Madison

Steve Markham
North Carolina State University

Robert Nash
Vanderbilt University

Anthony Paoni
Northwestern University

Oya Tukel
Cleveland State University

Anthony Warren
The Pennsylvania State University

I also need to thank my husband, Alex, for his love and support despite my neglect of him during the writing of this book. Finally, the biggest debt of gratitude is certainly owed to the many students of the Technological Innovation and New Product Development courses I have taught at New York University, Boston University, and University of California at Santa Barbara. Not only did these students read, challenge, and help improve many earlier drafts of the work, but they also contributed numerous examples that have made the text far richer than it would have otherwise been. I thank them wholeheartedly for their patience and generosity.

Melissa A. Schilling

Brief Contents

Contents

Chapter 9
Protecting Innovation 165

PART THREE
IMPLEMENTING TECHNOLOGICAL
INNOVATION STRATEGY 187

Chapter 10
Organizing for Innovation 189

Chapter 11
Managing the New Product Development
Process 213

Chapter **One**

Introduction

THE IMPORTANCE OF TECHNOLOGICAL INNOVATION

technological innovation
The act of introducing a new device, method, or material for application to commercial or practical objectives.

In many industries **technological innovation** is now the most important driver of competitive success. Firms in a wide range of industries rely on products developed within the past five years for more than one-third of their sales and profits. For example, Baxter, a leading manufacturer of medical equipment and supplies, earned 37 percent of its 2002 sales from products introduced within the previous five years. The percentage of sales from products developed within the past five years has hit as high as 45 percent at 3M in recent years.

The increasing importance of innovation is due in part to the globalization of markets. Foreign competition has put pressure on firms to continuously innovate in order to produce differentiated products and services. Introducing new products helps firms protect their margins, while investing in process innovation helps firms lower their costs. Advances in information technology also have played a role in speeding the pace of innovation. Computer-aided design and computer-aided manufacturing have made it easier and faster for firms to design and produce new products, while flexible manufacturing technologies have made shorter production runs economical and have reduced the importance of production economies of scale.[1] These technologies help firms develop and produce more product variants that closely meet the needs of narrowly defined customer groups, thus achieving differentiation from competitors. A prime example is Sony, which produces more than 75 models of its Walkman portable stereo that differ in size, color, music format (e.g., MP3, minidisk, CD, cassette, radio signal), and other features. Sony's portfolio of Walkman models enables it to penetrate every conceivable market niche.[2] While producing multiple product variations used to be expensive and time-consuming, Sony uses flexible manufacturing technologies to seamlessly transition from producing one product model to the next, and to adjust production schedules with real-time information on demand. The company further reduces production costs by using common components in many of the models.

As firms such as Sony adopt these new technologies and increase their pace of innovation, they raise the bar for competitors, triggering an industrywide shift to shortened development cycles and more rapid new product introductions. The net results are greater market segmentation and rapid product obsolescence.[3] Product life cycles (the time between a product's introduction and its withdrawal from the market or replacement by a next-generation product) have become as short as 4 to 12 months for software, 12 to 24 months for computer hardware and consumer electronics, and 18 to 36 months for large home appliances.[4] This spurs firms to focus increasingly on innovation as a strategic imperative—a firm that does not innovate quickly finds its margins diminishing as its products become obsolete.

THE IMPACT OF TECHNOLOGICAL INNOVATION ON SOCIETY

If the push for innovation has raised the competitive bar for industries, arguably making success just that much more complicated for organizations, its net effect on society is more clearly positive. Innovation enables a wider range of goods and services to be delivered to people worldwide. It has made the production of food and other necessities more efficient, yielded medical treatments that improve health conditions, and enabled people to travel to and communicate with almost every part of the world.

gross domestic product
The total annual output of an economy as measured by its final purchase price.

The aggregate impact of technological innovation can be observed by looking at **gross domestic product** (GDP). The gross domestic product of an economy is its total annual output, measured by final purchase price. Figure 1.1 shows the average GDP per capita (that is, GDP divided by the population) for the world, and also for developed economies, transitional economies, and developing countries, from 1971 to 2003. The figures have been converted into U.S. dollars and adjusted for inflation. As shown in the figure, the average world GDP per capita has risen steadily since 1971, particularly in the developed economies. Data dating to the 1920s for the United States show the same pattern.

In a series of studies of economic growth conducted at the National Bureau of Economic Research, economists showed that the historic rate of economic growth in GDP could not be accounted for entirely by growth in labor and capital inputs. Economist Robert Merton Solow argued that this unaccounted for residual growth represented technological change: Technological innovation increased the amount of

FIGURE 1.1
Gross Domestic Product per Capita, 1971–2003 (in 2000 $US)

Source: *Science and Engineering Indicators 2002.* National Science Board.

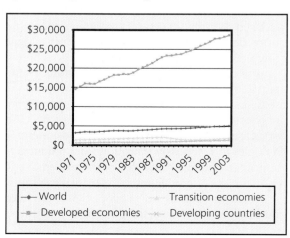

output achievable from a given quantity of labor and capital. This explanation was not immediately accepted; many researchers attempted to explain the residual away in terms of measurement error, inaccurate price deflation, or labor improvement. But in each case the additional variables were unable to eliminate this residual growth component. A consensus gradually emerged that the residual did in fact capture technological change. Solow received a Nobel Prize for his work in 1981, and the residual became known as the Solow Residual.[5] While GDP has its shortcomings as a measure of standard of living, it does relate very directly to the amount of goods consumers can purchase. Thus, to the extent that goods improve quality of life, we can ascribe some beneficial impact of technological innovation.

Sometimes technological innovation results in negative **externalities**. Production technologies may create pollution that is harmful to the surrounding communities; agricultural and fishing technologies can result in erosion, elimination of natural habitats, and depletion of ocean stocks; medical technologies can result in unanticipated consequences such as antibiotic-resistant strains of bacteria or moral dilemmas regarding the use of genetic modification. However, technology is, in its purest essence, knowledge—knowledge to solve our problems and pursue our goals.[6] Technological innovation is thus the creation of new knowledge that is applied to practical problems. Sometimes this knowledge is applied to problems hastily, without full consideration of the consequences and alternatives, but overall it will probably serve us better to have more knowledge than less.

While the government plays a significant role in investing in technological innovation, among member countries of the Organization for Economic Cooperation and Development (OECD), the majority of R&D funds come from industry. Furthermore, the percentage of R&D funds that come from industry (versus government) has been growing at a quick pace (see Figure 1.2). These figures include R&D funds paid to university scientists and private research organizations, in addition to funds utilized within firms. The statistics indicate that industry bears much of the responsibility for technological innovation.

externalities
Costs (or benefits) that are borne (or reaped) by individuals other than those responsible for creating them. Thus, if a business emits pollutants in a community, it imposes a negative externality on the community members; if a business builds a park in a community, it creates a positive externality for community members.

FIGURE 1.2
Percentage of R&D Funds from Industry, Government, and Other Sources, for OECD countries,* 1982–1998

Source: *Science and Engineering Indicators 2002.* National Science Board.

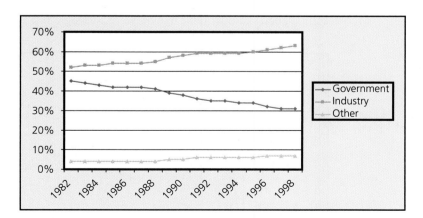

*OECD countries include Australia, Austria, Belgium, Canada, Czech Republic, Denmark, Finland, France, Germany, Greece, Hungary, Iceland, Ireland, Italy, Japan, Korea, Luxembourg, Mexico, Netherlands, New Zealand, Norway, Poland, Portugal, Slovak Republic, Spain, Sweden, Switzerland, Turkey, United Kingdom, and United States.

INNOVATION BY INDUSTRY: THE IMPORTANCE OF STRATEGY

In the frenetic race to innovate, many firms charge headlong into new product development without clear strategies or well-developed processes for choosing and managing projects. Such firms often initiate more projects than they can effectively support, choose projects that are a poor fit with the firm's resources and objectives, and suffer long development cycles and high project failure rates as a consequence (see the accompanying Research Brief for a recent study of the length of new product development cycles). While innovation is popularly depicted as a freewheeling process that is unconstrained by rules and plans, study after study has revealed that successful innovators have clearly defined innovation strategies and management processes.[7]

The Innovation Funnel

Most innovative ideas do not become successful new products. Many studies suggest that only one out of several thousand ideas results in a successful new product: Many projects do not result in technically feasible products and of those that do, many fail to earn a commercial return. According to one study that combined data from prior studies of innovation success rates with data on patents, venture capital funding, and surveys, it takes about 3,000 raw ideas to produce one significantly new and success-ful commercial product.[8] The pharmaceutical industry demonstrates this well—only one out of every 10,000 compounds succeeds as a new pharmaceutical, with an overall time from discovery to market of 12 years, and a total cost of approximately $350 mil-lion! The innovation process is thus often conceived of as a funnel, with many poten-tial new product ideas going in the wide end, but very few making it through the development process (see Figure 1.3).

The Strategic Management of Technological Innovation

Improving a firm's innovation success rate requires a well-crafted strategy. A firm's innovation projects should align with its resources and objectives, leveraging its core competencies and helping it achieve its strategic intent. A firm's organizational

FIGURE 1.3
The Innovation Funnel

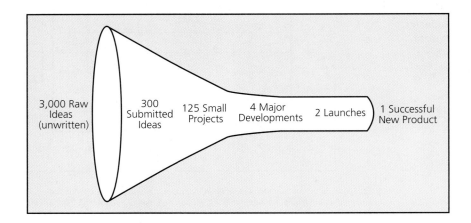

Research Brief   How Long Does New Product Development Take?

In a study of 116 firms developing business-to-business innovations (that is, new products that are sold to businesses rather than consumers), Abbie Griffin examined the length of time it took firms to develop a new product from initial concept to market introduction. She found that the length of the new product development cycle varied with the innovativeness of the project. On average, *incremental improvements* to an existing product took only 8.6 months from concept to market introduction. *Next generation improvements* (large improvements to existing products) took significantly longer, clocking in at 22 months. The development of *new-to-the-firm product lines* took an average of 36 months, and the development of *new-to-the-world products* or technologies took the longest, averaging 53 months. Griffin also found that about half of the companies had reduced their cycle time by an average of 33 percent over the last five years.

Source: Adapted from A. Griffin, "Product Development Cycle Time for Business-to-Business Products," *Industrial Marketing Management* 31, pp. 291–304.

structure and control systems should encourage the generation of innovative ideas while also ensuring efficient implementation. A firm's new product development process should maximize the likelihood of projects being both technically and commercially successful. To achieve these things, a firm needs (*a*) an in-depth understanding of the dynamics of innovation, (*b*) a well-crafted innovation strategy, and (*c*) well-designed processes for implementing the innovation strategy. We will cover each of these in turn (see Figure 1.4).

In Part One, we will cover the foundations of technological innovation, gaining an in-depth understanding of how and why innovation occurs in an industry, and why some innovations rise to dominate others. First, we will look at the sources of innovation in Chapter Two. We will address questions such as: Where do great ideas come from? How can firms harness the power of individual creativity? What role do customers, government organizations, universities, and alliance networks play in creating innovation? In this chapter we will first explore the role of creativity in the generation of novel and useful ideas. We then look at various sources of innovation, including the role of individual inventors, firms, publicly sponsored research, and collaborative networks.

In Chapter Three, we will review models of types of innovation (such as radical versus incremental, or architectural versus modular) and patterns of innovation (including s-curves of technology performance and diffusion, and technology cycles). We will address questions such as: Why are some innovations much harder to create and implement than others? Why do innovations often diffuse slowly even when they appear to offer a great advantage? What factors influence the rate at which a technology tends to improve over time? Familiarity with these types and patterns of innovation will help us distinguish how one project is different from another and the underlying factors that shape the project's likelihood of technical or commercial success.

FIGURE 1.4
The Strategic Management of Technological Innovation

In Chapter Four, we will turn to the particularly interesting dynamics that emerge in industries characterized by increasing returns, where strong pressures to adopt a single dominant design can result in standards battles and winner-take-all markets. We will address questions such as: Why do some industries choose a single dominant standard rather than enabling multiple standards to coexist? What makes one technological innovation rise to dominate all others, even when other seemingly superior technologies are offered? How can a firm avoid being locked out? Is there anything a firm can do to influence the likelihood of its technology becoming the dominant design?

In Chapter Five, we will discuss the impact of entry timing, including first-mover advantages, first-mover *dis*advantages, and the factors that will determine the firm's optimal entry strategy. This chapter will address such questions as: What are the advantages and disadvantages of being first to market, early but not first, and late? What determines the optimal timing of entry for a new innovation? This chapter reveals a number of consistent patterns in how timing of entry impacts innovation success, and it outlines what factors will influence a firm's optimal timing of entry, thus beginning the transition from understanding the dynamics of technological innovation to formulating technology strategy.

In Part Two, we will turn to formulating technological innovation strategy. Chapter Six will cover the basics of how a firm can assess its current position and define its strategic direction for the future. This chapter will addresses such questions as: What are the firm's sources of sustainable competitive advantage? Where in the firm's value chain do its strengths and weaknesses lie? What are the firm's core competencies, and how should it leverage and build upon them? What is the firm's strategic intent—that is, where does the firm want to be 10 years from now? Only once the firm has thoroughly appraised where it is currently can it formulate a coherent technological innovation strategy for the future.

In Chapter Seven, we will examine a variety of methods of choosing innovation projects. These include quantitative methods such as discounted cash flow and options valuation techniques, qualitative methods such as screening questions and balancing the research and development portfolio, as well as methods that combine qualitative and quantitative approaches such as conjoint analysis and data envelopment analysis. Each of these methods has its advantages and disadvantages, leading many firms to use a multiple-method approach to choosing innovation projects.

In Chapter Eight, we will examine collaboration strategies for innovation. This chapter addresses questions such as: Should the firm partner on a particular project or go solo? How does the firm decide which activities to do in-house and which to access through collaborative arrangements? If the firm chooses to work with a partner, how should the partnership be structured? How does the firm choose and monitor partners? We will begin by looking at the reasons a firm might choose to go solo versus working with a partner. We then will look at the pros and cons of various partnering methods, including joint ventures, alliances, licensing, outsourcing, and participating in collaborative research organizations. The chapter also reviews the factors that should influence partner selection and monitoring.

In Chapter Nine, we will address the options the firm has for appropriating the returns to its innovation efforts. We will look at the mechanics of patents, copyright, trademarks, and trade secrets. We will also address such questions as: Are there ever times when it would benefit the firm to not protect its technological innovation so vigorously? How does a firm decide between a wholly proprietary, wholly open, or partially open strategy for protecting its innovation? When will open strategies have advantages over wholly proprietary strategies? This chapter examines the range of protection options available to the firm, and the complex series of trade-offs a firm must consider in its protection strategy.

In Part Three, we will turn to implementing the technological innovation strategy. This begins in Chapter 10 with an examination of how the organization's size and structure influences its overall rate of innovativeness. The chapter addresses such questions as: Do bigger firms outperform smaller firms at innovation? How do formalization, standardization, and centralization impact the likelihood of generating innovative ideas and the organization's ability to implement those ideas quickly and efficiently? Is it possible to achieve creativity and flexibility at the same time as efficiency and reliability? How do multinational firms decide where to perform their development activities? How do multinational firms coordinate their development activities toward a common goal when the activities occur in multiple countries? This chapter examines how organizations can balance the benefits and trade-offs of flexibility, economies of scale, standardization, centralization, and tapping local market knowledge.

In Chapter 11, we will review a series of "best practices" that have been identified in managing the new product development process. This includes such questions as: Should new product development processes be performed sequentially or in parallel? What are the advantages and disadvantages of using project champions? What are the benefits and risks of involving customers and/or suppliers in the development process? What tools can the firm use to improve the effectiveness and efficiency of its new product development processes? How does the firm assess whether its new product development process is successful? This chapter provides an extensive review of methods that have been developed to improve the management of new product development projects and to measure their performance.

Chapter 12 builds on the previous chapter by illuminating how team composition and structure will influence project outcomes. This chapter will addresses questions such as: How big should teams be? What are the advantages and disadvantages of choosing highly diverse team members? Do teams need to be collocated? When should teams be full-time and/or permanent? What type of team leader and management practices should be used for the team? This chapter provides detailed guidelines for constructing new product development teams that are matched to the type of new product development project underway.

Finally, in Chapter 13, we will look at innovation deployment strategies. This chapter will address such questions as: How do we accelerate the adoption of the technological innovation? How do we decide whether to use licensing or OEM agreements? Does it make more sense to use penetration pricing or a market-skimming price? What strategies can the firm use to encourage distributors and complementary goods providers to support the innovation? This chapter complements traditional marketing, distribution, and pricing courses by looking at how a deployment strategy can be crafted that especially targets the needs of a new technological innovation.

Summary of Chapter

1. Technological innovation is now often the single most important competitive driver in many industries. Many firms receive more than one-third of their sales and profits from products developed within the past five years.

2. The increasing importance of innovation has been driven largely by the globalization of markets and the advent of advanced technologies that enable more rapid product design and allow shorter production runs to be economically feasible.

3. Technological innovation has a number of important effects on society, including fostering increased GDP, enabling greater communication and mobility, and improving medical treatments.

4. Technological innovation may also pose some negative externalities, including pollution, resource depletion, and other unintended consequences of technological change.

5. While government plays a significant role in innovation, industry provides the majority of R&D funds that are ultimately applied to technological innovation.

6. Successful innovation requires an in-depth understanding of the dynamics of innovation, a well-crafted innovation strategy, and well-developed processes for implementing the innovation strategy.

Discussion Questions

1. Why is innovation so important for firms to compete in many industries?

2. What are some advantages of technological innovation? Disadvantages?

3. Why do you think so many innovation projects fail to generate an economic return?

Endnotes

1. J. P. Womack, D. T. Jones, and D. Roos, *The Machine That Changed the World* (New York: Rawson Associates, 1990).

2. The automobile industry provides another example. In the mid-1960s the best-selling car in the United States was the Chevrolet Impala. The platform on which it was based sold approximately 1.5 million units. In 1991 the best-selling car in the United States was the Honda Accord, which sold about 400,000 units. Thus, in a market that is larger than it was in 1965, the volume per model has declined by a factor of four.

3. W. Qualls, R. W. Olshavsky, and R. E. Michaels, "Shortening of the PLC—an Empirical Test," *Journal of Marketing* 45 (1981), pp. 76–80.

4. M. A. Schilling and C. E. Vasco, "Product and Process Technological Change and the Adoption of Modular Organizational Forms," in *Winning Strategies in a Deconstructing World,* eds. R. Bresser, M. Hitt, R. Nixon, and D. Heuskel (Sussex, England: John Wiley & Sons, 2000), pp. 25–50.

5. N. Crafts, "The First Industrial Revolution: A Guided Tour for Growth Economists," *The American Economic Review* 86, no. 2 (1996), pp. 197–202; R. Solow, "Technical Change and the Aggregate Production Function," *Review of Economics and Statistics* 39 (1957), pp. 312–20; and N. E. Terleckyj, "What Do R&D Numbers Tell Us about Technological Change?" *American Economic Association* 70, no. 2 (1980), pp. 55–61.

6. H. A. Simon, "Technology and Environment," *Management Science* 19 (1973), pp. 1110–21.

7. S. Brown and K. Eisenhardt, "The Art of Continuous Change: Linking Complexity Theory and Time-Paced Evolution in Relentlessly Shifting Organizations," *Administrative Science Quarterly* 42 (1997), pp. 1–35; K. Clark and T. Fujimoto, *Product Development Performance* (Boston: Harvard Business School Press, 1991); R. Cooper, "Third Generation New Product Processes," *Journal of Product Innovation Management* 11 (1994), pp. 3–14; D. Doughery, "Reimagining the Differentiation and Integration of Work for Sustained Product Innovation," *Organization Science* 12 (2001), pp. 612–31; and M. A. Schilling and C. W. L. Hill, "Managing the New Product Development Process: Strategic Imperatives," *Academy of Management Executive* 12, no. 3 (1998), pp. 67–81.

8. G. Stevens and J. Burley, "3,000 Raw Ideas Equals 1 Commercial Success!" *Research Technology Management* 40, no. 3 (1997), pp. 16–27.

Part One

Industry Dynamics of Technological Innovation

In this section, we will explore the industry dynamics of technological innovation, including:

- The sources from which innovation arises, including the role of individuals, organizations, government institutions, and networks.
- The types of innovations and common industry patterns of technological evolution and diffusion.
- The factors that determine whether industries experience pressure to select a dominant design, and what drives which technologies to dominate others.
- The effects of timing of entry, and how firms can identify (and manage) their entry options.

This section will lay the foundation that we will build upon in Part Two, Formulating Technological Innovation Strategy.

Industry Dynamics of Technological Innovation

Chapter **Two**

Sources of Innovation

Segway Human Transporter

In January 2001, an Internet news story leaked that iconoclastic inventor Dean Kamen had devised a fantastic new invention—a device that could affect the way cities were built, and even change the world. Shrouded in secrecy, the mysterious device, code-named "Ginger" and "IT," became the talk of the technological world and the general public, as speculation about the technology grew wilder and wilder. In December of that year, Kamen finally unveiled his invention, the Segway Human Transporter.[1] Based on an elaborate combination of motors, gyroscopes, and a motion control algorithm, the Segway HT was a self-balancing, two-wheeled scooter. Though to many it looked like a toy, the Segway represented a significant advance in technology. John Doerr, the venture capitalist behind Amazon.com and Netscape, predicted it would be bigger than the Internet.

Segway's Inventor: Dean Kamen

The Segway was the brainchild of Dean Kamen, an inventor with more than 150 U.S. and foreign patents, whose career began in his teenage days of devising mechanical gadgets in his parents' basement.[2] Kamen never graduated from college, though he has since received numerous honorary degrees. He is described as tireless and eclectic, an entrepreneur with a seemingly boundless enthusiasm for science and technology. Kamen has received numerous awards for his inventions, including the Kilby award, the Hoover Medal, and the National Medal of Technology. Most of his inventions have been directed at advancing health care technology. In 1988, he invented the first self-service dialysis machine for people with kidney failure. Kamen had rejected the original proposal for the machine brought to him by Baxter, one of the world's largest medical equipment manufacturers. To Kamen, the solution was not to come up with a new answer to a known problem, but to instead reformulate the problem: "What if you can find the technology that not only fixes the valves but also makes the whole thing as simple as plugging a cassette into a VCR? Why do patients have to continue to go to these centers? Can we make a machine that can go in the home, give the patients back their dignity, reduce the cost, reduce the trauma?"[3] The result was the HomeChoice dialysis machine, which won *Design News'* 1993 Medical Product of the Year award.

In 1999, Kamen's company, DEKA Research, introduced the IBOT Mobility System, an extremely advanced wheelchair incorporating a sophisticated balancing system that enabled users to climb stairs and negotiate sand, rocks, and curbs. According to Kamen, the IBOT "allowed a disabled person, a person who cannot walk, to basically do all the ordinary things that you take for granted that they can't do even in a wheelchair, like go up a curb."[4] It was the IBOT's combination of balance and mobility that gave rise to the idea of the Segway.

Developing the Segway

Building the Segway required solving a number of design challenges. Kamen's philosophy toward problem solving is "kissing frogs." DEKA's engineers are expected to produce, evaluate, and eliminate many different design concepts in order to explore a wide range of potential solutions.[5] The company also embraces a process that attempts to balance "ideation" people with "execution" people. According to Doug Field, vice president of development and operations, "ideation" people generate an abundance of ideas and want to try them all out, using experiential learning in an effort to better understand options. They ask "what if?" Execution people prefer to develop clear definitions of requirements in hopes of getting "it right the first time," asking questions like "should we do it?"[6]

The development and commercial production of the Segway also required a number of external partnerships. Venture capitalists invested $90 million to help fund the Segway's development. Silicon Sensing Systems helped DEKA develop the Segway's gyroscopic sensor systems, while Michelin provided unique "Balance" tires. Pacific Science helped to create Segway's electric motor, and Saft assisted in the development of a "smart-charging" battery. DEKA also had to work closely with government regulators to try to ensure that the Segway would be legal to operate on city sidewalks.

By early 2003, Segway had been adopted for several commercial and industrial applications. Several cities were testing the Segway as a vehicle for police officers and postal workers. Some companies were experimenting with using the Segway in place of the small carts they used for transportation within a facility, and Disney had introduced the Segway as a unique transportation option on its cruise lines and private islands. DEKA's management hoped the Segway's use in these settings would legitimize it the public's perceptions, so that the Segway would be viewed as a vehicle and a tool, and not a toy. "We don't play, we ride," said Gary Bridge, Segway LLC's senior vice president of marketing.[7]

Discussion Questions

1. What factors do you think enable Dean Kamen and his company, DEKA Research, to come up with novel innovations such as the IBOT or Segway?
2. What are the advantages and disadvantages of Kamen's philosophy of "kissing frogs"?

3. What role did external organizations play in helping Kamen translate his creative inspiration for the Segway into a commercial innovation?

OVERVIEW

Innovation can arise from many different sources. It can originate with individuals, as in the familiar image of the lone inventor or users who design solutions for their own needs. Innovation can also come from the research efforts of universities, government laboratories and incubators, or private nonprofit organizations. One primary engine of innovation is firms. Firms are well-suited to innovation activities because they typically have greater resources than individuals and a management system to marshal those resources toward a collective purpose. Firms also face strong incentives to develop differentiating new products and services, which may give them an advantage over nonprofit or government-funded entities.

An even more important source of innovation, however, does not arise from any one of these sources, but rather the linkages between them. Networks of innovators that leverage knowledge and other resources from multiple sources are one of the most powerful agents of technological advance.[8] We can thus think of sources of innovation as composing a complex system wherein any particular innovation may emerge primarily from one or more components of the system or the linkages between them (see Figure 2.1).

In the sections that follow, we will first consider the role of creativity as the underlying process for the generation of novel and useful ideas. We will then consider how creativity is transformed into innovative outcomes by the separate components of the innovation system (e.g., individuals, firms, etc.), and through the linkages between different components (e.g., firm's relationships with their customers, technology transfer from universities to firms, etc.).

FIGURE 2.1
Sources of Innovation as a System

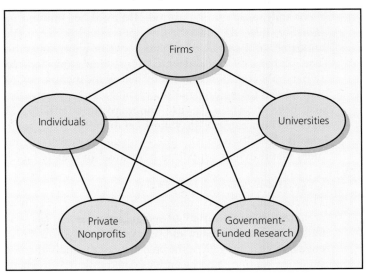

CREATIVITY

creativity
The ability to produce novel and useful work.

Innovation begins with the generation of new ideas. The ability to generate new and useful ideas is termed creativity. **Creativity** is defined as the ability to produce work that is useful and novel. Novel work must be different from work that has been previously produced and surprising in that it is not simply the next logical step in a series of known solutions.[9] The degree to which a product is novel is a function both of how different it is from prior work (e.g., a minor deviation versus a major leap) and of the audience's prior experiences.[10] A product could be novel to the person who made it, but known to most everyone else. In this case, we would call it reinvention. A product could be novel to its immediate audience, yet be well-known somewhere else in the world. The most creative works are novel at the individual producer level, the local audience level, and the broader societal level.[11]

Individual Creativity

An individual's creative ability is a function of his or her intellectual abilities, knowledge, style of thinking, personality, motivation, and environment.[12] The most important intellectual abilities for creative thinking include the ability to look at problems in unconventional ways, the ability to analyze which ideas are worth pursuing and which are not, and the ability to articulate those ideas to others and convince others that the ideas are worthwhile. The impact of knowledge on creativity is somewhat double-edged. If an individual has too little knowledge of a field, he or she is unlikely to understand it well enough to contribute meaningfully to it. On the other hand, if an individual knows a field too well, that person can become trapped in the existing logic and paradigms, preventing him or her from coming up with solutions that require an alternative perspective. Thus, an individual with only a moderate degree of knowledge of a field might be able to produce more creative solutions than an individual with extensive knowledge of field.[13] This may explain in part why an inventor such as Dean Kamen has come up with significant innovations in fields as diverse as medical equipment and transportation, despite little former training in either field. With respect to *thinking styles,* the most creative individuals prefer to think in novel ways of their own choosing, and can discriminate between important problems and unimportant ones. The personality traits deemed most important for creativity include self-efficacy (a person's confidence in his or her own capabilities), tolerance for ambiguity, and a willingness to overcome obstacles and take reasonable risks.[14] Intrinsic motivation has also been shown to be very important for creativity.[15] That is, individuals are more likely to be creative if they work on things they are genuinely interested in and enjoy. Finally, to fully unleash an individual's creative potential often requires an environment that provides support and rewards for creative ideas.

Organizational Creativity

The creativity of the organization is a function of creativity of the individuals within the organization and a variety of social processes and contextual factors that shape the way those individuals interact and behave.[16] An organization's overall creativity level is thus not a simple aggregate of the creativity of the individuals it employs. The organization's structure, routines, and incentives could thwart individual creativity or amplify it.

The most familiar method of a company tapping the creativity of its individual employees is the suggestion box. In 1895, John Patterson, founder of National Cash Register (NCR), created the first sanctioned suggestion box program to tap the ideas of the hourly worker.[17] The program was considered revolutionary in its time. The originators of adopted ideas were awarded $1. In 1904, employees submitted 7,000 ideas, of which one-third were adopted. Other firms have created more elaborate systems for capturing employee ideas. For instance, Honda of America utilizes an employee-driven idea system (EDIS) whereby employees submit their ideas and are rewarded primarily through recognition rather than monetarily for ideas that are approved. Unlike traditional suggestion boxes, the employee who submits the idea is responsible for following through on the suggestion, overseeing its progress from concept to implementation. Honda of America reports that more than 75 percent of all ideas are implemented.[18] Bank One, one of the largest holding banks in the United States, has created an employee idea program called "One Great Idea." Employees access the company's idea repository through the company's **intranet.** There they can submit their ideas and actively interact and collaborate on the ideas of others.[19] Through active exchange, the employees can evaluate and refine the ideas, improving their fit with the diverse needs of the organization's stakeholders.

intranet
A private network, accessible only to authorized individuals. It is like the Internet but operates only within ("intra") the organization.

Idea collection systems (such as suggestion boxes) are relatively easy and inexpensive to implement, but are only a first step in unleashing employee creativity. Today companies such as Intel, Motorola, 3M, and Hewlett-Packard go to much greater lengths to tap the creative potential embedded in employees, including investing in creativity training programs. Such programs encourage managers to develop verbal and nonverbal cues that signal employees that their thinking and autonomy is respected. These cues shape the culture of the firm and are often more effective than monetary rewards—in fact, sometimes monetary rewards undermine creativity by encouraging employees to focus on extrinsic rather than intrinsic motivation.[20] The programs also often incorporate exercises that encourage employees to use creative mechanisms such as developing alternative scenarios, using analogies to compare the problem with another problem that shares similar features or structure, and restating the problem in a new way. One product design firm, IDEO, even encourages employees to develop mock prototypes of potential new products out of inexpensive materials such as cardboard or styrofoam and pretend to use the product, exploring potential design features in a tangible and playful manner (IDEO is discussed in greater depth in Chapter 11).

TRANSLATING CREATIVITY INTO INNOVATION

Innovation is more than the generation of creative ideas; it is the implementation of those ideas into some new device or process. Innovation requires combining a creative idea with resources and expertise that make it possible to embody the creative idea in a useful form. We will first consider the role of individuals as innovators, including innovation by inventors who specialize in creating new products and processes, and innovation by end users. We then will look at innovation activity that is organized by firms, universities, and government institutions.

The Inventor

The familiar image of the inventor as an eccentric and doggedly persistent scientist may have some basis in cognitive psychology. Analysis of personality traits of inventors suggests these individuals are likely to be interested in theoretical and abstract thinking, and have an unusual enthusiasm for problem solving. Their tendency toward introversion may cause them to be better at manipulating concepts than at interacting socially.[21] Such personality traits appear to suggest that the capacity to be an inventor is an innate ability of an individual. Others, however, disagree with this conclusion and argue that inventors are made, not born.[22] One 10-year study of inventors concludes that the most successful inventors possess the following traits:

1. They have mastered the basic tools and operations of the field in which they invent, but they have not specialized solely on that field; instead they have pursued two or three fields simultaneously, permitting them to bring different perspectives to each.
2. They are curious and more interested in problems than solutions.
3. They question the assumptions made in previous work in the field.
4. They often have the sense that all knowledge is unified. They seek global solutions rather than local solutions, and are generalists by nature.[23]

These traits were demonstrated by Dean Kamen in the opening illustration. They are also illustrated in the following quotes by Nobel laureates. Sir MacFarlane Burnet, Nobel Prize-winning immunologist noted, "I think there are dangers for a research man being too well trained in the field he is going to study,"[24] and Peter Debye, Nobel Prize-winning chemist, noted, "At the beginning of the Second World War, R. R. Williams of Bell Labs came to Cornell to try to interest me in the polymer field. I said to him, 'I don't know anything about polymers. I never thought about them.' And his answer was, 'That is why we want you.'"[25] The global search for global solutions is aptly illustrated by Thomas Edison, who did not set out to invent just a lightbulb: "The problem then that I undertook to solve was . . . the production of the multifarious apparatus, methods, and devices, each adapted for use with every other, and all forming a comprehensive system."[26]

Such individuals may spend a lifetime developing numerous creative new devices or processes, though they may patent or commercialize few. The qualities that make someone inventive do not necessarily make them entrepreneurial; many inventors do not actively seek to patent or commercialize their work. Many of the most well-known inventors (e.g., Alexander Graham Bell, Thomas Alva Edison, Albert Einstein, Benjamin Franklin), however, had both inventive and entrepreneurial traits.[27]

Innovation by Users

Innovation often originates with those who create solutions for their own needs. Users often have both a deep understanding of their unmet needs and the incentive to find ways to fulfill them.[28] Users may alter the features of existing products, approach existing manufacturers with product design suggestions, or develop new products themselves. For example, the extremely popular small sailboat, the Laser, was designed without any formal market research or concept testing. Instead it was the creative inspiration of three former Olympic sailors, Ian Bruce, Bruce Kirby, and Hans Vogt. They designed the boat based on their own preferences: simplicity, maximum performance, transportability, durability, and low cost. The resulting sailboat became

The first snowboards were not developed by major sports equipment manufacturers seeking to leverage their capabilities by developing a new sport. Instead, they were developed by individuals who sought new ways of fulfilling their own desires for gliding over snow.

Snowboarding traces its history to the early 1960s, when a number of individuals developed an assortment of snowboard precursors, whose designs would ultimately give rise to the modern snowboard.[29] Some of the most notable of these individuals included Tom Sims, Sherman Poppen, Jake Burton Carpenter, Dimitrije Milovich, Mike Olson and Chuck Barfoot. In 1963, Tom Sims, an avid skier and skateboarder, made his first "ski board" in wood shop class. Sims and Bob Weber would go on to design snowboards and found the company known as Sims. Another very early developer was Sherman Poppen. In 1965 as a toy for his daughter, Poppen attached two skis together into what he called a "snurfer." The toy turned out to be so popular that Poppen began organizing informal competitions for snurfer enthusiasts. Jake Burton Carpenter was one such enthusiast, and he began developing a version of the snurfer with rubber straps to act as bindings, giving the user greater control. This led to the founding of his Vermont-based company, Burton, which rose to become a dominant force in snowboarding.

By the early 70s, several other individuals were developing snowboards, often driven by a desire to more closely replicate the action and feel of skateboarding or surfing rather than skiing. In 1975, Dimitrije Milovich set up one of the earliest snowboard companies, Winterstick, to sell his swallowtailed snowboards based on a surfboard design. He gained considerable exposure when *Newsweek* covered him in March of that same year, and *Powder* magazine gave him a two-page photo spread.[30] About the same time, Mike Olson and Chuck Barfoot were also developing their own snowboard prototypes, which would evolve to become the snowboard lines of Gnu and Barfoot.

By the mid-1980s, snowboarding was beginning to be allowed in major ski resorts, and ski manufacturers such as K2 and Rossignol were eyeing this growing market. The skiing industry had peaked in the 1970s and had since seen slumping demand. Snowboarding offered a way to revitalize the industry because it promised to tap a new market (largely skateboarders and surfers) rather than cannibalizing existing ski sales. By the late 1980s, K2 had a successful line of snowboards, and Rossignol was working the kinks out of its snowboarding line (early Rossignols received a lackluster response due to their more skilike feel). Even Mistral, a Swiss windsurfing company, was designing and selling snowboards. By 2001, there were approximately 5.3 million snowboarding participants in the United States alone (see Figure 2.2), and the U.S. market for snowboarding equipment had surpassed $235 million in annual sales.[31] What had begun as the creation of a few renegade sportsmen had developed into a significant industry.

FIGURE 2.2
U.S. Snowboarding Participants (in millions, 1988–2001)

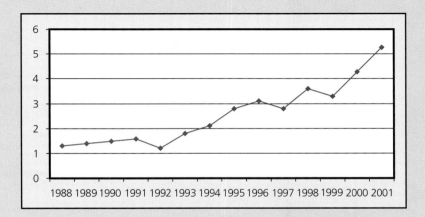

hugely successful; throughout the 1970s and 1980s, 24 Laser sailboats were produced every day.[32] User innovations can also blossom into new industries. For example, consider the development of snowboards, as described in the accompanying Theory in Action section.

Research and Development by Firms

basic research
Research targeted at increasing scientific knowledge for its own sake. It may or may not have any long-term commercial application.

applied research
Research targeted at increasing knowledge for a specific application or need.

development
Activities that apply knowledge to produce useful devices, materials, or processes.

One of the most obvious sources of firm innovation is the firm's own research and development efforts. Though the terms *research* and *development* are often lumped together, they actually represent different kinds of investment in innovation-related activities. *Research* can refer to both basic research and applied research. **Basic research** is effort directed at increasing understanding of a topic or field without a specific immediate commercial application in mind. This research advances scientific knowledge, which may (or may not) turn out to have long-run commercial implications. **Applied research** is directed at increasing understanding of a topic to meet a specific need. In industry, this research typically has specific commercial objectives. **Development** refers to activities that apply knowledge to produce useful devices, materials, or processes. Thus, the term *research and development* refers to a range of activities that extend from early exploration of a domain to specific commercial implementations.

Studies show that firms consider their in-house R&D to be their most important source of innovation (see Figure 2.3). This perception also appears to be supported by evidence on R&D spending and firm sales: a firm's R&D intensity (its R&D expenditures as a percentage of its revenues) has a strong positive correlation with its sales growth rate, sales from new products, and profitability.[33]

During the 1950s and 1960s, scholars of innovation emphasized a *science-push* approach to research and development.[34] This approach assumed that innovation proceeded linearly from scientific discovery, to invention, to engineering, then manufacturing activities, and finally marketing. According to this approach, the primary sources of innovation were discoveries in basic science that were translated into

FIGURE 2.3

Firms' Rank Ordering of the Importance of Sources for Research and Development Work, 1999

Source: E. Roberts, "Benchmarking Global Strategic Management of Technology," *Research Technology Management,* March–April 2001, pp. 25–36

	Rank Order of Sources of Research Work	Rank Order of Sources of Development Work
1	Central corporate research	Internal R&D within divisions
2	Internal R&D within divisions	Central corporate research
3	Sponsored university research	Suppliers' technology
4	Recruited students	Joint ventures/alliances
5	Continuing education	Licensing
6	University liaison programs	Customers' technology
7	Consultants/contract R&D	Continuing education
8	Joint ventures/alliances	Acquisition of products

commercial applications by the parent firm. This linear process was soon shown to have little applicability to real-world products. In the mid-1960s, another model of innovation gained prominence: the *demand-pull* model of research and development. This approach argued that innovation was driven by the perceived demand of potential users. Research staff would develop new products in efforts to respond to customer problems or suggestions. This view, however, was also criticized as being too simplistic. Rothwell, for example, points out that different phases of innovation are likely to be characterized by varying levels of science push and demand pull.[35]

Most current research suggests that firms that are successful innovators utilize multiple sources of information and ideas, including:

- In-house research and development, including basic research.
- Linkages to customers or other potential users of innovations.
- Linkages to an external network of firms that may include competitors, complementors, and suppliers.
- Linkages to other external sources of scientific and technical information, such as universities and government laboratories.[36]

Firm Linkages with Customers, Suppliers, Competitors, and Complementors

Firms often form alliances with customers, suppliers, complementors, and even competitors to jointly work on an innovation project or to exchange information and other resources in pursuit of innovation. Collaboration might occur in the form of alliances, participation in research consortia, licensing arrangements, contract research and development, joint ventures, and other arrangements. The advantages and disadvantages of different forms of collaboration are discussed in Chapter Eight. Collaborators can pool resources such as knowledge and capital, and they can share the risk of a new product development project.

The most frequent collaborations are between firms and their customers, suppliers, and local universities.[37] Several studies indicate that firms consider users their most valuable source of new product ideas.[38] The use of such collaborations is consistent across North America, Europe, and Japan, though Japanese firms may be somewhat more likely to collaborate extensively with their customers (see Figure 2.4).

FIGURE 2.4
Percentage of Companies That Report Extensive Collaboration with Customers, Suppliers, and Universities

Source: E. Roberts, "Benchmarking Global Strategic Management of Technology," *Research Technology Management,* March–April 2001, pp. 25–36

	North America	Europe	Japan
Collaborates with:			
Customers	44%	38%	52%
Suppliers	45	45	41
Universities	34	32	34

complementors
Producers of complementary goods or services (e.g., for video game console producers such as Sony or Nintendo, game developers are complementors).

Firms may also collaborate with competitors and complementors. **Complementors** are organizations (or individuals) that produce complementary goods, such as lightbulbs for lamps, or DVD movies for DVD players. In some industries, firms produce a range of goods and the line between competitor and complementor can blur. For instance, Kodak competes with Fuji in both the camera and film markets, yet Fuji's film is also a complement for Kodak's cameras and vice versa. This can make the relationships between firms very complex. In some circumstances, firms might be bitter rivals in a particular product category, and yet engage in collaborative development in that product category or complementary product categories.

For example, when Palm Computer developed its PalmPilot, it decided to produce both the operating system for the device (Palm OS) and the hardware. Palm Computing had been founded to produce applications software for personal digital assistants (PDAs), but its founder, Jeff Hawkins, did not believe any of the existing PDA models on the market possessed the right combination of features, so he designed one himself—even going so far as to carry a block of wood in his pocket that he would occasionally pull out and pretend to use as a PDA. PalmPilots quickly attained a dominant share of the PDA market, and the bulk of Palm's revenues came from hardware sales.

Palm's management believed the key to long-run success was controlling the dominant PDA operating system, just as Microsoft had controlled the dominant operating system for personal computers. Palm thus began to license its Palm OS to various companies in both the personal user and enterprise markets. The more companies that produced PDA hardware and applications for the Palm OS, the better were Palm's chances of staying the dominant market standard. However, the products produced by these companies were also competitors for Palm's own hardware and applications products, putting the company in a tricky position. Sony, for example, was one of Palm's most important licensees for the Palm OS and collaborated with Palm in several development projects, yet Sony was also one of Palm's biggest competitors in hardware. While some industry analysts argued that Palm should exit the hardware business so as to avoid alienating existing and potential producers of Palm OS PDAs, giving up hardware sales would have substantially reduced Palm's revenues. Palm opted instead to try to sustain its delicate balance of competitor-and-complementor with its licensees. In 2002, Palm announced it would gradually separate the company into two independent companies, PalmSource (the operating system unit) and PalmSolutions (the hardware unit).

External versus Internal Sourcing of Innovation

Critics have often charged that firms are using external sources of technological innovation rather than investing in original research. But empirical evidence suggests that external sources of information are more likely to be complements to rather than substitutes for in-house research and development. Research by the Federation of British Industries indicated firms that had their own research and development were also the heaviest users of external collaboration networks. Presumably doing in-house R&D helps to build the firm's **absorptive capacity,** enabling it to better assimilate and utilize information obtained externally.[39] Absorptive capacity refers to the firm's ability to understand and use new information (absorptive capacity is discussed in more detail in Chapter Four).

absorptive capacity
The ability of an organization to assimilate and utilize new knowledge.

Universities and Government-Funded Research

Another important source of innovation comes from public research institutions such as universities, government laboratories, and incubators. A significant share of companies report that research from public and nonprofit institutions enabled them to develop innovations that they would not have otherwise developed.[40]

Universities

Many universities encourage their faculty to engage in research that may lead to useful innovations. Typically the intellectual property policies of a university embrace both patentable and unpatentable innovations, and the university retains sole discretion over the rights to commercialize the innovation. If an invention is successfully commercialized, the university typically shares the income with the individual inventor(s).[41] To increase the degree to which university research leads to commercial innovation, many universities have established **technology transfer offices.**

technology transfer offices
Offices designed to facilitate the transfer of technology developed in a research environment to an environment where it can be commercially applied.

In the United States, the creation of university technology transfer offices accelerated rapidly after the Bayh-Dole Act was passed in 1980. This act allowed universities to collect royalties on inventions funded with taxpayer dollars. Before this, the federal government was entitled to all rights from federally funded inventions.[42] While the revenues from the university technology transfer activities are still quite small in comparison to university research budgets, their importance is growing rapidly. Universities also contribute significantly to innovation through the publication of research results that are incorporated into the development efforts of other organizations and individuals.

Government-Funded Research

science parks
Regional districts, typically set up by government to foster R&D collaboration between government, universities, and private firms.

Governments of many countries actively invest in research through their own laboratories, the formation of science parks and incubators, and grants for other public or private research entities. For example, the U.S. government was the main provider of research and development funds in the 1950s and 1960s, accounting for as much as 66.5 percent in 1964. Its share has fallen significantly since then, and in 2000, U.S. government spending accounted for only 26.3 percent of the nation's R&D spending. However, the decline in the government share of spending is largely due to the rapid increase in industry R&D funding rather than a real decline in the absolute amount spent by the government. U.S. government funding for R&D in 2000 was at its highest level ever—$69.6 billion (see Figure 2.5), while about $180 billion was spent by industry on R&D.

incubators
Institutions designed to nurture the development of new businesses that might otherwise lack access to adequate funding or advice.

In the United States, industry spending on R&D dwarfs that spent by government (as shown in Figure 2.6). However, the ratio of R&D funding provided by industry compared to government funding varies significantly by country as shown in Figure 2.6.

One way governments support the research and development efforts in both the public and private sectors is through the formation of **science parks** and **incubators.** Since the 1950s, national governments have actively invested in developing science parks to foster collaboration between national and local government institutions, universities, and private firms. These science parks often include institutions designed to nurture the development of new businesses that might otherwise lack access to

FIGURE 2.5
U.S. Spending on R&D by Source (in billions of constant 1996 U.S. dollars)

Source: *Science and Engineering Indicators 2002,* National Science Board.

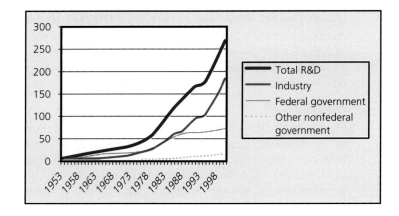

FIGURE 2.6
Percent of R&D Funds by Source and Country, 1999

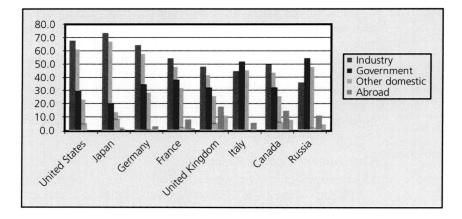

adequate funding and technical advice. Such institutions are often termed *incubators.* Incubators help overcome the market failure that can result when a new technology has the potential for important societal benefits, but its potential for direct returns is highly uncertain.[43]

Notable examples of science parks with incubators include:

- Stanford Research Park, established near Stanford University in 1951.
- Research Triangle Park, established in North Carolina in 1959.
- Sophia Antipolis Park, established in Southern France in 1969.
- Cambridge Science Park, established in Cambridge, England, in 1972.

These parks create fertile hotbeds for new startups and a focal point for the collaboration activities of established firms. Their proximity to university laboratories and other research centers ensures ready access to scientific expertise. Such centers also help university researchers implement their scientific discoveries in commercial applications.[44] Such parks often give rise to technology clusters that have long-lasting and self-reinforcing advantages (discussed later in the chapter).

FIGURE 2.7
Top 20 U.S. Nonprofit R&D Performers, 1997

Nonprofit Organization	R&D Expenditures (in $US millions)	Nonprofit Organization	R&D Expenditures (in $US millions)
Howard Hughes Medical Institute	$352.00	Beth Israel Deaconess Medical Center	$83.41
Mayo Foundation/St. Mary's Hospital, Rochester, MN	156.72	Charles Stark Draper Laboratory, Inc.	60.60
SRI International	146.14	The Salk Institute for Biological Studies	56.08
Memorial Sloan Kettering Cancer Center	115.23	Ludwig Institute for Cancer Research	54.50
Research Triangle Institute	112.90	Analytic Services, Inc.	51.77
Fred Hutchinson Cancer Research Center	100.47	Harbor-UCLA Research and Education Institute	46.69
SEMATECH, Inc.	97.70	Children's Hospital of Philadelphia	45.72
Dana-Farber Cancer Institute (Children's Cancer Research Foundation)	91.00	Rand Corporation	43.00
		Population Council	42.23
		Summer Institute of Linguistics, Inc.	41.00
Brigham and Women's Hospital	87.79	Whitehead Institute for Biomedical Research	40.71

Private Nonprofit Organizations

Private nonprofit organizations, such as private research institutes, nonprofit hospitals, private foundations, professional or technical societies, academic and industrial consortia, and trade associations, also contribute to innovation activity in a variety of complex ways. Many nonprofit organizations perform their own research and development activities, some fund the research and development activities of other organizations but do not do it themselves, and some nonprofit organizations do both in-house research and development and fund the development efforts of others. Nonprofit organizations spent $8.8 billion on R&D performed in-house in 2000, and funded an additional $2 billion in R&D conducted by others.[45]

In the United States, the top 20 nonprofit organizations that conduct a significant amount of research and development include such organizations as the Howard Hughes Medical Institute, the Mayo Foundation, the Memorial Sloan Kettering Cancer Center, SEMATECH, and Rand Corporation (see Figure 2.7).

INNOVATION IN COLLABORATIVE NETWORKS

As the previous sections indicate, there is a growing recognition of the importance of collaborative research and development networks for successful innovation.[46] Such collaborations include (but are not limited to) joint ventures, licensing and second-sourcing agreements, research associations, government-sponsored joint research programs, value-added networks for technical and scientific interchange, and informal networks.[47] Collaborative research is especially important in high-technology sectors, where it is unlikely that a single individual or organization will possess all of the resources and capabilities necessary to develop and implement a significant innovation.[48]

Sometimes geographical proximity appears to play a role in the formation and innovative activity of collaborative networks. Well-known regional clusters such as Silicon Valley's semiconductor firms, lower Manhattan's multimedia cluster, and the Modena, Italy, knitwear district aptly illustrate this point. This has spurred considerable interest in the factors that lead to the emergence of a cluster. City and state governments, for example, might like to know how to foster the creation of a technology cluster in their region in order to increase employment, tax revenues, and other economic benefits. For firms, understanding the drivers and benefits of clustering is useful for developing a strategy that ensures the firm is well-positioned to benefit from clustering.

Technology Clusters

technology clusters
Regional clusters of firms that have a connection to a common technology, and may engage in buyer, supplier, and complementor relationships, as well as research collaboration.

complex knowledge
Knowledge that has many underlying components, many interdependencies between those components, or both.

tacit knowledge
Knowledge that cannot be readily codified (documented in written form).

Technology clusters may span a region as narrow as a city or as wide as a group of neighboring countries.[49] Clusters often encompass an array of industries that are linked through relationships between suppliers, buyers, and producers of complements. One primary reason for the emergence of regional clusters is the benefit of proximity in knowledge exchange. Though advances in information technology have made it easier, faster, and cheaper to transmit information great distances, several studies indicate that knowledge does not always transfer readily via such mechanisms.

Proximity and interaction can directly influence firms' ability and willingness to exchange knowledge. First, knowledge that is **complex** or **tacit** may require frequent and close interaction to be meaningfully exchanged.[50] Firms may need to interact frequently to develop common ways of understanding and articulating the knowledge before they are able to transfer it.[51] Second, closeness and frequency of interaction can influence a firm's *willingness* to exchange knowledge. When firms interact frequently, they can develop trust and reciprocity norms. Firms that interact over time develop greater knowledge of each other, and their repeated interactions give them information as to the likelihood of their partner behaving opportunistically. A shared understanding of the rules of engagement emerges, wherein each partner understands its obligations with respect to how much knowledge is exchanged, how that knowledge can be used, and how the firms are expected to reciprocate.[52]

Firms that are proximate thus have an advantage in sharing information that can lead to greater innovation productivity. This can, in turn, lead to other self-reinforcing geographical advantages. A cluster of firms with high innovation productivity can lead to more new firms starting up in the immediate vicinity and can attract other firms to the area.[53] As firms grow, divisions may be spun off into new firms, entrepreneurial employees may start their own enterprises, and supplier and distributor markets emerge to service the cluster. Successful firms also attract new labor to the area and help to make the existing labor pool more valuable by enabling individuals to gain experience working with the innovative firms. The increase in employment and tax revenues in the region can lead to improvements in infrastructure (such as roads and utilities), schools, and other markets that service the population (such as shopping malls, grocery stores, health care providers, etc.).

A big part of the reason that knowledge tends to be regionally localized is that knowledge is, to a large extent, held by people, and people are often only reluctantly mobile. In a well-known study, Annalee Saxenian found that engineers in Silicon Valley were more loyal to their craft than to any particular company, but they were also very likely to stay in the region even if they changed jobs.[54] This was due in part to the labor market for their skills in the region, and in part due to the disruption in an individual's personal life if he or she were to move out of the region. Thus, if for some reason an innovative activity commences in a geographic locale, the knowledge and expertise that accumulates might not spread readily into other geographic locales, leading to a localized cluster of technological expertise.[55]

Studies have indicated that while many innovative activities appear to have some geographic component, the degree to which innovative activities are geographically clustered depends on things such as:

- The nature of the technology, such as its underlying knowledge base or the degree to which it can be protected by patents or copyright, and the degree to which its communication requires close and frequent interaction.
- Industry characteristics, such as the degree of market concentration or stage of the industry life cycle, transportation costs, the availability of supplier and distributor markets.
- The cultural context of the technology, such as the population density of labor or customers, infrastructure development, or national differences in the way technology development is funded or protected.

For example, one study that examined the spatial distribution of technology sectors in different countries found that pharmaceutical development was highly clustered in the United Kingdom and France, but much more spatially diffused in Italy and Germany.[56] The same study found, however, that the manufacture of clothing demonstrated high clustering in Italy, but not in France, Germany, or the United Kingdom. While the clustering of pharmaceutical development may have been influenced by the national systems of research funding and the need to share complex technological expertise, the formation of textile clusters may have been due more to cultural factors that influenced the historical rise of industrial districts.

Technological Spillovers

technological spillovers
A positive externality from R&D resulting from the spread of knowledge across organizational or regional boundaries.

While the work on technology clusters has tended to emphasize the "stickiness" of knowledge, a related body of research has focused on explaining the spread of knowledge across organizational or regional boundaries. This topic is known as technological spillovers. **Technological spillovers** occur when the benefits from the research activities of one firm (or nation or other entity) spill over to other firms (or nations or other entities). Spillovers are thus a positive externality of research and development efforts. Evidence suggests that technology spillovers are a significant influence on innovative activity. For example, in a series of studies conducted in the 1980s and 1990s, Adam Jaffe and his coauthors found that both a firm's patenting activities and profits were influenced by the R&D spending of other firms and universities in its geographical region.[57]

Research Brief Knowledge Brokers

Andrew Hargadon and Robert Sutton point out that some firms play a particularly pivotal role in the innovation network–that of knowledge brokers. **Knowledge brokers** are individuals or firms that transfer information from one domain to another in which it can be usefully applied. The knowledge broker puts existing information to use in new and profitable ways. Hargadon and Sutton provide the example of Robert Fulton, who after observing the use of steam engines in mines, realized this technology could be used to propel boats and subsequently developed the first successful steamboat.[58] While Fulton did not claim to have invented the steamboat (there had been at least 30 years of prior development on steamboats), Fulton's design was the first to combine existing technologies into a successful product.

In a network of firms, a knowledge broker may be a firm that connects clusters of firms that would otherwise share no connection. By serving as the bridge between two different knowledge networks, the knowledge broker is in a position to find unique combinations from the knowledge possessed by the two groups. This can enable knowledge brokers to be exceptionally prolific in generating innovation. Consider Thomas Edison's laboratory. Edison's strategy of borrowing from different industries to create products that would ultimately serve many markets resulted in innovations in telegraphs, telephones, phonographs, generators, lightbulbs, vacuum pumps, and many others.[59]

Knowledge brokers may not create breakthroughs in any single technology, but instead may exploit the potential synergies of combining existing technologies. While this might at first seem to limit the scope of a knowledge broker's potential, research suggests that most innovation is not due to the discovery of something fundamentally new, but is instead the result of novel recombinations of known concepts and materials.[60] Thus, the knowledge broker's key expertise may lie not in a particular domain of science, but instead in the ability to recognize and capture potential solutions that may be matched to problems in an unexpected way.

knowledge brokers
Individuals or organizations that transfer information from one domain to another in which it can be usefully applied.

Whether R&D benefits will spill over is partially a function of the strength of protection mechanisms such as patents, copyrights, and trade secrets (methods of protecting innovation are discussed in greater detail in Chapter Nine). Since the strength of protection mechanisms varies significantly across industries and countries, the likelihood of spillovers varies also.[61] The likelihood of spillovers is also a function of the nature of the underlying knowledge base (for example, as explained in the previous section, tacit knowledge may not flow readily across firm boundaries) and the mobility of the labor pool.[62]

Summary of Chapter

1. Creativity is the underlying process for innovation. Creativity enables individuals and organizations to generate new and useful ideas. Creativity is considered a function of intellectual abilities, knowledge, thinking styles, personality traits, intrinsic motivation, and environment.

2. Innovation sometimes originates with individual inventors. The most prolific inventors tend to be trained in multiple fields, be highly curious, question previously made assumptions, and view all knowledge as unified. The most well-known inventors tend to have both inventive and entrepreneurial traits.

3. Innovation can also originate with users who create solutions to their own needs. The rise of the snowboarding industry provides a rich example.

4. Firms, research and development is considered a primary driver of innovation. In the United States, firms spend significantly more on R&D than government institutions spend on R&D, and firms consider their in-house R&D their most important source of innovation.

5. Firms often collaborate with a number of external organizations (or individuals) in their innovation activities. Firms are most likely to collaborate with customers, suppliers, and universities, though they also may collaborate with competitors, producers of complements, government laboratories, nonprofit organizations, and other research institutions.

6. Many universities have a research mission, and in recent years universities have become more active in setting up technology transfer activities to directly commercialize the inventions of faculty. Universities also contribute to innovation through the publication of research findings.

7. Government also plays an active role in conducting research and development (in its own laboratories), funding the R&D of other organizations, and creating institutions to foster collaboration networks and to nurture start-ups (e.g., science parks and incubators). In some countries, government-funded research and development exceeds that of industry-funded research.

8. Private nonprofit organizations (such as research institutes and nonprofit hospitals) are another source of innovation. These organizations both perform their own R&D and fund R&D conducted by others.

9. Probably the most significant source of innovation does not come from individual organizations or people, but from the collaborative networks that leverage resources and capabilities across multiple organizations or individuals. Collaborative networks are particularly important in high-technology sectors.

10. Collaboration is often facilitated by geographical proximity, which can lead to regional technology clusters.

11. Technology spillovers are positive externality benefits of R&D, such as when the knowledge acquired through R&D spreads to other organizations.

Discussion Questions

1. What are some of the advantages and disadvantages of (*a*) individuals as innovators, (*b*) firms as innovators, (*c*) universities as innovators, (*d*) government institutions as innovators, (*e*) nonprofit organizations as innovators?

2. What traits appear to make individuals most creative? Are these the same traits that lead to successful inventions?

3. Could firms identify people with greater capacity for creativity or inventiveness in their hiring procedures?

4. To what degree do you think the creativity of the firm is a function of the creativity of individuals, versus the structure, routines, incentives, and culture of the firm? Provide an example of a firm that does a particularly good job at nurturing and leveraging the creativity of its individuals.

5. Several studies indicate that the use of collaborative research agreements is increasing around the world. What are some reasons collaborative research is becoming more prevalent?

Endnotes

1. J. Bender, D. Condon, S. Gadkari, G. Shuster, I. Shuster, and M. A. Schilling, "Designing a New Form of Mobility: Segway Human Transporter," New York University teaching case, 2003.

2. E. I. Schwartz, "The Inventor's Play-Ground," *Technology Review* 105, no. 8 (2002), pp. 68–73.

3. Ibid.

4. *The Great Inventor.* Retrieved November 19, 2002, from www.cbsnews.com.

5. Schwartz, "The Inventor's Play-Ground."

6. M. Watson, "Seminar on Segway Scooter Focuses on Design Process," Knight Ridder Tribune Business News, January 11, 2003, p. 1.

7. Ibid.

8. R. Rothwell, "Factors for Success in Industrial Innovations, Project SAPPHO—A Comparative Study of Success and Failure in Industrial Innovation," SPRU, University of Sussex, Brighton, U.K., 1972; and L. Smith-Doerr, J. Owen-Smith, K. W. Koput, and W. W. Powell, "Networks and Knowledge Production: Collaboration and Patenting in Biotechnology," in *Corporate Social Capital,* eds. R. Leenders and S. Gabbay (Norwell, MA: Kluwer Academic Publishers, 1999), pp. 331–50.

9. F. Barron, *Creative Person and Creative Process* (New York: Holt, Rinehart, and Winston, 1969); D. W. MacKinnon, "Personality and the Realization of Creative Potential," *American Psychologist* 17 (1965), pp. 484–95; R. Oshse, *Before the Gates of Excellence: The Determinants of Creative Genius* (New York: Cambridge University Press, 1990); and T. Lubart, "Creativity," in *Thinking and Problem Solving,* ed. R. J. Sternberg (New York: Academic Press, 1994), pp. 289–332.

10. M. Boden, *The Creative Mind: Myths and Mechanisms* (New York: Basic Books, 1992).

11. Lubart, "Creativity."

12. R. J. Sternberg and T. I. Lubart, "The Concept of Creativity: Prospects and Paradigms," in *Handbook of Creativity,* ed. R. J. Sternberg (Cambridge, England: Cambridge University Press, 1999).

13. P. A. Frensch and R. J. Sternberg, "Expertise and Intelligent Thinking: When Is It Worse to Know Better?" in *Advances in the Psychology of Human Intelligence,* vol. 5, ed. R. J. Sternberg (Hillsdale, NJ: Erlbaum, 1989), pp. 157–158.

14. T. I. Lubart, "Product-Centered Self-Evaluation and the Creative Process," unpublished doctoral dissertation, New Haven, CT: Yale University Press, 1994; and Sternberg and Lubart, "The Concept of Creativity."

15. T. M. Amabile, *The Social Psychology of Creativity* (New York: Springer-Verlag, 1983); and T. M. Amabile, *Creativity in Context* (Boulder, CO: Westview, 1996).

16. R. W. Woodman, J. E. Sawyer, and R. W. Griffin, "Toward a Theory of Organizational Creativity," *Academy of Management Review* 18 (1993), pp. 293–321.

17. C. Gorski and E. Heinekamp, "Capturing Employee Ideas for New Products," in *The PDMA Toolbook for New Product Development,* P. Belliveau, A. Griffin, and S. Somermeyer (New York: John Wiley & Sons, 2002).

18. Gorski and Heinekamp, "Capturing Employee Ideas for New Products;" and R. E. Mcdermott, R. J. Mikulak, and M. R. Beauregard, *Employee Driven Quality: Releasing the Creative Spirit of Your Organization Through Suggestion Systems* (White Plains, NY: Quality Resource, 1993).

19. Gorski and Heinekamp, "Capturing Employee Ideas for New Products."

20. Woodman, Sawyer, and Griffin, "Toward a Theory of Organizational Creativity;" and Amabile, *The Social Psychology of Creativity.*

21. A. H. Church and J. Waclawski, "The Relationship between Individual Personality Orientation and Executive Leadership Behavior," *Journal of Occupational and Organizational Psychology* 71, no. 2 (1998), pp. 99–125.

22. R. S. Root-Bernstein, "Who Discovers and Who Invents," *Research Technology Management* 32, no. 1 (1989), pp. 43–51.

23. Ibid.

24. Sir MacFarlane, Burnett, *Changing Patterns, an Atypical Autobiography* (Melbourne and London: Heinemann, 1968), p. 35.

25. P. Debye, interview in *The Editors of International Science and Technology, The Way of the Scientist. Interviews from the World of Science and Technology* (New York: Simon and Schuster, 1966), p. 80.

26. T. P. Hughes, "How Did the Heroic Inventors Do It?" *American Heritage of Invention and Technology,* Fall, 1985, p. 21.

27. B. Z. Khan and K. I. Sokoloff, "Schemes of Practical Utility: Entrepreneurship and Innovation Among 'Great Inventors' in the United States, 1790–1865," *Journal of Economic History* 53, no. 2 (1993), p. 289.

28. E. Von Hippel, "Innovation by User Communities: Learning from Open-Source Software," *Sloan Management Review* 42, no. 4 (2001), pp. 82–86.

29. M. A. Schilling, A. Eng, and M. Velasquez, "Madd Snowboards," in *Strategic Management: Competitiveness and Globalization,* eds. M. Hitt, D. Ireland, and B. Hoskisson, 4th ed. (St. Paul, MN: West Publishing, 2000).

30. Transworld Snowboarding, Snowboard History Timeline, www.twsnow.com.

31. Statistics from the National Sporting Goods Association.

32. R. J. Thomas, *New Product Success Stories: Lessons from Leading Innovators* (New York: John Wiley & Sons, Inc., 1995).

33. E. Roberts, "Benchmarking Global Strategic Management of Technology," *Research Technology Management,* March–April 2001, pp. 25–36.

34. M. Dodgson, *The Management of Technological Innovation* (New York: Oxford University Press, 2000).

35. Ibid.

36. C. Freeman, "Networks of Innovators: A Synthesis of Research Issues," *Research Policy* 20 (1991), pp. 499–514; Rothwell, "Factors for Success in Industrial Innovations, Project SAPPHO"; and R. Rothwell, C. Freeman, A. Horseley, V. T. B. Jervis, A. B. Robertson, and J. Townsend, "SAPPHO Updated-Project SAPPHO Phase II," *Research Policy* 3 (1974), pp. 258–91.

37. Roberts, "Benchmarking Global Strategic Management of Technology."

38. R. G. Cooper and E. Kleinschmidt, "An Investigation into the New Product Process: Steps, Deficiencies, and Impact," *Journal of Product Innovation Management* 3, no. 2 (1986), pp. 71–85; and E. Yoon and G. Lilien, "Characteristics of the Industrial Distributor's Innovation Activities: An Exploratory Study," *Journal of Product Innovation Management* 5, no. 3 (1988), pp. 227–40.

39. W. M. Cohen and D. A. Levinthal, "Absorptive Capacity: A New Perspective on Learning and Innovation," *Administrative Science Quarterly* March 1990, pp. 128–152.

40. M. Biese and H. Stahl, "Public Research and Industrial Innovations in Germany," *Research Policy* 28 (1999), pp. 397–422; and E. Mansfield, "Academic Research and Industrial Innovation. Research Policy," 20 (1991), pp. 1–12.

41. A. Silverman, "Understanding University Patent Policies," *JOM* 55, no. 1 (2003), p. 64.

42. D. Rahm and V. Hansen, "Technology Policy 2000: University to Industry Transfer," *International Journal of Public Administration* 22, no. 8 (1999), pp. 1189–211.

43. M. Colombo and M. Delmastro, "How Effective Are Technology Incubators? Evidence from Italy," *Research Policy* 31 (2001), pp. 1103–22.

44. Ibid.

45. Data obtained from the National Science Foundation.

46. G. Ahuja and C. M. Lampert, "Entrepreneurship in the Large Corporation: A Longitudinal Study of How Established Firms Create Breakthrough Inventions," *Strategic Management Journal* 22 (2001), pp. 521–43; T. J. Allen, *Managing the Flow of Technology: Technology Transfer and the Dissemination of Technological Information Within the R&D Organization* (Cambridge, MA: MIT Press, 1977); R. S. Burt, *Structural Holes* (Cambridge, MA: Harvard University Press, 1992); C. Freeman, "Networks of Innovators: A Synthesis of Research Issues," *Research Policy* 20 (1991), pp. 499–514; S. C. Gilfillan, *The Sociology of Invention* (Chicago: Follett, 1935); and A. B. Hargadon and R. I. Sutton, "Technology Brokering and Innovation in a Product Development Firm," *Administrative Science Quarterly* 42 (1997), pp. 716–49.

47. K. Imai and Y. Baba, 1989, "Systemic Innovation and Cross-Border Networks: Transcending Markets and Hierarchies to Create a New Techno-Economic System," OECD, Conference on Science Technology and Economic Growth, Paris; and C. Freeman, "Networks of Innovators: A Synthesis of Research Issues," *Research Policy* 20 (1991), pp. 499–514.

48. J. Hegedoorn, "Inter-Firm R&D Partnerships—an Overview of Major Trends and Patterns Since 1960," *Research Policy* 31 (2002), pp. 477–92.

49. M. E. Porter, "Location, Competition, and Economic Development: Local Clusters in a Global Economy," *Economic Development Quarterly* 14, no. 1 (2000), pp. 15–34.

50. P. Almeida and B. Kogut, "Localization of Knowledge and the Mobility of Engineers in Regional Networks," *Management Science* 45 (1999), pp. 905–17; P. Bourdieu, "The Forms of Capital," in *Handbook of Theory and Research for the Sociology of Education,* ed. J. G. Richardson (Westport, CT: Greenwood Press, 1986), pp. 241–58; M. S. Granovetter, "Problems of Explanation in Economic Sociology," in *Networks and Organizations: Structure, Form, and Action,* eds. N. Nohria and R. Eccles (Boston: Harvard Business School Press, 1992), pp. 25–56; and M. T. Hansen, "The Search-Transfer Problem: The Role of Weak Ties in Sharing Knowledge across Organization Subunits," *Administrative Science Quarterly* 44 (1999), pp. 82–112.

51. U. Zander and B. Kogut, "Knowledge and the Speed of the Transfer and Imitation of Organizational Capabilities: An Empirical Test," *Organization Science* 6 (1995), pp. 76–92; and G. Szulanski, "Exploring Internal Stickiness: Impediments to the Transfer of Best Practice Within the Firm," *Strategic Management Journal* 17 (winter special issue) (1996), pp. 27–43.

52. J. H. Dyer and K. Nobeoka, "Creating and Managing a High-Performance Knowledge-Sharing Network: The Toyota Case," *Strategic Management Journal* 21 (2000), pp. 345–67; and E. Von Hippel, "Cooperation between Rivals: Informal Know-How Trading," *Research Policy* 16 (1987), pp. 291–302.

53. T. Stuart and O. Sorenson, "The Geography of Opportunity: Spatial Heterogeneity in Founding Rates and the Performance of Biotechnology Firms," *Research Policy* 32 (2003), p. 229.

54. A. Saxenian, *Regional Advantage: Culture and Competition in Silicon Valley and Route 128* (Cambridge, MA/London: Harvard University Press, 1994).

55. P. Almeida and B. Kogut, "Localization of Knowledge and the Mobility of Engineers in Regional Networks," *Management Science* 45 (1999), pp. 905–17.

56. S. Breschi, "The Geography of Innovation: A Cross-Sector Analysis," *Regional Studies* 34, no. 3 (2000), pp. 213–29.

57. A. B. Jaffe, "Technological Opportunity and Spillovers of R&D: Evidence from Firms' Patents, Profits and Market Value," *American Economic Review* 76 (1986), pp. 984–1001; A. B. Jaffe, "Real Effects of Academic Research," *American Economic Review* 79 (1989), pp. 957–70; and A. B. Jaffee, M. Trajtenberg, and R. Henderson, "Geographic Localization of Knowledge Spillovers as Evidenced by Citations," *Quarterly Journal of Economics* 63 (1993), pp. 577–98.

58. A. Hargadon and R. Sutton, "Building an Innovation Factory," *Harvard Business Review* May–June, 2000, pp. 157–66.

59. A. B. Hargadon, "Firms as Knowledge Brokers: Lessons in Pursuing Continuous Innovation," *California Management Review* 40, no. 3 (1998), pp. 209–27.

60. S. C. Gilfillan, *The Sociology of Invention* (Chicago: Follett, 1935); R. R. Nelson and S. Winter, *An Evolutionary Theory of Economic Change* (Cambridge, MA: Harvard University Press, 1982); E. G. Penrose, *The Theory of the Growth of the Firm* (New York: Wiley, 1959); J. A. Schumpeter, *The Theory of Economic Development* (Cambridge, MA: Harvard University Press, 1934); and A. Usher, *A History of Mechanical Inventions* (Cambridge, MA: Harvard University Press, 1954).

61. W. Cohen, A. Goto, A. Nagata, R. Nelson, and J. Walsh, "R&D Spillovers, Patents and the Incentives to Innovate in Japan and the United States," *Research Policy* 31 (2002), pp. 1349–67.

62. Almeida and Kogut, "Localization of Knowledge and the Mobility of Engineers in Regional Networks."

Chapter **Three**

Types and Patterns
of Innovation

Ericsson's Gamble on 3G Wireless

Ericsson was founded in Sweden in 1876 as a repair shop for telegraph equipment and grew to become one of the leading manufacturers of advanced telecommunication equipment in the world. Some of its more noteworthy innovations included a dial telephone introduced in 1931 that became the standard for the UK post office, Stockholm's first mobile phone system in 1956, and in 1988, the world's first Global System for Mobile Communications (GSM) cellular telephone service. GSM would go on to become the most widely used wireless platform by the late 1990s. At the end of 2002, Ericsson was the largest supplier of mobile telecommunication systems in the world; approximately 40 percent of all mobile calls were made through Ericsson systems.

In 1999, most wireless telecommunication leaders had set their sights on the third generation (3G) of mobile telephony. The first generation (in the 1970s and 1980s) had been analog voice communication; the second generation of the 1990s had enabled voice and text transmission over digital networks. However, by the late 1990s, the market for second-generation handsets and networks was maturing and sales were beginning to decline. Wireless telephone producers and service providers thus began envisioning the introduction of a third generation of wireless communication technology that would utilize broadband channels. This increased bandwidth would give mobile phones far greater data transmission capabilities that would enable activities such as videoconferencing and accessing the most advanced Internet sites.[1]

As of spring 2001, Ericcson appeared well positioned to be a market leader in 3G technology. It had already won 22 infrastructure contracts, close to 70 percent of all infrastructure contracts awarded in the world. However, in its focus on pioneering the 3G marketplace, Ericsson had fallen behind in the 2G wireless market and had seen a significant erosion in its profits. In fact, in 2001, Ericsson lost more than $2 billion, bringing its return on assets down from 8.4 percent in 2000 to −8.5 percent in 2001. Some industry observers argued that research and development of new-generation wireless systems were soaking up most of Ericsson's resources and had caused the company to lose sight of the current marketplace. Many people felt the company's move toward 3G was too early, while others praised Ericsson's strategy for its long-term vision. After all, 2G margins were declining precipitously, and sales of new 3G network equipment and handsets offered the potential of reviving the industry.

By mid-2002, it was clear that the transition to 3G networks was going to be even more complex and risky than originally anticipated. Though Ericsson and other 3G network system providers such as Nokia had counted on the increased efficiency of their systems to persuade telecom operators to adopt them, major problems such as a lack of affordable 3G handsets and competing 3G network standards had significantly dampened the pace of the rollout. European mobile operators had led the race in upgrading to 3G networks, and the initial optimism over 3G had spurred operators to spend billions of euros on operating licenses from government auctions. However, this spending left the companies so deeply in debt that they lost investor support to roll out 3G networks at the pace they had originally intended.[2] Operators such as Spain's Telefonica SA, Finland's Sonera, and Germany's MobilCom all announced they would scale back or suspend their investments in 3G networks, sending a shudder through network providers.

Worse news still were the rumors that consumers might not find 3G capabilities to be valuable. In late 2002, a report from Japan's DoCoMo, the world's first company to offer 3G services, indicated most individuals used such features as picture messaging only for the first two months after getting their 3G handset—after which the novelty had apparently worn off. Other desirable features, such as videoconferencing, turned out to be impractical for users because they rapidly drained the battery power.[3] The future of 3G, and the companies that had bet their futures on it, looked precarious.

Discussion Questions

1. Is 3G a radical innovation or an incremental innovation?
2. What factors do you think will influence the rate at which 3G technologies are adopted by operators and mobile phone consumers?
3. Is Ericsson trying to offer more technological capability than consumers really need?
4. Is Ericsson's focus on 3G technologies a good strategy? Why or why not?

OVERVIEW

The previous chapters pointed out that technological innovation can come from many sources and take many forms. Different types of technological innovations offer different opportunities for organizations and society, and they pose different demands upon producers, users, and regulators. While there is no single agreed-upon taxonomy to describe different kinds of technological innovations, in this chapter we will review several dimensions that are often used to categorize technologies. These dimensions are useful for understanding some key ways that one innovation may differ from another.

technology trajectory
The path a technology takes through its lifetime. This path may refer to its rate of performance improvement, its rate of diffusion, or other change of interest.

The path a technology follows through time is termed its **technology trajectory.** Technology trajectories are most often used to represent the technology's rate of performance improvement or its rate of adoption in the marketplace. Though many factors can influence these technology trajectories (as discussed in both this chapter and the following chapters), some patterns have been consistently identified in technology trajectories across many industry contexts and over many periods. Understanding these patterns of technological innovation provides a useful foundation that we will build upon in the later chapters on formulating technology strategy.

The chapter begins by reviewing the dimensions used to distinguish types of innovations. It then describes the s-curve patterns so often observed in both the rate of technology improvement and the rate of technology diffusion to the market. In the last section, the chapter describes research suggesting that technological innovation follows a cyclical pattern composed of distinct and reliably occurring phases.

TYPES OF INNOVATION

Technological innovations are often categorized into different types such as "radical" versus "incremental." Different types of innovation require different kinds of underlying knowledge and have different impacts on the industry's competitors and customers. Four of the dimensions most commonly used to categorize innovations are described here: product versus process innovation, radical versus incremental, competence enhancing versus competence destroying, and architectural versus component.

Product Innovation versus Process Innovation

Product innovations are embodied in the outputs of an organization—its goods or services. For example, both Ericsson's development of third-generation wireless networks and the provision of new third-generation wireless services by telecommunications operators are product innovations. Process innovations are innovations in the way an organization conducts its business, such as in the techniques of producing or marketing goods or services. Process innovations are often oriented toward improving the effectiveness or efficiency of production by, for example, reducing defect rates or increasing the quantity that may be produced in a given time. For example, a process innovation at a biotechnology firm might entail developing a genetic algorithm that can quickly search a set of disease-related genes to identify a target for therapeutic intervention. In this instance, the process innovation (the genetic algorithm) can speed up the firm's ability to develop a product innovation (a new therapeutic drug).

New product innovations and process innovations often occur in tandem. First, new processes may enable the production of new products. For example, as discussed later in the chapter, the development of new metallurgical techniques enabled the development of the bicycle chain, which in turn enabled the development of multiple-gear bicycles. Second, new products may enable the development of new processes. For example, the development of advanced workstations has enabled firms to implement computer-aided-manufacturing processes that increase the speed and efficiency of production. Finally, a product innovation for one firm may simultaneously be a process innovation for another. For example, when United Parcel Service (UPS) helps a customer develop a more efficient distribution system, the new distribution system is simultaneously a product innovation for UPS and process innovation for its customer.

Though product innovations are often more visible than process innovations, both are extremely important to an organization's ability to compete. Throughout the remainder of the book, the term *innovation* will be used to refer to both product and process innovations.

Radical Innovation versus Incremental Innovation

One of the primary dimensions used to distinguish types of innovation is the continuum between radical versus incremental innovation. A number of definitions have been posed for **radical innovation** and **incremental innovation,** but most hinge on the degree to which an innovation represents a departure from existing practices.[4] Thus radicalness might be conceived as the combination of *newness* and the degree of *differentness*. A technology could be new to the world, new to an industry, new to a firm, or new merely to an adopting business unit. A technology could be significantly different from existing products and processes or only marginally different. The most radical innovations would be new to the world and exceptionally different from existing products and processes. The introduction of wireless telecommunication products aptly illustrates this—it embodied significantly new technologies that required new manufacturing and service processes. Incremental innovation is at the other end of the spectrum. An incremental innovation might not be particularly new or exceptional; it might have been previously known to the firm or industry, and involve only a minor change from (or adjustment to) existing practices. For example, changing the configuration of a cell phone from one that has an exposed keyboard to one that has a flip cover or offering a new service plan that enables more free weekend minutes would represent incremental innovations.

The radicalness of innovation is also sometimes defined in terms of risk. Since radical innovations often embody new knowledge, producers and customers will vary in their experience and familiarity with the innovation, and in their judgment of its usefulness or reliability.[5] The development of 3G technologies is again illustrative. For companies to develop and offer 3G wireless telecommunications service required a significant investment in new networking equipment and an infrastructure capable of carrying a much larger bandwidth of signals. It also required developing phones with greater display and memory capabilities, and either increasing the phone's battery power or increasing the efficiency of the phone's power utilization. Any of these technologies could potentially pose serious obstacles. It was also unknown to what degree customers would ultimately value broadband capability in a wireless device. Thus, the move to 3G required managers to assess several different risks simultaneously, including technical feasibility, reliability, costs, and demand.

Finally, the radicalness of an innovation is relative, and may change over time or with respect to different observers. An innovation that was once considered radical may eventually be considered incremental as the knowledge base underlying the

radical innovation
An innovation that is very new and different from prior solutions.

incremental innovation
An innovation that makes a relatively minor change from (or adjustment to) existing practices.

innovation becomes more common. For example, while the first steam engine was a monumental innovation, today their construction seems relatively simple. Furthermore, an innovation that is radical to one firm may seem incremental to another. Although both Kodak and Sony introduced digital cameras for the consumer market within a year of each other (Kodak's DC40 was introduced in 1995, and Sony's Cyber-Shot Digital Still Camera was introduced in 1996), the two companies' paths to the introduction were quite different. Kodak's historical competencies and reputation were based on its expertise in chemical photography, and thus the transition to digital photography and video required a significant redirection for the firm. Sony, on the other hand, had been an electronics company since its inception, and had a substantial level of expertise in digital recording and graphics before producing a digital camera. Thus, for Sony, a digital camera was a straightforward extension of its existing competencies.

Competence Enhancing Innovation versus Competence Destroying Innovation

competence enhancing (destroying) innovation
An innovation that builds on (renders obsolete) existing knowledge and skills. Whether an innovation is competence enhancing or competence destroying depends on whose perspective is being taken. An innovation can be competence enhancing to one firm, while competence destroying for another.

Innovations can also be classified as **competence enhancing** versus **competence destroying.** An innovation is considered to be competence enhancing from the perspective of a particular firm if it builds on the firm's existing knowledge base. For example, each generation of Intel's microprocessors (e.g., 286, 386, 486, Pentium, Pentium II, Pentium III, Pentium 4) builds on the technology underlying the previous generation. Thus, while each generation embodies innovation, these innovations leverage Intel's existing competencies, making them more valuable.

An innovation is considered to be competence destroying from the perspective of a particular firm if the technology does not build on the firm's existing competencies or renders them obsolete. For example, from the 1600s to the early 1970s, no self-respecting mathematician or engineer would have been caught without his or her slide rule. Slide rules are lightweight devices, often constructed of wood, that use logarithm scales to solve complex mathematical functions. They were used to calculate everything from the structural properties of a bridge to the range and fuel use of an aircraft. Specially designed slide rules for businesses had, for example, scales for doing loan calculations or determining optimal purchase quantities. During the 1950s and 1960s, Keuffel & Esser was the preeminent slide-rule maker in the United States, producing 5,000 slide rules a month. However, in the early 1970s, a new innovation relegated the slide rule to collectors and museum displays within just a few years: the inexpensive handheld calculator. Keuffel & Esser had no background in the electronic components that made electronic calculators possible and was unable to transition to the new technology. By 1976, Keuffel & Esser withdrew from the market.[6] Whereas the inexpensive handheld calculator built on the existing competencies of companies such as Hewlett-Packard and Texas Instruments (and thus for them would be competence enhancing), for Keuffel & Esser, the calculator was a competence destroying innovation.

Architectural Innovation versus Component Innovation

Most products and processes are hierarchically nested systems, meaning that at any unit of analysis, the entity is a system of components, and each of those components is, in turn, a system of finer components, until we reach some point at which the components are elementary particles.[7] For example, a bicycle is a system of components such as a frame, wheels, tires, seat, brakes, and so on. Each of those components is also a system of components: the seat might be a system of components that includes a metal and plastic frame, padding, a nylon cover, and so on.

An innovation may entail a change to individual components, to the overall architecture within which those components operate, or both. An innovation is considered a **component innovation** (or **modular innovation**) if it entails changes to one or more components, but does not significantly affect the overall configuration of the system.[8] In the example above, an innovation in bicycle seat technology (such as the incorporation of gel-filled material for additional cushioning) does not require any changes in the rest of the bicycle architecture.

In contrast, an **architectural innovation** entails changing the overall design of the system or the way that components interact with each other. An innovation that is strictly architectural may reconfigure the way that components link together in the system, without changing the components themselves.[9] Most architectural innovations, however, create changes in the system that reverberate throughout its design, requiring changes in the underlying components in addition to changes in the ways those components interact. Architectural innovations often have far-reaching and complex influences on industry competitors and technology users.

For example, the transition from the high-wheel bicycle to the safety bicycle was an architectural innovation that required (and enabled) the change of many components of the bicycle and the way in which riders propelled themselves. In the 1800s, bicycles had extremely large front wheels. Because there were no gears, the size of the front wheel directly determined the speed of the bicycle since the circumference of the wheel was the distance that could be traveled in a single rotation of the pedals. However, by the start of the 20th century, improvements in metallurgy had enabled the production of a fine chain and a sprocket that was small enough and light enough for a human to power. This enabled bicycles to be built with two equally sized wheels, while using gears to accomplish the speeds that the large front wheel had enabled. Because smaller wheels meant shorter shock-absorbing spokes, the move to smaller wheels also prompted the development of suspension systems and pneumatic (air-filled) tires. The new bicycles were lighter, cheaper, and more flexible. This architectural innovation led to the rise of companies such as Dunlop (which invented the pneumatic tire) and Raleigh (which pioneered the three-speed, all-steel bicycle), and transformed the bicycle from a curiosity into a practical transportation device.

For a firm to initiate or adopt a component innovation may require that the firm have knowledge only about that component. However, for a firm to initiate or adopt an architectural innovation typically requires that the firm have architectural knowledge about the way components link and integrate to form the whole system. Firms must be able to understand how the attributes of components interact, and how changes in some system features might trigger the need for changes in many other design features of the overall system or the individual components.

Though the dimensions described above are useful for exploring key ways that one innovation may differ from another, these dimensions are not independent, nor do they offer a straightforward system for categorizing innovations in a precise and consistent manner. Each of the above dimensions shares relationships with others—for example,

component (or modular) innovation
An innovation to one or more components that does not significantly affect the overall configuration of the system.

architectural innovation
An innovation that changes the overall design of a system or the way its components interact with each other.

architectural innovations are often considered more radical and more competence destroying than component innovations. Furthermore, where an innovation lies on the dimension of competence enhancing versus destroying, architectural versus component, or radical versus incremental depends on the time frame and industry context from which it is considered. Thus, while the dimensions above are valuable for understanding innovation, they should be considered relative dimensions whose meaning is dependent on the context in which they are used.

We now will turn to exploring patterns in technological innovation. Numerous studies of innovation have revealed recurring patterns in how new technologies emerge, evolve, are adopted, and are displaced by other technologies. We begin by examining technology s-curves.

TECHNOLOGY S-CURVES

Both the rate of a technology's performance improvement and the rate at which the technology is adopted in the marketplace repeatedly have been shown to conform to an s-shape curve. Though s-curves in technology performance and s-curves in technology diffusion are related (improvements in performance may foster faster adoption, and greater adoption may motivate further investment in improving performance), they are fundamentally different processes. S-curves in technology improvement are described first, followed by s-curves in technology diffusion. This section also explains that despite the allure of using s-curves to predict when new phases of a technology's life cycle will begin, doing so can be misleading.

S-curves in Technological Improvement

Many technologies exhibit an s-curve in their performance improvement over their lifetimes.[10] When a technology's performance is plotted against the amount of effort and money invested in the technology, it typically shows slow initial improvement, then accelerated improvement, then diminishing improvement (see Figure 3.1). Performance improvement in the early stages of a technology is slow because the fundamentals of the technology are poorly understood. Great effort may be spent exploring different paths of improvement or different drivers of the technology's improvement. However, as scientists or firms gain a deeper understanding of the technology, improvement begins to accelerate. Developers target their attention toward those activities that reap the greatest improvement per unit of effort, enabling performance to increase rapidly. However, at some point, diminishing returns to effort begin to set in. As the technology begins to reach its inherent limits, the cost of each marginal improvement increases, and the s-curve flattens.

Often a technology's s-curve is plotted with performance (e.g., speed, capacity, power, etc.) against time, but this must be approached with care. If the effort invested is not constant over time, the resulting s-curve can obscure the true relationship. If effort is relatively constant over time, plotting performance against time will

FIGURE 3.1
S-curve of Technology Performance

result in the same characteristic curve as plotting performance against effort. However, if the amount of effort invested in a technology decreases or increases over time, the resulting curve could appear to flatten much more quickly, or not flatten at all. For instance, one of the more well-known technology trajectories is described by an axiom that became known as Moore's Law. In 1965, Gordon Moore, cofounder of Intel, noted that the density of transistors on integrated circuits had doubled every year since the integrated circuit was invented. That rate has since slowed to doubling every 18 months, but the rate of acceleration is still very steep. Figure 3.2 reveals a sharply increasing performance curve.

However, Intel's rate of investment (research and development dollars per year) has also been increasing rapidly, as shown in Figure 3.3. Not all of Intel's R&D expense goes directly to improving microprocessor power, but it is reasonable to assume that Intel's investment specifically in microprocessors would exhibit a similar pattern of increase. Figure 3.4 shows the big gains in transistor density have come at a big cost in terms of effort invested. Though the curve does not yet resemble the traditional s-curve, its rate of increase is not as sharp as when the curve is plotted against years. Most estimates (including those of Gordon Moore himself) predict that transistor miniaturization will reach its physical limits about 2017.

discontinuous technology
A technology that fulfills a similar market need by building on an entirely new knowledge base.

Technologies do not always get the opportunity to reach their limits; they may be rendered obsolete by new, **discontinuous technologies.** A new innovation is discontinuous when it fulfills a similar market need, but does so by building on an entirely new knowledge base.[11] For example, the switch from propeller-based planes to jets, from silver-halide (chemical) photography to digital photography, from carbon copying to photocopying, and from vinyl records (or analog cassettes) to compact discs were all technological discontinuities.

Initially, the technological discontinuity may have lower performance than the incumbent technology. For instance, one of the earliest automobiles, introduced in 1771 by Nicolas Joseph Cugnot, was never put into commercial production

FIGURE 3.2
Improvements in Intel's Microprocessor Transistor Density over Time

Year	Transistors	Intel CPU
1971	2,250	4004
1972	2,500	8008
1974	5,000	8080
1978	29,000	8086
1982	120,000	286
1985	275,000	386™
1989	1,180,000	486™ DX
1993	3,100,000	Pentium®
1997	7,500,000	Pentium II
1999	24,000,000	Pentium III
2000	42,000,000	Pentium 4

FIGURE 3.3

Graph of Transistor Density versus Cumulative R&D Expense, 1972–2000

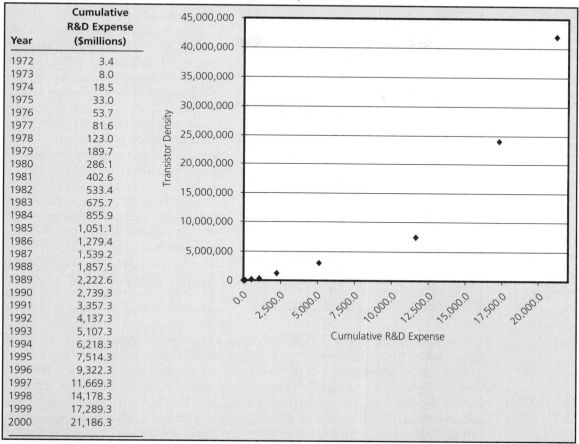

Year	Cumulative R&D Expense ($millions)
1972	3.4
1973	8.0
1974	18.5
1975	33.0
1976	53.7
1977	81.6
1978	123.0
1979	189.7
1980	286.1
1981	402.6
1982	533.4
1983	675.7
1984	855.9
1985	1,051.1
1986	1,279.4
1987	1,539.2
1988	1,857.5
1989	2,222.6
1990	2,739.3
1991	3,357.3
1992	4,137.3
1993	5,107.3
1994	6,218.3
1995	7,514.3
1996	9,322.3
1997	11,669.3
1998	14,178.3
1999	17,289.3
2000	21,186.3

because it was much slower and harder to operate than a horse-drawn carriage. It was three-wheeled, steam-powered, and could travel at 2.3 miles per hour. A number of steam- and gas-powered vehicles were introduced in the 1800s, but it was not until the early 1900s that automobiles began to be produced in quantity.

In early stages, effort invested in a new technology may reap lower returns than effort invested in the current technology, and firms are often reluctant to switch. However, if the disruptive technology has a steeper s-curve (see Figure 3.4a) or an s-curve that increases to a higher performance limit (see Figure 3.4b), there may come a time when the returns to effort invested in the new technology are much higher than effort invested in the incumbent technology. New firms entering the industry are likely to choose the disruptive technology, and incumbent firms face the difficult choice of trying to extend the life of their current technology or investing in switching to the new technology. If the disruptive technology has much greater performance potential for a given amount of effort, in the long run it is likely to displace the incumbent technology, but the rate at which it does so can vary significantly.

FIGURE 3.4
Technology
S-curves—
Introduction of
Discontinuous
Technology

**technology
diffusion**
The spread of
a technology
through a
population.

S-curves in Technology Diffusion

S-curves are also often used to describe the diffusion of a technology. Unlike s-curves in technology performance, S-curves in **technology diffusion** are obtained by plotting the cumulative number of adopters of the technology against time. This yields an s-shape curve because adoption is initially slow when an unfamiliar technology is introduced to the market, it accelerates as the technology becomes better understood and utilized by the mass market, and eventually the market is saturated so the rate of new adoptions declines. For instance, when electronic calculators were introduced to the market, they were first adopted by the relatively small pool of scientists and engineers. This group had previously used slide rules. Then the calculator began to penetrate the larger markets of accountants and commercial users, followed by the still larger market that included students and the general public. After these markets had become saturated, fewer opportunities remained for new adoptions.[12]

One rather curious feature of technology diffusion is that it typically takes far more time than information diffusion.[13] For example, Mansfield found that it took 12 years for half the population of potential users to adopt industrial robots, even though these potential users were aware of the significant efficiency advantages the robots offered.[14] If a new technology is a significant improvement over existing solutions, why do some firms shift to it more slowly than others? The answer may lie in the complexity of the knowledge underlying new technologies, and in the development of complementary resources that make those technologies useful. Although some of the knowledge necessary to utilize a new technology might be transmitted through manuals or other documentation, other aspects of knowledge necessary to fully realize the potential of a technology might be built up only through experience. Some of the knowledge about the technology might be *tacit* and require transmission from person to person through extensive contact. Many potential adopters of a new technology will not adopt it until such knowledge is available to them, despite their awareness of the technology and its potential advantages.[15]

Furthermore, many technologies become valuable to a wide range of potential users only after a set of complementary resources are developed for them. For example, while the first electric light was invented in 1809 by Humphry Davy, an English chemist, it did not become practical until the development of bulbs within which the arc of light would be encased (first demonstrated by James Bowman Lindsay in 1835) and vacuum pumps to create a vacuum inside the bulb (the mercury vacuum pump was invented by Herman Sprengel in 1875).These early lightbulbs burned for only a few hours. Thomas Alva Edison built on the work of these earlier inventors when, in 1880, he invented filaments that would enable the light to burn for 1,200 hours.

The role of complementary resources and other factors influencing the diffusion of technological innovations are discussed further in Chapters 4, 5, and 13.

S-curves as a Prescriptive Tool

Several authors have argued that managers can use the s-curve model as a tool for predicting when a technology will reach its limits and as a prescriptive guide for whether and when the firm should move to a new, more radical technology.[16] Firms can use data on the investment and performance of their own technologies, or data on the overall industry investment in a technology and the average performance achieved by multiple producers. Managers could then use these curves to assess whether a technology appears to be approaching its limits or to identify new technologies that might be emerging on s-curves that will intersect the firm's technology s-curve. Managers could then switch s-curves by acquiring or developing the new technology. However, as a prescriptive tool, the s-curve model has several serious limitations.

Limitations of S-curve Model as a Prescriptive Tool

First, it is rare that the true limits of a technology are known in advance, and there is often considerable disagreement among firms about what a technology's limits will be. Second, the shape of a technology's s-curve is not set in stone. Unexpected changes in the market, component technologies, or complementary technologies can shorten or extend the life cycle of a technology. Furthermore, firms can influence the shape of the s-curve through their development activities. For example, firms can sometimes stretch the s-curve through implementing new development approaches or revamping the architecture design of the technology.[17]

Christensen provides an example of this from the disk-drive industry. A disk drive's capacity is determined by its size multiplied by its areal recording density, thus, density has become the most pervasive measure of disk-drive performance. In 1979, IBM had reached what it perceived as a density limit of ferrite-oxide-based disk drives. It abandoned its ferrite-oxide-based disk drives and moved to developing thin-film technology, which had greater potential for increasing density. Hitachi and Fujitsu continued to ride the ferrite-oxide s-curve, ultimately achieving densities that were eight times greater than the density that IBM had perceived to be a limit.

Finally, whether switching to a new technology will benefit a firm depends on a number of factors, including (*a*) the advantages offered by the new technology, (*b*) the new technology's fit with the firm's current abilities (and thus the amount of effort that would be required to switch, and the time it would take to develop new competencies), (*c*) the new technology's fit with the firm's position in complementary resources (e.g., a firm may lack key complementary resources, or may earn a significant portion of its revenues from selling products compatible with the incumbent technology), and (*d*) the expected rate of diffusion of the new technology. Thus, a firm that follows an s-curve model too closely could end up switching technologies earlier or later than it should.

Research Brief The Diffusion of Innovation and Adopter Categories

S-curves in technology diffusion are often explained as a process of different categories of people adopting the technology at different times. One typology of adopter categories that gained prominence was proposed by Everett M. Rogers.[18] Figure 3.5 shows each of Rogers' adopter categories on a technology diffusion s-curve. The figure also shows that if the non-cumulative share of each of these adopter groups is plotted on the vertical axis with time on the horizontal axis, the resulting curve is typically bell shaped (though in practice it may be skewed right or left).

INNOVATORS

Innovators are the first individuals to adopt an innovation. Extremely adventurous in their purchasing behavior, they are comfortable with a high degree of complexity and uncertainty. Innovators typically have access to substantial financial resources (and thus can afford the losses incurred in unsuccessful adoption decisions). Though they are not always well-integrated into a particular social system, innovators play an extremely important role in the diffusion of an innovation because they are the individuals that bring new ideas into the social system. Rogers estimated that the first 2.5 percent of individuals to adopt a new technology were in this category.

EARLY ADOPTERS

The second category of adopters are the early adopters. Early adopters are well-integrated into their social system and have the greatest potential for opinion leadership. Early adopters are respected by their peers and know that to retain that respect they must make sound innovation adoption decisions. Other potential adopters look to early adopters for information and advice, thus early adopters make excellent missionaries for new products or processes. Rogers estimated that the next 13.5 percent of individuals to adopt an innovation (after innovators) were in this category.

EARLY MAJORITY

Rogers identifies the next 34 percent of individuals in a social system to adopt a new innovation as the early majority. The early majority adopts innovations slightly before the average member of a social system. They are typically not opinion leaders, but they interact frequently with their peers.

LATE MAJORITY

The next 34 percent of the individuals in a social system to adopt an innovation are the late majority, according to Rogers. Like the early majority, the late majority constitutes one-third of the individuals in a social system. Those in the late majority approach innovation with a skeptical air and may not adopt the innovation until they feel pressure from their peers. The late majority may have scarce resources, thus making them reluctant to invest in adoption until most of the uncertainty about the innovation has been resolved.

LAGGARDS

The last 16 percent of the individuals in a social system to adopt an innovation are termed *laggards.* They may base their decisions primarily upon past experience rather than influence from the social network, and they possess almost no opinion leadership. They are highly skeptical of innovations and innovators, and they must feel certain that a new innovation will not fail before adopting it.

continued

concluded

FIGURE 3.5
Technology Diffusion S-curve with Adopter Categories

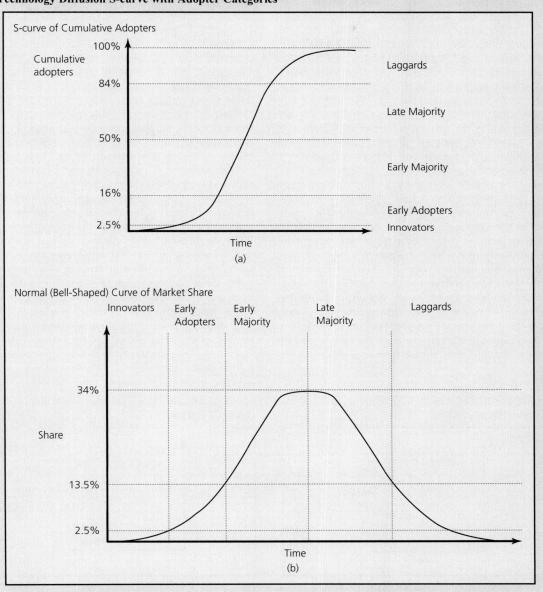

S-curve of Cumulative Adopters

(a)

Normal (Bell-Shaped) Curve of Market Share

(b)

In many industries—including microprocessors, software, motorcycles, and electric vehicles—the slope of technology improvement has been steeper than the slope of the trajectory of customer needs.[19] Firms often add features (speed, power, etc.) to products faster than customers' capacity to absorb them. Why would firms provide higher performance than that required by the bulk of their customers? The answer appears to lie in the market segmentation and pricing objectives of a technology's providers. As competition in an industry drives prices and margins lower, firms often try to shift sales into progressively higher tiers of the market. In these tiers, high performance and feature-rich products can command higher margins. Though customers may also expect to have better-performing products over time, their ability to fully utilize such performance improvements is slowed by the need to learn how to use new features and adapt their work and lifestyles. Thus, while both the trajectory of technology improvement and the trajectory of customer demands are upward sloping, the trajectory for technology improvement is steeper (for simplicity, the technology trajectories are drawn in Figure 3.6 as straight lines and plotted against time in order to compare them against customer requirements).

In Figure 3.6, the technology trajectory begins at a point where it provides performance close to that demanded by the mass market, but over time it increases faster than the expectations of the mass market as the firm targets the high-end market. As the price of the technology rises, the mass market may feel it is overpaying for technological features it does not value. In Figure 3.7, the low-end market is not being served; it either pays far more for technology that it does not need, or it goes without. It is this market that Andy Grove, former CEO of Intel, refers to as segment zero.

For Intel, segment zero was the market for low-end personal computers (those less than $1,000). While segment zero may seem unattractive in terms of margins, if it is neglected, it can become the breeding ground for companies that provide lower-end versions of the technology. As Grove notes, "The overlooked, underserved, and seemingly unprofitable end of the market can provide fertile ground for massive competitive change."[20]

As the firms serving low-end markets with simpler technologies ride up their own trajectories (which are also steeper than the slope of the trajectories of customer expectations), they can eventually reach a performance level that meets the demands of the mass market, while offering a much lower price than the premium technology (see Figure 3.7). At this point, the firms offering the premium technology may suddenly find they are losing the

FIGURE 3.6
Trajectories of Technology Improvement and Customer Requirements

FIGURE 3.7
Low-End Technology's Trajectory Intersects Mass Market Trajectory

continued

bulk of their sales revenue to industry contenders that do not look so low-end anymore. For example, by 1998, the combination of rising microprocessor power and decreasing prices enabled personal computers priced under $1,000 to capture 20 percent of the market. Intel now pays very close attention to segment zero.

Grove describes how this same scenario also played out in the textbook publishing industry. In the early 1980s, a relatively small portion of instructors used course packets created at a copy center such as Kinko's. The course packets were rather shabby. The copy quality of articles was often not good, and the course packets had no page numbers, no indexing system, and dull paper or card-stock covers. The instructors typically used them because they wanted more control over the content and sequencing of material—and they wanted it badly enough to sacrifice the advantages of a professionally produced textbook. However, by the late 1990s, course packets produced by copy centers had become significantly more sophisticated. Digital printing and copying technologies enabled copy centers to produce high-quality course packets with crisp print, numbered pages, glossy covers, and often even tables of contents and indexes. As these copying options proliferated (as did copyright clearinghouses that facilitate the transfer of copyright privileges), many instructors began to move away from textbooks, assembling their own course packets from articles, book chapters, cases, and their own course notes.

In response, publishing companies began targeting the market that had been publishing's segment zero by designing their own customized textbook systems. One of the most widely used of these systems in the late 1990s was McGraw-Hill's Primis. Primis allows instructors to assemble their own textbook from a database of book chapters, articles, cases, and other materials.[21] The materials are entered into a database and coded so that an instructor may choose materials and decide on their order, and a table of contents and indexing system is electronically generated. Books can be printed and shipped to bookstores within 5 to 10 days.

TECHNOLOGY CYCLES

The s-curve model above suggests that technological change is cyclical: Each new s-curve ushers in an initial period of turbulence, followed by rapid improvement, then diminishing returns, and ultimately is displaced by a new technological discontinuity.[22] The emergence of a new technological discontinuity can overturn the existing competitive structure of an industry, creating new leaders and new losers. Schumpeter called this process creative destruction, and argued that it was the key driver of progress in a capitalist society.[23]

Several studies have tried to identify and characterize the stages of the technology cycle in order to better understand why some technologies succeed and others fail, and whether established firms or new firms are more likely to be successful in introducing or adopting a new technology.[24] One technology evolution model that rose to prominence was proposed by Utterback and Abernathy. They observed that a technology passed through distinct phases. In the first phase (what they termed the *fluid phase*), there was considerable uncertainty about both the technology and its market. Products or services based on the technology might be crude, unreliable, or expensive, but might suit the needs of some market niches. In this phase, firms experiment with

dominant design
A product design that is adopted by the majority of producers, typically creating a stable architecture on which the industry can focus its efforts.

different form factors or product features to assess the market response. Eventually, however, producers and customers begin to arrive at some consensus about the desired product attributes, and a **dominant design** emerges.[25] The dominant design establishes a stable architecture for the technology and enables firms to focus their efforts on process innovations that make production of the design more effective and efficient or on incremental innovations to improve components within the architecture. Utterback and Abernathy termed this phase the *specific phase* because innovation in products, materials, and manufacturing processes are all specific to the dominant design. For example, in the United States the vast majority of energy production is based on the use of fossil fuels (e.g., oil, coal), and the methods of producing energy based on these fuels are well established. On the other hand, technologies that produce energy based on renewable resources (e.g., solar, wind, hydrogen) are still in the fluid phase. Organizations such as Royal Dutch/Shell, General Electric, and Ballard Power are experimenting with various forms of solar photo-cell technologies, wind-turbine technologies, and hydrogen fuel cells in efforts to find methods of using renewable resources that meet the capacity and cost requirements of serving large populations.

Building on the Utterback and Abernathy model, Anderson and Tushman studied the history of the U.S. minicomputer, cement, and glass industries through several cycles of technological change. Like Utterback and Abernathy, Anderson and Tushman found that each technological discontinuity inaugurated a period of turbulence and uncertainty (which they termed the *era of ferment*) (see Figure 3.8). The new technology might offer breakthrough capabilities, but there is little agreement about what the major subsystems of the technology should be or how they should be configured together. Thus, while the new technology displaces the old (Anderson and Tushman refer to this as substitution), there is considerable design competition as firms experiment with different forms of the technology. Just as in the Utterback and Abernathy model, Anderson and Tushman found that a dominant design always arose to command the majority of the market share unless the next discontinuity arrived too soon and disrupted the cycle, or several producers patented their own proprietary technologies and refused to license to each other. Anderson and Tushman also found that the dominant design was never in the same form as the original discontinuity, but it was also never on the leading edge of the technology. Rather than maximizing

FIGURE 3.8
The Technology Cycle

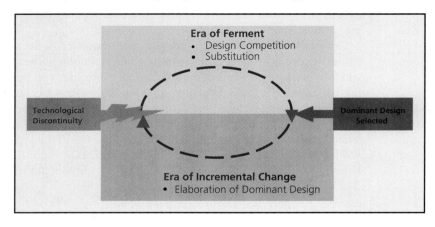

performance on any individual dimension of the technology, the dominant design tended to bundle together a combination of features that best fulfilled the demands of the majority of the market.

In the words of Anderson and Tushman, the rise of a dominant design signals the transition from the era of ferment to the *era of incremental change*.[26] In this era, firms focus on efficiency and market penetration. Firms may attempt to achieve greater market segmentation by offering different models and price points. They may also attempt to lower production costs by simplifying the design or improving the production process. This period of accumulating small improvements may account for the bulk of the technological progress in an industry, and it continues until the next technological discontinuity.

Understanding the knowledge that firms develop during different eras lends insight into why successful firms often resist the transition to a new technology, even if it provides significant advantages. During the era of incremental change, many firms cease to invest in learning about alternative design architectures and instead invest in refining their competencies related to the dominant architecture. Most competition revolves around improving components rather than altering the architecture; thus, companies focus their efforts on developing component knowledge and knowledge related to the dominant architecture. As firms' routines and capabilities become more and more wedded to the dominant architecture, the firms become less able to identify and respond to a major architectural innovation. For example, the firm might establish divisions based on the primary components of the architecture and structure the communication channels between divisions based on how those components interact. In the firm's effort to absorb and process the vast amount of information available to it, it is likely to establish filters that enable it to identify the information most crucial to its understanding of the existing technology design.[27] As the firm's expertise, structure, communication channels, and filters all become oriented around maximizing its ability to compete in the existing dominant design, they become barriers to the firm recognizing and reacting to a new technology architecture.

While many industries appear to conform to this model in which a dominant design emerges, there are exceptions. In some industries, heterogeneity of products and production processes are a primary determinant of value, and thus a dominant design is undesirable.[28] For example, art and cuisine may be examples of industries in which there is more pressure to do things differently than to settle upon a standard.

Summary of Chapter

1. Different dimensions have been used to distinguish types of innovation. Some of the most widely used dimensions include product versus process innovation, radical versus incremental innovation, competence-enhancing versus competence-destroying innovation, and architectural versus component innovation.

2. A graph of technology performance over cumulative effort invested often exhibits an s-shape curve. This suggests that performance improvement in a new technology is initially difficult and costly as the fundamental principles of the technology are worked out, it then begins to accelerate as the technology becomes better understood, and finally diminishing returns set in as the technology approaches its inherent limits.

3. A graph of a technology's market adoption over time also typically exhibits an s-shape curve. Initially the technology may seem uncertain and there may be great costs or risks for potential adopters. Gradually, the technology becomes more certain (and its costs may be driven down), enabling the technology to be adopted by larger market segments. Eventually the technology's diffusion slows as it reaches market saturation or is displaced by a newer technology.

4. The rate at which a technology improves over time is often faster than the rate at which customer requirements increase over time. This means technologies that initially met the demands of the mass market may eventually exceed the needs of the market. Furthermore, technologies that initially served only low-end customers (segment zero) may eventually meet the needs of the mass market and capture the market share that originally went to the higher-performing technology.

5. Technological change often follows a cyclical pattern. First, a technological discontinuity causes a period of turbulence and uncertainty and producers and consumers explore the different possibilities enabled by the new technology. As producers and customers begin to converge on a consensus of the desired technological configuration, a dominant design emerges. The dominant design provides a stable benchmark for the industry, enabling producers to turn their attention to increasing production efficiency and incremental product improvements. This cycle begins again with the next technological discontinuity.

6. The first design based on the initial technological discontinuity rarely becomes the dominant design. There is usually a period in which firms produce a variety of competing designs of the technology before one design emerges as dominant.

7. The dominant design rarely embodies the most advanced technological features available at the time of its emergence. It is instead the bundle of features that best meets the requirements of the majority of producers and customers.

Discussion Questions

1. What are some reasons that established firms might resist adopting a new technology?

2. Are well-established firms or new entrants more likely to (*a*) develop and/or (*b*) adopt new technologies? Why?

3. Think of an example of an innovation you have studied at work or school. How would you characterize it on the dimensions described at the beginning of the chapter?

4. What are some reasons that both technology improvement and technology diffusion exhibit s-shape curves?

5. Why do technologies often improve faster than customer requirements? What are the advantages and disadvantages to a firm of developing a technology beyond the current state of market needs?

6. In what industries would you expect to see particularly short technology cycles? In what industries would you expect to see particularly long technology cycles? What factors might influence the length of technology cycles in an industry?

Endnotes

1. D. Krause, G. Austin, and M. A. Schilling, "Ericsson: Positioning for 3G," Boston University teaching case, 2001.

2. A. Latour, D. Pringle, and J. Drucker, "A Global Journal Report: Wireless Concerns in Europe Suspend '3G' Investments," *The Wall Street Journal,* July 2002, p. A2.

3. J. Yoshida, "From White Knight to White Elephant," *Asia Computer Weekly,* October 21, 2002, p. 1.

4. R. L. Daft and S. W. Becker, *Innovation in Organizations* (New York: Elsevier, 1978); T. D. Duchesneau, S. Cohn, and J. Dutton, *A Study of Innovation in Manufacturing: Determination, Processes and Methodological Issues,* vol. 1 (Social Science Research Institute, University of Maine, 1979); and J. Hage, *Theories of Organization* (New York: Wiley Interscience, 1980).

5. R. D. Dewar and J. E. Dutton, "The Adoption of Radical and Incremental Innovations: An Empirical Analysis," *Management Science* 32 (1986), pp. 1422–33; and J. Dutton and A. Thomas, "Relating Technological Change and Learning by Doing," in *Research on Technological Innovation, Management and Policy,* ed. R. Rosenbloom (Greenwich, CT: JAI Press, 1985), pp. 187–224.

6. C. Scuria-Fontana, "The Slide Rule Today: Respect for the Past; History of the Slide Rule," *Mechanical Engineering-CIME,* July 1990, pp. 122–24.

7. H. Simon, "The Architecture of Complexity," *Proceedings of the American Philosophical Society* 106 (1962), pp. 467–82.

8. L. Fleming and O. Sorenson, "Navigating the Technology Landscape of Innovation," *Sloan Management Review* 44, no. 2 (2003), p. 15; and M. A. Schilling, "Towards a General Modular Systems Theory and Its Application to Interfirm Product Modularity," *Academy of Management Review* 25 (2000), pp. 312–34.

9. R. Henderson and K. Clark, "Architectural Innovation: The Reconfiguration of Existing Product Technologies and the Failure of Established Firms," *Administrative Science Quarterly* 35 (1990), pp. 9–30.

10. R. Foster, *Innovation: The Attacker's Advantage* (New York: Summit Books, 1986).

11. Ibid.

12. R. Brown, "Managing the 's' Curves of Innovation," *Journal of Consumer Marketing* 9 (1992), pp. 61–72.

13. E. Rogers, *Diffusion of Innovations,* 4th ed. (New York: Free Press, 1995).

14. E. Mansfield, "Industrial Robots in Japan and the USA," *Research Policy* 18 (1989), pp. 183–92.

15. P. A. Geroski, "Models of Technology Diffusion," *Research Policy* 29 (2000), pp. 603–25.

16. Foster, *Innovation;* and E. H. Becker and L. M. Speltz, "Putting the S-curve Concept to Work," *Research Management* 26 (1983), pp. 31–33.

17. C. Christensen, *Innovation and the General Manager* (New York: Irwin/McGraw-Hill, 1999).

18. E. M. Rogers, *Diffusion of Innovations,* 3rd ed. (New York: Free Press, 1983).

19. Christenson, *Innovation and the General Manager.*

20. A. S. Grove, "Managing Segment Zero," *Leader to Leader,* 1999, p. 11.

21. N. Venkatraman, "The College Textbook Marketplace in the 1990s: McGraw-Hill's Launch of Primis," Boston University teaching case, 1997.

22. P. Anderson and M. Tushman, "Technological Discontinuities and Dominant Designs: A Cyclical Model of Technological Change," *Administrative Science Quarterly* 35 (1990), pp. 604–34.

23. J. Schumpeter, *Capitalism, Socialism and Democracy* (New York: Harper Brothers, 1942).

24. See for example, J. M. Utterback and W. J. Abernathy, "A Dynamic Model of Process and Product Innovation," *Omega, the International Journal of Management Science* 3 (1975), pp. 639–56; and D. Sahal, *Patterns of Technological Innovation* (Reading, MA: Addison-Wesley Publishing Co., 1981).

25. Utterback and Abernathy, "A Dynamic Model of Process and Product Innovation"; F. F. Suarez and J. M. Utterback, "Dominant Designs and the Survival of Firms," *Strategic Management Journal* 16 (1995), pp. 415–30; and J. M. Utterback and F. F. Suarez, "Innovation, Competition and Industry Structure," *Research Policy* 22 (1993), pp. 1–21.

26. P. Anderson and M. Tushman, "Technological Discontinuities and Dominant Designs: A Cyclical Model of Technological Change," *Administrative Science Quarterly* 35 (1990), pp. 604–34.

27. R. Henderson and K. Clark, "Architectural Innovation: The Reconfiguration of Existing Product Technologies and the Failure of Established Firms," *Administrative Science Quarterly* 35 (1990), pp. 9–30.

28. M. E. Porter, "The Technological Dimension of Competitive Strategy," in *Research on Technological Innovation, Management and Policy,* ed. R. S. Rosenbloom (Greenwich, CT: JAI Press, 1983); and S. Klepper, "Entry, Exit, Growth, and Innovation over the Product Life Cycle," *American Economic Review* 86 (1996), pp. 562–83.

Chapter **Four**

Standards Battles and Design Dominance

The Rise of Microsoft

Since the early 1980s, Microsoft's Windows has controlled an overwhelming share of the personal computer operating system market. An operating system is the main program on a computer, which enables it to run other programs. Operating systems are responsible for recognizing the input from a keyboard, sending output to the display, tracking files and directories on the disk drives, and controlling peripheral devices. Because the operating system determines how other software applications must be designed, Microsoft's dominance in the operating system market made it extraordinarily powerful in the software industry. However, Microsoft's emergence as a software superpower was due largely to the unfolding of a unique set of circumstances. Had these events played out differently, Microsoft's dominance might have never been.

In 1980, the dominant operating system for personal computers was CP/M. CP/M was invented by Gary Kildall and marketed by Kildall's company, Digital Research. Kildall had been retained by Intel in 1972 to write software for Intel's 4004, the first true microprocessor in that it could be programmed to do custom calculations. Later that year, Intel began to sell the 8008 to designers who would use it as a computer, and Kildall was hired to write a programming language for the chip, called PL/M (Programming Language/Microcomputers).[1]

Then Memorex and Shugart began offering floppy disks (which IBM had invented) as a replacement for punch cards, and Kildall acquired one of these drives. However, no existing program would make the disk drive communicate with Intel's microprocessor, so he wrote a disk operating system that he called Control Program/Microprocessor (CP/M).[2] CP/M could be adapted to any computer based on Intel microprocessors.

Before 1980, IBM, the world's largest computer producer, had not been interested in developing a personal computer. IBM managers could not imagine the personal computer market ever amounting to more than a small niche of hobbyists. However, when businesses began adopting Apple computers to do basic accounting or word processing, IBM began to get nervous. IBM suddenly realized that the personal computer market might become a significant industry, and if it wanted to be a major player in that market it needed to act fast. IBM's managers did not believe they had time to develop their own microprocessor and operating system, so they based their personal computer on Intel microprocessors and planned to use Kildall's CP/M operating system. There are many stories of why Kildall did not sign with IBM. One story is that Kildall was out flying his plane when IBM came around, and though the IBM managers left their names with Kildall's wife, Dorothy McEwen, they did not state the nature of their business, and Kildall did not get back to them for some time. Another version of the story posits that Kildall was reluctant to become tied into any long-term contracts with the massive company, preferring to retain his independence. Yet a third version claims that Kildall was simply more interested in developing advanced technologies than in the strategic management of the resulting products. Whatever the reason, Kildall did not sign with IBM.

Pressed for time, IBM turned to Bill Gates, who was already supplying other software for the system, and asked if he could provide an operating system as well. Though Gates did not have an operating system at that time, he replied that he could supply one. Gates bought a 16-bit operating system (basically a clone of CP/M) from Seattle Computer Company, and reworked the software to match IBM's machines. The product was called Microsoft DOS. With DOS bundled on every IBM PC (which sold more than 250,000 units the first year), the product had an immediate and immense installed base. Furthermore, the companies that emerged to fulfill the unmet demand for IBM PCs with clones also adopted Microsoft DOS to ensure that their products were IBM PC-compatible. Because it replicated CP/M, Microsoft DOS was compatible with the range of software that had been developed for the CP/M operating system. Furthermore, after it was bundled with the IBM PC, more software was developed for the operating system, creating an even wider availability of complementary goods. Microsoft DOS was soon entrenched as the industry standard, and Microsoft was the world's fastest-growing software company.

"We were able to get the technology out into the market early to develop a standard. We were effective in soliciting software vendors to write to that platform to solidify the standard," said B. J. Whalen, Microsoft product manager. "Once you get it going, it's a snowball effect. The more applications you have available for a platform, the more people will want to use that platform. And of course, the more people that want to use that platform, the more software vendors will want to write to that platform."

Later Microsoft would develop a graphical interface named Windows that closely replicated the user-friendly functionality of Apple computers. By bundling Windows with DOS, Microsoft was able to transition its base of DOS customers over to the Windows system. Microsoft also worked vigorously to ensure that compatible applications were developed for DOS and Windows, making applications itself and also encouraging third-party developers to support the platform. Microsoft was able to leverage its dominance with Windows into a major market share in many other software markets (e.g., word processing, spreadsheet programs, presentation programs) and influence over many aspects of the computer software and hardware industries. However, had Kildall signed with IBM, or had Compaq and other computer companies been unable to clone the IBM personal computer, the software industry might look very different today.

Discussion Questions

1. What factors led to Microsoft's emergence as the dominant personal computer operating system provider? Is Microsoft's dominance due to luck, skill, or some combination of both?
2. How might the computing industry look different if Gary Kildall had signed with IBM?
3. Does having a dominant standard in operating systems benefit or hurt consumers? Does it benefit or hurt computer hardware producers?

OVERVIEW

dominant design
A single product or process architecture that dominates a product category—usually 50 percent or more of the market. A dominant design is a "de facto standard," meaning that while it may not be officially enforced or acknowledged, it has become a standard for the industry.

The previous chapter described recurrent patterns in technological innovation, and one of those patterns was the emergence of a **dominant design.** As Anderson and Tushman pointed out, the technology cycle almost invariably exhibits a stage in which the industry selects a dominant design. Once this design is selected, producers and customers focus their efforts on improving their efficiency in manufacturing, delivering, marketing, or deploying this dominant design, rather than continuing to develop and consider alternative designs. In this chapter, we first will examine why industries experience strong pressure to select a single technology design as dominant. We then will consider the multiple dimensions of value that will shape which technology designs rise to dominance.

WHY DOMINANT DESIGNS ARE SELECTED

Why do many markets coalesce around a single dominant design rather than support a variety of technological options? One primary reason is that many industries exhibit increasing returns to adoption, meaning that the more a technology is adopted, the more valuable it becomes.[3] Complex technologies often exhibit increasing returns to adoption in that the more they are used, the more they are improved. A technology that is adopted usually generates revenue that can be used to further develop and refine the technology. Furthermore, as the technology is used, greater knowledge and understanding of the technology accrue, which may then enable improvements both in the technology itself and in its applications. Finally, as a technology becomes more widely adopted, complementary assets are often developed that are specialized to operate with the technology. These effects can result in a self-reinforcing mechanism that increases the dominance of a technology regardless of its superiority or inferiority to competing technologies. Two of the primary sources of increasing returns are (1) learning effects and (2) network externalities.

Learning Effects

Ample empirical evidence shows that the more a technology is used, the more it is developed and the more effective and efficient it becomes.[4] As a technology is adopted, it generates sales revenues that can be reinvested in further developing and refining the technology. Furthermore, as firms accumulate experience with the technology, they find ways to use the technology more productively, including developing an organizational context that improves the implementation of the technology. Thus, the more a technology is adopted, the better it should become.

One example of learning effects is manifest in the impact of cumulative production on cost and productivity—otherwise known as the *learning curve*. As individuals and producers repeat a process, they learn to make it more efficient, often producing new technological solutions that may enable them to reduce input costs or waste rates. Organizational learning scholars typically model the learning curve as a function of cumulative output: performance increases, or cost decreases, with the number of units of production, usually at a decreasing rate (see Figure 4.1). For example, in studies of industries as diverse as aircraft production and pizza franchises, researchers have consistently found that the cost of producing a unit (for example, a pizza or an airplane) falls as the number of units produced increases.

The standard form of the learning curve is formulated as $y = ax^{-b}$, where y is the number of direct labor hours required to produce the xth unit, a is the number of direct labor hours required to produce the first unit, x is the cumulative number of units produced, and b is the learning rate. This pattern has been found to be consistent with production data on a wide range of products and services, including the production of automobiles, ships, semiconductors, pharmaceuticals, and even heart surgery techniques.[5] Learning curves have also been identified using a variety of performance measures, including productivity, total costs per unit, accidents per unit, and waste per unit.[6]

Though learning curves are found in a wide range of organizational processes, there are substantial differences in the rates at which organizations learn.[7] Both managers

FIGURE 4.1
Standard Learning Curve Forms

and scholars are very interested in understanding why one firm reaps great improvement in a process while another exhibits almost no learning. Many studies have examined various reasons for this variability, including looking at how the firm's learning rate is affected by process-improvement projects, intentional innovation, or contact with customers and suppliers.[8] The results suggest the learning rate can be influenced by factors such as the nature of the task, firm strategy, and the firm's prior experience.

Prior Learning and Absorptive Capacity

A firm's investment in prior learning can accelerate its rate of future learning by building the firm's absorptive capacity.[9] Absorptive capacity refers to the phenomenon whereby as individuals learn, they also increase their future ability to assimilate information. A firm's prior related experience shapes its ability to recognize the value of new information, and to utilize that information effectively. For example, in developing a new technology, a firm will often try a number of unsuccessful configurations or techniques before finding a solution that works well. This experimentation builds a base of knowledge in the firm about how key components behave, what alternatives are more likely to be successful than others, what types of projects the firm is most successful at, and so on. This knowledge base enables the firm to more rapidly assess the value of related new materials, technologies, and methods. The effects of absorptive capacity suggest that firms that develop new technologies ahead of others may have an advantage in staying ahead. Firms that forgo investment in technology development may find it very difficult or expensive to develop technology in a subsequent period. This explains, in part, why firms that fall behind the technology frontier find it so difficult to catch up.

At the aggregate level, the more firms that are using a given technology and refining it, the more absorptive capacity that is being generated related to that technology, making development of that technology (and related technologies) more effective and efficient. Furthermore, as firms develop complementary technologies to improve the productivity or ease of utilization of the core technology, the technology becomes more attractive to other firms. In sum, learning effects suggest that early technology offerings often have an advantage because they have more time to develop and become enhanced than subsequent offerings. (However, as we shall discuss in Chapter Five, it is also possible to be *too early* to a market!)

---

network externalities
Also termed *positive consumption externalities,* this is when the value of a good to a user increases with the number of other users of the same or similar good.

Network Externalities

Many markets are characterized by **network externalities,** or positive consumption externalities.[10] In a market characterized by network externalities, the benefit from using a good increases with the number of other users of the same good. The classic examples of markets demonstrating network externality effects are those involving physical networks, such as railroads or telecommunications. Railroads are more valuable as the size of the railroad network (and therefore the number of available destinations) increases. Similarly, a telephone is not much use if only a few people can be called with it—the amount of utility the phone provides is directly related to the size of the network.

installed base
The number of users of a particular good. For instance the installed base of a particular video game console refers to the number of those consoles that are installed in homes worldwide.

Network externalities can also arise in markets that do not have physical networks. For example, a user's benefit from using a good may increase with the number of users of the same good when compatibility is important. The number of users of a particular technology is often referred to as its **installed base.** A user may choose a computer platform based on the number of other users of that platform, rather than on the technological benefits of a particular platform, because it increases the ease of exchanging files. For example, many people choose a computer that uses the Windows operating system and an Intel microprocessor because the "Wintel" (*Win*dows and In*tel*) platform has the largest installed base, thus maximizing the number of people with which the user's files will be compatible. Furthermore, the user's training in a particular platform becomes more valuable as the size of the installed base of the platform increases. If the user must invest considerable effort in learning to use a computer platform, the user will probably choose to invest this effort in learning the format he or she believes will be most widely used.

complementary goods
Additional goods and services that enable or enhance the value of another good. For example, the value of a video game console is directly related to the availability of complementary goods such as video games, peripheral devices, and services such as online gaming.

Network externalities also arise when **complementary goods** are important. Many products are only functional or desirable when there is a set of complementary goods available for them (e.g., videotapes for VCRs, film for cameras, etc.). Some firms make both a good and its complements (e.g., Kodak produces both cameras and film), whereas others rely on other companies to provide complementary goods or services for their products (e.g., computer manufacturers often rely on other vendors to supply service and software to customers). Products that have a large installed base are likely to attract more developers of complementary goods. This was demonstrated in the opening vignette: Once the Windows operating system had the largest installed base, most producers of complementary software applications chose to design their products to be optimized to work with Windows. Since the availability of complementary goods will influence users' choice among competing platforms, the availability of complementary goods influences the size of the installed base. A self-reinforcing cycle ensues (see Figure 4.2).

The effect of this cycle is vividly demonstrated by Microsoft's dominance of the operating system market, and later the graphical user interface market. Microsoft's early advantage in installed base led to an advantage in the availability of complementary goods. These network externality advantages enabled Windows to

FIGURE 4.2
The Self-Reinforcing Cycle of Installed Base and Availability of Complementary Goods

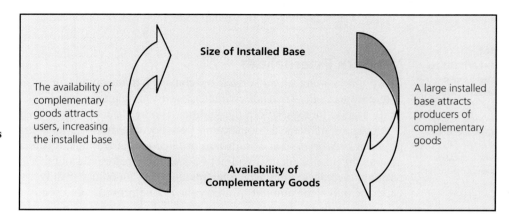

In 1982, Sony Corporation and Philips Electronics had joined forces for the development and launch of the compact disc, the digital format that replaced the vinyl LP. The compact disc remained the dominant standard in the audio consumer market for more than 20 years, and Sony and Philips split the royalties from every compact disc player ever sold. However, by the late 1990s, the compact disc market was saturated, and the consumer electronics industry was eager for the introduction of a new generation of audio technology. A successful new audio format was expected to usher in a new era of growth in the audio electronics market. The new format would also help combat music piracy by making it difficult to share music over the Internet.

In 1996, a group of record companies and consumer electronics manufacturers including Hitachi, JVC, Matsushita, Mitsubishi, Pioneer, Seagram's Universal Music Group, and Time Warner, gathered to form a consortium to back a new audio standard called DVD audio. DVD audio players and disks were planned to replace the compact disc standard by offering higher-fidelity music with surround sound. Actual players would not reach the market, however, until 2000. In 1999, Sony and Philips unveiled their own high-fidelity audio format. However, their new format would be an extension to the compact disc format, enabling Sony and Philips to continue to control the royalties for the new disks and players.[11]

Sony and Philips Super Audio CD systems were initially priced much higher than the consortium's DVD audio players ($5,000 for a Super Audio CD player versus $1,000 for a DVD audio player), consistent with Sony and Philips claim that the system was targeting audiophiles rather than the mass market. However, the price of both systems began to drop and rapidly converge after their introduction, and many feared a format war (akin to the VHS versus Beta video format battle) was inevitable. Ultimately, many manufacturers decided to hedge their bets by producing universal players that would support both formats. By the end of 2002, major manufacturers such as Pioneer and Yamaha had introduced universal players priced at less than $1,000.

lock several would-be contenders such as Geoworks and NeXT (and, some would argue, Apple) out of the market.

Firms can also attempt to influence the selection of a dominant design by building coalitions around a preferred technology.[12] This is aptly illustrated in the accompanying Theory in Action.

While the preceding has emphasized the emergence of dominant designs through market forces, occasionally a dominant design is put in place through government regulation.

Government Regulation

In some industries, the consumer welfare benefits of having compatibility among technologies has prompted government regulation, and thus a legally induced adherence to a dominant design. This has often been the case for the utilities, telecommunications, and television industries, to name a few.[13] For example, in 1953 the U.S. Federal Communications Commission (FCC) approved the National Television Systems Committee (NTSC) color standard in television broadcasting to ensure that individuals with monochrome television sets would be able to receive the color television programs broadcast by networks (though they would see them in black and white). That standard was still in place in 2003. Similarly, in 1998, while a battle was being fought in the United States over wireless technology formats, the European Union (EU) adopted a single wireless telephone standard (the general standard for mobile communications, or GSM). By choosing a uniform standard, the EU could avoid the proliferation of incompatible standards and facilitate exchange both within and across national borders. Where government regulation imposes a single standard on an industry, the technology design embodied in that standard necessarily dominates the other technology options available to the industry. The consumer welfare impact of dominant designs is explored further in the Theory in Action section at the end of this chapter.

The Result: Winner-Take-All Markets

All these forces can encourage the market toward natural monopolies. While some alternative platforms may survive by focusing on niche markets, the majority of the market may be dominated by a single (or few) design(s). A firm that is able to lock in its technology as the dominant design of a market usually earns huge rewards and may dominate the product category through several product generations. When a firm's technology is chosen as a dominant design, not only does the firm have the potential to earn near-monopoly rents in the short run, but the firm also is in a good position to shape the evolution of the industry, greatly influencing what future generations of products will look like. However, if the firm supports a technology that is not chosen as the dominant design, it may be forced to adopt the dominant technology, effectively forfeiting the capital, learning, and brand equity invested in its original technology. Even worse, a firm may find itself locked out of the market if it is unable to adopt the dominant technology. Such standards battles are high-stakes games—resulting in big winners and big losers.

path dependency
When end results depend greatly on the events that took place leading up to the outcome. It is often impossible to reproduce the results that occur in such a situation.

Increasing returns to adoption also imply that technology trajectories are characterized by **path dependency,** meaning that relatively small historical events may have a great impact on the final outcome. Though the technology's quality and technical advantage undoubtedly influence its fate, other factors, unrelated to the technical superiority or inferiority, may also play important roles.[14] For instance, timing may be crucial; early technology offerings may become so entrenched that subsequent technologies, even if considered to be technically superior, may be unable to gain a foothold in the market. How and by whom the technology is sponsored may also impact adoption. If, for example, a large and powerful firm aggressively sponsors a technology (perhaps even pressuring suppliers or distributors to support the technology) that technology may gain a controlling share of the market, locking out alternative technologies.

The influence of a dominant design can also extend beyond its own technology cycle. As the dominant design is adopted and refined, it influences the knowledge that is accumulated by producers and customers, and it shapes the problem-solving techniques used in the industry. Firms will tend to use and build on their existing knowledge base rather than entering unfamiliar areas.[15] This can result in a very "sticky" technological paradigm that directs future technological inquiry in the area.[16] Thus, a dominant design is likely to influence the nature of the technological discontinuity that will eventually replace it.

Such winner-take-all markets demonstrate very different competitive dynamics than markets in which many competitors can coexist relatively peacefully. These markets also require very different firm strategies to achieve success. Technologically superior products do not always win—the firms that win are usually the ones that know how to manage the multiple dimensions of value that shape design selection.

MULTIPLE DIMENSIONS OF VALUE

increasing returns
When the *rate of return* (not just gross returns) from a product or process increases with the size of its installed base.

The value a new technology offers a customer is a composite of many different things. We first consider the value of the stand-alone technology, and then show how the stand-alone value of the technology combines with the value created by the size of the installed base and availability of complementary goods.[17] In industries characterized by **increasing returns,** this combination will influence which technology design rises to dominance.

A Technology's Stand-alone Value

The value a new technology offers to customers can be driven by many different things, such as the functions it enables the customer to perform, its aesthetic qualities, its ease of use, and so on. To help managers identify the different aspects of utility a new technology offers customers, W. Chan Kim and Renee Mauborgne developed a "Buyer Utility Map."[18] They argue that it is important to consider six different utility levers, as well as six stages of the buyer experience cycle, to understand a new technology's utility to a buyer.

The stages they identify are *purchase, delivery, use, supplements, maintenance,* and *disposal.* The six utility levers they consider are *customer productivity, simplicity, convenience, risk, fun and image,* and *environmental friendliness.* Creating a grid with stage and levers yields a 36-cell utility map (see Figure 4.3). Each cell offers an opportunity to offer a new value proposition to a customer.

A new technology might offer a change in value in a single cell or in a combination of cells. For example, when retailers establish an online ordering system, the primary new value proposition they are offering is greater *simplicity* in the *purchase* stage. On the other hand, as shown in Figure 4.3, the introduction of the Honda Insight hybrid-electric vehicle offered customers greater productivity (in the form of gas savings), image benefits and environmental friendliness in the customer's use, supplements, and maintenance stages while providing the same simplicity and convenience of regular gasoline-only powered vehicles.

Kim and Mauborgne's model is designed with an emphasis on consumer products, but their mapping principle can be easily adapted to emphasize industrial products or different aspects of buyer utility. For example, rather than having a single entry for customer productivity, the map could have rows for several dimensions of productivity such as speed, efficiency, scalability, reliability, and so on. The map provides a guide for managers to consider multiple dimensions of technological value and multiple stages of the customer experience. Finally, the new benefits have to be considered with respect to the cost to the customer of obtaining or using the technology—it is the ratio of benefits to cost that determines value.

FIGURE 4.3
The Buyer Utility Map with Honda Insight Example

Source: Adapted from W. C. Kim and R. Mauborgne, "Knowing a Winning Business Idea When You See One," *Harvard Business Review,* September–October 2000.

	Purchase	Delivery	Use	Supplements	Maintenance	Disposal
Customer productivity			Save money on gasoline			
Simplicity			Operates like a regular combustion engine vehicle			
Convenience			Does not have to be plugged into electrical outlet	Can purchase fuel at regular gas stations	Maintenance is similar to regular combustion engine vehicle	
Risk						
Fun and image			Connotes image of environmental responsibility			
Environmental friendliness			Emits lower levels of pollutants	Requires less use of fossil fuels		

Network Externality Value

In industries characterized by network externalities, the value of a technological innovation to users will be a function not only of its stand-alone benefits and cost, but also the value created by the size of its installed base and the availability of complementary goods (see Figure 4.4(a)).[19] Thus, the value to consumers of using the Windows operating system is due in part to the technology's stand-alone value (for example, the ability of the operating system to make it easy for consumers to use the computer), the installed base of the operating system (and thus the number of computers with which the user can easily interact), and the availability of compatible software. Visualizing the value of technological innovations in this way makes it clear why even innovations that offer significant improvements in technological functionality often fail to displace existing technologies that are already widely adopted: Even if a new innovation has a significant advantage in functionality, its overall value may be significantly less than the incumbent standard. This situation is poignantly illustrated in the case of NeXT computers. In 1985, Steve Jobs and five senior managers of Apple Computer founded NeXT Incorporated. They unveiled their first computer in 1988. With a 25MHz Motorola 68030, 8MB of RAM, the machine was significantly more powerful than most other personal computers available. It offered advanced graphics capability and even ran an object-oriented operating system (called NextStep) that was considered extremely advanced. However, the machine was not compatible with the IBM-compatible personal computers (based on Intel's microprocessors and Microsoft's operating system) that had become the dominant standard. The machine thus would not run the vast majority of

FIGURE 4.4
Components of Value

(a) Combined value of stand-alone technological utility, installed base, and complementary goods offered by existing technology.

(b) New technology competes only on the value of its stand-alone utility.

(c) New technology that is compatible with existing technology's installed base and complementary goods.

software applications on the market. A small contingent of early adopters bought the NeXT personal computers, but the general market rejected them due to a dire lack of software and uncertainty about the company's viability. The company discontinued its hardware line in 1993 and ceased development of NextStep in 1996.

As shown in Figure 4.4(b), it is not enough for a new technology's stand-alone utility to exceed that of the incumbent standard. The new technology must be able to offer greater overall value. For the new technology to compete on its stand-alone utility alone, that utility must be so great that it eclipses the combined value of an existing technology's stand-alone utility, its installed base, and its complementary goods.

In some cases, the new technology may be made compatible with the existing technology's installed base and complementary goods as in Figure 4.4(c). In this case, a new technology with only a moderate functionality advantage may offer greater overall value to users. Sony and Philips are employing this strategy with their new audio format, Super Audio CD (SACD), a high-density multichannel audio format based on a revolutionary "scalable" bit-stream technology known as Direct Stream Digital (DSD). Anticipating that users would be reluctant to replace their existing compact disc players and compact disc music collections, Sony and Philips made the new Super Audio CD technology (discussed in the Theory in Action section earlier in the chapter) compatible with existing compact disc technology. The Super Audio CD players include a feature that enables them to play standard CDs, and the recorded Super Audio CDs include a CD audio layer in addition to the high-density layer, enabling them to be played on standard CD systems. Customers can thus take advantage of the new technology without giving up the value of their existing CD players and music libraries.

When users are comparing the value of a new technology to an existing technology, they are weighing a combination of objective information (e.g., actual technological benefits, actual information on installed base or complementary goods), subjective information (e.g., perceived technological benefits, and perceived installed base or complementary goods), and expectations for the future (e.g., anticipated technological benefits, anticipated installed base and complementary goods). Thus, each of the primary value components described above also has corresponding perceived or anticipated value components (see Figure 4.5). In Figure 4.5(a), the perceived and anticipated value components map proportionately to their corresponding actual components. However, as depicted in Figure 4.5(b), this need not be the case. For instance, perceived installed base may greatly exceed actual installed base, or customers may expect that a technology will eventually have a much larger installed base than competitors and thus the value accrued from the technology's installed base is expected to grow much larger than it is currently.

Firms can take advantage of the fact that users rely on both objective and subjective information in assessing the combined value offered by a new technology. For example, even a technology with a small installed base can achieve a relatively large mind share through heavy advertising by its backers. Producers can also shape users' expectations of the future installed base and availability of complements through announcements of preorders, licensing agreements, and distribution arrangements. For example, when Sega and Nintendo were battling for dominance in the 16-bit video game console market, they went to great lengths to manage impressions of their installed base and market share, often to the point of deception. At the end of 1991,

FIGURE 4.5
Actual, Perceived, and Expected Components of Value

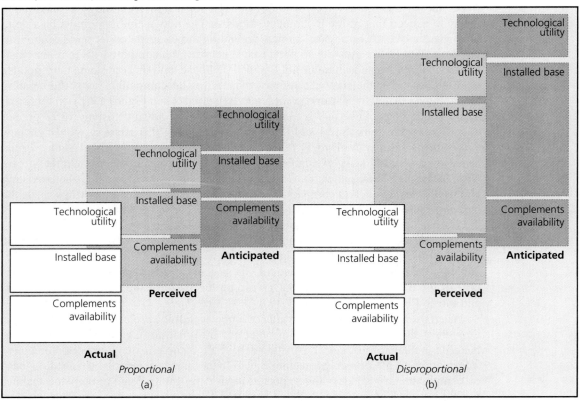

Nintendo claimed it had sold 2 million units of the Super Nintendo Entertainment System in the U.S. market. Sega disagreed, arguing that Nintendo had sold 1 million units at most. By May 1992, Nintendo was claiming a 60 percent share of the 16-bit market, and Sega was claiming a 63 percent share![20] Since perceived or expected installed base may drive subsequent adoptions, a large perceived or expected installed base can lead to a large actual installed base.

Such a tactic also underlies the use of "vaporware"—products that are not actually on the market and may not even exist but are advertised—by many software vendors. By building the impression among customers that a product is ubiquitous, firms can prompt rapid adoption of the product when it actually is available. Vaporware may also buy a firm valuable time in bringing its product to market. If other vendors beat the firm to market and the firm fears that customers may select a dominant design before its offering is introduced, it can use vaporware to attempt to persuade customers to delay purchase until the firm's product is available. The video game console industry also provides an excellent example here. When Sega and Sony introduced their 32-bit video game consoles (the Saturn and PlayStation, respectively), Nintendo was still a long way from introducing its next-generation console. In an effort to forestall consumer purchases of 32-bit systems, Nintendo began aggressively promoting its development of a 64-bit system (originally named Project Reality) in 1994, though the product would not actually reach the market until September 1996. The project underwent so many delays that some industry observers dubbed it "Project Unreality."[21] Nintendo was successful in persuading many customers to wait for its Nintendo 64, and the system was ultimately relatively successful.

Nintendo, however, was never able to reclaim dominance over the video game industry. By the time the Nintendo 64 had gained significant momentum, Sony was developing its even more advanced PlayStation2. Sony's experience in VCRs and compact discs had taught it to manage the multiple dimensions of value very well: Sony's PlayStation2 offered more than double the processing power of the Nintendo 64, it was backward compatible (helping the PlayStation2 tap the value of customers' existing PlayStation game libraries), and Sony sold it for a price that many speculated was less than the cost of manufacturing the console ($299). Sony also invested heavily to ensure that many game titles would be available at launch, and it used its distribution leverage and advertising budget to ensure the product would seem ubiquitous at its launch.

Competing for Design Dominance in Markets with Network Externalities

Graphs illustrate how differing technological utilities and network externality returns to market share impact the competition for design dominance. The following figures examine whether network externalities create pressure for a single dominant design versus a few dominant designs by considering the rate at which value increases with the size of the installed base, and how large of an installed base is necessary before most of the network externality benefits are achieved. In Figure 4.6(a), the curve represents the increase in network externality benefits of a technology as its market share rises. Initially, the benefits may increase slowly. For example, whether a cell phone can reach 1 percent of the population or 5 percent is fairly insignificant—the reach of the phone service has to become much wider before the phone has much value. However, beyond some threshold level, the network externality returns to market share begin to increase rapidly, until at some point, most of the benefits have been obtained and the rate of return decreases. In Figure 4.6(b), a base level of technological utility has been added to the graph, shifting the entire graph up. This becomes relevant later when two technologies that have different base levels of technological utility are considered.

When two technologies compete for dominance, customers will compare the overall value yielded (or expected) from each technology, as discussed in the previous section. In Figure 4.7, two technologies, A and B, each offer similar technological utility, and have similarly shaped network externality returns curves. The curve for

FIGURE 4.6
Network Externality Returns to Market Share

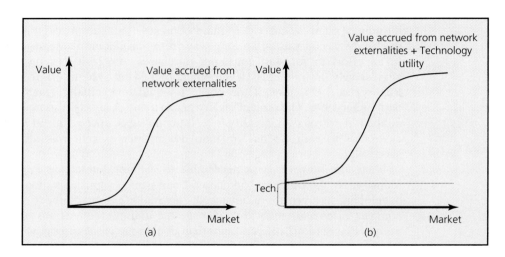

FIGURE 4.7
Network Externality Returns and Technological Utility: Competing Designs

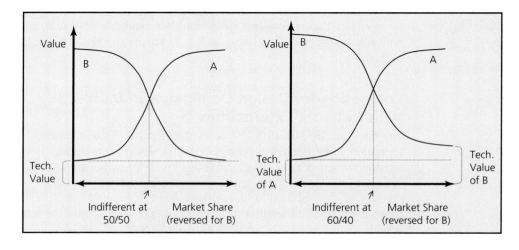

B is drawn with the market share dimension reversed so that we can compare the value offered by the two different technologies at different market share splits, that is, when A has a 20 percent market share, B has an 80 percent market share, and so on. This graph shows that at every point where A has less than 50 percent market share (and thus B has greater than 50 percent market share), B will yield greater overall value, making B more attractive to customers. On the other hand, when A has greater than 50 percent market share (and B thus has less than 50 percent market share), A yields more overall value. When each technology has exactly 50 percent market share, they yield the same overall value. However, if both technologies earn similar network externality returns to market share, but one technology offers greater stand-alone utility, the indifference point will be shifted in its favor. In the righthand graph in Figure 4.7, technology B offers a greater level of stand-alone technological utility, shifting its overall value curve up. In this graph, technology A must have greater than 60 percent market share (and B must have less than 40 percent market share) for A to offer more overall value than B.

Another interesting scenario arises when customers attain their desired level of network externality benefits at lower levels of market share, depicted graphically in Figure 4.8. In this case, customers may face a relatively large indifference region within which neither technology clearly dominates. This may be the case with the video game console industry: While customers may experience some network externality benefits to a console having significant share (more game titles, more people to play against), those benefits might be achieved by a console without attaining a majority of the market. For example, while Sony has a majority share of the U.S. video game market and neither Nintendo's GameCube nor Microsoft's Xbox has greater than a 20 percent market share, there is still an abundance of game titles for all three consoles and a significant pool of people to play games against. Such markets may not experience great pressure to select a single dominant design; two or more platforms may successfully coexist.

FIGURE 4.8
Network Externality Value Is Fully Tapped at Minority Market Share Levels

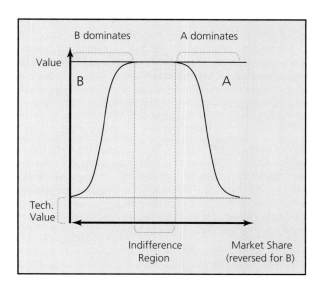

Traditionally, economics has emphasized the consumer welfare benefits of competitive markets; however, increasing returns make this a complicated issue. This is exemplified by the antritrust suits brought against Microsoft. While some analysts argued that Microsoft had clearly engaged in anticompetitive behavior and had damaged consumers, others argued that Microsoft had behaved appropriately, and that its overwhelming share of the personal computer operating system market was good for consumers since it created greater compatibility among computers and more software applications. So how does a regulatory body decide when a firm has become too dominant? One way to think about this is to compare the network externality returns to market share with corresponding monopoly costs. Network externality returns refers to the value customers reap as a larger portion of the market adopts the same good (e.g., there is likely to be greater availability of complementary goods, more compatibility among users, more revenues can be channeled into further developing the technology, etc.). Monopoly costs refer to the costs users bear as a larger portion of the market adopts the same good (e.g., a monopolist may charge higher prices, there may be less product variety, innovation in alternative technologies may be stifled, etc.). Network externality returns to market share often exhibit the s-shape described in the previous section. Monopoly costs to market share, however, are often considered to be exponentially increasing. Plotting them on the same graph (as in Figure 4.9) reveals how network externality benefits and monopoly costs trade off against one another.

In Figure 4.9, so long as technology A's market share remains less than X, the combination of technological utility and network externality benefits exceeds the monopoly costs, even if X represents a very large share of the market. However, as technology A's market share climbs beyond X, the monopoly costs now exceed the value of the technology utility

FIGURE 4.9
Network Externality Benefits and Monopoly Costs

and network externality benefits. A number of factors can shift where these two curves cross. If the technology utility for A were higher, the curves would cross at a point greater than X. If the network externality returns curve began to flatten at a lower market share (as was demonstrated earlier with the video game console industry), then the curves would cross at a market share less than X.

The steepness of the monopoly cost curve is largely a function of the firm's discretionary behavior. A firm can choose not to exploit its monopoly power, thus flattening the monopoly costs curve. For instance, one of the most obvious assertions of monopoly power is typically exhibited in the price charged for a good. However, a firm can choose not to charge the maximum price that customers would be willing to pay for a good. For example, many people would argue that Microsoft does not charge the maximum price for its Windows operating system that the market would bear. However, a firm can also assert its monopoly power in more subtle ways, by controlling the evolution of the industry through selectively aiding some suppliers or complementors more than others, and many people would argue that in this respect, Microsoft has taken full advantage of its near-monopoly power.

Summary of Chapter

1. Many technologies demonstrate increasing returns to adoption, meaning that the more they are adopted, the more valuable they become.

2. One primary source of increasing returns is learning curve effects. The more a technology is produced and used, the better understood and developed it becomes, leading to improved performance and reduced costs.

3. Another key factor creating increasing returns is network externality effects. Network externality effects arise when the value of a good to a user increases with the size of the installed base. This can be due to a number of reasons, such as need for compatibility or the availability of complementary goods.

4. In some industries, the consumer welfare benefits of having a single standard have prompted government regulation, such as the European Union's mandate to use the GSM cellular phone standard.

5. Increasing returns can lead to winner-take-all markets where one or a few companies capture nearly all the market share.

6. The value of a technology to buyers is multidimensional. The stand-alone value of a technology can include many factors (such as productivity, simplicity, etc.) and the technology's cost. In increasing returns industries, the value will also be significantly affected by the technology's installed base and availability of complementary goods.

7. Customers weigh a combination of objective and subjective information. Thus, a customer's perceptions and expectations of a technology can be as important as (or more important than) the actual value offered by the technology.

8. Firms can try to manage customers' perceptions and expectations through advertising and public announcements of preorders, distribution agreements, and so on.

9. The combination of network externality returns to market share and technological utility will influence at what level of market share one technology will dominate another. For some industries, the full network externality benefits are attained at a minority market share level; in these industries, multiple designs are likely to coexist.

Discussion Questions

1. What are some of the sources of increasing returns to adoption?

2. What are some examples of industries not mentioned in the chapter that demonstrate increasing returns to adoption?

3. What are some of the ways a firm can try to increase the overall value of its technology, and its likelihood of becoming the dominant design?

4. What determines whether an industry is likely to have one or a few dominant designs?

5. Are dominant designs good for consumers? Competitors? Complementors? Suppliers?

Endnotes

1. P. Korzeniowski, "DOS: Still Thriving after All These Years," *Software Magazine* 10, no. 6 (1990), pp. 83–112.

2. S. Veit, "What Ever Happened to . . . Gary Kildall?" *Computer Shopper* 14, no. 11 (1994), pp. 608–14.

3. W. B. Arthur, *Increasing Returns and Path Dependency in the Economy* (Ann Arbor, MI: University of Michigan Press, 1994).

4. For examples of this, see M. Lapre, A. S. Mukherjee, and L. N. Van Wassenhove, "Behind the Learning Curve: Linking Learning Activities to Waste Reduction," *Management Science* 46 (2000), pp. 597–611; F. K. Levy, "Adaptation in the Production Process," *Management Science* 11 (1965), pp. B136–54; and L. E. Yelle, "The Learning Curve: Historical Review and Comprehensive Survey," *Decision Sciences* 10 (1979), pp. 302–28.

5. L. Argote, *Organizational Learning: Creating, Retaining and Transferring Knowledge* (Boston: Kluwer Academic Publishers, 1999); N. W. Hatch and D. C. Mowery, "Process Innovation and Learning by Doing in Semiconductor Manufacturing," *Management Science* 44, no. 11 (1998), pp. 1461–77; and M. A. Schilling, P. Vidal, R. Ployhart, and A. Marangoni, "Learning by Doing Something Else: Variation, Relatedness, and the Learning Curve," *Management Science* 49 (2003), pp. 39–56.

6. For examples, see L. Argote, "Group and Organizational Learning Curves: Individual, System and Environmental Components," *British Journal of Social Psychology* 32 (1993), pp. 31–52; Argote, *Organizational Learning;* N. Baloff, "Extensions of the Learning Curve—Some Empirical Results," *Operations Research Quarterly* 22, no. 4 (1971), pp. 329–40; E. D. Darr, L. Argote, and D. Epple, "The Acquisition, Transfer and Depreciation of Knowledge in Service Organizations: Productivity in Franchises," *Management Science* 41 (1995), pp. 1750–62; L. Greenberg, "Why the Mine Injury Picture Is Out of Focus," *Mining Engineering* 23 (1971), pp. 51–53; Hatch and Mowery, "Process Innovation and Learning by Doing in Semiconductor Manufacturing"; A. Mukherjee, M. Lapre, and L. Wassenhove, "Knowledge Driven Quality Improvement," *Management Science* 44 (1998), pp. S35–S49; and Yelle, "The Learning Curve."

7. Argote, *Organizational Learning.*

8. J. Dutton and A. Thomas, "Treating Progress Functions as a Managerial Opportunity," *Academy of Management Review* 9 (1984), pp. 235–47; Levy, "Adaptation in the Production Process"; and Mukherjee, Lapre, and Wassenhove, "Knowledge Driven Quality Improvement."

9. W. M. Cohen and D. A. Levinthal, "Absorptive Capacity: A New Perspective on Learning and Innovation," *Administrative Science Quarterly,* March 1990, pp. 128–52.

10. M. Katz and C. Shapiro, "Technology Adoption in the Presence of Network Externalities," *Journal of Political Economy* 94 (1986), pp. 822–41; M. Schilling, "Technological Lock Out: An Integrative Model of the Economic and Strategic Factors Driving Technology Success and Failure," *Academy of Management Review* 23 (1998), pp. 267–84; and M. Thum, "Network Externalities, Technological Progress, and the Competition of Market Contracts," *International Journal of Industrial Organization* 12 (1994), pp. 269–89.

11. J. Brinkley, "Disk vs. Disk: The Fight for the Ears of America," *New York Times,* August 8, 1999.

12. J. Wade, "Dynamics of Organizational Communities and Technological Bandwagons: An Empirical Investigation of Community Evolution in the Microprocessor Market," *Strategic Management Journal* 16 (1995), pp. 111–34.

13. Schilling, "Technological Lock Out"; and F. F. Suarez, "Battles for Technological Dominance: An Integrative Framework," *Research Policy* 33, pp. 271–86.

14. W. B. Arthur, "Competing Technologies, Increasing Returns, and Lock-In by Historical Events," *The Economic Journal,* March 1989, pp. 116–31; R. W. England, "Three Reasons for Investing Now in Fossil Fuel Conservation: Technological Lock-In,

Institutional Inertia, and Oil Wars," *Journal of Economic Issues,* September 1994, pp. 755–76; and Katz and Shapiro, "Technology Adoption in the Presence of Network Externalities."

15. G. Dosi, "Sources, Procedures, and Microeconomic Effects of Innovation," *Journal of Economic Literature* 26 (1988), p. 1130.

16. Ibid., pp. 1120–71.

17. M. A. Schilling, "Technological Leapfrogging: Lessons from the U.S. Video Game Console Industry," *California Management Review* 45, no. 3 (2003), pp. 6–32; and Suarez, "Battles for Technological Dominance."

18. W. C. Kim and R. Mauborgne, "Knowing a Winning Business Idea When You See One," *Harvard Business Review,* September–October 2000, pp. 129–38.

19. Schilling, "Technological Leapfrogging."

20. A. Brandenberger, 1995b. "Power Play (B): Sega in 16-Bit Video Games," Harvard Business School case #9-795-103.

21. A. Brandenberger, 1995c. "Power Play (C): 3DO in 32-Bit Video Games," Harvard Business School case #9-795-104; and Schilling, "Technological Leapfrogging."

Chapter **Five**

Timing of Entry

The Personal Digital Assistant Industry

In January 2000, analysts were estimating that worldwide handheld computer shipments had reached 5.7 million in 1999. The personal digital assistant (PDA) industry, despite its troubled childhood, was blossoming into a substantial market. But many potential entrants had mixed feelings about the PDA industry. As PDA technology evolved from early offerings in the late 1980s and early 1990s, it left in its wake the remains of many failed startups. Nearly all the companies who had competed in the PDA market—even those that survived—had been singed by the unrealized expectations of the PDA market, and they considered future opportunities with great caution.

In the Beginning

In 1966, Gene Roddenberry's "Star Trek" introduced what some have called the first PDA design mock-up. There were to be no paper or pencils on the Enterprise. Crew members wrote on electronic tablets and used a handheld tricorder to access, process, and display information.[1] Such portable processing power sparked the imagination of millions and may well have been the inspiration for today's PDAs.

However, it was not until the early 1990s that technology began to deliver on this inspiration. At that time, most speculators believed that pen-based computing would be the next wave of the future. In 1993, Forrester Research Inc. predicted that 298,000 handheld computers would be shipped that year, a number that would increase to 4 million by 1996. BIS Strategic Decisions estimated that 96,000 PDAs would be shipped in 1993 and 2.6 million units by 1997. In early 1994, industry observers were predicting that 1994 would be the "year of the pen,"[2] and that the two leading operating systems, Microsoft's Pen for Windows and GO's PenPoint, were poised to battle for the spoils.

From 1990 to 1993, a small flurry of companies entered PDA development. The players included well-known computer makers such as Apple, IBM, Hewlett-Packard, and Motorola, as well as startups like GO Corporation, EO Inc. (which was bought by AT&T), and Momenta. Because they used pen-based input and because of their size, PDAs and their success rested upon the evolution of several enabling technologies, including handwriting recognition software, modems, and the miniaturization of power and memory.

Enabling Technologies

Several of these enabling technologies were not ready for use in PDA manufacture by 1993. Handwriting recognition software was a particular problem. Though accuracy rates had approached 95 percent, users still found the 5 percent inaccuracy to be very unsettling. Modems also posed problems. Many felt that the key feature of a PDA would be wireless connectivity. But in the early 1990s, modems were nicknamed "bricks" because they were large and heavy; achieving wireless connectivity in a PDA would have doubled the weight and size of most devices.[3]

Constraints on processing power and battery life also compromised the performance and/or size of the PDA. Even to replicate streamlined versions of office software products required significantly more memory and storage than was found on a typical electronic organizer. Additional memory and storage added to both the size and cost of the device. Greater processing power also required greater battery power, which affected the size of the end product.

Market Confusion about PDAs

Compounding the technological problems was a lack of market awareness about the functionality and *potential* functionality of pen-based PDAs. For PDAs to become viable in the market, companies had to sell large volumes to achieve the necessary economies of scale and recoup development costs. But the market was still very immature in the early 1990s. PDAs were expensive compared with desktop systems, and potential users were not sure about their performance, their compatibility with their current computer systems, or the availability of software. Not only were user needs poorly addressed, but there also was question about who the major market users would be. Some companies clearly envisioned the PDA as a mass-market consumer electronics device, while others saw it primarily as a tool for mobile executives. Still another group of companies envisioned the PDA for particular industries ("vertical markets") as a more specialized device that could allow inventory scanning or in-field sales estimates.

The Shakeout

In 1993, only a small market of early adopters were placing orders for the new PDAs. Then, Microsoft announced it would be entering the pen-based arena with its product, WinPad. Upon the announcement, many of the early customers withdrew their orders to see what Microsoft was going to do. Microsoft's previous experience in the computer industry was a strong indicator that if Microsoft entered PDAs, it would likely control the dominant standard and its products would have the greatest software compatibility. Furthermore, if a PDA had a Microsoft interface and software, it would capitalize on consumers' current training and experience with Microsoft products. As it turned out, however, Microsoft did not become serious about pen-based computing for several years, so its announcement stalled the market acceptance of PDA technology.

Many of the pen-based PDA companies began to falter by 1994. While several of them had made great technological progress and had working products, they did not yet have a revenue base coming in for the products, so many of the companies began to run out of capital. Momenta had been a front-runner in the pen-based computing market and had attracted several big-name executives (e.g., Delbert Yocam of Apple Computer), but it ran out of money and was dissolved by the fall of 1992. The breaking point for GO came in 1994, when after months of negotiations, Compaq chose to work with Microsoft instead of GO for its pen-based computers. Having lost $75 million, the company was bought by AT&T and absorbed into AT&T's EO Personal Communicator division. AT&T shut down the project shortly thereafter, noting that the handheld market had not turned out as well as it had expected, and projected that the industry was leaning more toward the smart cellular phones concept.[4]

As of 1996, price and features had still not reached an appropriate convergence for most vendors or users. AT&T, Compaq, IBM, Motorola, NCR, and Toshiba had all invested millions of dollars in developing pen computing hardware and software, but by 1996 they had all either scaled back dramatically or abandoned the market.[5]

Surviving Companies, Forging a Pen-Based Standard

Some companies and/or products survived the shakeout. Many of the vendors who focused on specialized devices for vertical markets weathered the storm quite well. Telxon, Psion, Fujitsu, Casio, and Sharp all continued to thrive. The big winner, however, was a relatively late entrant called Palm Computing. The founder of PalmPilot, Jeff Hawkins set out to design a product that was fast, simple, and would sell for less than $300. The product did not debut until January 1996, but 350,000 units were sold by the end of 1996, and a million units were sold within 18 months of its release. The PalmPilot had attracted the support of some 12,000 developers by January 1999,[6] and by the end of 1999, it controlled 77 percent of the worldwide market share for PDAs, and Microsoft's Windows CE operating system had a worldwide share of only 13 percent. Palm's share declined to 66 percent by the end of 2001, but that still represented a significant lead over the next contender, Microsoft's Windows CE.

By 2003, another major industry transition was on the horizon: smart phones. Smart phones integrated PDA functionality in a wireless telephone. Whereas some PDA models had wireless phone capabilities in the form of a clumsy phone module, smart phones would emphasize the styling characteristics of a mobile phone, and thus be more comfortable for use as a telecommunications device. However, unlike regular cell phones that have some organizer capabilities, smart phones have larger, sharper screens that can display regular Web pages rather than the small subset of Web pages designed to be readable on cell-phone displays.[7] Smart phone shipments were expected to reach almost 5 million units in 2002, amounting to $2.3 billion in sales.[8] Smart phones also had higher margins than PDAs. However, the convergence of PDAs and mobile phones also meant that companies that produced PDAs (such as Palm, Handspring, and Compaq) would now be pitted against very large and established mobile phone rivals such as Nokia, Samsung, and Ericsson.

Discussion Questions

1. Why did most of the early PDA companies fail, even if they had innovative and sophisticated product designs?
2. Could early PDA companies have done anything differently to survive?

3. Why was Palm successful where so many others had failed?
4. What does the emergence of smart phones mean for Palm?

OVERVIEW

first movers
The first entrants to sell in a new product or service category.

early followers
Entrants that are early to market, but not first.

late entrants
Entrants that do not enter the market until the time the product begins to penetrate the mass market or later.

The previous chapter pointed out that some industries are characterized by increasing returns to adoption, meaning that the more a technology is adopted, the more valuable it becomes. In such industries, timing can be crucial—a technology that is adopted earlier than others may reap self-reinforcing advantages such as greater funds to invest in improving the technology, greater availability of complementary goods, and less customer uncertainty. On the other hand, the same factors that cause increasing returns to adoption may make very early technologies unattractive: if there are few users of the technology or availability of complementary goods is poor, the technology may fail to attract customers. A number of other first-mover advantages, and disadvantages, can shape how timing of entry is related to likelihood of success.

Entrants are often divided into three categories: **first movers** (or pioneers), which are the first to sell in a new product or service category; **early followers** (also called early leaders), which are early to the market *but not first;* and **late entrants,** which enter the market when or after the product begins to penetrate the mass market. The research on whether it is better to be a first mover, early follower, or late entrant yields conflicting conclusions. Some studies that contrast early entrants (lumping first movers and early followers together) with late entrants find that early entrants have higher returns and survival rates, consistent with the notion of first-mover (or at least early-mover) advantage.[9] However, other research has suggested the first firm to market is often the first to fail, causing early followers to outperform first movers.[10] Still other research contends the higher returns of being a first mover typically offset the survival risk.[11] A number of factors influence how timing of entry affects firm survival and profits. In this chapter, we will first examine first-mover advantages and disadvantages. We will then look more closely at what factors determine the optimal timing of entry, and its implications for a firm's entry strategy.

FIRST-MOVER ADVANTAGES

Being a first mover may confer the advantages of brand loyalty and technological leadership, preemption of scarce assets, and exploitation of buyer switching costs.[12] Furthermore, in industries characterized by increasing returns, early entrants may accrue learning and network externality advantages that are self-reinforcing over time.[13]

Brand Loyalty and Technological Leadership

The company that introduces a new technology may earn a long-lasting reputation as a leader in that technology domain. Such a reputation can help sustain the company's image, brand loyalty, and market share even after competitors have introduced comparable products. The organization's position as technology leader also enables it to shape customer expectations about the technology's form, features, pricing, and other characteristics. By the time later entrants come to market, customer requirements may be well-established. If aspects that customers have come to expect in a technology are difficult for competitors to imitate (e.g., if they are protected by patent or copyright, or arise from the first mover's unique capabilities), being the technology leader can yield sustained **monopoly rents.** Even if the technology characteristics are imitable, the first mover has an opportunity to build brand loyalty before the entry of other competitors.

monopoly rents
The additional returns (either higher revenues or lower costs) a firm can make from being a monopolist, such as the ability to set high prices, or the ability to lower costs through greater bargaining power over suppliers.

Preemption of Scarce Assets

Firms that enter the market early can preemptively capture scarce resources such as key locations, government permits, access to distribution channels, and relationships with suppliers.

For example, companies that wish to provide any wireless communication service must license the rights to broadcast over particular radio frequencies from the government. In the United States, the Federal Communications Commission (FCC) is primarily responsible for allotting rights to use bands of radio frequencies (known as the spectrum) for any wireless broadcasting. The FCC first allocates different portions of the spectrum for different purposes (such as digital television broadcasting, third-generation wireless telecommunication, etc.) and different geographic areas. It then auctions off rights to use these segments to the highest bidders. This means that early movers in wireless services can preemptively capture the rights to use portions of the wireless spectrum for their own purposes, while effectively blocking other providers. By 2003, the proliferation of wireless services had caused the spectrum to become a scarce commodity, and the FCC was under pressure to allow the holders of wireless spectrum rights to sublet unused portions of their spectrum to other organizations.

Exploiting Buyer Switching Costs

Once buyers have adopted a good, they often face costs to switch to another good. For example, the initial cost of the good is itself a switching cost, as is the cost of complements purchased for the good. Additionally, if a product is complex, buyers must spend time becoming familiar with its operation; this time investment becomes a switching cost that deters the buyer from switching to a different product. If buyers face switching costs, the firm that captures customers early may be able to keep those customers even if technologies with a superior value proposition are introduced later. This is often the reason given for the dominance of the QWERTY typewriter keyboard. In 1867, Christopher Sholes began experimenting with building a typewriter. At that time, letters were struck on paper by mechanical keys. If two keys were struck in rapid succession, they often would jam. Key jamming was a particularly significant problem in the 1800s, because typewriters then were designed so that keys struck the back side of the paper; the typist might not realize he had been typing with jammed keys until after removing the page. Sholes designed his keyboard so that commonly used letter combinations were scattered as widely as possible over the keyboard. The QWERTY keyboard also puts a disproportionate burden on the left hand (3,000 English words can be typed with the left hand alone, while only 300 can be typed with the right hand alone). This positioning of keys would slow the typing of letter combinations, and thus reduce the likelihood of jamming the keys.[14]

Over time, many competing typewriter keyboards were introduced that boasted faster typing speeds or less tiring typing. For example, the Hammand and Blickensderfer "Ideal" keyboard put the most commonly used letters in the bottom row for easy access, and used only three rows total. Another example, the Dvorak keyboard, places all five vowels and the three most commonly used consonants in the home row, and common letter combinations require alternating hands frequently, reducing fatigue. However, QWERTY's early dominance meant typists were trained only on QWERTY keyboards. By the time Dvorak keyboards were introduced in 1932, tens of millions of typists were committed to QWERTY keyboards—the switching costs of learning how to type all over again were more than people were willing to bear.[15] Even after daisy-wheel keys (and later, electronic typewriters) removed all possibility of jamming keys, the QWERTY keyboard remained firmly entrenched. August Dvorak is said to have died a bitter man, claiming, "I'm tired of trying to do something worthwhile for the human race. They simply don't want to change!"[16]

Reaping Increasing Returns Advantages

In an industry with pressures encouraging adoption of a dominant design, the timing of a firm's investment in new technology development may be particularly critical to its likelihood of success. For example, in an industry characterized by increasing returns to adoption, there can be powerful advantages to being an early provider; a technology that is adopted early may rise in market power through self-reinforcing positive feedback mechanisms, culminating in its entrenchment as a dominant design. Intel is an apt example of this.

Intel's Ted Hoff invented the first microprocessor in 1971, and in 1975, Bill Gates and Paul Allen showed that it could run a version of BASIC that Gates had written. Gates' BASIC became widely circulated among computer enthusiasts, and as BASIC was adopted and applications developed for it, the applications were simultaneously optimized for Intel's architecture. IBM's adoption of Intel's 8088 microprocessor in its PC introduction secured Intel's dominant position, and each of Intel's subsequent generations of products has set the market standard.[17]

FIRST-MOVER DISADVANTAGES

Despite the great attention that first-mover advantages receive, there are also arguments for not entering a market too early. In a historical study of 50 product categories, Gerard Tellis and Peter Golder found that market pioneers have a high failure rate—roughly 47 percent—and that the mean market share of market pioneers is 10 percent.[18] By contrast, early leaders (firms that enter after market pioneers but assume market leadership during the early growth phase of the product life cycle) averaged almost three times the market share of market pioneers.[19] Tellis and Golder point out that the market may often perceive first movers to have advantages because it has misperceived who the first mover really was. For example, while today few people would dispute Procter & Gamble's claim that it "created the disposable diaper market,"[20] in actuality, Procter & Gamble entered the disposable market almost 30 years after Chux, a brand owned by a subsidiary of Johnson & Johnson. In the mid-1960s, *Consumer Reports* ranked both products as best buys. However, over time Pampers became very successful and Chux disappeared, and eventually people began to reinterpret history.

Other studies have found that first movers earn greater revenues than other entrants, but that they also face higher costs, causing them to earn significantly lower profits in the long run.[21] First movers typically bear the bulk of the research and development expenses for their product or service technologies, and they must also often pay to develop suppliers and distribution channels, plus consumer awareness. A later entrant often can capitalize on the research and development investment of the first mover, fine-tune the product to customer needs as the market becomes more certain, avoid any mistakes made by the earlier entrant, and exploit **incumbent inertia.**[22] Later entrants can also adopt newer and more efficient production processes while early movers are either stuck with earlier technologies or must pay to rebuild their production systems.[23]

incumbent inertia
The tendency for incumbents to be slow to respond to changes in the industry environment due to their large size, established routines, or prior strategic commitments to existing suppliers and customers.

Research and Development Expenses

Developing a new technology often entails significant research and development expenses, and the first to develop and introduce a technology typically bears the brunt of this expense. By the time a firm has successfully developed a new technology, it may have borne the expense not only of that technology, but also the expense of exploring technological paths that did not yield a commercially viable product. This firm also typically bears the cost of developing necessary production processes and complementary goods that are not available on the market. Since the new product development failure rate can be as high as 95 percent, being the first to develop and introduce an unproven new technology is expensive and risky.

By contrast, later entrants often do not have to invest in exploratory research. Once a product has been introduced to the market, competitors can often ascertain how the product was created. The later entrant can also observe the market's response to particular features of the technology and decide how to focus its development efforts. Thus, the later entrant can both save development expense and produce a product that achieves a closer fit with market preferences.

Undeveloped Supply and Distribution Channels

When a firm introduces a new-to-the-world technology, often no appropriate suppliers or distributors exist. The firm may face the daunting task of developing and producing its own supplies and distribution service, or assisting in the development of supplier and developer markets. For example, when DEKA Research began developing its self-balancing IBOT wheelchair, it needed a type of ball bearing for which there were no suppliers. DEKA was forced to develop a machine to mold the bearings. According to Dean Kamen, the company's founder, "Nobody here planned to invent new ball bearings, but in order to make this engine practical we have to develop a bearing technology that doesn't exist."[24]

enabling technologies
Component technologies that are necessary for the performance or desirability of a given innovation.

Immature Enabling Technologies and Complements

When firms develop technologies, they often rely on other producers of **enabling technologies.** For instance, the opening vignette demonstrated that even though producers of personal digital assistants (PDAs) had created palm-size devices with significant computing power, the potential of these devices would be delivered only if battery and modem technologies were further developed. Since few PDA manufacturers were

Fuel cells create electricity from a reaction between hydrogen and oxygen, and are much more efficient than internal combustion gasoline engines. Whereas a typical internal combustion engine converts less than 20 percent of the energy potential of gasoline into power for the automobile, fuel cells capture 40 percent to 60 percent of the energy potential of their fuel source, which can be any hydrogen-rich liquid or gas.[25] Hydrogen is one of the most abundant elements on earth and can be obtained in a number of ways, including electrolysis of water or steam conversion of methanol. Furthermore, the only waste products of hydrogen fuel cells are water vapor and carbon dioxide. Hydrogen thus offers an inexhaustible and environmentally friendly fuel source.[26] Utilizing hydrogen to power vehicles (among other things) offers the promise of reducing reliance on dwindling fossil fuel reserves while dramatically decreasing the environmental impact of automobiles. Many of the key players in fuel cell development envision a "hydrogen economy" whereby automobiles with hydrogen fuel cells are used to supply power to homes and offices, eventually replacing the existing electrical power grids.

Fuel cells were developed more than 150 years ago, but were initially too bulky and expensive to be used in automobiles. In the 1970s, however, the energy crisis sparked a resurgence in fuel cell development, and a number of prototypes emerged through the late 1970s and 1980s. By the 1990s, several auto manufacturers, including Toyota and Daimler-Benz (now DaimlerChrysler), had developed automobiles powered by fuel cells and were planning commercial production. A number of serious obstacles, however, stood in the way of fuel cell adoption by the mass market. The most serious of these was the lack of a complementary refueling infrastructure. Before fuel cell vehicles could be promoted to the mass market, refueling options had to be developed that would be convenient and easy for consumers to use. This was no small feat—the existing fuel stations that were ubiquitous in almost every corner of the globe could not handle a gaseous fuel such as hydrogen. While liquid gasoline can be stored in almost any type of container, hydrogen gas is liquid only under very high pressure and has very small molecules. It would rapidly leak out of existing gasoline storage containers. Both fueling stations and automobiles would need to be able to keep compressed hydrogen in a pressurized tank. Furthermore, many of the existing gasoline stations were owned or otherwise connected to oil companies. Since it was not yet clear what role oil companies would play in the hydrogen economy, many suspected that oil companies would use their resources and lobbying power to resist the adoption of hydrogen fuel cells. To unleash the power of the "hydrogen economy" vision would not only require heavy investment in new infrastructure, but it would also require resolving or overcoming the conflicting interests of numerous stakeholders, including government, utilities, auto manufacturers, oil producers, and consumers.

actually involved in the development of batteries or modems, they were reliant on the development efforts of other firms.

As discussed in Chapter Four, many products also require complementary goods to be useful or valuable. Computers need software, cameras need film, automobiles need service, gasoline, and roads. When new technologies are introduced to a market, important complements may not yet be fully developed, thus hindering adoption of the innovation. The development of vehicles powered by hydrogen fuel cells (see the accompanying Theory in Action) provides an excellent example of how a lack of complementary technologies and infrastructure can pose serious obstacles for early movers.

Uncertainty of Customer Requirements

A first mover to the market may face considerable uncertainty about what product features customers will ultimately desire and how much they will be willing to pay for them. For a very new product technology, market research may be of little help. Customers may have little idea of the value of the technology or the role it would play in their lives. As a consequence, first movers may find that their early product offerings must be revised as the market begins to reveal customer preferences.

For instance, when Kodak introduced the 8 mm video camera in the late 80s, it expected that customers would flock to the design's smaller size and superior recording ability. Instead, consumers rejected the product. The 8 mm video cameras were more expensive, and consumers had not yet recognized a need for this product and were unsure of what value it could provide. Kodak decided to withdraw from the market. However, by the early 1990s, consumers had become more comfortable with the concept of 8mm video camera technology, and several competitors (most notably Sony) successfully entered this market.

First movers have an opportunity to shape customer preferences by establishing the precedent for product design in the newly emerging market and by investing in customer education. Customer education efforts are expensive, however. If the product is slow to begin to reap revenues for the sponsoring firm, it may collapse under the weight of its R&D and marketing expenses, as illustrated in the opening vignette of the personal digital assistants industry. Figure 5.1 provides a number of product categories with their first movers, prominent followers, and which of these were ultimately more successful.

FIGURE 5.1
First Movers and Followers— Who Wins?

Source: R. M. Grant, *Contemporary Strategy Analysis* (Malden, MA: Blackwell Publishers, 1998); D. Teece, *The Competitive Challenge: Strategies for Industrial Innovation and Renewal* (Cambridge: Ballinger 1987); and M. A. Schilling, "Technology Success and Failure in Winner-Take-All Markets; Testing a Model of Technological Lock Out," *Academy of Management Journal* 45, pp. 387–98.

Product	First Mover	Notable Follower(s)	The Winner
8 mm video camera	Kodak	Sony	Follower
Disposable diaper	Chux	Pampers Kimberly Clark	Follower
Float glass	Pilkington	Corning	First mover
Groupware	Lotus	AT&T	First mover
Instant camera	Polaroid	Kodak	First mover
Microprocessors	Intel	AMD Cyrix	First Mover
Microwave	Raytheon	Samsung	Follower
Personal computer	MITS (Altair)	Apple IBM	Followers
Personal computer operating system	Digital Research	Microsoft (MS-DOS)	Follower
Spreadsheet software	VisiCalc	Microsoft (Excel) Lotus	Followers
VCR	Ampex/Sony	Matsushita	Follower
Video game console	Magnavox	Atari Nintendo	Follower
Web browser	NCSA Mosaic	Netscape Microsoft (Internet Explorer)	Followers
Word processing software	MicroPro (WordStar)	Microsoft (MS Word) Wordperfect	Followers
Workstation	Xerox Alto	Sun Microsystems Hewlett-Packard	Followers

FACTORS INFLUENCING OPTIMAL TIMING OF ENTRY

In very early market stages, a technology may be underdeveloped and its fit with customer needs unknown. In late market stages, a technology may be well-understood, but competitors may have already captured controlling shares of the market. How does a firm decide whether to attempt to pioneer a technology category or to wait while others do so? The answer will depend on several factors, including customer certainty, the margin of improvement offered by the new technology, the state of enabling technologies and complementary goods, the threat of competitive entry, the degree to which the industry exhibits increasing returns, and the firm's resources.

1. How certain are customer preferences?

When new-to-the-world technologies are first developed, customers may have difficulty understanding the technology and its role in their life. Both producers and customers may face considerable ambiguity about the importance of various features of the technology. As producers and customers gain experience with the technology, features that initially seemed compelling may turn out to be unnecessary, and features that had seemed unimportant may turn out to be crucial. For example, many of the companies that raced to establish an online presence in the e-commerce frenzy of the late 1990s believed that their websites needed exciting graphics and sounds to be competitive. Graphics and sound, however, turned out to be the downfall of many early websites. Many customers did not have high-speed Internet access or computers with enough processing power to quickly download the websites, making multimedia websites an annoyance rather than an attraction.

The reverse scenario is demonstrated in Sony's introduction of the PlayStation2. When Sony introduced its multifeatured PlayStation2, many industry analysts believed that Sony had overestimated consumer interest in having a game console that would play music CDs or DVD movies. It turned out, however, that Sony may have *underestimated* the desirability of these features. Video game consoles are typically sold at cost (or at a loss) in order to rapidly build an installed base. Profits are then made on game royalties. However, when consumers realized that the PlayStation2 was a very affordable combination of game console and high-quality DVD player, many consumers bought the system for its DVD capabilities first and game capabilities second. Many of these consumers bought very few games, causing Sony's strategy of subsidizing the console with the intention of making money on the games to backfire. Observing this, Microsoft disabled DVD playback on its Xbox unless consumers purchased an add-on DVD playback kit.

Not all pioneers face customer uncertainty—some innovations are developed in response to well-understood customer needs. Customer requirements may have been long known even if the method of meeting them was not. For example, the developers of Tagamet (a medication for patients with chronic heartburn or ulcers) faced very little customer uncertainty. Customers wanted an affordable, easy-to-use solution to their stomach discomfort. Once a method of achieving this objective had been developed, tested, and approved, its developers raced the product to market in hopes of patenting it and securing market share ahead of competing products. Other things being equal, less customer uncertainty favors earlier timing of entry.

2. How much improvement does the innovation provide over previous solutions?

The degree to which the technology represents an improvement over previous technologies increases a firm's likelihood of successful early entry. That is, when a technology makes a dramatic improvement over previous generations or different technologies that serve similar functions, it will more rapidly gain customer acceptance. There will be less ambiguity about the value of the technology and more early adoptions (as well as more support by complementary goods providers); as a consequence, customer expectations should become known sooner, and adoptions should be more rapid.

3. Does the innovation require enabling technologies, and are these technologies sufficiently mature?

As mentioned earlier, many innovations rely on crucial enabling technologies to ensure their performance. A high-definition television set is of little value if networks are incapable of broadcasting in high definition; cellular phones or portable stereos would have little value if small and long-lasting batteries were unavailable. A developer must identify which enabling technologies will affect the performance of the new innovation and assess the degree to which those technologies are mature enough (or *will be* mature enough) to deliver the desired performance. More mature enabling technologies allow earlier entry; less mature enabling technologies may favor waiting for enabling technologies to be further developed.

4. Do complementary goods influence the value of the innovation, and are they sufficiently available?

If the value of an innovation hinges critically on the availability and quality of complementary goods, then the state of complementary goods determines the likelihood of successful entry. Not all innovations require complementary goods, and many more innovations can utilize existing complementary goods. For example, though numerous innovations in 35 mm cameras have been introduced in the last few decades, almost all have remained compatible with standard rolls of 35 mm film, thus availability of that complementary good was ensured. If, on the other hand, the innovation requires the development of new complementary goods, then a pioneer must find a way to ensure their availability. Some firms have the resources and capabilities to develop both a good and its complements, while others do not. If the firm's innovation requires complementary goods that are not available on the market, and the firm is unable to develop those complements, successful early entry is unlikely.

5. How high is the threat of competitive entry?

If there are significant entry barriers or few potential competitors with the resources and capabilities to enter the market, the firm may be able to wait while customer requirements and the technology evolve. Over time, one would expect customer expectations to become more certain, enabling technologies to improve, and support goods and services to be developed, thus increasing the likelihood that sponsored technologies will possess a set of attributes that meet consumer demands. However, if the technology proves to be valuable, other firms are also likely to be attracted to the market. Thus, if entry barriers are low, the market could quickly become quite

Research Brief　Whether and When to Enter?

In a study of 30 years of data on entry into the medical diagnostic imaging industry, Will Mitchell examined the factors that drive whether and when a firm that is an incumbent in one subfield of an industry chooses to enter a newly emerging subfield of the industry.[27] For instance, what determines whether and when a manufacturer of coventional X-ray machines decides to go into magnetic resonance imaging (MRI) equipment? While new goods offer opportunities for growth, they can cannibalize existing products, and they also require an investment in new skills. Incumbents often are slow to enter new technical subfields.[28] They may be intentionally waiting for industry turbulence to subside, or they may be unintentionally slowed by factors that create inertia, such as the difficulty in altering well-established routines and strategic commitments to the firm's existing supplier and customer base.

Mitchell pointed out that entry barriers and imitability of a new product (for example, whether it can be effectively protected by patents) interact to create different incentives for timing. First, if only one firm can produce an inimitable good, it can enter if and when it wants. However, if several firms could produce a good that will subsequently be inimitable, they may race to do so to capture the market. In such a circumstance, being early confers a significant advantage. Finally, if the good is expected to be highly imitable (for example, if it would be difficult to effectively protect with patents because competitors could easily invent around the patent), then firms will prefer to wait while others bear the expense of developing and introducing the good. There are disincentives to being early to market.[29]

Mitchell found that firms that had more specialized assets that would be useful in the new subfield (for example, a well-established distribution system that could be used for the new imaging equipment) were more likely to enter the new subfield. A firm was also more likely to enter if the products it currently produced were threatened by the new products (i.e., if the new technology was likely to displace the firm's current technology as the dominant choice in the market). Furthermore, the incumbent was likely to enter *earlier* if its core products were threatened and there were several potential rivals.

competitive, and entering a market that has already become highly competitive can be much more challenging than entering an emerging market.[30] Margins may already have been driven down to levels that require competitors to be highly efficient, and access to distribution channels may be limited. If the threat of competitive entry is high, the firm may need to enter earlier to establish brand image, capture market share, and secure relationships with suppliers and distributors. This is discussed further in the Research Brief above.

6. Is the industry likely to experience increasing returns to adoption?

In industries that have increasing returns to adoption due to strong learning curve effects or network externalities, allowing competitors to get a head start in building installed base can be very risky. If a competitor's offering builds a significant installed base, the cycle of self-reinforcing advantages could make it difficult for the firm to ever catch up. Furthermore, if there are forces encouraging adoption of a single dominant design, a competitor's technology may be selected. If protection mechanisms such as patents prevent the firm from offering a compatible technology, the firm may be locked out.[31]

7. Can the firm withstand early losses?

As was discussed earlier, a first mover often bears the bulk of the expense and risk of developing and introducing a new innovation. First movers thus often need significant amounts of capital that either is available internally (in the case of large firms) or can be accessed externally (e.g., through the debt or equity markets). Furthermore, the first mover must be able to withstand a significant period with little sales revenue from the product. Even in the case of successful new technologies, often a considerable period elapses between the point at which a first mover introduces a new innovation and the point at which the innovation begins to be adopted by the mass market. The s-curve shape of technology diffusion (discussed in Chapter Three and Chapter 13), illustrates this aptly. New innovations tend to be adopted very slowly at first, while innovators and early adopters try the technology and communicate their experience to others. This slow initial takeoff of new innovations has caused the demise of many startup firms. For example, in the PDA industry, startups such as GO Corporation and Momenta had received accolades for their technology designs, but were unable to withstand the long period of market confusion about PDAs and ultimately ran out of capital. Companies such as IBM and Compaq survived because they were large and diversified, and thus not reliant on PDA revenues. Palm was a relatively late mover in the PDA industry so it did not have to withstand as long of a takeoff period, but even Palm was forced to seek external capital and was acquired by U.S. Robotics, which was later bought by 3COM. It was not until 2000 that Palm was spun out.

On the other hand, firms with significant resources also may be able to more easily catch up to earlier entrants.[32] By spending aggressively on development and advertising, and leveraging relationships with distributors, a late entrant may be able to rapidly build brand image and take market share away from earlier movers. For example, though Nestlé was very late to enter the freeze-dried coffee market with Taster's Choice, the company was able to use its substantial resources to both develop a superior product and rapidly build market awareness. It was thus able to quickly overtake the lead from General Foods' Maxim.[33]

8. Does the firm have resources to accelerate market acceptance?

A firm with significant capital resources not only has the capability to withstand a slow market takeoff, but also can invest such resources in accelerating market takeoff. The firm can invest aggressively in market education, supplier and distributor development, and development of complementary goods and services. Each of these strategies can accelerate the early adoption of the innovation, giving the firm much greater discretion over entering early.[34] These strategies are discussed in more detail in Chapter 13. Thus, a firm's capital resources can give it some influence on the shape of the adoption curve.

9. Is the firm's reputation likely to reduce the uncertainty of customers, suppliers, and distributors?

In addition to capital resources, a firm's reputation and credibility can also influence its optimal timing of entry.[35] A firm's reputation can send a strong signal about its likelihood of success with a new technology. Customers, suppliers, and distributors will use the firm's track record to assess its technological expertise and market prowess. Customers may use the firm's reputation as a signal of the innovation's quality, and thus face less ambiguity about adopting the innovation. A firm with a well-respected reputation for successful technological leadership is also more likely to attract suppliers and distributors.[36] This was aptly demonstrated in the opening vignette with Microsoft's announcement that it would enter the personal digital assistant market: Many distributors decided to wait for Microsoft's product since Microsoft's track record suggested the company would be likely to dominate the new market. Other things being equal, an entrant with a strong reputation can attract adoptions earlier than entrants without strong reputations.

STRATEGIES TO IMPROVE TIMING OPTIONS

As should now be clear, managing the timing of entry into the market is a complex matter. If the technology has a clear advantage to consumers, entering the market early may give the entrant a path dependent advantage that is nearly impossible for competitors to overcome. If, on the other hand, a firm enters a market very early and the advantages of the technology are not very clear to consumers, there is a strong possibility that the technology will receive a tepid welcome. Confounding this risk is the fact that watchful competitors may be able to use the firm's failure to their advantage, refining the technology the firm has introduced to the market and making any corrections necessary to improve the technology's market acceptance. The later entrant may be able to enter at a lower cost because it can capitalize on the research and development of the early firm, and use knowledge of the market gained from observing the early entrant's experience.

In the above, it is assumed that timing of entry is a matter of *choice* for the firm. However, implicit in this assumption is a corollary assumption that the firm is capable of producing the technology at any point in the time horizon under consideration. For this to be true, the firm must possess the core capabilities required to produce the technology to consumer expectations, or be able to develop them quickly. Furthermore, if the firm intends to refine an earlier entrant's technology and beat the earlier entrant to market with a new version of this technology, it must have *fast-cycle development processes*. If a firm has very fast-cycle development processes, the firm not only has a better chance at being an early entrant, but it can also use experience gained through customers' reactions to its technology to quickly introduce a refined version of its technology that achieves a closer fit with customer requirements. In essence, a firm with very fast development deployment processes should be able to take advantage of both first- and second-mover advantages. The research on new product development cycle time indicates that development time can be greatly shortened by using strategic alliances, cross-functional new product development teams, and **parallel development processes**. Chapter 11 will deal specifically with how firms can ensure that their innovations are deployed rapidly to the market.

parallel development process
When multiple stages of the new product development process occur simultaneously.

Summary of Chapter

1. A first mover may be able to build brand loyalty and a reputation for technological leadership, preemptively capture scarce resources, and exploit buyer switching costs.

2. First movers may also benefit from increasing returns to adoption due to learning curve effects and network externalities.

3. Some studies, however, argue that first movers may have higher failure rates. First movers have to bear the brunt of R&D expenses and may face considerable consumer ambiguity. Second movers can capitalize on the R&D and marketing efforts of the first mover, producing a technology that costs less to develop and that corrects for any of the first mover's mistakes.

4. First movers may also face poorly developed supplier markets, distribution channels, and availability of complementary goods, all of which can increase the challenge of successfully launching their new product or service. Enabling technologies may also be immature, hindering the new technology's performance.

5. The biggest disadvantage many first movers face is uncertainty over customer requirements. Customers themselves may be uncertain about what features or form they desire in a new innovation. A firm may have to withstand significant losses before customer preferences become more certain.

6. The optimal timing of entry is thus a function of several factors, including the margin of advantage offered by the new innovation, the state of enabling technologies and complements, the state of customer expectations, the threat of competitive entry, whether the industry faces increasing returns, and a firm's resources.

7. Firms that have fast-cycle development processes have more options when it comes to timing. Not only does a fast-cycle developer have an advantage in introducing innovations earlier, but it also can be its own fast follower by quickly introducing refined versions of its own technology.

Discussion Questions

1. What are some advantages of entering a market early? Are there any advantages to entering a market late?

2. Name a successful (*a*) first mover, (*b*) early follower, and (*c*) late entrant. Identify unsuccessful examples of each.

3. What factors might make some industries harder to pioneer than others? Are there industries in which there is no penalty for late entry?

Endnotes

1. T. Halfhill, E. Perratore, D. Pountain, and B. Ryan, "PDAs Arrive but Aren't Quite Here Yet," *Byte* 18, no. 11 (1993), p. 66.
2. M. Okumura, "Is 1994 'Year of the Pen'?" *Computing Canada* 20, no. 3 (1994), p. 38.
3. T. Schmidt, "Discord in Hardwareland," *Network World* 13, no. 8 (1996), p. 47.
4. D. Hwang, "EO Seeks New CEO: Rossman to Step Down," *Computer Reseller News,* February 28, 1994, p. 10.
5. Schmidt, "Discord in Hardwareland."
6. S. Brull, "Reading the Palm Market Right," *Business Week* 3611 (1999), p. 95.
7. R. Pegoraro, "Even the Best of the Phone-PDA Combos Aren't Good Enough," *Washington Post,* January 27 (2002), p. H.07.

8. Salomon Smith Barney, "Smart Handheld Device Market Segments, Worldwide, 1998–2004E," October 18, 2000.

9. R. Agarwal, "Technological Activity and Survival of Firms," *Economics Letters* 52 (July 1996), pp. 101–08; R. Agarwal, "Survival of Firms over the Product Life Cycle," *Southern Economic Journal* 63, no. 3 (1997), pp. 571–84; and R. Agarwal and G. Michael, "The Evolution of Markets and Entry, Exit, and Survival of Firms," *Review of Economics and Statistics* 78 (November 1996), pp. 489–98.

10. P. Golder and G. Tellis, "Pioneer Advantage: Marketing Logic or Marketing Legend?" *Journal of Marketing Research* 30 (May 1993), pp. 158–70.

11. W. Robinson and M. Sungwook, "Is the First to Market the First to Fail? Empirical Evidence for Industrial Goods Businesses," *Journal of Marketing Research* 39 (2002), pp. 120–28.

12. M. Lieberman and D. Montgomery, "First Mover Advantages: A Survey," *Strategic Management Journal* 9 (1988), pp. 41–58.

13. Ibid.; and M. Spence, "The Learning Curve and Competition," *Bell Journal of Economics* 12 (1981), pp. 49–70.

14. Diamond, "The Curse of QWERTY," *Discover* 18, no. 4 (1997), pp. 34–42.

15. P. A. David, "Clio and the Economics of QWERTY," *American Economic Review* 75 (1985), pp. 332–38.

16. Diamond, "The Curse of QWERTY."

17. C. Ferguson and C. Morris, *Computer Wars* (New York: Random House, 1993).

18. P. N. Golder and G. Tellis, "Pioneer Advantage: Marketing Logic or Marketing Legend," *Journal of Marketing Research* 20 (1993), pp. 158–70.

19. G. Tellis and P. Golder, "First to Market, First to Fail? Real Causes of Enduring Market Leadership," *Sloan Management Review,* Winter 1996, pp. 65–75.

20. Procter & Gamble Annual Report, 1977.

21. W. Boulding and M. Christen, "First-Mover Disadvantage," *Harvard Business Review,* October 2001.

22. M. Lieberman and D. Montgomery, "First Mover Advantages: A Survey," *Strategic Management Journal* 9 (1988), pp. 41–58.

23. Boulding and Christen, "First-Mover Disadvantage."

24. E. I. Schwartz, "The Inventor's Play-Ground," *Technology Review* 105, no. 8 (2002), p. 69.

25. www.doe.gov.

26. J. Rifkin, "The Hydrogen Economy," *E Magazine,* January–February 2003, pp. 26–37.

27. W. Mitchell, "Whether and When? Probability of Incumbent's Entry into Emerging Technical Subfields," *Administrative Science Quarterly* 38 (1989), pp. 208–30.

28. F. M. Scherer, *Industrial Market Structure and Economic Performance,* 2nd ed. (Chicago: Rand McNally, 1980).

29. M. Katz and C. Shapiro, "Technology Adoption in the Presence of Network Externalities," *Journal of Political Economy* 94 (1986), pp. 822–41.

30. G. L. Lilien and E. Yoon, "The Timing of Competitive Market Entry: An Exploratory Study of New Industrial Products," *Management Science* 36 (1990), pp. 568–85; R. Makadok, "Can First-Mover and Early-Mover Advantages Be Sustained in an Industry with Low Barriers to Entry/Imitation?" *Strategic Management Journal* 19 (1998), pp. 683–96; and R. W. Shaw and S. A. Shaw, "Late Entry, Market Shares and

Competitive Survival: The Case of Synthetic Fibers," *Managerial and Decision Economics* 5 (1984), pp. 72–79.

31. W. B. Arthur, "Competing Technologies, Increasing Returns, and Lock-In by Historical Events," *The Economic Journal,* March 1989, pp. 116–31; and M. Schilling, "Technological Lock Out: An Integrative Model of the Economic and Strategic Factors Driving Technology Success and Failure," *Academy of Management Review* 23 (1998), pp. 267–84.

32. J. Shamsie, C. Phelps, and J. Kuperman, "Better Late than Never: A Study of Late Entrants in Household Electrical Equipment," *Strategic Management Journal* 25 (2003), pp. 69–84.

33. D. A. Aaker and G. S. Day, "The Perils of High-Growth Markets," *Strategic Management Journal* 7 (1986), pp. 409–21; Shamsie, Phelps, and Kuperman, "Better Late than Never"; V. Shankar, G. S. Carpenter, and L. Krishnamurthi, "Late Mover Advantage: How Innovative Late Entrants Outsell Pioneers," *Journal of Marketing Research* 35, no. 1 (1998), pp. 54–70; and G. L. Urban, T. Carter, S. Gaskin, and Z. Mucha, "Market Share Rewards to Pioneering Brands: An Empirical Analysis and Strategic Implications," *Management Science* 32 (1986), pp. 645–59.

34. M. A. Schilling, "Technological Leapfrogging: Lessons from the U.S. Video Game Console Industry," *California Management Review* 45, no. 3 (2003), pp. 6–32.

35. D. A. Shepherd and M. Shanley, *New Venture Strategy: Timing, Environmental Uncertainty and Performance* (London: Sage, 1998).

36. Schilling, "Technological Leapfrogging."

Part Two

Formulating Technological Innovation Strategy

In this section, we will cover the key aspects of formulating a technological innovation strategy, including:

- Assessing the firm's position and defining its strategic direction.
- Choosing innovation projects in which to invest, including both quantitative and qualitative valuation techniques.
- Deciding whether and how the firm will collaborate on development activities, choosing a collaboration mode, and choosing and monitoring partners.
- Crafting a strategy for protecting—or diffusing—a technological innovation through such methods as patents, trademarks, copyrights, and trade secrets.

Formulating Technological Innovation Strategy

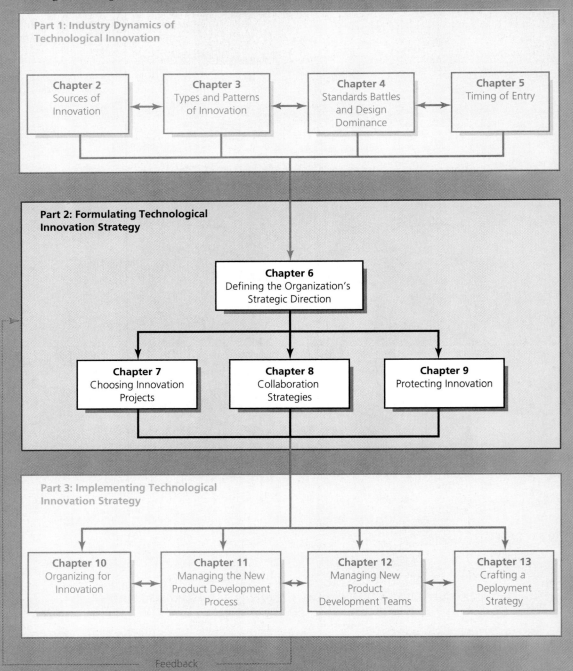

Chapter **Six**

Defining the Organization's Strategic Direction

Redefining Handspring—Are Smart Phones a Smart Move?

In 2001, Handspring's line of personal digital assistants (PDAs) was second only to Palm Computer's PalmPilots in worldwide market share. Handspring, however, had yet to turn a profit. Price wars and slumping sales had decimated margins in the PDA industry and left producers with large quantities of rapidly obsolescing inventory. Economic conditions had forced Handspring to mark down even its more advanced models. In late 2001, Handspring made a startling announcement: It would discontinue development on its Visor line of personal digital assistants, and instead refocus on a new product, a smart phone called the Treo. Smart phones are handheld devices with the functionality of PDAs but the ergonomic and aesthetic styling of a mobile phone. Smart phones appeared to have great growth potential and were also expected to have higher margins. However, entering the smart phone market required developing new capabilities, targeting new customer segments, and creating new distribution channels. Perhaps even more ominously, it meant pitting the company against very large and established rivals such as Nokia, Samsung, and Ericsson.

Handspring's History

Jeff Hawkins founded Palm Computing, the company that had introduced the extremely successful PalmPilot line of PDAs. U.S. Robotics acquired Palm in 1995, bringing badly needed capital to fund development costs, and in 1997, 3Com acquired U.S. Robotics. In 1998, Hawkins and Donna Dubinsky left the company and started a new venture that would produce PDAs based on the Palm operating system: Handspring.[1] They positioned Handspring to the public and investors as the same people doing the same thing, this time just better. The executive team's mantra was "Innovate, innovate, and innovate. Yet keep it small, simple, affordable, and connected."

Handspring entered the PDA market in mid-1999 with its Visor device. The Visor was priced lower than Palm's PDAs, and with its Springboard module, it offered more functions than Palm's devices. The module allowed the PDA to be expanded by inserting a range of components, such as mobile phones, digital cameras, pagers, modems, or MP3 players, and additional software applications.[2] Handspring launched a global marketing program for its Visor and Springboard modules, selling through a variety of distribution channels that included the World Wide Web, value-added resellers, international distribution agencies, and retailers. Handspring's largest retailers were Best Buy, Staples, and CompUSA, which accounted for 14 percent, 13 percent, and 10 percent of sales, respectively. Competing primarily on design and price, the consumer segment was Handspring's primary target while the business segment received only a secondary focus.

Before long it became apparent that the Springboard modules, initially praised by consumers and feared by competitors, were not going to revolutionize the PDA market. The Springboard modules never achieved strong market acceptance because they were expensive and could only make the Visor devices imitate, and not replace, other devices. This lack of a compelling differentiating factor, combined with an increasingly competitive PDA market, had moved Handspring into a very vulnerable competitive position. Since the fall of 2000, investors had seen Handspring's stock price drop from a high of $95 to as low as $0.56 a share. Facing increasingly difficult economic conditions and a third straight year of increasing operating losses, Handspring had to do something drastic. Though Handspring had already made one foray into merging cell phone and PDA capabilities with the VisorPhone (a Springboard module that acted as a cell phone), that product had received a lukewarm welcome. The module was expensive, and the combination of the module and the PDA was bulky and awkward. This time the company decided to commit fully to the smart phone concept by introducing a product that would put phone capability and styling first, with PDA functionality second: the Treo.

Treo

"The theme for the company is Treo," said Ed Colligan, chief operating officer of Handspring. The Treo is a single device that integrates the functionality of a cell phone, PDA, and pager with "always on" capability.[3] Unlike regular cell phones that have some organizer capabilities, smart phones such as the Treo had larger, sharper screens that could display regular Web pages rather than the small subset of Web pages designed to be readable on cell-phone displays.[4] At its launch, it was heralded as the smart phone with the tightest integration of these functions and capabilities. Notably, the Treo did *not* include a Springboard module.

Betting the Farm

Treo represented more than just an additional product in Handspring's portfolio—Handpring was "betting the farm" on the success of the new device. As stated by CEO Donna Dubinsky, Handspring would be "transitioning out of the organizer business and into the communicator business."[5] Handspring would continue to support the Visor so long as there was demand, but it would direct all its development and promotion effort toward the Treo. Some analysts wondered why Handspring would abandon the Visor platform, risking alienating third-party developers for the platform and rendering all Springboard development and inventory obsolete.[6]

Treo also represented a shift in market focus for Handspring. Though individual consumers would still be targeted, the Treo would be primarily targeted at the enterprise market. Management believed the integration of phone, PDA, and pager made the Treo an appealing corporate productivity tool and the growth potential in the business-to-business market was greater than that in the business-to-consumer market. At a major corporate software convention in Las Vegas, Ed Colligan stated, "We believe that this is a really compelling enterprise device for wireless voice and data. I think as we build critical mass in the enterprise with the Treo, you'll see more applications. It takes a breakthrough device to get developers going."

Handspring shipped 47,000 units of the Treo in the first quarter of 2002, and Wall Street responded warmly, pushing Handspring's stock price up 34 percent. By the end of the year, Handspring had sold 250,000 Treos. This was a paltry number, however, when compared to the 1 million Visors that Handspring had sold in its first year of operations. By early 2003, Handspring's stock was still trading at less than a dollar a share, and the company had cut its workforce by 40 percent. Still, most analysts applauded Handspring's bold move, and believed that Handspring was right about converged devices being the future. The real question was whether Handspring could survive the painful transition. As stated by Steve Baker, analyst at the NPD Techworld research firm, "The product category just wasn't ready for Handspring yet. I think it's ready for them now; it's just going to be a slow build. The question is, do they have they staying power."[7]

Discussion Questions

1. How does Handspring's move into smart phones change the nature of the external threats and opportunities that Handspring faces?
2. What new resources and capabilities will Handspring have to develop to be successful in the smart phone market?
3. Why do you think Handspring chose to discontinue the Visor line when it moved to smart phones, rather than supporting both product lines?
4. Was Handspring's move to smart phones too early? Too ambitious?

OVERVIEW

The first step in formulating a company's technological innovation strategy is to assess its current position and define its strategic direction for the future. What are the firm's key strengths and weaknesses? Does it have any sources of sustainable competitive advantage? What are the firm's core competencies, and what kind of value propositions do those core competencies offer to customers? How do managers want those value propositions to evolve? What key resources and capabilities does the firm need to develop or acquire to meet its long-term objectives?

A coherent technological innovation strategy both leverages and enhances the firm's existing competitive position, and it provides direction for the future development of the firm. Formulating a technological innovation strategy first requires an accurate appraisal of where the firm currently is. It then requires articulating an ambitious strategic intent—one that creates a gap between a company's existing resources and capabilities and those required to achieve its intent.[8] The ability of the firm to cohesively leverage all its resources around a unified vision can enable it to create a competitive advantage that is very difficult for competitors to imitate.[9]

ASSESSING THE FIRM'S CURRENT POSITION

To assess the firm's current position in the marketplace, it is useful to begin with some standard tools of strategic analysis for analyzing the external and internal environment of the firm.

External Analysis

The two most commonly used tools for analyzing the external environment of the firm include Porter's five-force model and stakeholder analysis.

Porter's Five-Force Model

In this model, the attractiveness of an industry and a firm's opportunities and threats are identified by analyzing five forces (see Figure 6.1):

1. **The degree of existing rivalry.** An industry's degree of rivalry is influenced by a number of factors. First, the number and relative size of competitors will shape the nature of rivalry. In general, the more firms competing that are of comparable size, the more competitive the industry will be. There are, however, exceptions to this generality. For example, **oligopolistic industries** (those that have a few large competitors) can be fiercely competitive if firms choose to engage in price wars (as happened in the personal digital assistants industry). On the other hand, oligopolistic industries can have a low degree of rivalry if the competitors choose to avoid competing head-to-head in the same market segments, or if they engage in tacit price collusion. Rivalry is also influenced by the degree to which competitors are differentiated from each other. For example, the lack of any significantly differentiating feature in its Visor line was one reason Handspring had become so vulnerable to price competition. If competitors are

oligopolistic industries
Highly consolidated industries with a few large competitors.

FIGURE 6.1
Porter's Five-Force Model

Source: M. A. Porter, *Competitive Strategy* (New York: Free Press, 1980).

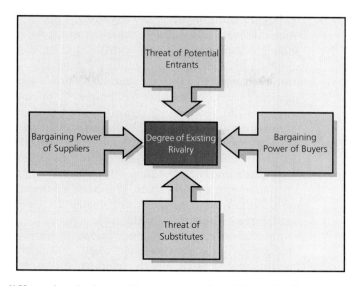

highly differentiated, they will experience less direct rivalry because their products are likely to appeal to different market segments. Demand conditions also influence degree of rivalry. When demand is increasing, there are more revenues to go around and firms will experience less competitive pressure. On the other hand, when demand is declining, firms have to compete for a shrinking pool of revenues, and competition can become very aggressive. In declining industries, high **exit barriers** (e.g., fixed capital investments, emotional attachment to the industry, etc.) can also intensify rivalry by making firms reluctant to abandon the industry.

exit barriers
Costs or other commitments that make it difficult for firms to abandon an industry (e.g., large fixed asset investments, emotional commitment to the industry, etc.).

2. **Threat of potential entrants.** The threat of potential entrants is influenced by both the degree to which the industry is likely to attract new entrants (i.e., is it profitable, growing, or otherwise alluring?) and the height of **entry barriers.** Entry barriers can include such factors as large start-up costs, brand loyalty, difficulty in gaining access to suppliers or distributors, government regulation, threat of retaliation by existing competitors, and many others. While profitability and growth may attract new entrants, entry barriers will deter them. For example, while high projected growth in the smart phone market attracts potential entrants to this market, the challenge of competing against large, well-established and efficient competitors such as Nokia and Ericsson deters many entrants. To effectively compete against these companies requires that an entrant be able to manufacture, advertise, and distribute on a large scale, suggesting significant start-up costs for an entrant to achieve a competitive position. However, some of these capabilities could be obtained through partnerships with other firms, such as having contract manufacturers handle production and having mobile phone service providers handle distribution, thereby lowering start-up costs.

entry barriers
Conditions that make it difficult or expensive for new firms to enter an industry (e.g., government regulation, large start-up costs, etc.).

3. **Bargaining power of suppliers.** The degree to which the firm relies on one or a few suppliers will influence its ability to negotiate good terms. If there are few suppliers or suppliers are highly differentiated, the firm may have little choice in

its buying decision, and thus have little leverage over the supplier to negotiate prices, delivery schedules, or other terms. On the other hand, if suppliers are very abundant and/or are not highly differentiated, the firm may be able to force the suppliers to bid against one another for the sale. The amount the firm purchases from the supplier is also relevant. If the firm's purchases constitute the bulk of a supplier's sales, the supplier will be heavily reliant upon the firm and the supplier will have little bargaining power. Likewise, if the supplier's sales constitute a large portion of the firm's purchases, the firm will be heavily reliant upon the supplier and the supplier will have more bargaining power. For example, manufacturers that sell to Wal-Mart often have little bargaining power because Wal-Mart's enormous volume often makes its purchases a significant portion of a manufacturer's yearly sales. Wal-Mart's suppliers typically have little bargaining power. When Intel sells to personal computer manufacturers, on the other hand, it typically wields considerable supplier bargaining power. When computer manufacturers consider potential suppliers for microprocessors, they often have little choice but to go with Intel—many consumers demand their systems include Intel microprocessors, and the majority of personal computer hardware and software has been optimized for the Intel architecture. If the firm faces **switching costs** that make it difficult or expensive to change suppliers, this will also increase the supplier's bargaining power. Finally, if the firm can backward **vertically integrate** (i.e., produce its own supplies) this will lessen supplier bargaining power, and if the supplier can threaten to forward vertically integrate into the firm's business, this will increase the supplier's bargaining power.

switching costs
Factors that make it difficult or expensive to change suppliers or buyers, such as investments in specialized assets to work with a particular supplier or buyer.

vertical integration
Getting into the business of one's suppliers (backward vertical integration) or one's buyers (forward vertical integration). For example, a firm that begins producing its own supplies has practiced backward vertical integration, and a firm that buys its distributor has practiced forward vertical integration.

4. **Bargaining power of buyers.** Many of the same factors that influence the bargaining power of suppliers have an analogous role with the bargaining power of buyers. The degree to which the firm is reliant on a few customers will increase the customer's bargaining power, and vice versa. If the firm's product is highly differentiated, buyers will typically experience less bargaining power, and if the firm's product is undifferentiated, buyers will typically experience greater bargaining power. If buyers face switching costs, this is likely to lower their bargaining power, and if the firm faces switching costs to work with other buyers, this will increase the buyer's bargaining power. Finally, if the buyers can threaten to backward vertically integrate, this will increase their bargaining power, and if the firm can threaten to forward vertically integrate, it will lower customer bargaining power.

5. **Threat of substitutes.** Substitutes are products or services that are not considered competitors, but fulfill a strategically equivalent role for the customer. For example, Starbucks may consider other coffeehouses as competitors, but other social destinations (such as bars or restaurants) or beverages (such as soft drinks or beer) as substitutes. The more potential substitutes there are, and the closer they are in function to the firm's product or service, the greater the threat of substitution. Furthermore, the threat of substitutes will also be shaped by the relative price. For example, while traveling by bus versus air is not particularly comparable in terms of speed, traveling by bus is often considerably less expensive; thus, it poses a threat of substitution, particularly for shorter distances to be traveled. Note that

FIGURE 6.2
Stakeholder Analysis

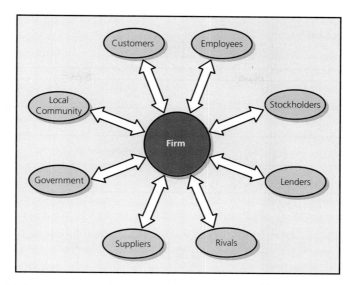

distinguishing between a competitor and a substitute depends on how the industry is defined. For example, if one considers the *airline* industry as the unit of analysis, then bus service is a substitute for airlines. However, if one were considering the *transportation* industry as the unit of analysis, then bus services would be competitors of airlines.

complements

Products or services that enhance the usefulness or desirability of another product.

Recently, Porter has acknowledged a sixth force: the role of **complements**. As has been discussed in several of the earlier chapters, complements are products that enhance the usefulness or desirability of a good. For example, software is an important complement for computers, and gasoline is an important complement for automobiles. The availability, quality, and price of complements will influence the threats and opportunities posed by the industry.

Stakeholder Analysis

stakeholder

Any entity that has an interest ("stake") in the organization.

Stakeholder models are often used for both strategic and normative purposes. A strategic *stakeholder analysis* emphasizes the stakeholder management issues that are likely to impact the firm's financial performance, while a *normative stakeholder analysis* emphasizes the stakeholder management issues the firm ought to attend to due to their ethical or moral implications.[10] Typically, the first step of a stakeholder analysis is to identify all the parties that will be affected by the behavior of the firm (and thus have a "stake" in the firm). For each party, the firm identifies what that stakeholder's interests are, what resources they contribute to the organization, what claims they are likely to make on the organization, and which will be most important from the firm's perspective. Stakeholders include (but are not limited to) stockholders, employees, customers, suppliers, lenders, the local community, government, and rivals (see Figure 6.2).

Internal Analysis

The analysis of the internal environment of the firm most often begins with identifying the firm's strengths and weaknesses. Sometimes this task is organized by examining

FIGURE 6.3
Porter's Value Chain

Source: M. E. Porter, *Competitive Advantage* (New York: Free Press, 1985).

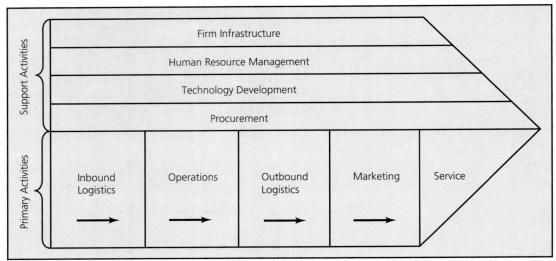

each of the activities of the value chain (see Figure 6.3).[11] In Michael Porter's model of a value chain, activities are divided into primary activities and support activities. Primary activities include *inbound logistics* (all activities required to receive, store, and disseminate inputs), *operations* (activities involved in the transformation of inputs into outputs), *outbound logistics* (activities required to collect, store, and distribute outputs), *marketing and sales* (activities to inform buyers about products and services and to induce their purchase), and *service* (after-sales activities required to keep the product or service working effectively). Support activities include *procurement* (the acquisition of inputs, but not their physical transfer as that would be covered in inbound logistics), *human resource management* (activities such as recruiting, hiring, training, and compensating personnel), *technology development* (activities involved in developing and managing equipment, hardware, software, procedures and knowledge necessary to transform inputs into outputs), and *infrastructure* (functions such as accounting, legal counsel, finance, planning, public affairs, government relations, quality assurance, and general management necessary to ensure smooth functioning of the firm). This generic model can be adapted to better fit a particular firm's needs. For example, for a biotechnology firm or software developer, research and development is likely to be a primary activity and inbound logistics may be insignificant.

Each activity can then be considered from the view of how it contributes to the overall value produced by the firm, and what the firm's strengths and weaknesses are in that activity. For example, Figure 6.4 illustrates what a value-chain analysis might look like for Take2 Interactive Software, which produces the Grand Theft Auto video game. In the figure, research and development is considered a primary activity, but the support activity of the technology development is not considered. Because all the

FIGURE 6.4

Example of Value-Chain Analysis for Take2 Interactive Software

Value-Chain Activity	Strengths	Weaknesses
Inbound Logistics Insignificant; few inputs necessary.		
Research & Development Ability to incorporate state-of-the-art graphics capabilities, sound, and innovative themes significantly differentiates the product in the eyes of the consumer.	Take2's game maximized the polygon processing potential of the PlayStation2 console, making play more lifelike. Parallel development processes kept the development cycles short.	Lack of experience in developing online games could become major liability if market for playing games over the Internet takes off.
Operations Company focuses on producing a few very high-quality games, introducing a new version every year. Once designed, games are manufactured by the video game console producers (e.g., Sony).	Concentrating on a few games enables firm to focus significant resources on ensuring game is a hit.	Concentrating on a few games could be risky—if game fails may have no revenues to support operations. Take2 is completely reliant on console manufacturers for right to develop compatible games, and for manufacture of games.
Outbound Logistics Products are sold through game retailers (e.g., Gamestop), general merchandisers (e.g., Best Buy), and occasionally through bundling arrangements with video console producers, avoiding expense of maintaining own retail stores. Signed an exclusive deal with Sony to offer Grand Theft Auto exclusively for PlayStation2.	Existing retailers already have excellent market penetration, providing rapid and wide deployment of the games. Since Sony PlayStation2 is the No. 1 video game console, signing an exclusive with Sony enables tapping a large market.	Using retailers gives company little discretion over store placement, promotion, and pricing. Exclusive deal with Sony may prove a liability if Xbox or GameCube become more popular.
Marketing Helps build customer awareness of products, builds brand image, accelerates sales. Uses websites, advertisements in gaming magazines, billboards. Grand Theft Auto targeted toward the adult market.	GTA had successfully established an image as being leading edge, and was the No. 1 game in 2002.	Some consumers, retailers, and regulatory agencies criticized Grand Theft Auto's violence and sexual images, potentially tarnishing the company's image.
Service Phone line for technical support helps customers resolve problems in using the product.	Have had relatively few returns or warranty problems.	

continued

concluded		
Firm Infrastructure Legal department negotiates license rights for games.		Copyright infringement suits by other games producers becoming more frequent.
Human Resource Management Hiring and retaining skilled and creative developers is crucial for the production of high-quality games. Company had 932 full-time employees in 2002.	Employees are not unionized. Employee stock option plan improves loyalty and morale.	
Procurement Have to acquire rights to use copyright-protected characters and music.	Thus far have been very successful in obtaining rights to use copyrighted materials.	

Source: S. Balasubramanian, A. Kim, L. Lei, and S. Singh, "Beyond the Mayhem: Take-Two Interactive Software," New York University teaching case, 2003.

tacit resources
Resources of an intangible nature (such as knowledge) that cannot be readily codified.

socially complex resources
Resources or activities that emerge through the interaction of multiple individuals.

causal ambiguity
The relationship between a resource and the outcome it produces is poorly understood (the *causal* mechanism is *ambiguous*).

game manufacturing is performed by the console producers rather than by Take2, its primary technology activities center on design of the games, which is covered in the research and development section.

Once the key strengths and weaknesses are identified, the firm can assess which strengths have the potential to be a source of sustainable competitive advantage. This helps the firm gain valuable perspective on which of its activities and resources should be further leveraged in its articulation of its strategic intent for the future.

To be a potential source of sustainable competitive advantage, resources must be *rare, valuable, durable,* and *inimitable*.[12] Resources that are rare and valuable may yield a competitive advantage, but that advantage will not be sustainable if the firm is incapable of keeping the resources, or if other firms are capable of imitating them. For example, a positive brand image can be a rare and valuable resource, but it requires ongoing investment to sustain. If a firm lacks the capital to reinvest in its brand image, it will erode. Furthermore, many valuable resources are quickly imitated by other firms. Technological advances are reverse-engineered, skillful marketing campaigns are copied, innovative human resource practices are adopted by imitators, and so on. Some resources, however, are not readily imitable. For example, if valuable resources are **tacit** (i.e., they cannot be readily codified in written form), path dependent (i.e., they are dependent on a particular historical sequence of events), **socially complex** (i.e., they arise through the complex interaction of multiple people), or **causally ambiguous** (i.e., it is unclear how the resource gives rise to value), they will be extremely difficult to imitate.[13] For example, *talent* is typically considered to be a tacit and causally ambiguous resource. It is thought to be an inherent trait that cannot be trained, and the mechanisms by which individuals acquire it or tap it are poorly understood. A first-mover advantage is a path-dependent advantage that cannot be copied—once a firm has become the first mover in a category, other firms no longer have the opportunity to be first. Once the firm has established a baseline internal analysis, it can move on to identifying its core competencies and formulate its strategic intent.

IDENTIFYING CORE COMPETENCIES AND CAPABILITIES

core competencies (or core capabilities)
A set of integrated and harmonized abilities that distinguish the firm in the marketplace.

The terms *competency* and *capability* are frequently intermingled in the existing literature on strategy and technological innovation. While several authors have attempted to distinguish such terms as *core competencies, distinctive competencies,* or *core capabilities,* these efforts have sometimes created more confusion than clarity.[14] For example, Prahalad and Hamel use the term **core competency** to refer to a harmonized combination of multiple resources and skills that distinguish a firm in the marketplace, and they use the term *capabilities* to distinguish more elemental skills (such as logistics management or advertising) that might contribute to a competency. By contrast, other authors have argued that core competencies are more elemental technological or production skills, while capabilities are more broadly based and may encompass the firm's entire value chain.[15] This confusion is not really surprising given the near semantic equivalence of the terms *competence* and *capability.* Many dictionaries define both in terms of *abilities*, and some definitions use competence in their definitions of capabilities and vice versa. For example, a capability might be defined in terms of a talent or ability in which one has competence, and competency is often defined in terms of whether one's physical or intellectual capabilities are adequate for a task. The efforts to distinguish these terms more likely reflects (*a*) differences in how various authors envision competencies or capabilities becoming *core* or *distinctive*, and (*b*) their efforts to discriminate between elemental abilities that serve as components of more integrative abilities. For example, an ability to read textbooks might be considered a component ability of the ability to excel in school. Excelling in school requires combining the ability to read textbooks with a host of other skills such as taking notes, participating in class discussions, integrating previous experience with new ideas and models, completing assignments, and so on. In this text, the terms *competency* and *capability* are used interchangeably, but the book will attempt to distinguish what various authors have considered makes competencies or capabilities *core*, and to illustrate how the core competencies or capabilities are achieved through integrating a variety of more basic capabilities.

Core Competencies

A company's core competencies are typically considered to be those that differentiate it strategically. A core competency is more than just a core technology. A core competency arises from a firm's ability to combine and harmonize multiple primary abilities in which the firm excels into a few key building blocks of specialized expertise. Competencies often combine different kinds of abilities, such as abilities in managing the market interface (e.g., advertising, distribution), building and managing an effective infrastructure (e.g., information systems, logistics management), and technological abilities (e.g., applied science, process design).[16] This combination and harmonization of multiple abilities make core competencies difficult to imitate. Consider, for example, Sony's core competency in miniaturization.[17] This competency arises from the harmonization of multiple technologies (e.g., liquid crystal displays, semiconductors, etc.) and is leveraged into multiple markets (including televisions, radios, personal digital assistants, etc.). A firm's core competencies also depend on building high-quality relationships across different functions and business units.

Prahalad and Hamel compare core competencies to roots, from which grow core products such as major components or subassemblies. Core products, in turn, give rise to business units, whose fruit are the various end products of the company (see Figure 6.5).

FIGURE 6.5
Visualizing the Firm's Core Competencies, Core Products, Business Units, and End Products

Source: Adapted from C. K. Prahalad and G. Hamel, "The Core Competence of the Corporation," *Harvard Business Review*, May–June 1990, pp. 79–91.

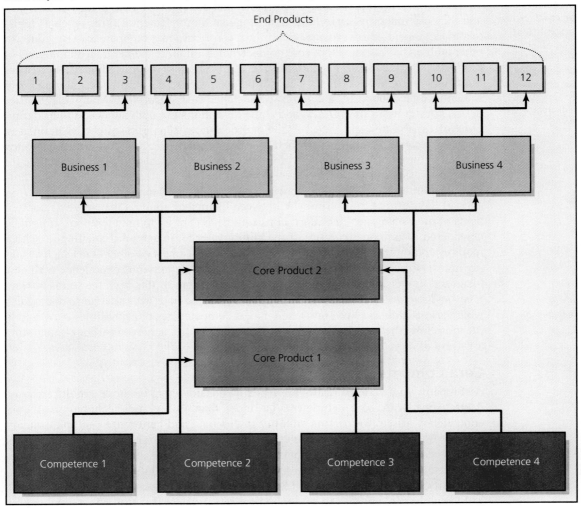

Several core competencies may underlie an individual business unit, and several business units may draw upon the same core competency. This indicates the organization's structure and incentives must encourage cooperation and exchange of resources across strategic business unit boundaries. If managers or resources are wed too closely to their business units, there will be underinvestment in the development and leverage of core competencies.[18] Prahalad and Hamel go so far as to argue that strategic business units should be expected to bid for people in the firm who have particular skills to contribute to a project. Rather than viewing individuals as being employed by a particular strategic business unit, individuals should be considered corporate assets that can be redeployed across the organization.

Prahalad and Hamel offer the following tests to identify the firm's core competencies:

1. Is it a significant source of competitive differentiation? Does it provide a unique signature to the organization? Does it make a significant contribution to the value a customer perceives in the end product? For example, Sony's skills in miniaturization have an immediate impact on the utility customers reap from its portable products.

2. Does it transcend a single business? Does it cover a range of businesses, both current and new? For example, Honda's core competence in engines enables the company to be successful in businesses as diverse as automobiles, motorcycles, lawn mowers, and generators.

3. Is it hard for competitors to imitate? In general, competencies that arise from the complex harmonization of multiple technologies will be difficult to imitate. The competence may have taken years (or decades) to build. This combination of resources and embedded skills will be difficult for other firms to acquire or duplicate.

According to Prahalad and Hamel, few firms are likely to be leaders in more than five or six core competencies. If a company has compiled a list of 20 to 30 capabilities, it probably has not yet identified its true core competencies. For an example of a step-by-step procedure for identifying core competencies, see the accompanying Research Brief. By viewing the business as a portfolio of core competencies, managers are better able to focus on value creation and meaningful new business development, rather than cost cutting or opportunistic expansion.[19]

The Risk of Core Rigidities

Sometimes the very things that a firm excels at can enslave it, making the firm rigid and overly committed to inappropriate skills and resources.[20] Incentive systems may evolve that favor activities that reinforce the firm's core competencies. The organizational culture may reward employees who are most closely connected to core competencies with higher status and better access to other organizational resources. While these systems and norms can prove beneficial in reinforcing and leveraging the firm's existing core competencies, they can also inhibit the development of new core competencies. For example, a firm's emphasis on a scientific discipline that is central to its core competency can make the firm less attractive to individuals from other disciplines. Rewards for engaging in core competency activities can discourage employees from pursuing more exploratory activities. Finally, as noted in Chapter Four,

Research Brief — Identifying the Firm's Core Competencies

In their 1995 article, "Putting Core Competency Thinking into Practice," Mark Gallon, Harold Stillman, and David Coates offer a step-by-step program for discovering and cultivating a firm's core competencies.[21] The program has six modules:

MODULE 1—STARTING THE PROGRAM

The firm should assemble a steering committee, appoint a program manager, and communicate the overall goals of the project to all members of the firm. The program manager should organize teams that will be responsible for circulating throughout the firm to compile an exhaustive inventory of capabilities.

MODULE 2—CONSTRUCTING AN INVENTORY OF CAPABILITIES

The capabilities identified by the teams should be categorized by type. The teams should assess their strength, importance, and criticality to firm operations.

MODULE 3—ASSESSING CAPABILITIES

The list of capabilities should be organized by both their criticality and the current level of expertise within the firm for each of the capabilities.

MODULE 4—IDENTIFYING CANDIDATE COMPETENCIES

The capabilities should be carefully distilled into an array of possible competencies for the firm to focus on and cultivate. No options should be thrown out at this point; all possibilities should be carefully considered.

MODULE 5—TESTING THE CANDIDATE CORE COMPETENCIES

Each candidate core competency should be tested against Prahalad and Hamel's original criteria: Does it provide customer-perceived value? Does it extend into multiple existing or new markets? Is it difficult to imitate?

MODULE 6—EVALUATING THE CORE COMPETENCY POSITION

After choosing the core competencies, the firm must assess to what degree it has ownership of these competencies relative to its competitors. This is the point at which the firm can identify any areas in which it needs to develop or acquire missing pieces of a particular competency.

---

knowledge accumulation tends to be very path dependent. Firms that have well-developed knowledge sets along a particular trajectory may find it very hard to assimilate or utilize knowledge that appears unrelated to that trajectory, potentially limiting the firm's flexibility.[22]

Dynamic Capabilities

In fast-changing markets, it can be extremely useful for a firm to develop a core competency in responding to change. Whereas in Prahalad and Hamel's model, core competencies relate to sets of specific core products, it is also possible for a firm to develop core competencies that are not specific to any set of technologies or products, but rather to a set of abilities that enable it to quickly reconfigure its organizational structure and routines in response to new opportunities.[23] Such competencies are termed **dynamic capabilities**. Dynamic capabilities enable firms to quickly adapt to emerging markets or major technological discontinuities. For example, Corning has made its own evolvability one of its most important core competencies. It invests heavily in research in areas likely to provide scientific breakthroughs (such as opal glasses and their solvents). It develops pilot plants to experiment with new products

dynamic capabilities
A set of abilities that make a firm more agile and responsive to change.

and production processes.[24] It even manages its relationships with alliance partners not as individual relationships focused on particular projects, but rather as an integrative and flexible system of capabilities that extend the firm's boundaries.[25]

STRATEGIC INTENT

A firm's purpose is to create value. This entails more than just improving operations or cutting costs; it means leveraging corporate resources to create more performance for customers, more well-being for employees, and more returns for shareholders. This is accomplished through developing new businesses and markets, and leveraging corporate resources, all guided by the firm's *strategic intent*.[26]

A company's strategic intent is a long-term goal that is ambitious, builds upon and stretches the firm's existing core competencies, and draws from all levels of the organization. Hamel and Prahalad's examples include Canon's obsession with overtaking Xerox in copiers, Apple's mission of ensuring that every individual has a personal computer, or Yahoo's goal of becoming the world's largest Internet shopping mall. Typically a strategic intent looks 10 to 20 years ahead and establishes clear milestones for employees to target.[27] This forward-looking orientation is crucial; without it companies can easily become focused on markets they have served in the past. Focusing on the firm's existing markets results in the development of products and services that meet current market requirements, rather than future market requirements. Successful and innovative firms question existing price-performance assumptions. They lead customers by developing and introducing products that extend well beyond current market requirements and help mold the market's expectations for the future.[28]

Once the strategic intent has been articulated, the company should be able to identify the resources and capabilities required to close the gap between the strategic intent and the current position (see Figure 6.6). This includes identifying any technological gap. Articulating the company's strategic intent enables the company to focus its development efforts and choose the investments necessary to develop strategic technologies and incorporate them into the company's new products.[29] Many companies

FIGURE 6.6
Identifying the Resource and Capability Gap

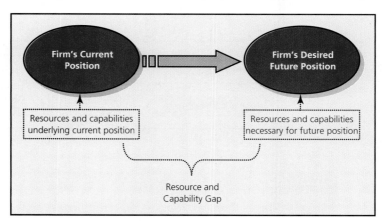

Firm's Current Position

Firm's Desired Future Position

Resources and capabilities underlying current position

Resources and capabilities necessary for future position

Resource and Capability Gap

Theory in Action   The Balanced Scorecard

Robert Kaplan and David Norton point out that a firm's methods of measuring performance will strongly influence whether and how the firm pursues its strategic objectives. They argue that effective performance measurement must be more than simple reliance on financial indicators; it must be a coherent and integral part of the management process. They proposed a method, the "balanced scorecard," that they argue can motivate breakthrough improvements in product, process, customer, and market development.[30] The balanced scorecard (see Figure 6.7) emphasizes four perspectives the firm should take in formulating goals that target critical success factors and in defining measures:

1. **Financial perspective.** Goals might include such things as "meet shareholder's expectations" or "double our corporate value in seven years." Measures might include return on capital, net cash flow, and earning's growth.

FIGURE 6.7
The Balanced Scorecard

Source: Adapted from R. Kaplan and D. Norton, "Putting the Balanced Scorecard to Work," *Harvard Business Review,* September–October 1993, pp. 134–47.

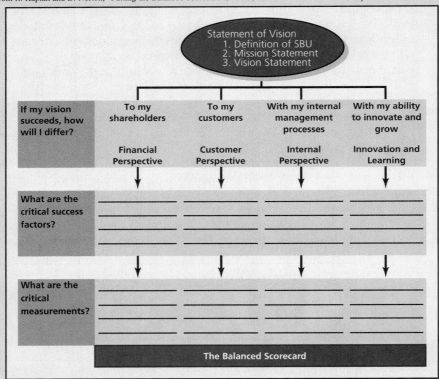

2. **Customer perspective.** Goals might be to "improve customer loyalty," "offer best-in-class customer service," or "increase customer satisfaction." Measures might include market share, percent of repeat purchases, customer satisfaction surveys, and so on.

3. **Internal perspective.** Goals might include such things as "reduce internal safety incidents," "build best-in-class franchise teams," or "improve inventory management." Measures might include the number of safety incidents per month, franchise quality ratings, stockout rates, and inventory costs.

4. **Innovation and learning perspective.** Goals might include such things as "accelerate and improve new product development" or "improve employee skills." Measures might include the percentage of sales from products developed within the past five years, average length of the new product development cycle, or employee training targets.

Kaplan and Norton acknowledge that the balanced scorecard model often has to be adapted to fit different markets and businesses, but many firms (including IBM, Philips Electronics, Apple, and Advanced Micro Electronics) in many different industries (including electronics, petrochemicals, and health care) are finding the balanced scorecard useful.[31] In fact, a 2002 survey by Bain & Company found that approximately 50 percent of Fortune 1,000 companies in the United States and 40 percent in Europe use some version of the balanced scorecard.[32]

are now pairing the articulation of their strategic intent with a multidimensional performance measurement system, such as the balanced scorecard, as discussed in the Theory in Action section.

Summary of Chapter

1. The first step in establishing a coherent strategy for the firm is assessing the external environment. Two commonly used models of external analysis are Porter's five-force model and stakeholder analysis.

2. Porter's five-force model entails assessing the degree of existing rivalry, threat of potential entrants, bargaining power of suppliers, bargaining power of customers, and threat posed by substitutes. Recently Porter added a sixth force, the role of complements.

3. Stakeholder analysis involves identifying any entity with an interest in the firm, what it wants from the company, and what claims it can make on the company.

4. To analyze the internal environment, firms often begin by identifying strengths and weaknesses in each activity of the value chain. The firm can then identify which strengths have the potential to be a source of sustainable competitive advantage.

5. Next the firm identifies its core competencies. Core competencies are integrated combinations of abilities that distinguish the firm in the marketplace. Several core competencies may underlie each business unit, and several business units may draw upon the same core competency.

6. Sometimes core competencies can become core rigidities that limit the firm's ability to respond to a changing environment.

7. Dynamic capabilities are competencies that enable a firm to quickly reconfigure the firm's organizational structure or routines in response to change in the firm's environment or opportunities.

8. A firm's strategic intent is the articulation of an ambitious long-term (10 to 20 years out) goal or set of goals. The firm's strategic intent should build upon and stretch its existing core competencies.

9. Once the firm articulates its strategic intent, managers should identify the resources and capabilities that the firm must develop or acquire to achieve its strategic intent.

10. The balanced scorecard is a measurement system that encourages the firm to consider its goals from multiple perspectives (financial, customer, business process, and innovation and learning), and establish measures that correspond to each of those perspectives.

Discussion Questions

1. What is the difference between a *strength, a competitive advantage,* and a *sustainable competitive advantage*?

2. What makes an ability (or set of abilities) a *core competency*?

3. Why is it necessary to perform an external and internal analysis before the firm can identify its true core competencies?

4. Pick a company you are familiar with. Can you identify some of its core competencies?

5. How is the idea of "strategic intent" different from models of strategy that emphasize achieving a fit between the firm's strategies and its current strengths, weaknesses, opportunities, and threats (SWOT)?

6. Can a strategic intent be too ambitious?

Endnotes

1. P. Tjahyadikarta and M. A. Schilling, "Palm Economy," Boston University teaching case #2001-01, and forthcoming in M. Hitt, D. Ireland, and B. Hoskisson, *Strategic Management: Competitiveness and Globalization,* 5th ed. (St. Paul, MN: West Publishing, 2001).

2. Stephanie Miles, "Is Palm Ready for the Handheld Challenge?" *CNET News.com,* September 13, 1999.

3. "Always on" refers to devices that are capable of remaining continuously connected to the Internet.

4. R. Pegoraro, "Even the Best of the Phone-PDA Combos Aren't Good Enough," *Washington Post,* January 27, 2002, p. H-7.

5. M. Moore, "Treo Melds Phone, Wireless Net, PDA in 'Star Trek' Style," *Houston Chronicle,* January 24, 2002.

6. J. Sullivan, "Handspring Bets the Farm on Treo—Then Postpones It," *Wireless Data News,* January 30, (2002), pp. 1+.

7. J. Fortt, "Handspring Combats Liabilities, Stakes Hope on New Wireless Product," *Knight Ridder Tribune Business News,* March 3, 2003, p. 1.

8. G. Hamel and C. K. Prahalad, "Strategic Intent," *Harvard Business Review,* May–June 1991, pp. 63–76.

9. C. K. Prahalad, "The Role of Core Competencies in the Corporation," *Research Technology Management,* November–December 1993, pp. 40–47.

10. S. L. Berman, A. Wicks, S. Kotha, and T. M. Jones, "Does Stakeholder Orientation Matter? The Relationship between Stakeholder Management Models and Firm Financial Performance," *Academy of Management Journal* 42 (1999), pp. 488–507; T. Donaldson, and L. Preston, "The Stakeholder Theory of the Corporation: Concepts, Evidence, and Implications," *Academy of Management Review* 20 (1995), pp. 65–91; and W. Evan and R. E. Freeman, "A Stakeholder Theory of the Modern Corporation: Kantian Capitalism," in *Ethical Theory in Business,* eds. T. Beauchamp and N. Bowie (Englewood Cliffs, NJ: Prentice Hall, 1983), pp. 75–93.

11. M. E. Porter, *Competitive Advantage* (New York: Free Press, 1985).

12. J. Barney, "Firm Resources and Sustained Competitive Advantage," *Journal of Management* 17 (1991), pp. 99–120.

13. R. Reed and R. J. DeFillippi, "Causal Ambiguity, Barriers to Imitation, and Sustainable Competitive Advantage," *Academy of Management Review* 15, no. 1 (1990), pp. 88–102.

14. R. Burgelman, M. Madique, and S. Wheelwright, *Strategic Management of Technological Innovation* (New York: McGraw-Hill, 2001); M. Hitt and R. D. Ireland, "Corporate Distinctive Competence, Strategy, Industry and Performance," *Strategic Management Journal* 6 (2001), pp. 273–93; D. Leonard-Barton, "Core Capabilities and Core Rigidities: A Paradox in Managing New Product Development," *Strategic Management Journal* 13 (1992), pp. 111–25; B. McKelvey and H. E. Aldrich, "Populations, Organizations, and Applied Organizational Science," in *Administrative Science Quarterly* 28 (1983), pp. 101–28; C. K. Prahalad and G. Hamel, "The Core Competence of the Corporation," *Harvard Business Review,* May–June 1990, pp. 79–91; C. C. Snow and L. G. Hrebiniak, "Strategy, Distinctive Competence, and Organizational Performance," *Administrative Science Quarterly* 25 (1980), pp. 317–35; and G. Stalk, P. Evans, and L. E. Shulman, "Competing on Capabilities: The New Rules of Corporate Strategy," *Harvard Business Review,* March–April 1992, pp. 57–69.

15. Stalk, Evans, and Shulman, "Competing on Capabilities."

16. M. Gallon, H. Stillman, and D. Coates, "Putting Core Competency Thinking into Practice," *Research Technology Management,* May–June 1995, pp. 20–28.

17. Prahalad, "The Role of Core Competencies in the Corporation."

18. Prahalad and Hamel, "The Core Competence of the Corporation."

19. Prahalad, "The Role of Core Competencies in the Corporation."

20. Leonard-Barton, "Core Capabilities and Core Rigidities."

21. Gallon, Stillman, and Coates, "Putting Core Competency Thinking into Practice."

22. G. Dosi, "Sources, Procedures, and Microeconomic Effects of Innovation," *Journal of Economic Literature,* September 26, 1988, p. 1130; and M. Tripsas and G. Gavetti, "Capabilities, Cognition, and Inertia: Evidence from Digital Imaging," *Strategic Management Journal* 21 (2000), p. 1147.

23. A. King and C. Tucci, "Incumbent Entry into New Market Niches: The Role of Experience and Managerial Choice in the Creation of Dynamic Capabilities," *Management Science* 48 (2002), pp. 171–86; and K. M. Eisenhardt and J. A. Martin, "Dynamic Capabilities: What Are They?" *Strategic Management Journal* 21 (2000), pp. 1105–21.

24. M. B. Graham and A. T. Shuldiner, *Corning and The Craft of Innovation* (New York: Oxford University Press, 2001); and C. L. Tucci, "Corning and the Craft of Innovation," *Business History Review* 75 (2001), pp. 862–65.

25. C. A. Bartlett and A. Nanda, "Corning, Inc.: A Network of Alliances," Harvard Business School case #9-391-102, 1990.

26. Prahalad, "The Role of Core Competencies in the Corporation."

27. Hamel and Prahalad, "Strategic Intent."

28. Prahalad, "The Role of Core Competencies in the Corporation."

29. K. Marino, "Developing Consensus on Firm Competencies and Capabilities," *Academy of Management Executive* 10, no. 3 (1996), pp. 40–51.

30. R. Kaplan and D. Norton, "Putting the Balanced Scorecard to Work," *Harvard Business Review,* September–October 1993, pp. 134–47; and R. Kaplan and D. Norton, "The Balanced Scorecard—Measures That Drive Performance," *Harvard Business Review,* January–February 1992, pp. 71–80.

31. Kaplan and Norton, "Putting the Balanced Scorecard to Work."

32. A. Gumbus and B. Lyons, "The Balanced Scorecard at Philips Electronics," *Strategic Finance* 84, no. 5 (2002), pp. 45–49.

Chapter **Seven**

Choosing Innovation Projects

Boeing's Sonic Cruiser[1]

At the end of 2002, the airline and aircraft industries were facing difficult times. Still reeling from the abrupt business slowdown after the September 11, 2001, terrorist attacks, the whole industry seemed to be struggling under its own weight. The U.S. government had stepped in to provide some short-term assistance, but U.S. Airways and United Airlines had both declared bankruptcy, clouding longer-term industry prospects. Internationally, state-sponsored carriers were requesting higher subsidies and private carriers were suffering losses similar to the U.S. domestic fleet. In the midst of this bleak landscape, Boeing had to decide whether it would continue the development and launch of its new commercial aviation concept, the Sonic Cruiser. While many in the company thought the Sonic Cruiser was key to Boeing's leadership in the commercial airline market, others did not think the Sonic Cruiser would make it off the drawing board.

The Sonic Cruiser

Boeing's new aircraft design, the Sonic Cruiser, was a midsize jet targeted for a 2006 release. With its focus on increasing both the speed and flying range of a plane, it aimed to radically change the way airlines and passengers think about air travel. When the design was unveiled March 29, 2001, analysis had indicated the initial version of the delta-winged Sonic Cruiser would accommodate 200 to 250 passengers, fly between 6,000 and 9,000 nautical miles, and travel at a speed between Mach 0.95 and Mach 0.98—15 to 20 percent faster than existing models. It would also deliver its speed advantage with about the same fuel burn per passenger as conventional aircraft with similar seating capacity, a performance level previously thought impossible. With its huge speed advantage, the new airplane would cut travel times by approximately 20 percent, or one hour for every 3,000 miles traveled. And because it could travel at altitudes well above existing commercial airplanes (around 45,000 feet, about 10,000 feet higher than typical commercial airliners) the airlines would be less affected by traffic congestion, an emerging industry concern.[2] Continental's CEO Gordon Bethune noted: "If they can do what they say they can, we will be first to order. It will change the way that we see the market. But operating costs? That is a big bet." Some industry insiders had speculated that the new plane could cost 12 to 15 percent more to operate than the Boeing 767 that it would replace.[3]

The Market

The principal customers in the commercial aircraft market are the airlines and air cargo carriers that directly purchase the planes. Their buying decisions depend on the product's ability to serve the needs of the airlines' end consumers most efficiently. The variables that go into this decision involve operating costs over specific distance ranges with forecasted levels of passengers and cargo. As of 2002, the largest U.S. carriers all utilized a hub system. Hubs were strategically located airports that airlines would use as transfer points for their passengers and cargo.[4] Funneling the bulk of airline traffic through key hubs enabled airlines to serve more destinations with the same number of aircraft. Customers traveling from lower-traffic locales would first be brought to the hub on a smaller aircraft, then consolidated onto larger aircraft for transport between the major hubs.[5] By contrast, some smaller carriers such as Southwest, Midwest Express, and Europe's Easyjet, were organized around a direct routing model that transferred passengers directly from their origination to destination (point-to-point), often utilizing smaller airports. Southwest had performed well in the late 1990s, proving that it was possible to be successful with a point-to-point air travel strategy featuring low cost and no frills. Midwest, a smaller (35 aircraft) operator focused exclusively on the business traveler, had not fared as well. Since the Sonic Cruiser was a midsize jet with speed and cost advantages that would be fully realized only across long distances, it was particularly well-suited for a point-to-point model.

Complementarity of models within a family of aircraft also influenced the purchase decision. There were significant advantages to airlines that operated only one or a few types of aircraft. For each different type, pilots and maintenance staff had to be continuously trained to ensure safety, parts had to be kept in inventory, and maintenance crews had to be able to provide support. A diverse fleet of aircraft dramatically increased the complexity and cost of operating the airline. Most airlines attempted to fulfill their aircraft needs within families of aircraft designed to be operated and serviced in similar ways to reduce these costs. For example, Southwest operated only Boeing 737 family aircraft and JetBlue only Airbus A320,[6] both in an effort to simplify operations and increase efficiency. On the other hand, airlines also had to consider the danger of being single sourced not only for aircraft but also for replacement parts and technical assistance. As a whole, the industry had a keen interest in keeping at least two suppliers active to ensure competitive prices and reliable sources of supplies.[7]

Boeing had been careful to position the Sonic Cruiser as a supplement to its existing lines, and had committed to continuing the manufacture of the 7x7 line in conjunction with the Sonic Cruiser. However, it hoped that the Sonic Cruiser would allow major airlines to add point-to-point routes to existing hub-based services. To that end, Boeing was working to ensure that the Sonic Cruiser's take-off and landing noise would be 30 percent less than that of the 767,[8] and below proposed noise standards, expected to go into effect in 2006 (noise ordinances limited the range of aircraft that could be operated in airports near residential areas).

Most of the major carriers around the world had fleets composed of both Boeing and Airbus aircraft, though flight patterns varied significantly. European carriers had large webs of inter-European routes requiring short-haul aircraft. Additionally, these carriers were often government subsidized, and therefore expected to purchase Airbus products if possible. Asia was a different story—the routes were longer, and with no regional aircraft manufacturer, this business was up for grabs.

In 2002, the airline industry was under considerable pressure. Ticket sales were down 9 percent from 2001 levels, and the industry was forced to reduce capacity to keep the load factor (the percentage of total seats occupied) constant. However, even reducing capacity had not preserved the margins that the airlines earned on each seat. Business travel had dropped precipitously, and low-cost Web-based vacation tickets were not filling the revenue void. Thus, airlines were focused on reducing costs. Many airlines eliminated perks on flights such as meal service or free headphones. Several airlines were fighting to win wage concessions from their unions. Fuel costs were also, as always, a serious concern. Fluctuations in fuel costs had a significant impact on an airline's bottom line. It was estimated that every $.01 change in the average annual price per gallon of jet fuel caused a change of almost $28 million in United's annual fuel costs.[9]

To reduce capacity, aircraft were put into storage. In September 2002, *Valueline* reported the existence of more than 1,900 aircraft in storage in the Nevada desert. About 350 were of aircraft types still in production. It was expected that any increase in demand for air travel or air cargo would be met with those aircraft rather than by a surge in orders for either Boeing or Airbus products. Despite these concerns, Boeing's forecasts were optimistic. Boeing estimated the worldwide aircraft fleet would double to almost 33,000 jets by 2021. This fleet would include at least 8,500 aircraft that were already in use in 2002, 6,700 new airplanes to replace aging craft, and just over 17,200 new airplanes due to market growth. This estimate was based on a forecast of 4.9 percent growth in world air travel, plus 6.4 percent growth in the cargo market. Latin America was expected to be the fastest-growing market. Airlines were expected to invest $1.8 trillion in new commercial airplanes (about 24,000 airplanes) over the 20 years from 2001 to 2021. Of that total, 18 percent (or 4,240 aircraft) were expected to be for smaller regional jets (below 90 seats); 57 percent (or 13,765 aircraft) for larger regional jets and single-aisle airplanes; 21 percent (or 4,980 aircraft) for intermediate-size airplanes; and 4 percent (or about 945 aircraft) for 747 and larger airplanes. Boeing also estimated that the commercial aviation support services market would be worth about $3.1 trillion over the next 20 years, with annual revenues considerably greater than that for the new airplane market.[10]

Developing the Sonic Cruiser

The technological and economic hurdles facing the Sonic Cruiser were daunting. The plane was expected to cost $10 billion to develop—significantly more than the development cost of a more traditional aircraft. The initial phase of development required scanning the market and finding the available technologies. Jeff Luckey, supplier management director of the Sonic Cruiser program, stated this was "particularly important because it will be impossible to achieve the promised Sonic Cruiser results with current material and manufacturing technologies." Although no concrete supply contracts for the Sonic Cruiser existed yet, suppliers were quickly signing technology agreements with Boeing's development team to secure a place in the project. As Walt Gillette, Boeing's development program manager, remarked, "Competition is a wonderful thing. As soon as we started talking about this being a mostly composite airplane we began to get very interesting proposals from the aluminum manufacturers regarding new alloys with better properties and economics."[11]

The development of new technologies and capabilities was a serious consideration in the decision about whether to move forward with the aircraft. As noted by Gillette, "Industry experience indicates that if the company doesn't create a new airplane every 12 to 15 years, the needed skills and experience will be gone. Too many of the people who created the last new airplane will have retired or moved on to other companies, and their skills and experience will not have been passed on to the next generation of Boeing employees."[12] In December 2002, no airline had yet placed an order for the Sonic Cruiser, and Gillette had to decide whether to proceed with development or just roll the technologies developed for it into Boeing's existing product lines.[13]

Discussion Questions

1. What factors must go into Boeing's decision about whether to continue developing—and launching—the Sonic Cruiser?
2. What are the challenges in estimating the potential returns of the project?
3. What method, or combination of methods, do you think Boeing should use to evaluate the project?
4. Should Boeing continue developing the Sonic Cruiser? If so, should Boeing attempt to commercially produce and launch the Sonic Cruiser?

OVERVIEW

Developing innovative new products and services is expensive and time-consuming. It is also extremely risky—most studies have indicated that the vast majority of development projects fail. Firms have to make difficult choices about which projects are worth the investment, and then they have to make sure those projects are pursued with a rigorous and well-thought-out development process. In this chapter, we will explore the various methods used to evaluate and choose innovation projects. The methods

capital rationing
The allocation of a finite quantity of resources over different possible uses.

range from informal to highly structured, and from entirely qualitative to strictly quantitative. We will start by considering the role of **capital rationing** in the R&D investment decision, and then will cover various methods used to evaluate projects including strictly quantitative methods, qualitative methods, and approaches that combine quantitative and qualitative techniques.

THE DEVELOPMENT BUDGET

While many project valuation methods seem to assume that all valuable projects will be funded, most firms face serious constraints in capital and other resources, forcing them to choose between multiple valuable projects (or obtain external financing as discussed in the Theory in Action section). Many firms use a form of *capital rationing* in formulating their new product development plans. Under capital rationing, the firm sets a fixed research and development budget (often some percentage of the previous year's sales), and then uses a rank ordering of possible projects to determine which will be funded. Firms might establish this budget based on industry benchmarks or historical benchmarks of the firm's own performance.

R&D intensity
The ratio of R&D expenditures to sales.

To provide a sense of what firms in different industries spend on R&D, Figure 7.1 shows the R&D expenditures as a percent of sales (also termed **R&D intensity**) for U.S. firms in different industries. Some industries (notably communications, pharmaceuticals, computers, scientific services, and software) spend considerably more than other industries.

There is also considerable variation within each of the industries in the amount that individual firms spend. For example, as shown in Figure 7.2, Dell Computer's R&D intensity is significantly lower than the industry average for computer and peripheral equipment producers (1.5 percent versus 6.4 percent), and Ford Motor spends considerably more than the industry average for motor vehicle producers (4.5 percent versus 2.9 percent). Figure 7.2 also reveals the impact of firm size on R&D budgets. For example, while Microsoft's R&D intensity is almost five times higher than General Motors', General Motors' total R&D budget is more than 40 percent larger than Microsoft's due to General Motors' significantly larger sales base.

The rank ordering used in capital rationing may be established by any number of methods, including quantitative methods, such as discounted cash flow analysis or options analysis, or qualitative methods, such as screening questions and portfolio mapping, or a combination of multiple methods. Knowing the requirements, strengths, and weaknesses of each method helps managers make sound decisions about which valuation techniques to employ.

QUANTITATIVE METHODS FOR CHOOSING PROJECTS

Quantitative methods of analyzing new projects usually entail converting projects into some estimate of future cash returns from a project. Quantitative methods enable managers to use rigorous mathematical and statistical comparisons of projects, though the quality of the comparison is ultimately a function of the quality of the original

FIGURE 7.1
R&D as a Percentage of Sales for Selected Industries, 1999

Source: National Science Foundation, Division of Science Resources Studies, "Research and Development in Industry: 1999, Early Release Tables," project officer Raymond Wolfe, Arlington, VA, 2001.

Industry	R&D as a Percent of Sales	Industry	R&D as a Percent of Sales
Manufacturing	3.2%	**Nonmanufacturing**	2.2%
Communications equipment	11.6	Scientific R&D services	32.1
Pharmaceuticals and medicines	10.5	Software	16.7
Navigational, measuring, electromedical, and control instruments	9.1	Computer systems design and related services	11.0
Semiconductor and other electronic components	8.3	Architectural, engineering, and related services	6.8
Medical equipment and supplies	7.7	Health care services	6.4
Computers and peripheral equipment	6.4	Management of companies and enterprises	5.7
Resin, synthetic rubber, fibers, and filament	4.2	Trade	5.5
Machinery	3.3	Construction	3.1
Other chemicals	3.2	Newspaper, periodical, book, and database information	2.0
Aerospace products and parts	3.2		
Motor vehicles, trailers, and parts	2.9	Mining, extraction, and support activities	1.9
Electrical equipment, appliances, and components	2.3	Finance, insurance, and real estate	0.5
Basic chemicals	2.0	Transportation and warehousing	0.5
Plastics and rubber products	1.9	Broadcasting and telecommunications	0.4
Nonmetallic mineral products	1.5	Utilities	0.1
Paper, printing, and support activities	1.4		
Fabricated metal products	1.4		
Textiles, apparel, and leather	0.7		
Furniture and related products	0.7		
Wood products	0.5		
Food	0.4		
Primary metals	0.4	**All industries**	2.7

FIGURE 7.2
R&D Expenditures and R&D Intensity for Selected U.S. Firms, 2001

Company	R&D Expenditures (billions $US)	R&D Intensity (R&D/sales)
Dell Computer	$0.5	1.5%
Ford Motor	7.3	4.5
General Electric	2.3	1.8
General Motors	6.2	3.5
Johnson & Johnson	3.6	10.9
Microsoft	4.4	17.4

estimates. The accuracy of such estimates can be questionable—particularly in highly uncertain or rapidly changing environments. The most commonly used quantitative methods include discounted cash flow methods and real options.

While large firms can fund innovation projects internally, new technology start-ups must often obtain external financing. This can sometimes be daunting. Because technology start-ups often have both an unproven technology and an unproven business concept (and sometimes an unproven management team), they typically face a much higher cost of capital than larger competitors, and their options for obtaining capital can be very limited. In the first few stages of start-up and growth, entrepreneurs may have to turn to friends, family, and personal debt. Start-ups might also be able to obtain some initial funding through government agencies. If the idea and the management team seem promising enough, the entrepreneur can tap "angel investors" and venture capitalists as both sources of funds and mentoring.

FAMILY, FRIENDS, AND CREDIT CARDS

When a new venture is starting out, often the technology and/or management is unproven, making the venture appear very risky. In this stage, entrepreneurs must often rely on friends and family members that are willing to provide initial funding either in the form of a loan or an exchange for equity in the company. Alternatively, the entrepreneur may try to obtain debt financing from a local bank. A very large number of start-ups are actually funded with credit cards, resulting in a very high rate of interest!

GOVERNMENT GRANTS AND LOANS

Some new ventures obtain start-up funds from government sources. In the United States, the Small Business Administration (SBA) is designed to foster entrepreneurship and innovation by administering grants, loans, and venture capital programs from many different federal agencies including the Department of Commerce, Department of Agriculture, Department of Energy, NASA, and others. Similarly, in the United Kingdom, the Enterprise Fund administers a series of programs designed to fund small to medium-size technology firms, and in Germany there are more than 800 federal and state government programs established to finance new firms.[14]

ANGEL INVESTORS

Angel investors are private investors who fund projects without utilizing a venture capital limited partnership structure. They are often wealthy individuals who have been very successful in business, and who enjoy the thrill of vicarious entrepreneurship afforded by investing in—and sometimes mentoring—start-up firms. Angels typically fund projects that are $1 million or less. While angel investors lose money in a significant share of their investments, those investments that pay off can earn very high returns. Angels are usually not listed in public directories, but are identified through professional networks (such as through one's former colleagues, professors, lawyers, etc.). A large number of start-ups obtain "seed-stage" (before there is a real product or company organized) financing from angel investors. While it is difficult to get data on angel investing because most of the transactions are not publicly reported, estimates put the average angel investor deal somewhere between $350,000 and $700,000.[15] According to Jeffrey Sohl, director of the Center for Venture Research at the University of New Hampshire, angel investors funded approximately 50,000 deals in 2000.[16]

VENTURE CAPITAL

For projects that require more than $1 million, entrepreneurs often turn to venture capital, either from independent venture capital firms or corporate venture capital sources.

Independent venture capital firms manage a pool of funds that they invest in projects they believe to have rapid growth potential. Many venture capital firms specialize in particular industries, making them better able to evaluate the potential of start-ups in that industry. The venture capital funds are likely to be provided in a complex debt-equity hybrid contract that essentially looks more like equity if the firm performs well, or debt if the firm performs poorly.[17] If and when the business is successful, the

continued

venture capitalist can cash out of the investment by negotiating an initial public offering or a buyout of the company by another firm. Venture capitalists are very selective, and reject the vast majority of proposals considered. However, for those projects that are funded, the support of the venture capitalist provides a number of valuable benefits including credibility among other investors (and thus better access to capital) and mentoring. While some venture capitalists specialize in providing seed-stage funding, venture capitalists are more likely to provide funding during early stages—after the company has been organized and the product has shown early signs of success, but before it is able to sustain its development activities and growth through its own revenues. In 2002, the average venture capital deal was almost $10.5 million, and the vast majority of those deals were in the biotechnology, computer hardware and software, and wireless telecommunications industries.[18]

Corporate venture capital is provided by firms that wish to take a minority equity stake in another firm's technology development, often to gain access to cutting-edge technology that they may wish to develop further should it prove technically and commercially promising. Such firms may establish an internal venturing group that is closely tied to the firm's own development operations, or they may create a dedicated external fund that has more independence from the firm's own operations.[19] The benefit of the former structure is that the firm should be better able to use its own expertise and resources to help the new venture succeed. However, under this structure, the entrepreneur may have concerns about the larger firm expropriating the entrepreneur's proprietary technology. Under the latter structure, the independence of the external venture fund provides some reassurance that the entrepreneur's technology will not be stolen, but it also limits the ability of the entrepreneur to leverage any of the larger firm's nonfinancial resources.[20] According to Venture Economics, 233 companies had venture capital programs (such as Eastman Kodak's Eastman Ventures, General Electric's GE Equity, and Intel's Intel Capital) in March 2003, down from a high of 488 in 2000. These programs tend to invest in sectors that closely mirror those invested in by independent venture capital firms.[21]

Discounted Cash Flow Methods

net present value (NPV)
The discounted cash inflows of a project minus the discounted cash outflows.

internal rate of return (IRR)
The rate of return yielded by a project, normally calculated as the discount rate that makes the net present value of an investment equal zero.

Many firms use some form of discounted cash flow analysis to evaluate projects. Discounted cash flows are quantitative methods for assessing whether the anticipated future benefits are large enough to justify expenditure, given the risks. Discounted cash flow methods take into account the payback period, risk, and time value of money. The two most commonly used forms of discounted cash flow analysis for evaluating investment decisions are **net present value (NPV)** and **internal rate of return (IRR).** Both methods rely on the same basic discounted cash flow mechanics, but they look at the problem from different angles. NPV asks, "Given a particular level of expenditure, particular level(s) and rate of cash inflows, and a discount rate, what is this project worth today?" IRR asks instead, "Given a particular level of expenditure and particular level(s) and rate of cash inflows, what rate of return does this project yield?" For either method, managers must use estimates of the size and timing of expenditures and cash inflows. Both methods enable the decision maker to incorporate some basic measure of risk. For example, riskier projects may be examined using a higher discount factor in NPV analysis. Managers also often calculate discounted cash flow measures using best-case and worst-case cash flow estimates.

Net Present Value (NPV)

To calculate the NPV of a project, managers first estimate the costs of the project and the cash flows the project will yield (often under a number of different "what if" scenarios). Costs and cash flows that occur in the future must be discounted back to the current period to account for risk and the time value of money. The present value of cash inflows can then be compared to the present value of cash outflows:

$$\text{NPV} = \text{Present value of cash inflow} - \text{Present value of cash outflows}$$

If this value is greater than 0, then the project generates wealth given the assumptions made in calculating its costs and cash inflows.

To find the present value of cash inflow and outflows, each cash flow must be discounted back to the current period using a discount rate (see Figure 7.3). If there is a single expenditure at the beginning of the project (year 0), the original expenditure can be compared directly to the present value of the future expected cash flows. In the example in Figure 7.3, the present value of the future cash flows (given a discount rate of 6 percent) is $3,465.11. Thus, if the initial cost of the project were less than $3,465.11, the net present value of the project is positive. If there are cash outflows for multiple periods (as is common with most development projects), those cash outflows would have to be discounted back to the current period.

If the cash inflows from the development project were expected to be the same each year (as they were in Figure 7.3) we can use the formula for calculating the present value of an annuity rather than discounting each of the cash inflows individually. This is particularly useful when cash inflows are expected for many years. The present value of C dollars per period, for t periods, with discount rate r is given by the following formula:

$$\text{Annuity present value} = C \times \frac{1 - \{1/(1+r)^t\}}{r}$$

FIGURE 7.3
Example of Present Value of Future Cash Flows

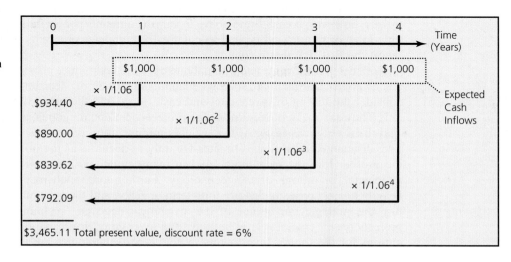

This amount can then be compared to the initial investment. If the cash flows are expected in perpetuity (forever), then a simpler formula can be used:

$$\text{Perpetuity present value} = C \times 1/r$$

discounted payback period

The time required to break even on a project using discounted cash flows.

The present value of the costs and future cash flows can also be used to calculate the **discounted payback period** (that is, the time required to break even on the project using discounted cash flows). Suppose for the example above, the initial investment required was $2,000. Using the discounted cash inflows, the cumulative discounted cash flows for each year are:

Year	Cash Flow
1	$ 934.40
2	1,833.40
3	2,673.02
4	3,465.11

Thus, the investment will be paid back sometime between the end of year two and the end of year three. The accumulated discounted cash flows by the end of year two are $1,833.40, so we need to recover $166.60 in year three. Since the discounted cash flow expected for year three is $839.62, we will have to wait $166.60/$839.61 ≈ .20 of a year. Thus, the payback period is just over two years and two months.

Internal Rate of Return (IRR)

The internal rate of return of a project is the discount rate that makes the net present value of the investment zero. Managers can compare this rate of return to their required return to decide if the investment should be made. Calculating the IRR of a project typically must be done by trial and error, substituting progressively higher interest rates into the NPV equation until the NPV is driven down to zero. Calculators and computers can perform this trial and error. This measure should be used cautiously, however; if cash flows arrive in varying amounts per period, there can be multiple rates of return, and typical calculators or computer programs will often simply report the first IRR that is found.

Both net present value and internal rate of return techniques provide concrete financial estimates that facilitate strategic planning and trade-off decisions. They explicitly consider the timing of investment and cash flows, and the time value of money and risk. They can make the returns of the project seem unambiguous, and managers may find them very reassuring. However, this minimization of ambiguity may be deceptive; discounted cash flow estimates are only as accurate as the original estimates of the profits from the technology, and in many situations it is extremely difficult to anticipate the returns of the technology. Furthermore, such methods discriminate heavily against projects that are long term or risky, and the methods may fail to capture the strategic importance of the investment decision. Technology development projects play a crucial role in building and leveraging firm capabilities, and creating options for the future. Investments in new core technologies are investments in the organization's capabilities and learning, and they create opportunities for the firm that might otherwise be unavailable.[22] Thus, standard discounted cash flow analysis has the potential to severely undervalue a development project's contribution to the firm. For example, Intel's investment in DRAM technology might have been considered a total loss by NPV methods (Intel exited the DRAM business after Japanese competitors drove the price of DRAM to levels Intel could not match). However, the investment in DRAM technology laid the foundation for Intel's ability to develop microprocessors—and this business has proved to be enormously profitable for Intel. To better incorporate strategic implications in the new product development investment decision, some managers and scholars have recently begun promoting the idea of treating new product development decisions as **real options,** as described below.

real options
The application of stock option valuation methods to investments in nonfinancial assets.

Real Options

When a firm develops new core technologies, it is simultaneously investing in its own learning and in the development of new capabilities. Thus, development projects can create valuable future opportunities for the firm that would otherwise be unavailable.[23] Even development projects that appear unsuccessful (as Intel's DRAM discussed above) may prove to be very valuable when they are considered from the perspective of the options they create for the future of the firm. Some managers and scholars have begun arguing that new product development decisions should be evaluated as "real options."

To understand real options, it is first useful to consider the financial model upon which they are based—stock options. A call option on a stock enables an investor to purchase the right to buy the stock at a specified price (the "exercise price") in the future. If, in the future, the stock is worth more than the exercise price, the holder of the option will typically exercise the option by buying the stock. If the stock is worth more than the exercise price plus the price paid for the original option, the option holder makes money on the deal. If the stock is worth less than the exercise price, the option holder will typically choose not to exercise the option, allowing it to expire. In this case, the option holder loses the amount of money paid for the initial option. If, at the time the option is exercised, the stock is worth more than the exercise price but not more than the exercise price plus the amount paid for the original option, the stockholder will typically exercise the option. Even though the stockholder loses money on the deal (some portion of the price paid for the original option), he or she loses less than if he or she allowed the option to expire (the entire price paid for the original option).

In "real options," the assets underlying the value of the option are nonfinancial resources.[24] An investor who makes an initial investment in basic R&D or in breakthrough technologies is, it is argued, buying a real call option to implement that technology later should it prove to be valuable.[25] Figure 7.4 provides examples of investment decisions that can be viewed as real call options. With respect to research and development:

- The cost of the R&D program can be considered the price of a call option.
- The cost of future investment required to capitalize on the R&D program (such as the cost of commercializing a new technology that is developed) can be considered the exercise price.
- The returns to the R&D investment are analogous to the value of a stock purchased with a call option.[26]

FIGURE 7.4
Examples of Real Call Options

Source: Adapted from K. D. Miller and T. B. Folta, "Option Value and Entry Timing," *Strategic Management Journal,* 23 (2002), pp. 655–65.

Investment Providing the Option	Nature of Option	Benefits from Exercising the Option	Exercise Price	Factors Affecting the Duration
License to commercialize technology	Right to commercialize a technology	• Stream of cash flows from commercialization • Manufacturing experience • Marketing and distribution experience	Cost of manufacturing, marketing, and distribution	• Patent time limit • Availability of substitutes
Equity stake in a partner	Right to acquire partner	• Cash flows • Capabilities of partner	Cost of acquiring partner	• Takeover bid by another partner or outside firm
R&D capability	Right to develop and commercialize technology	• Cash flows • Technological expertise	Cost of implementing the technology	• Competitors' replication or substitution of R&D capabilities

FIGURE 7.5
The Value of a Call Option at Expiration

If the stock price is less than the exercise price at point of expiration, call value is equal to zero.

If the stock price is greater than the exercise price, the value of the call is equal to the stock price minus the exercise price.

As shown in Figure 7.5, the value of a call stock option is zero as long as the price of the stock remains less than the exercise price. If the value of the stock rises above the exercise price, however, the value of the call rises with the value of the stock, dollar for dollar (thus the value of the call rises at a 45-degree angle).[27]

Options are valuable when there is uncertainty, and because technology trajectories are uncertain, an options approach may be useful. Though there has not yet been much empirical work in the area, several authors have developed methodologies and applications of options analysis to valuing technology development investments.[28] Also, some evidence shows that an options approach results in better technology investment decisions than a cash flow analysis approach.[29]

Other authors, however, warn against liberal application of the approach, pointing out that technology investment scenarios often do not conform to the same capital market assumptions upon which the approach is based.[30] For instance, implicit in the value of options is the assumption that one can acquire or retain the option for a small price, and then wait for a signal to determine if the option should be exercised.[31] While this assumption might hold true for an outside firm investing venture capital in another firm's innovation effort, it would be rare for this assumption to hold for a company investing in its own development efforts. In the case of a firm undertaking solo new product development, it may not be possible to secure this option at a small price; it may require full investment in the technology before a firm can determine if the technology will be successful.[32] Furthermore, while the value of a stock is independent of the call holder's behavior (that is, the call holder can simply wait and observe whether the value of the stock rises or falls), the value of an R&D investment is not independent of the investor's behavior. A firm's degree of investment, its development capabilities, its complementary assets, and its strategies can all significantly influence the future returns of the development project.[33] Therefore, rather than simply waiting and observing the value of the investment, the investor is an active driver of the value of the investment.

QUALITATIVE METHODS FOR CHOOSING PROJECTS

Most new product development projects require the evaluation of a significant amount of qualitative information. Many factors in the choice of development projects are extremely difficult to quantify, or quantification could lead to misleading results. Almost all firms utilize some form of qualitative assessment of potential projects, ranging from informal discussions to highly structured approaches.

Screening Questions

As a starting point, a management team is likely to discuss the potential costs and benefits of a project, and the team may create a list of screening questions that are used to structure this discussion. These questions might be organized into categories such as the role of the customer, the role of the firm's capabilities, and the project's timing and cost.[34] Some examples are provided below:

Role of Customer

Market

- Who are the most likely customers of the new product?
- How big is this market? Are there other likely markets for the product?
- What type of marketing will be required to create customer awareness?

Use
- How will customers use the product?
- What new benefits will the product provide the customer?
- What other products are customers likely to consider as substitutes for this product?

Compatibility and Ease of Use
- Will the product be compatible with the customer's existing complements?
- Will the product require significant new learning on the part of the customer?
- How will the customer perceive the product's ease of use?
- Will the product require the customer to bear other costs?

Distribution and Pricing
- Where will the customer buy the product?
- Will the product require installation or assembly?
- How much are customers likely to be willing to pay for the product?

Role of Capabilities

Existing Capabilities
- Does the new project leverage the firm's core competencies or sources of sustainable competitive advantage?
- Will the project render some of the firm's existing competencies obsolete or cannibalize existing products? If so, does the firm have a transition strategy to handle possible cash-flow implications?
- Does the firm have the necessary manufacturing capabilities, and if not, will those capabilities be developed in-house or acquired externally (e.g., outsourcing)?
- Will the firm need to hire employees with new skills?

Competitors' Capabilities
- Do one or more competitors have better capabilities for developing this project?
- If the company does not develop this technology, are competitors likely to?
- Will the company be able to protect its intellectual property through patents, copyright, trademarks, or trade secrets?
- Should the firm seek to form a collaboration with a potential competitor?

Future Capabilities
- Will the project help the firm build new capabilities that will allow it to achieve its strategic intent?
- What other products/markets will the new capabilities enable the firm to develop?
- Is this project a platform that will lead to a family of new products?

Project Timing and Cost

Timing

- How long will the project take to complete?
- Is the firm likely to be first to market? Is pioneering the technology a desirable strategy?
- Is the market ready for the product? (For example, are enabling and complementary technologies well-developed? Will customers perceive the value of the technology?)
- If the firm misses its target deadlines, what impact will this have on the potential value of the project?
- Are there already appropriate suppliers and distribution channels?

Cost Factors

- How much will the project cost? What is the potential variability in these costs?
- What will the manufacturing costs be? At what rate are these costs expected to decline with experience?
- Will the firm need to bear other costs related to customer adoption (e.g., production of complements, installation, technical support, etc.)?

After creating a list of questions, managers can use the questions to structure debate about a project, or they can create a scoring mechanism (such as a scaled response to each question such as "Project fits closely with existing competencies" to "Project fits poorly with existing competencies") that can then be weighted according to importance and used in subsequent analysis.

While screening questions such as the one above do not always provide concrete answers about whether or not to fund a project, they enable a firm to consider a wider range of issues that may be important in the firm's development decisions. Consider Boeing's development of the Sonic Cruiser as discussed in the opening vignette: Even if quantitative analysis suggests that the project will not be profitable, the project may be *necessary* when considered with respect to the role of capabilities. As noted by Gillette, "If the company doesn't create a new airplane every 12 to 15 years, the needed skills and experience will be gone. Too many of the people who created the last new airplane will have retired or moved on to other companies, and their skills and experience will not have been passed on to the next generation of Boeing employees."[35] Thus, Boeing's development of the Sonic Cruiser is expected to be valuable to the firm even if the only return from the project is the enhancement of the firm's development capabilities. Such value would be difficult to assess via quantitative methods, but is revealed clearly by qualitative analysis.

Mapping the Company's R&D Portfolio

Many companies attempt to manage new product development as a balanced portfolio of projects at different stages in development.[36] Companies may use a project map (similar to that depicted in Figure 7.6) to aid this process. Four types of development projects commonly appear on this map—advanced R&D, breakthrough, platform, and derivative projects. Over time a particular technology may migrate

FIGURE 7.6
The Project Map

Source: Adapted from S. C. Wheelwright, and K. B. Clark, *Revolutionizing Product Development* (New York: Free Press, 1992).

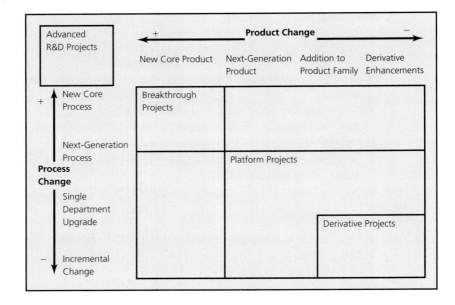

through these different types of projects. Advanced R&D projects are the precursor to commercial development projects and are necessary to develop cutting-edge strategic technologies. Breakthrough projects involve development of products that incorporate revolutionary new product and process technologies. For example, while Honda's work on hydrogen fuel cells might be considered an advanced R&D project since it is still a significant distance from a commercial application, the company's development of its hybrid-electric vehicle, the Insight, would be considered a breakthrough project. The Insight incorporated revolutionary new technology in a commercialized application.

Platform projects typically offer fundamental improvements in the cost, quality, and performance of a technology over preceding generations. Derivative projects involve incremental changes in products and/or processes. A platform project is designed to serve a core group of consumers, whereas derivative projects represent modifications of the basic platform design to appeal to different niches within that core group. For example, Hunter's Care Free humidifier is a platform that offers several derivative versions to appeal to different customer segments. The water storage tank comes in different sizes (e.g., 2.0 gallon, 2.5 gallon, 3.0 gallon); some models include a digital humidistat; and some also include Nite Glo lights. However, all of the models are based on the same Permawick filter design and fan system. Similarly, Toyota's Camry is a platform for a family of car models that includes the Camry LE, Camry SE, and Camry XLE. While all the models are based on the same basic design, each offers a different combination of features to appeal to different market segments. These variations on the Camry theme are derivative products.

Companies that use the project map categorize all their existing projects and projects under consideration by the resources they require (e.g., engineers, time, capital, etc.) and by how they contribute to the company's product line. The company can then map the project types and identify gaps in the development strategy.[37] Managers can also use the map to identify their desired mix of projects, and allocate resources accordingly. The mix of projects represented on such a map should be consistent both with the company's resources and with its strategic intent.

Mapping the company's R&D portfolio encourages the firm to consider both short-term cash flow needs and long-term strategic momentum in its budgeting and planning. For instance, a firm that invests heavily in derivative projects that may be immediately commercialized with little risk may appear to have good returns on its R&D investment in the short run, but then be unable to compete when the market shifts to newer technology. On the other hand, a firm that invests heavily in advanced R&D or breakthrough projects may be on the leading edge of technology, but run into cash flow problems from a lack of revenues generated from recently commercialized platform or derivative projects. As once noted by Jack Welch, former CEO of General Electric, "You can't grow long term if you can't eat short term. Anyone can manage short. Anyone can manage long. Balancing those two things is what management is."[38]

This is poignantly illustrated in the pharmaceutical industry, where high project failure rates, long product development cycles, and reliance on patent protection can cause a firm to suddenly find it has a devastating gap in its product pipeline. A 2001 study by the Tufts Center for the Study of Drug Development indicated that developing a new prescription drug took 10 to 15 years and cost about $800 million. Also, many of the world's largest pharmaceutical companies have become increasingly reliant on a few blockbuster drugs for a significant share of their revenues (see Figure 7.7). Taken together, these factors indicate that if pharmaceutical companies do not balance their research and development portfolios very carefully, they could experience extreme volatility in their sales revenue.

Q-Sort

Q-sort is a simple method for ranking objects or ideas on a number of different dimensions. The Q-sort method has been used for purposes as diverse as identifying personality disorders to establishing scales of customer preferences. Individuals in a group are each given a stack of cards with an object or idea on each card. In the case of new product development, each card could identify a potential project. Then a series of project selection criteria are presented (e.g., technical feasibility, market impact, fit with strategic intent), and for each criteria, the individuals sort their cards in rank order (e.g., best fit with strategic intent) or in categories (e.g., technically feasible versus infeasible) according to that criteria. Individuals then compare their rank orderings and use these comparisons to structure a debate about the projects. After several rounds of sorting and debating, the group is expected to arrive at a consensus about the best projects.[39]

COMBINING QUANTITATIVE AND QUALITATIVE INFORMATION

As demonstrated above, both quantitative methods and qualitative methods offer a number of benefits to managers in choosing development projects. Thus, many firms use a combination of methods to arrive at an investment decision.[40] For example, a

FIGURE 7.7
Pharmaceutical Firms' Reliance on a Few Blockbuster Products, 2000

Source: Adapted from R. J. Franco, *Pharmaceutical Executive* 22, no. 11 (2002), pp. 74–80.

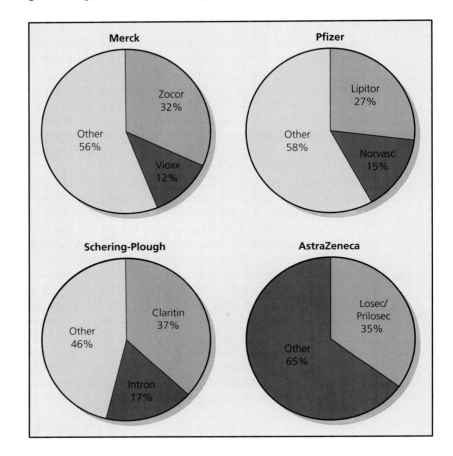

firm might have screening questions that require quantitative analysis in addition to qualitative responses. Firms might also use quantitative methods to estimate the cash flows anticipated from a project when balancing their R&D portfolio on a project map. There are also valuation techniques that attempt to translate qualitative assessments into quantitative measures, such as conjoint analysis and data envelopment analysis, as discussed below.

Conjoint Analysis

conjoint analysis
A family of techniques that enables assessment of the weight individuals put on different attributes of a choice.

Conjoint analysis is a family of techniques (including discrete choice, choice modeling, hierarchical choice, trade-off matrices, and pairwise comparisons) used to estimate the specific value individuals place on some attribute of a choice, such as the relative value of features of a product or the relative importance of different outcomes of a development project. While individuals may find it very difficult to accurately assess the weight they put on individual attributes of a decision, conjoint analysis enables these weights to be derived statistically. Conjoint analysis enables a subjective assessment of a complex decision to be decomposed into quantitative scores of the relative importance of different criteria.

Theory in Action Courtyard by Marriot

In the mid-1980s, Marriott was facing a nearly saturated market for full-service, upscale hotels. Marriott's managers knew that the only way to sustain the company's 20 percent annual sales growth rate was to expand its product line. Marriott's management believed there was a market opportunity in the moderately priced ($35 to $60 a night) hotel category. The dominant chains in this category (e.g., Holiday Inn, Howard Johnson) tended to receive poor marks for customer satisfaction, and Marriott's managers believed that a chain that provided newer facilities and more consistent service would be enthusiastically received by customers. They also knew, however, that the company's most valuable resource was its well-established brand name, and they were reluctant to hastily affix the Marriott name to a scaled-down version of its hotels.

The company constructed a carefully structured plan for evaluating potential designs for a midprice hotel line. The company first conducted focus groups to identify different customer segments and the major factors that influenced their purchase decisions. The factors identified included external surroundings, room, food, lounge, services, leisure activities, and security. Within each major factor, there were several specific attributes that could take on multiple levels of product or service quality. For example, within the "services" factor, one of the attributes was "reservations," and the company had two levels: "call the hotel directly" or "call an 800 reservation number." A sample of hotel customers was selected to participate in a research group whereby each participant was given a fictional $35 with which to build their own hotel. Each participant was given seven cards (one card for each

of the major factors identified above). On the card was listed each of the specific attributes and their possible levels, along with a price for each level. The participants would evaluate one card at a time, selecting the features they desired. If participants went over the $35 budget, they were required to eliminate some features or choose a less expensive level of service. This technique helped management understand customer priorities and the trade-offs made by different customer segments. Based on these priorities, the managers then developed a series of hotel profiles offering different combinations of features and levels of service. Participants were then asked to rate each of these profiles. The managers could then use regression to assess how different levels of service within a specific attribute influenced customer ratings of the hotel overall. For example, as illustrated in Figure 7.8, after the hotel profiles are rated by the participants, the values for the levels in the profiles and the participant ratings can be entered into a spreadsheet. The ratings can then be regressed on the attribute levels, yielding a model that estimates the relative importance of each attribute.

Based on their conjoint analysis, Marriott's managers came up with the Courtyard concept: relatively small hotels (about 150 rooms) with limited amenities, small restaurants, small meeting rooms, enclosed courtyards, high security features, well-landscaped exteriors, and rates of $40 to $60 a night. Courtyard by Marriott turned out to be very successful. By the end of 2002, there were 533 Courtyard hotels (508 of those were in the United States), and their average occupancy rate of 72 percent was well above the industry average.

continued

concluded

FIGURE 7.8
Hotel Profiles and Ratings for Conjoint Analysis

Hotel Profile 1	Hotel Profile 2	Hotel Profile 3 ...
Reservations		
1-800 number (1)	Call hotel directly (0)	1-800 number (1)
Room Service		
Full-menu, 24 hours a day (5)	Limited menu, offered 6 A.M. to midnight (3)	No room service (1)
Newspaper Delivery		
None (0)	Daily (1)	None (0)
Etc.		

Attributes	Reservations	Room Service	Newspaper Delivery	Etc.	Overall Rating (1–10)
Participant 1					
Hotel Profile 1	1	5	0		8
Hotel Profile 2	0	3	1		7
Hotel Profile 3	1	1	0		5
Participant 2					
Hotel Profile 1	1	5	0		7
Hotel Profile 2	0	3	1		9
Hotel Profile 3	1	1	0		4
Etc.					

Source: Adapted from R. J. Thomas, *New Product Success Stories* (New York: John Wiley & Sons, 1995).

The most common use of conjoint analysis is to assess the relative importance to customers of different product attributes—these values can then be used in development and pricing decisions. For example, potential customers might be given a series of cards describing different models of a camera with different features and prices. The individuals are then asked to rate each in terms of its desirability (for example, on a scale of 1 to 10) or asked to order the models in terms of which they would most likely buy. Multiple regression is then used to assess the degree to which each attribute influences the overall rating, resulting in the assignment of specific weights to individual criteria. These weights provide a quantitative assessment of the trade-offs that customers implicitly consider in their evaluation of products. The firm can then use these weights in a series of "what if" scenarios to consider the implications of different product configurations. For example, Marriott used conjoint analysis to determine what features customer would most value in a moderately priced hotel. This analysis enabled Marriott to develop its very successful line of Courtyard by Marriott hotels (see the accompanying Theory in Action).

Data Envelopment Analysis

data envelopment analysis (DEA)
A method of ranking projects based on multiple decision criteria by comparing them to a hypothetical efficiency frontier.

Data envelopment analysis (DEA) is a method of assessing a potential project (or other decision) using multiple criteria that may have different kinds of measurement units.[41] For instance, for a particular set of potential projects, a firm might have cash flow estimates, a ranking of the project's fit with existing competencies, a ranking of the project's potential for building desired future competencies, a score for its technical feasibility, and a score for its customer desirability. Each of these measures captures something that is qualitatively different, and the numbers assigned to them are based on different units of measure. While the first measure is in dollars and is a nearly continuous measure, the second two measures are rank orders and thus are categorical measures with little information about what the difference is between one level of rank and another. The last two measures are scores that might be based on a ranking system or scaling system (e.g., a Likert measure that goes from one to seven).

efficiency frontier
The range of hypothetical configurations that optimize a combination of features.

Data envelopment analysis uses linear programming to combine these different measures from the projects to create a hypothetical **efficiency frontier** that represents the best performance on each measure. It can also consider which measures are inputs (such as costs) versus outputs (expected benefits). It then measures the distance of each project from this frontier to give it an efficiency value. These values can then be used to rank order the projects or identify projects that clearly dominate others.[42] For example, Figure 7.9 shows a DEA ranking of projects evaluated by the Advanced Technologies Group of Bell Laboratories. The Advanced Technologies Group chose to evaluate projects in terms of three measures of discounted cash flows expected from the project

FIGURE 7.9
DEA Ranking of the Advanced Technologies Group's 10 Most Attractive Projects and Every 50th Project Thereafter

Source: Adapted from J. D. Linton, S. T. Walsch, and J. Morabito, "Analysis, Ranking and Selection of R&D Projects in a Portfolio," *R&D Management* 32, no. 2 (2002), pp. 139–48.

Rank	Intellectual Property	Product Market	Investment	Cash Flow (most likely)	Cash Flow (optimistic)	Cash Flow (pessimistic)
1	2.25	1.5	$4,322	$1,296,700	$1,353,924	$1,184,192
2	1.5	1.5	850	525,844	551,538	493,912
3	1.5	1.5	1	4	4	3
4	2.25	2.25	478	545,594	822,164	411,082
5	1.5	1.5	1	15	15	11
6	1.5	2.25	65	89,144	178,289	0
7	1.5	1.5	1,068	685,116	1,027,386	342,558
8	1.5	1.5	4	3,766	4,707	2,824
9	1.5	1.5	20	4,800	4,800	−96
10	1.5	2.25	2	23	27	18
50	1.5	2.25	9	116	139	93
100	1.5	1.5	15	60	72	48
150	2.25	2.25	40	5,531	13,829	2,766
200	2.25	1.5	38	90	135	45

(most likely, optimistic scenario, pessimistic scenario), the investment required, and each project's desirability from the perspective of intellectual property benefits and product market benefits. For the latter two measures, projects were given a score of 1, 1.5, or 2.25 based on the group's model for intellectual property and product market benefits. As shown, the DEA method enabled Bell Laboratories to rank order different projects, despite the fact that they offered different kinds of benefits and risks.

The biggest advantage of DEA is that it enables comparisons of projects using multiple kinds of measures. However, just as with several of the methods described previously, the results of DEA are only as good as the data utilized. Managers bear the responsibility of determining which measures are most important to include and of ensuring that the measures are accurate.

Summary of Chapter

1. Firms often use a combination of quantitative and qualitative methods to evaluate which projects should be funded. Though some methods assume that all valuable projects will be funded, resources are typically constrained and firms must use capital rationing.

2. The most commonly used quantitative methods of evaluating projects are discounted cash flow methods such as net present value (NPV) or internal rate of return (IRR). While both methods enable the firm to create concrete estimates of returns of a project and account for the time value of money, the results are only as good as the cash flow estimates used in the analysis (which are often unreliable). Both methods also tend to heavily discount long-term or risky projects, and can undervalue projects that have strategic implications that are not well-reflected by cash flow estimates.

3. Some firms now use a real options approach to assessing projects. Real options better account for the long-run strategic implications of a project. Unfortunately, many new product development investment decisions do not conform to the assumptions inherent in an options valuation approach.

4. One commonly used qualitative method of assessing development projects is to subject the project to a series of screening questions that consider the project from multiple angles. These questions may be used merely to structure the discussion of a project or to create rating scales that are then utilized in an approach that combines qualitative and quantitative assessment.

5. A company's portfolio of projects typically includes projects of different types (e.g., advanced R&D, breakthrough, platform, and derivative projects) that have different resource requirements and different rates of return. Companies can use a project map to assess what their balance of projects is (or should be) and allocate resources accordingly.

6. Q-sort is a qualitative method of assessing projects whereby individuals rank each project under consideration according to a series of criteria. Q-sort is most commonly used to provide a format for discussion and debate.

7. Conjoint analysis is method of converting qualitative assessments of a choice into quantitative weights of the different criteria underlying the choice. It is most often used for assessing how customers value different product attributes.

8. Data envelopment analysis (DEA) is another method that combines qualitative and quantitative measures. DEA enables projects that have multiple criteria in different measurement units to be ranked by comparing them to a hypothetical efficiency frontier.

Discussion Questions

1. What are the advantages and disadvantages of discounted cash flow methods such as NPV and IRR?
2. For what kind of development projects might a real options approach be appropriate? For what kind of projects would it be inappropriate?
3. Why might a firm use both qualitative and quantitative assessments of a project?
4. Identify a development project you are familiar with. What methods do you believe were used to assess the project? What methods do you believe *should have been* used to assess the project?
5. Will different methods of evaluating a project typically yield the same conclusions about whether to fund its development? Why or why not?

Endnotes

1. Adapted from A. Juliano, P. Karsson, and B. O'Connell, "Boeing's Sonic Cruiser: Thinking Fast or Just Not Thinking?" New York University teaching case, 2003.
2. Boeing, 2001, *Boeing Focuses Commercial Airplanes Long-Range Product Strategy.* Retrieved November 20, 2002, from www.boeing.com/news/releases/2001/q1/news_release_010329a.html.
3. H. Banks, "Paper Plane," *Forbes,* May 28, 2001, pp. 52–53.
4. Air Transport Association, *Online Airline Handbook,* October 10, 2002.
5. Ibid.
6. JetBlue, 2002, *Fact Sheet.* Retrieved November 20, 2002, from www.jetblue.com/learnmore/factsheet.html.
7. Air Transport Association, *Online Airline Handbook.*
8. Boeing, 2002, *Boeing Provides Sonic Cruiser Technology Progress Report.* Retrieved November 20, 2002, from www.boeing.com/news/releases/2002/q3/nr_020724h.html.
9. UAL 10K.
10. "Boeing Sees $4.9 Trillion Market, 'Point-to-Point' Flying," *Airline Financial News* 20, no. 29 (2002), p. 1.
11. Boeing, 2002, *Boeing Provides Sonic Cruiser Technology Progress Report.*
12. L. Gunter, 2002, "The Need for Speed," *Boeing Frontiers.* Retrieved November 20, 2002, from www.boeing.com/news/frontiers/archive/2002/july/i_ca2.html.
13. H. Jung, "Sonic Cruiser Idea Is Grounded. Boeing to Opt for Efficiency over Speed," *Houston Chronicle,* December 22, 2002, p. 2.
14. B. Hall, "The Financing of Research and Development," *Oxford Review of Economic Policy* 18 (2002), pp. 35–51.
15. www.ventureeconomics.com; www.nvca.org; and V. Tenorio, "As Techs Sink, Angels Rush Out," *The Deal,* September 9, 2001.
16. Tenorio, "As Techs Sink, Angels Rush Out."
17. Hall, "The Financing of Research and Development."

18. Data obtained from the VC Deal Database. For more information on venture capital, see the National Venture Capital Association at www.nvca.org.

19. P. A. Gompers, "Corporations and the Financing of Innovation: The Corporate Venturing Experience," *Economic Review—Federal Reserve Bank of Atlanta* 87, no. 4 (2002), pp. 1–18.

20. G. Dushnitsky, "Limitations to External Knowledge Acquisition: The Paradox of Corporate Venture Capital," doctoral dissertation, New York University, 2003.

21. M. Sheahan, "Corporate Spin Can't Mask the VC Units' Blunders," *Venture Capital Journal,* March 1, 2003.

22. B. Kogut and N. Kulatilaka, "Options Thinking and Platform Investments: Investing in Opportunity," *California Management Review* 36, no. 2 (1994), pp. 52–72.

23. Ibid.

24. M. Amram and N. Kulatilaka, *Real Options: Managing Strategic Investment in an Uncertain World* (Boston: Harvard Business School Press, 1999); and K. D. Miller and T. B. Folta, "Option Value and Entry Timing," *Strategic Management Journal* 23 (2002), pp. 655–65.

25. D. Hurry, A. T. Miller, and E. H. Bowman, "Calls on High-Technology: Japanese Exploration of Venture Capital Investments in the United States," *Strategic Management Journal* 13 (1992), pp. 85–101.

26. G. Mitchell and W. Hamilton, "Managing R&D as a Strategic Option," *Research Technology Management* 31, no. 3 (1988), pp. 15–23.

27. S. A. Ross, R. W. Westerfield, and B. D. Jordan, *Fundamentals of Corporate Finance* (Boston: Irwin, 1993).

28. M. Amran and N. Kulatilaka, *Real Options* (Boston: Harvard Business School Press, 1999); F. P. Boer, "Valuation of Technology Using Real Options," *Research Technology Management* 43 (2000), pp. 26–31; and R. T. McGrath, "Assessing Technology Projects Using Real Options Reasoning," *Research Technology Management* 43 (July–August, 2000), pp. 35–50.

29. M. Benaroch and R. Kauffman, "Justifying Electronic Banking Network Expansion Using Real Options Analysis," *MIS Quarterly* 24 (June 2000), pp. 197–226.

30. M. Perlitz, T. Peske, and R. Schrank, "Real Options Valuation: The New Frontier in R&D Evaluation?" *R&D Management* 29 (1999), pp. 255–70.

31. E. H. Bowman and D. Hurry, "Strategy through the Option Lens: An Integrated View of Resource Investments and the Incremental-Choice Process," *Academy of Management Review* 18 (1993), pp. 760–82.

32. M. A. Schilling, "Technological Lock Out: An Integrative Model of the Economic and Strategic Factors Driving Success and Failure," *Academy of Management Review* 23 (1998), pp. 267–85.

33. T. Chan, J. A. Nickerson, and H. Owan, "Strategic Management of R&D Pipelines," Washington University working paper, 2003.

34. K. R. Allen, *Bringing New Technology to Market* (Upper Saddle River, NJ: Prentice Hall, 2003).

35. Gunter, 2002, "The Need for Speed."

36. Y. Wind and V. Mahajan, "New Product Development Process: A Perspective for Reexamination," *Journal of Product Innovation Management* 5 (1988), pp. 304–10.

37. S. C. Wheelwright and K. B. Clark, "Creating Project Plans to Focus Product Development," *Harvard Business Review,* March–April 1992.

38. J. A. Byrne, "Jack," *Business Week,* June 8, 1998, p. 90.

39. Allen, *Bringing New Technology to Market;* and A. I. Helin and W. B. Souder, "Experimental Test of a Q-Sort Procedure for Prioritising R&D Projects," *IEEE Transactions on Engineering Management* EM-21 (1974), pp. 159–64.

40. R. G. Cooper, S. J. Edgett, and E. J. Kleinschmidt, "New Product Portfolio Management: Practices and Performance," *Journal of Product Innovation Management* 16 (1999), pp. 333–51.

41. A. W. Charnes, W. Cooper, and E. Rhodes, "Measuring the Efficiency of Decision Making Units," *European Journal of Operational Research* 2 (1978), pp. 429–44.

42. J. D. Linton, S. T. Walsch, and J. Morabito, "Analysis, Ranking and Selection of R&D Projects in a Portfolio," *R&D Management* 32, no. 2 (2002), pp. 139–48.

Chapter **Eight**

Collaboration Strategies

The XenoMouse

After spending seven years and $40 million in research and development, Abgenix had created a very special mouse.[1] The XenoMouse was a strain of genetically engineered mice capable of producing antibodies with human protein sequences.[2] While other companies had used mice to produce antibodies, most of these antibodies had failed to work against human illnesses because they were too mouselike. The XenoMouse used human genes to produce antibodies that closely resemble those a human would produce.[3] These antibodies had great potential for treating human illnesses, including cancer, arthritis, and organ transplant rejection. Major pharmaceutical and biotechnology companies were lined up to license access to XenoMouse, and the stock market was so enthusiastic about XenoMouse's prospects that it drove Abgenix's market capitalization up to $3 billion by 2000.

Abgenix had plans for two different ways to derive revenues from XenoMouse. First, it licensed pharmaceutical or biotechnology companies the rights to use XenoMouse to develop antibodies for a specific disease target the companies had identified. The companies would pay upfront fees, more fees at different development milestones, and then royalties on sales if drugs were successfully commercialized. Average fees before commercialization ranged from $7 million to $10 million, and royalties were 5 to 6 percent of sales.[4] Abgenix's second way of deriving revenues was to develop its own drugs through early stages of testing and then license the rights to develop and market the drug to another company. Both methods enabled Abgenix to earn upfront fees and royalties from sales, while avoiding the expense of establishing large manufacturing operations, a sales force, and other costs.

One of Abgenix's drug development programs, ABX-EGF, had shown particular promise in treating several different types of cancer, including colorectal cancer. ABX-EGF had eradicated human cancer tumors from every test mouse in which the tumors had been injected. This exciting finding had attracted several would-be collaborators; thus, Abgenix had to make some important decisions about whether, and how, it would use partners to further develop the ABX-EGF antibodies. Abgenix's managers identified three possible strategies—handing off ABX-EGF to a large pharmaceutical company, participating in a joint venture to further develop ABX-EGF with a biotechnology company, or further developing ABX-EGF on its own.

The Handing-Off Option

A large pharmaceutical company was interested in licensing the worldwide rights to the ABX-EGF technology. The company seemed like a good potential partner because it had the skills and resources necessary to guide ABX-EGF through the necessary testing and regulatory process, as well as commercially launching and marketing the drug if it were approved. The pharmaceutical company was willing to pay upfront fees and a royalty rate that was considered high by industry standards.[5]

The Joint Venture Option

A biotechnology firm was interested in a 50/50 joint venture with Abgenix. Abgenix and the biotech company would split the costs of developing ABX-EGF and bringing it through the testing, regulatory, and commercialization process. The two companies would then share the profits if the drug proved successful. Recognizing that Abgenix had already done significant work on the program, the biotechnology company agreed to make some additional upfront payments to Abgenix. Under this option, Abgenix would share more in the risks and rewards of ABX-EGF.

The Solo Development Option

Abgenix was also considering pursuing further development of ABX-EGF on its own. This option meant that Abgenix would need to develop the in-house capabilities to bring the product through the testing and regulatory process. Though, R. Scott Greer, chief executive officer, realized that Abgenix would most likely need a partner at some stage of the commercialization process, he also believed Abgenix could keep more of the potential value of ABX-EGF if it developed the drug on its own. Under this option, Abginex would bear most of the risk and reap most of the returns of the ABX-EGF project.

By late 2001, management at Abgenix was leaning toward developing the drug in-house and also had plans to build a large manufacturing facility. Analysts, however, were quick to point out that Abgenix was burning through its cash quickly, and after the stock market had soured in 2001, cash had gotten harder to come by. Adding still more urgency to the situation was the fact that heavy hitters such as Genentech and AstraZeneca were also developing their own drugs targeting the EGF pathway (the same cancer mechanism targeted by ABX-EGF).[6] Abgenix's decision had to account for the company's short-term cash needs, the ability to develop and commercialize ABX-EGF rapidly, and Abgenix's potential for long-term growth.

Discussion Questions

1. What are the pros and cons of Abgenix collaborating with a partner on ABX-EGF?
2. If Abgenix chooses collaboration, would it be better off licensing ABX-EGF to the pharmaceutical company or forming a joint venture with the biotech company?
3. How does Abgenix's decision about collaborating for ABX-EGF impact its prospects for its other drug development projects?

OVERVIEW

Firms frequently face difficult decisions about the scope of activities to perform in-house, and whether to perform them alone as a solo venture or to perform them collaboratively with one or more partners. As mentioned in Chapter Two, a significant portion of innovation arises not from any single individual or organization, but instead from the collaborative efforts of multiple individuals or organizations. Collaboration can often enable firms to achieve more, at a faster rate, and with less cost or risk than they can achieve alone. However, collaboration also often entails relinquishing some degree of control over development and some share of the expected rewards of innovation, plus it can expose the firm to risk of malfeasance by its partner(s). In this chapter, we will first consider the reasons that a firm might choose to engage in collaborative development or might choose to avoid it. We will then review some of the most common types of collaborative arrangements and their specific advantages and disadvantages.

REASONS FOR GOING SOLO

A firm might choose to engage in solo development of a project for a number of reasons. First, the firm may perceive no need to collaborate with other organizations—it may possess all the necessary capabilities and resources for a particular development project in-house. Alternatively, the firm may prefer to obtain complementary skills or resources from a partner, but there may be no available partner that is appropriate or willing to collaborate. A firm might also choose to develop a project as a solo venture if it is concerned that collaborating would put its proprietary technologies at risk, or if it seeks to have full control over the project's development and returns. Furthermore, a firm's solo development of a technological innovation might give it more opportunities to build and renew its capabilities.

1. Availability of Capabilities

Whether a firm chooses to partner on a project is largely determined by the degree to which it possesses all of the necessary capabilities in-house and the degree to which one or more potential partners have necessary capabilities. If a firm has all of the necessary capabilities for a project, it may have little need to collaborate with others and may opt to go it alone. Furthermore, if a firm finds that it lacks certain required capabilities but there are also no potential partners with such capabilities, it may be forced to develop the capabilities on its own.

For example, in the late 1970s Monsanto was interested in developing food crop seeds that were genetically modified to survive strong herbicides. Monsanto's Roundup, a powerful herbicide, had been introduced in 1974 and had been remarkably successful. However, Roundup killed almost all plants that it came into contact with and thus had to be applied with great care. If crops could be developed that were genetically modified to resist Roundup, the herbicide could be used more easily and in larger quantities. The biotechnology industry was still quite young, so there were no appropriate partners from which to acquire the necessary technologies. Monsanto decided to pursue the opportunity as a solo internal venture and declared that biotechnology was its new strategic focus.[7] In 1983, Monsanto successfully developed its first transgenic plant, but it would not be until 1995 that it would have its first genetically modified crop seed, Roundup Ready soybeans, approved for commercialization.[8] Though many environmental groups opposed both Roundup and the genetically modified Roundup Ready crops, the combination was enormously successful. By 2002, more than 130 million acres worldwide were planted with Monsanto's Roundup Ready soybean, corn, cotton, and canola seed.[9]

2. *Protecting Proprietary Technologies*

Firms sometimes avoid collaboration for fear of giving up proprietary technologies. Working closely with a partner might expose the company's existing proprietary technologies to the prying eyes of a would-be competitor. Furthermore, the firm may wish to have exclusive control over any proprietary technologies created during the development project. Consider Abgenix's decision about whether to collaborate with a partner in its development of a new cancer drug, as described in the opening vignette. While collaborating would give Abgenix needed cash and access to valuable development and marketing capabilities it did not possess, collaborating would also mean giving up exclusive control over the drugs developed.

3. *Controlling Technology Development and Use*

Sometimes firms choose not to collaborate because they desire to have complete control over their development processes and the use of any resulting new technologies. This desire might be for pragmatic reasons (e.g., the new technology is expected to yield high margins and the firm does not wish to share rents with collaborators) or cultural reasons (e.g., a company's culture may emphasize independence and self-reliance). Both of these reasons are demonstrated by Honda. While other auto manufacturers were enthusiastically forming **alliances** to collaborate on automobile design and the development of more efficient manufacturing processes, Honda was very cautious about forming collaborative relationships. Honda's decision not to join the Alliance of Automobile Manufacturers, the industry trade group that leads the fight against tougher fuel and emissions standards, had both pragmatic and cultural reasons. From a pragmatic standpoint, Honda worried that participating in the trade group would limit its discretion over its development of environmentally friendly automobiles, an area where Honda intended to be the market leader. This decision was

alliance
Alliance is a general term that can refer to any type of relationship between firms. Alliances may be short or long term and may include formally contracted agreements or be entirely informal in nature.

reinforced by Honda's culture that emphasized retaining complete control over the firm's technology development and direction. This is illustrated by Honda President Hiroyuki Yoshino's statement, "It's better for a person to decide about his own life rather than having it decided by others."[10]

4. Building and Renewing Capabilities

Firms may also choose to engage in solo development even when partnering could save time or money because they believe that development efforts are key to building and renewing their capabilities. Solo development of a technological innovation challenges the firm to develop new skills, resources, and market knowledge. As noted in Chapter Seven, the potential for creating and enhancing the organization's capabilities may be more valuable than the innovation itself. This was aptly demonstrated in the quote from Walt Gillette of Boeing about the development of the Sonic Cruiser: "Industry experience indicates that if the company doesn't create a new airplane every 12 to 15, years the needed skills and experience will be gone. Too many of the people who created the last new airplane will have retired or moved on to other companies, and their skills and experience will not have been passed on to the next generation of Boeing employees."[11]

Though there are several reasons a firm might choose to stick with solo development, there are also many reasons for firms to engage in collaborative development, and collaboration appears to be on the rise. In the next sections, we will discuss the advantages of collaboration and the strengths and weaknesses of various types of collaboration.

ADVANTAGES OF COLLABORATING

Collaborating on development projects can offer a firm a number of advantages. First, collaborating can enable a firm to obtain necessary skills or resources more quickly than developing them in-house.[12] It is not unusual for a company to lack some of the complementary assets required to transform a body of technological knowledge into a commercial product. Given time, the company can develop such complementary assets internally. However, doing so extends cycle time. Instead, a company may be able to gain rapid access to important complementary assets by entering into strategic alliances or licensing arrangements.[13] For example, when Apple was developing its LaserWriter, a high-resolution laser printer, it did not possess the technological expertise to produce the printer's engine, and developing such capabilities in-house would have taken a long time. Apple persuaded Canon, the market leader in printer engines, to collaborate on the project.[14] With Canon's help, Apple was able to bring the high-quality printer to market quickly.

Second, obtaining some of the necessary capabilities or resources from a partner rather than building them in-house can help a firm reduce its asset commitment and enhance its flexibility. This can be particularly important in markets characterized by rapid technological change. High-speed technological change causes product markets to rapidly transform. Product life cycles shorten, and innovation becomes the primary driver of competition. When technology is progressing rapidly, firms may seek to avoid committing themselves to fixed assets that may rapidly become obsolete. They may choose to become more narrowly specialized and to use linkages with other specialized firms to access resources they do not possess in-house.

Third, collaboration with partners can be an important source of learning for the firm. Close contact with other firms can facilitate both the transfer of knowledge between firms and the creation of new knowledge that individual firms could not have created alone.[15] By pooling their technological resources and capabilities, firms may be able to expand their knowledge bases and do so more quickly than they could without collaboration.

Fourth, one primary reason firms collaborate on a development project is to share the costs and risks of the project. This can be particularly important when a project is very expensive or its outcome highly uncertain.[16]

Finally, firms may also collaborate on a development project when such collaboration would facilitate the creation of a shared standard. Collaboration at the development stage can be an important way of ensuring cooperation in the commercialization stage of a technology, and such cooperation may be crucial for technologies in which compatibility and complementary goods are important. For example, in 1997 Nokia, Motorola, and Ericsson formed a nonprofit corporation called the WAP Forum, to establish a common wireless telecommunication format. WAP stands for Wireless Application Protocol. It is an open, global communication standard that is intended to enable users of mobile devices such as cell phones, pagers, and smart-phones to easily and quickly access information from the Internet. By establishing the WAP Forum, the companies hoped to prevent the emergence of multiple competing standards. In 2002, the WAP Forum merged with the Open Mobile Architecture initiative to form the Open Mobile Alliance (OMA). By early 2003, more than 200 mobile operators, equipment producers, and software developers had signed on to the standard.[17]

joint venture
A partnership between two or more firms involving a significant equity stake by the partners and often resulting in the creation of a new business entity.

Not all such ventures are so successful however. For example, in 1992, IBM, Apple, and Hewlett-Packard formed a **joint venture** called Taligent to jointly develop and promote an operating system that could overthrow Microsoft's Windows as the dominant standard in personal computer operating systems. After spending three years and $50 million developing and promoting the new operating system standard, the venture had failed to meet expectations and was ultimately dissolved.

Before the National Cooperative Research Act (NCRA) of 1984, collaborative research between firms had been restricted by antitrust regulation. However, the NCRA established that joint research and development was legal as long as collaborative efforts were not deemed anticompetitive. From 1985 to 2000, more than 800 research joint ventures (involving more than 4,200 businesses and organizations) were registered in the NCRA database (see Figure 8.1). Of the participating organizations, more than 3,000 were based in the United States, and half of the ventures involved companies from three industries: electronic and electrical equipment (18 percent), communications (16 percent), and transportation equipment (15 percent).[18]

Worldwide, use of technology or research alliances has more than doubled since 1980 (see Figure 8.2). In the year 2000, 574 new technology or research alliances were formed in six major sectors: information technology, biotechnology, advanced materials, aerospace and defense, automotive, and chemicals.[19]

FIGURE 8.1

New Research Joint Ventures Registered under the U.S. National Cooperative Research Act, 1985–2000

Source: Based on data from A. Link, "Federal Register Filings: The 2000 Update of the CORE Database," a report submitted to the National Science Foundation, Arlington, VA, 2001.

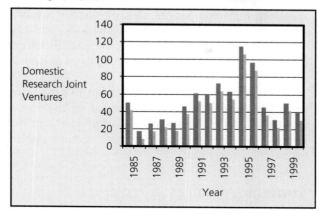

FIGURE 8.2

Wordwide Formation of New Technology or Research Alliances, 1980–2000

Source: J. Hagerdoon, Cooperative Agreements and Technology Indicators (CATI) database, unpublished tabulations (Maastricht, Netherlands: Maastricht Economic Research Institute on Innovation and Technology, 2001).

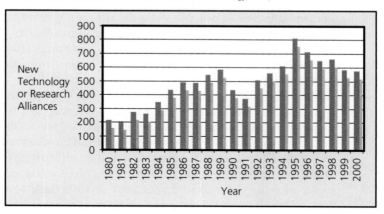

As firms forge collaborative relationships, they weave a network of paths between them that can act as conduits for information and other resources. By providing member firms access to a wider range of information (and other resources) than individual firms possess, interfirm networks can enable firms to achieve much more than they could achieve individually.[20] Thus, interfirm networks have become an increasingly important engine of innovation.[21] (Chapter Two provides a more in-depth discussion of technology clusters, knowledge spillovers, and technology brokering.)

TYPES OF COLLABORATIVE ARRANGEMENTS

Collaboration can include partnering with suppliers, customers, competitors, complementors, organizations that offer similar products in different markets, organizations that offer different products in similar markets, nonprofit organizations, government organizations, universities, or others. Collaboration can also be used for many different purposes, including manufacturing, services, marketing, or technology-based objectives. In North America, as many as 23 percent of all alliances are for research and development activities, compared to 14 percent in Western Europe and 12 percent in Asia.[22]

Collaboration arrangements can also take many forms, from very informal alliances to highly structured joint ventures or technology exchange agreements **(licensing)**. The most common forms of collaborative arrangements used in technological innovation include strategic alliances, joint ventures, licensing, outsourcing, and collective research organizations.

licensing
A contractual arrangement whereby one organization or individual (the licensee) obtains the rights to use the proprietary technology (or trademark, or copyright, etc.) of another organization or individual (the licensor).

Strategic Alliances

Firms may use strategic alliances to access a critical capability that is not possessed in-house or to more fully exploit their own capabilities by leveraging them in another firm's development efforts. Firms with different capabilities necessary for developing a new technology or penetrating a new market might form alliances to pool their resources so that collectively they can develop the product or market faster or less expensively. Even firms that have similar capabilities may collaborate in their development activities in order to share the risk of a venture or to speed up market development and penetration. Large firms might form alliances with small firms in order to take a limited stake in the smaller firm's development efforts, while small firms might form alliances with large forms to tap the larger firm's greater capital resources, distribution and marketing capabilities, or credibility.[23] For example, many large pharmaceutical firms have allied with small biotechnology firms for their mutual benefit: The pharmaceutical firms gain access to the drug discoveries of the biotechnology companies, and the biotechnology companies gain access to the capital resources, manufacturing, and distribution capabilities of the pharmaceutical firms.

Alliances can enhance a firm's overall level of flexibility.[24] Through an alliance, firms can establish a limited stake in a venture while maintaining the flexibility to either increase their commitment later or shift these resources to another opportunity.[25] Firms can use alliances to gain an early window on emerging opportunities that they may want to commit to more fully in the future. Alliances also enable a firm to rapidly adjust the type and scale of capabilities the firm can access, which can be very valuable in rapidly changing markets.

Alliances are also used to enable partners to learn from each other and develop new competencies. Alliance partners may hope to transfer knowledge between the firms or to combine their skills and resources to jointly create new knowledge. However, alliance relationships often lack the shared language, routines, and coordination that facilitate the transfer of knowledge—particularly the complex and tacit knowledge that is most likely to lead to sustainable competitive advantages.[26] To use alliances for learning requires a serious commitment of resources, such as a pool of dedicated people willing to travel between the home firm and partner firm, test-bed facilities, and active procedures for internalizing what has been learned.[27]

Yves Doz and Gary Hamel argue that it is useful to categorize a firm's alliance strategy along two dimensions.[28] The first dimension is the degree to which alliances practice **capability complementation** versus **capability transfer.** The second dimension is whether the firm manages each alliance individually or manages a collective network of alliances (see Figure 8.3).

In quadrant A are firms that forge an individual alliance to combine complementary technologies or skills needed for a project. For example, in the mid-1970s, General Electric (GE) and SNECMA (a French jet engine producer) formed a joint venture called CFM International to develop a new jet engine. The venture would combine GE's F101 turbojet with SNECMA's low-pressure fan expertise to create a powerful and fuel-efficient engine. Because the F101 was considered a sensitive military technology by the U.S. airforce, the venture was set up to carefully avoid the exchange of proprietary technology between the firms. GE would build the F101 portion as a sealed "black box," which could then be shipped to a separate assembly location. The resulting engine, the CFM-56, became the most successful jet engine in the history of aviation.[29]

In quadrant B are firms that use a network of alliances to combine complementary skills and resources. For example, Corning, known primarily as a producer of glass products, has created a web of alliances with partners that have complementary skills in order to extend its glass technology into fields as diverse as medical products, computer products, and fiber optics. Rather than attempting to internalize its partners' technologies, Corning views its relationships with its partners as a form of extended enterprise that form a flexible and egalitarian network of independent businesses.[30]

In quadrant C are firms that use individual alliances to transfer capabilities between them. Doz and Hamel provide the example of the alliance between JVC and Thomson. While both companies produce VCRs, Thomson wanted to glean product technology and manufacturing expertise from JVC, whereas JVC needed to learn how to penetrate the European market from Thomson. Both sides perceived an equitable opportunity for gain from exchanging capabilities.

capability complementation
Combining ("pooling") the capabilities and other resources of partner firms, but not necessarily transferring those resources between the partners.

capability transfer
Exchange of capabilities across firms in such a manner that partners can internalize the capabilities and use them independent of the particular development project.

FIGURE 8.3
Technology Alliance Strategies

Source: Adapted from Y. Doz and G. Hamel, "The Use of Alliances in Implementing Technology Strategies," in *Managing Strategic Innovation and Change,* eds, M. L. Tushman and P. Anderson (Oxford: Oxford University Press, 1997).

	Individual Alliance	**Network of Alliances**
Capability Complementation	A GE-SNECMA alliance	B Corning Glass alliances
Capability Transfer	C Thomson-JVC alliance	D Aspla

In quadrant D are firms that use a network of alliances to exchange capabilities and jointly develop new capabilities. The collective research organizations described later in the chapter (including Aspla and the National Center for Manufacturing Sciences) are examples of alliance networks in which a formal body has been created to govern the network. These organizations are designed to enable their member organizations to collectively create, share, and utilize knowledge.

The opportunities and flexibility that can be gained through using alliances can come at a cost. The potential for opportunism and self-interest exists for all parties of an alliance due to limited levels of mutual commitment.[31] Firms need to be constantly on guard to ensure that the alliance does not inadvertently result in giving too much away to a potential competitor. According to Doz and Hamel, while collegiality between partners can facilitate trust and communication, *too much* collegiality may be a warning sign that information gatekeepers within the firm are not being sufficiently vigilant.[32] Employees at all levels should be regularly informed about what information and resources are off-limits to the partner, and the firm should stringently monitor what information the partner requests and receives.[33]

The use of alliances is estimated to have grown by 25 percent a year since 1985, and estimates suggest the global value of alliances may reach as much as $40 trillion by 2005.[34]

Joint Ventures

Joint ventures are a particular type of strategic alliance that entails significant structure and commitment. While a strategic alliance can be any type of formal or informal relationship between two or more firms, a joint venture involves a significant equity investment from each partner and often results in establishment of a new separate entity. The capital and other resources to be committed by each partner are usually specified in carefully constructed contractual arrangements, as are the division of any profits earned by the venture.

For example, in May 2002, NEC Corporation and Fuji Heavy Industries (both of Japan) formed a joint venture called NEC Lamilion Energy to develop and manufacture high-performance batteries for environmentally friendly automobiles. The project would combine NEC's expertise in manganese lithium-ion cell technology with Fuji's battery pack technology to create rechargeable batteries for the automobiles. NEC and Fuji would have 51 percent and 49 percent stakes, respectively, in the $3.82 million venture.[35]

Licensing

Licensing is a contractual arrangement whereby one organization or individual (the *licensee*) obtains the rights to use the proprietary technology (or trademark, copyright, etc.) of another organization or individual (the *licensor*). Licensing enables a firm to rapidly acquire a technology (or other resource or capability) it does not possess. For example, when Microsoft realized it had lost precious time to Netscape and needed to get a Web browser to market fast, it licensed the software it needed to produce Internet Explorer from Spyglass Inc. Microsoft also bought several companies (including Vermeer Technologies, Colusa Software, and eShop Inc.) to provide other Internet utilities.

For the licensor, licensing can enable the firm's technology to penetrate a wider range of markets than it could on its own. For example, Delphi Automotive, a supplier to the automotive industry, had developed a software program that can simulate various aspects of machining, including turning, milling, and drilling. The software enabled manufacturers that do high-volume machining to identify ways of improving their machining processes. Delphi had developed the software for its own use, but then realized it could make more money by licensing the software to others.[36]

Licensing a technology from another firm is typically much less expensive for a licensee than developing a new technology in-house. As discussed in earlier chapters, new product development is both expensive and risky; through licensing, a firm can obtain a technology that is already technically or commercially proven. On the other hand, a technology that is available for license is typically available to many potential licensees and is unlikely to be the source of a sustainable competitive advantage.[37]

Licensing agreements typically impose many restrictions on the licensee, enabling the licensor to retain control over how the technology is used. However, over time licensees may gain valuable knowledge from working with the licensed technology that can enable them to later develop their own proprietary technologies. In the long run, the licensor's control over the technology may erode.

Sometimes firms license their technologies to preempt their competitors from developing their own competing technologies. This can be particularly important if competitors are likely to be able to imitate the primary features of the technology or if the industry has strong pressures for the adoption of a single dominant design (see Chapter Four and the accompanying Research Brief). By licensing out the technology to potential competitors, the licensor gives up the ability to earn monopoly rents on the technology. However, doing so may prevent potential competitors from developing their own proprietary technologies. Thus, licensing enables a firm to opt for a steady stream of royalties rather than gambling on the big gain—or big loss—of having its technology compete against others for market dominance.

Outsourcing

Firms that develop new technological innovations do not always possess the competencies, facilities, or scale to perform all the value-chain activities for the new innovation effectively or efficiently. Such firms might outsource activities to other firms. According to a survey conducted by *Purchasing* magazine, 66 percent of organizations polled say their spending on outsourcing increased between 10 percent and 1,000 percent from 1994 to 1999.[38] By 2003, worldwide spending on outsourcing services had exceeded $100 billion.[39]

contract manufacturing
When a firm hires another firm (often a specialized manufacturer) to manufacture its products.

One common form of outsourcing is the use of contract manufacturers. **Contract manufacturing** allows firms to meet the scale of market demand without committing to long-term capital investments or an increase in the labor force, thus giving the firm greater flexibility.[40] It also enables firms to specialize in those activities central to their competitive advantage while other firms provide necessary support and specialized resources the firm does not possess. Contract manufacturing further enables a firm to tap the greater economies of scale and faster response time of a dedicated manufacturer, thereby reducing costs and increasing organizational responsiveness to the environment.[41] For example, in 1999, Nortel Networks decided it needed to become

Research Brief   Using Alliances and Licensing to Establish a Standard

In a 1997 article, Charles Hill describes how a firm can use licensing or alliances to build momentum for its technology's adoption as a standard in winner-take-all markets. Hill describes a range of strategies, from "aggressive sole provider" to "aggressive multiple licensing," and the contingencies that determine which is likely to be the best choice (summarized in Figure 8.4). Hill argues that the primary factors that will determine the firm's optimal strategy include barriers to imitation, the presence of capable competitors, the availability of complementary goods, and whether the firm possesses the necessary capabilities to produce the technology and complementary goods in-house.

AGGRESSIVE SOLE PROVIDER

In this strategy, the firm attempts to establish itself as the sole supplier of a standard defining technology. The firm avoids licensing and alliances, positions its product or service aggressively through wide distribution and penetration pricing, and produces necessary complementary goods itself. If this strategy is successful, the firm keeps all the profits earned by the technology standard. However, this "going-it-alone" strategy is risky and expensive. This strategy makes sense when the barriers to imitation are high (competitors are unable to closely duplicate the technology's advantages) and the firm possesses all the capabilities in-house. Also, necessary complementary goods must either be readily available on the market or the firm must be able to produce them itself. This strategy also makes sense if there are no competitors that are likely to develop a superior technology, though some firms have been successful with this strategy even when there are highly capable competitors. For example, Intel has successfully pursued an aggressive sole provider strategy with its microprocessors despite ongoing pressure from highly capable competitors such as IBM and Motorola.

SELECTIVE PARTNERING

If there are high barriers to entry but the firm lacks an important capability or resource required to produce and support the technology on its own, the firm may enter strategic alliances with one or a few other organizations to jointly—and aggressively—promote the technology as a standard. This can be a particularly useful strategy if there is a particular rival that poses an obvious threat. Sony and Philips used this strategy in their development and promotion of the compact disc format.

PASSIVE MULTIPLE LICENSING

If there are low barriers to entry, multiple capable competitors, and the firm does not possess all the capabilities in-house to produce and support the technology (and complementary goods) on its own, it may make sense to license the technology to any firm interested, and let those licensees build the market. Passive licensing is an inexpensive way to build the technology's installed base and the availability of complementary goods, and it has the potential for coopting potential rivals. For example, Dolby has passively licensed its high-fidelity sound technology to all comers for a very reasonable fee, and thus potential rivals have little reason to attempt to develop a superior technology. Though Dolby earns only a few cents from every audio player sold with Dolby technology, the volume is huge and the company has almost zero overhead costs.

AGGRESSIVE MULTIPLE LICENSING

The aggressive multiple licensing strategy is like the passive multiple licensing strategy, but it also includes aggressive positioning on the part of the sponsoring firm. In this strategy, the firm both eagerly licenses out its technology to promote its adoption by rivals and vigorously produces and markets the technology itself. The objective is to both secure the technology's position as a

continued

concluded

standard *and* make the sponsoring firm the dominant producer of the technology. In this scenario, the firm possesses all necessary capabilities to produce and support the technology on its own, but low barriers to entry and the existence of many capable competitors mean that other firms are likely to challenge the firm's dominance.

Licensing the technology to such competitors prevents them from developing alternatives and builds momentum for the standard.

Source: C. W. L. Hill, "Establishing a Standard: Competitive Strategy and Technological Standards in Winner-Take-All Markets," *Academy of Management Executive* 11, no. 2 (1997), pp. 7–25.

FIGURE 8.4
Summary of Strategy Features and Contingencies Favoring Its Use

Competitive Strategy	Main Features	Contingencies Favoring Strategy
Aggressive Sole Provider	• Avoid licensing • Avoid alliances • Pursue aggressive positioning strategy • Diversify into production of complementary products if necessary	• High barriers to imitation • Firm possesses required complementary resources • Suppliers of complementary products exist (or diversification into their production is feasible) • Lack of capable competitors
Selective Partnering	• Enter into an alliance to jointly promote a standard	• Firm lacks critical complementary resources that partner possesses· • High barriers to imitation • Partner is also a potential capable competitor
Passive Multiple Licensing·	• License to all comers • Licensees develop the market	• Low barriers to imitation • Firm lacks complementary resources· • Many capable competitors
Aggressive Multiple Licensing	• License to many firms • Pursue aggressive positioning strategy	• Firm possesses required complementary resources • Barriers to imitation are low· • Many capable competitors

a much more agile company to respond to its rapidly changing environment.[42] From 1999 through 2001, Nortel implemented a program to outsource most of its in-house manufacturing to contract manufacturers.[43] During this time, Nortel closed or sold many of its manufacturing operations, shifting from a company that produces equipment to one that focuses on design and marketing of Internet and telecommunications solutions. According to Nortel CEO John Roth, greater use of contract manufacturing saved the company a significant amount of money, and made the company "faster, quicker, more in tune with the marketplace."[44]

Other activities, such as product design, process design, marketing, information technology, or distribution can also be outsourced from external providers. For example, large contract manufacturers such as Flextronics and Solectron now often help firms design products in addition to manufacturing them. Companies such as IBM or Siemens will provide a company a complete information technology solution, while United Parcel Service will take care of a company's logistics and distribution needs. Outsourcing can have a number of downsides, however. Reliance on outsourcing may cause the firm to forfeit important learning opportunities, potentially putting it at a disadvantage in the long run.[45] By not investing in development of in-house capabilities, a firm might not develop many of the skills and resources related to its products that enable the development of future product platforms. The firm risks becoming hollow.[46] In fact, Prahalad and Hamel argue that Korean firms such as Goldstar, Samsung, and Daewoo have explicit missions to capture investment initiative away from potential competitors by serving as contract manufacturers for them. This allows the Korean firms to use would-be competitors' funds to accelerate their own competence development, while the competitors' competencies erode.[47]

Outsourcing can also impose significant transaction costs for a firm.[48] Contract manufacturing, for example, requires a well-specified contract: Product design, cost, and quantity requirements must be clearly communicated and generally specified up front. The contracting firm may also have to go to great lengths to protect itself from having any proprietary technology expropriated by the contract manufacturer. In addition, the contract manufacturer may bear significant costs in ramping up production for a particular firm, and must therefore specify the contract to avoid being held up by the contracting firm after the manufacturer has made investments specific to the contract.[49]

Collective Research Organizations

In some industries, multiple organizations have established cooperative research and development organizations such as the Semiconductor Research Corporation or the American Iron and Steel Institute.[50] Collective research organizations may take a number of forms, including trade associations, university-based centers, or private research corporations.

Many of these organizations are formed through government or industry association initiatives. For example, the National Center for Manufacturing Sciences (NCMS) was formed in 1986 by the U.S. Defense Department, the Association for Manufacturing Technology, the Manufacturing Studies Board, General Motors, and 20 other manufacturing companies. Its purpose was to promote collaborations among industry, government, and academic organizations. By 1995, the center had 200 U.S., Canadian, and Mexican corporate members and was supporting approximately 100 projects at any particular time. Typical NCMS projects involve 15 to 20 organizations and run for two to four years.[51]

Other collective research organizations have been formed solely through the initiative of private companies. For example, in 2002, six Japanese electronics manufacturers (Fujitsu, Hitachi, Matsushita Electric Industrial, Mitsubishi Electric, NEC, and Toshiba) set up a collective research company called Aspla to develop designs for more advanced computer chips. Global competition had driven down margins on chips, resulting in major losses for many of the major Japanese electronics makers. Furthermore, research in advanced chip designs had become extremely expensive. The collaborative research organization would enable the companies to share the development expense and help the Japanese semiconductor industry retain its competitive edge. Each of the companies initially invested 150 million yen ($1.3 million) in the organization, and plans were for each to contribute about $85 million annually toward joint research.[52] The Japanese government also agreed to contribute $268 million.

CHOOSING A MODE OF COLLABORATION

Figure 8.5 summarizes some of the trade-offs between solo internal development and various modes of collaboration. Solo internal development is, on average, a relatively slow and expensive way of developing a technology. The firm bears all the costs and risks, and may spend considerable time learning about the new technology, refining its designs, and developing production or service processes to implement the new technology. However, a firm that engages in solo internal development retains total control over how the technology is developed and used. Solo internal development also offers great potential for the firm to leverage its existing competencies and to develop new competencies, but offers little to no potential for accessing another firm's competencies. Therefore, solo internal development might make sense for a firm that has strong competencies related to the new technology, has access to capital, and is not under great time pressure.

Because strategic alliances can take many forms, the speed, cost, and degree of control they offer varies considerably. Some strategic alliances may enable a firm to relatively quickly and cheaply gain access to another firm's technology, but give the firm a low level of control over that technology. Other strategic alliances might be aimed at utilizing the firm's own technology in a broader range of markets, which

FIGURE 8.5

Summary of Trade-offs between Different Modes of Development

	Speed	Cost	Control	Potential for Leveraging Existing Competencies	Potential for Developing New Competencies	Potential for Accessing Other Firms' Competencies
Solo Internal Development	Low	High	High	Yes	Yes	No
Strategic Alliances	Varies	Varies	Low	Yes	Yes	Sometimes
Joint Ventures	Low	Shared	Shared	Yes	Yes	Yes
Licensing In	High	Medium	Low	Sometimes	Sometimes	Sometimes
Licensing Out	High	Low	Medium	Yes	No	Sometimes
Outsourcing	Medium/High	Medium	Medium	Sometimes	No	Yes
Collective Research Organizations	Low	Varies	Varies	Yes	Yes	Yes

can be fast, cost-effective, and still enable the firm to retain a considerable amount of control. Most alliances offer opportunities for leveraging existing competencies or developing new competencies. Strategic alliances may or may not offer potential for accessing another firm's competencies depending on the alliance's purpose and structure.

By comparison, a joint venture is much more structured. While a joint venture typically involves developing a new technology and can take almost as long as solo internal development, it may be slightly faster due to the combination of the capabilities of multiple firms. Joint ventures enable partners to share the cost of the development effort, but they must also share control. Because joint ventures typically entail a long-term relationship between two or more firms that results in the development of a new product or business, joint ventures offer great potential for leveraging a firm's existing competencies, developing new competencies, and accessing its partners' competencies. Joint ventures may be more appropriate than a strategic alliance or solo internal development when the firm places great importance on access to other firms' competencies.

Licensing in technology offers a fast way to access a new technology that is typically lower in cost than developing it internally. The firm typically has limited discretion over what it can do with the technology, however, and thus has a low degree of control. Depending on the firm's capability mix and the nature of what it has licensed, licensing can sometimes offer the potential of leveraging a firm's existing competencies, developing new competencies, and accessing another organization's competencies. For example, many potential drugs or medical therapies are first developed in university research centers or medical schools. Pharmaceutical and biotechnology firms then license the right to explore whether the discovery has potential as a commercially viable medical treatment using their own drug development, testing, and manufacturing capabilities. Licensing the promising compounds or therapies enables the pharmaceutical and biotechnology firms to obtain drug targets quickly, thus helping them keep their pipelines full. It also helps the firms focus their development efforts on projects that have already demonstrated some treatment potential.

Licensing can also be good way for a firm to obtain enabling technologies that are necessary for its products or services, but that are not central to the firm's competitive advantage. For example, while producers of digital cameras need to be able to incorporate batteries that are long-lasting, light, and affordable in their camera designs, most camera producers do not perceive battery power as being central to their competitive advantage, and thus rely on externally sourced technology to meet this need. Licensing can also be an effective way for a firm that lacks technological expertise to gain initial market entry and experience that it can later build upon in developing its own technological capabilities.

Licensing out a technology offers a fast way for a firm to extend the reach of its technology that is nearly free and offers the potential for royalties. The firm relinquishes some control over the technology, but also retains a moderate amount of control through restrictions in the license agreement. Licensing out a technology explicitly leverages the firm's existing competencies by enabling the technology to be deployed in a wider range of products or markets than the firm participates in itself. It offers little opportunity for developing new competencies, however.

Sometimes licensing out a technology is a way of accessing another firm's competencies, as when a firm uses licensing to expand its technology into products or markets in which it has little expertise.

When a firm outsources design, production, or distribution of its technology, it is intentionally giving up a moderate amount of control to rapidly gain access to another firm's expertise and/or lower cost structure. While the firm pays to outsource activities, it typically pays less than it would to develop the capability of performing those activities in-house, and it gains access to those activities more quickly than it could develop them in-house. While outsourcing offers little opportunity for building new competencies, it can leverage the firm's existing competencies by enabling it to focus on those activities in which it earns its greatest returns. For example, Nike's strategy of outsourcing nearly all its athletic shoe production to contract manufacturers in Asia enables Nike to focus on its competitive advantages in design and marketing while tapping the lower labor and capital costs of its manufacturers. Thus, outsourcing might sometimes be appropriate for (*a*) firm activities that are not central to its competitive advantage, (*b*) activities that would cause the firm to give up crucial flexibility if performed in-house, or (*c*) activities in which the firm is at a cost or quality disadvantage.

Participation in a collective research organization is typically a long-term commitment rather than an effort to rapidly access capabilities or technology. As with strategic alliances, the nature of a firm's participation in a collective research organization can take many forms; thus, cost and control can vary significantly. Collective research organizations can be very valuable ways for the firm to leverage and build upon its existing competencies, as well as to learn from other participating organizations. Though collective research organizations may not yield immediate returns in the form of new products or services, participating in collective research organizations can be extremely useful in industries that have complex technologies and require considerable investment in basic science. By pooling their knowledge and effort, firms in collective research organizations can share the cost and risk of basic research, while accelerating the rate at which it yields useful new solutions.

CHOOSING AND MONITORING PARTNERS

Gaining access to another firm's skills or resources through collaboration is not without risks.[53] It may be difficult to determine if the resources provided by the partner are a good fit, particularly when the resource gained through the collaboration is something as difficult to assess as experience or knowledge. It is also possible that a collaboration partner will exploit the relationship, expropriating the company's knowledge while giving little in return. Furthermore, since managers can monitor and effectively manage only a limited number of collaborations, the firm's effectiveness at managing its collaborations will decline with the number of collaborations to which it is committed. This raises not only the possibility of diminishing returns to the number of collaborations, but also negative returns as the number of collaborations grows too large.[54] These risks can be minimized if the company limits the number of collaborations in which it engages, chooses its partners very carefully, and establishes appropriate monitoring and governance mechanisms to limit opportunism.[55]

Partner Selection

The success of collaborations will depend in large part on the partners chosen. A number of factors can influence how well suited partners are to each other, including their relative size and strength, the complementarity of their resources, the alignment of their objectives, and their similarity of values and culture.[56] These factors can be boiled down to two dimensions: resource fit and strategic fit.[57]

Resource fit refers to the degree to which potential partners have resources that can be effectively integrated into a strategy that creates value.[58] Such resources may be either complementary or supplementary. Most collaborations are motivated by the need to access resources the firm does not possess; such collaborations are based on the combination of complementary resources. Most of the examples in this chapter have entailed complementary resources, such as the combination of Apple's computer technology with Canon's printer engine technology, or the combination of Abgenix's drug leads with the development and distribution experience of larger biotechnology and pharmaceutical firms. Other collaborations seek supplementary stocks of resources that are similar to those possessed by the firm. The pooling of supplementary resources can enable partners to achieve market power or economies of scale. For example, British Petroleum and Mobil consolidated many of their operations in Europe to gain economies of scale and lower their cost structure.[59]

Strategic fit refers to the degree to which partners have compatible objectives and styles. The objectives of the partners need not be the same as long as the objectives can be achieved without harming the alliance or the partners. Not knowing a partner's true objectives or forging an alliance with a partner with incompatible objectives can result in conflict, wasted resources, and forfeited opportunities. Das and Teng provide an example of an alliance forged between General Motors and South Korea's Daewoo. While GM desired to use the alliance to drive down costs on its existing automobile models, Daewoo's objective was to develop new technologies and design new models. The alliance ultimately failed because of the incompatibility of GM's cost orientation and Daewoo's R&D orientation.[60]

Firms can also evaluate potential partners using many of the same tools used to evaluate the firm's own position and strategic direction (for a review of these, see Chapter Six). This includes assessing how collaboration with the partner is likely to impact the firm's opportunities and threats in its external environment; its internal strengths, weaknesses, or potential for sustainable competitive advantage; and the firm's ability to achieve its strategic intent.

Impact on Opportunities and Threats in the External Environment

Assessing the collaboration's impact on the firm's opportunities and threats includes asking such questions as:

1. How would the collaboration change the bargaining power of customers or suppliers?
2. Would the collaboration impact the threat of entry? For example, is the partner likely to become a new competitor? Does the partnership raise barriers to entry for other potential entrants?
3. Would the collaboration impact the firm's position vis-à-vis its rivals?

4. Would the collaboration influence the availability of complementary goods or the threat of substitutes?

Impact on Internal Strengths and Weaknesses

Assessing the collaboration's impact on the firm's strengths and weaknesses includes asking such questions as:

1. How would the collaboration leverage or enhance the firm's strengths? Does the collaboration put any of those strengths at risk?
2. How would the collaboration help the firm overcome its weaknesses?
3. Is the collaboration likely to yield a position of competitive advantage that is difficult for competitors to imitate? Is such a competitive advantage achievable without collaborating?
4. Would the collaboration leverage or enhance the firm's core capabilities?
5. Is the collaboration likely to impact the firm's financial strengths or weaknesses?

Impact on Strategic Direction

Assessing the fit of the collaboration with the firm's strategic direction includes asking such questions as:

1. How does this collaboration fit with the firm's statement of strategic intent?
2. Is the collaboration likely to help the firm close any resource or technology gap between where it is now and where it would like to be?
3. Are the objectives of the collaboration likely to change over time? How are such changes likely to be compatible or incompatible with the firm's strategic direction?

Partner Monitoring and Governance

governance
The act or process of exerting authority and/or control.

Successful collaboration agreements typically have clear, yet flexible monitoring and **governance** mechanisms.[61] Not surprisingly, the more resources put at risk by the collaboration (for example, the greater the upfront investment or the more valuable the intellectual property contributed to the collaboration), the more governance structure partner firms are likely to impose on the relationship.[62] Many collaboration agreements utilize legally binding contractual arrangements to ensure that partners (*a*) are fully aware of their rights and obligations in the collaboration and (*b*) have legal remedies available if a partner should violate the agreement. Such contracts typically include:

1. What each partner is obligated to contribute to the collaboration, including money, services, equipment, intellectual property, and so on.
2. How much control each partner has in the arrangement. For example, the contract may stipulate whether partners have the right to admit new partners to the relationship or change the terms of the agreement. It may also stipulate the rights partners will have over any proprietary products or processes developed in the course of the collaboration.
3. When and how proceeds of the collaboration will be distributed. For example, the collaboration agreement may stipulate whether cash, intellectual property rights, or other assets will be distributed and the schedule of such distribution.

Such contracts also often include mechanisms for monitoring each partner's adherence to the agreement, such as through regular review and reporting requirements.[63] Some collaboration agreements include provisions for periodic auditing either by the partner organizations or a third party. Many agreements also include provisions for terminating the relationship if the need for the alliance ends (for example, if the mission of the alliance is completed or the goals of the partner firms have changed) or partners encounter disputes they cannot resolve.[64] Markets and strategies change over time, and effective collaboration agreements should be flexible enough to be adapted in the event of change and provide a graceful exit strategy for members that no longer wish to participate in the collaboration.

Summary of Chapter

1. A number of factors will influence whether a firm chooses to collaborate on an innovation. Some of the most important include whether the firm (or a potential partner) has the required capabilities or other resources, the degree to which collaboration would make proprietary technologies vulnerable to expropriation by a potential competitor, the importance the firm places on controlling the development process and any innovation produced, and the role of the development project in building the firm's own capabilities or permitting it to access another firm's capabilities.

2. Firms may choose to avoid collaboration when they already possess the necessary capabilities and other resources in-house, they are worried about protecting proprietary technologies and controlling the development process, or they prefer to build capabilities in-house rather than access a partner firm's capabilities.

3. Some of the advantages of collaboration include sharing costs and risks of development, combining complementary skills and resources, enabling the transfer of knowledge between firms and the joint creation of new knowledge, and facilitating the creation of shared standards.

4. The term *strategic alliances* refers to a broad class of collaboration activities that may range from highly structured (e.g., joint ventures) to informal. Strategic alliances can enable simple pooling of complementary resources for a particular project, or they may enable the transfer of capabilities between partners. The transfer of capabilities often requires extensive coordination and cooperation.

5. A joint venture is a partnership between firms that entails a significant equity investment and often results in the creation of a new separate entity. Joint ventures are usually designed to enable partners to share the costs and risks of a project, and they have great potential for pooling or transferring capabilities between firms.

6. Licensing involves the selling of rights to use a particular technology (or other resource) from a licensor to a licensee. Licensing is a fast way of accessing (for the licensee) or leveraging (for the licensor) a technology, but offers little opportunity for the development of new capabilities.

7. Outsourcing enables a firm to rapidly access another firm's expertise, scale, or other advantages. Firms might outsource particular activities so that they can avoid the fixed asset commitment of performing those activities in-house.

Outsourcing can give a firm more flexibility and enable it to focus on its core competencies. Overreliance on outsourcing, however, can make the firm hollow.

8. Groups of organizations may form collective research organizations to jointly work on advanced research projects that are particularly large or risky.

9. Each form of collaboration mode poses a different set of trade-offs in terms of speed, cost, control, potential for leveraging existing competencies, potential for developing new competencies, or potential for accessing another firm's competencies. An organization should evaluate these trade-offs in formulating a collaboration strategy.

10. Successful collaboration requires choosing partners that have both a resource fit and strategic fit.

11. Successful collaboration also requires developing clear and flexible monitoring and governance mechanisms to ensure that partners understand their rights and obligations, and have methods of evaluating and enforcing each partner's adherence to these rights and obligations.

Discussion Questions

1. What are some advantages and disadvantages of collaborating on a development project?

2. How does the mode of collaborating (e.g., strategic alliance, joint venture, licensing, outsourcing, collective research organization) influence the success of a collaboration?

3. Identify an example of collaboration between two or more organizations. What were the advantages and disadvantages of collaboration versus solo development? What collaboration mode did the partners choose? What were the advantages and disadvantages of the collaboration mode?

4. If a firm decides it is in its best interest to collaborate on a development project, how would you recommend the firm choose a partner, a collaboration mode, and governance structure for the relationship?

Endnotes

1. R. Dolan, "Abgenix and the XenoMouse," Harvard Business School case #9-501-061, 2001.

2. www.abgenix.com.

3. J. Gillis, "Biotech Firms in Alliance; Creating Antibodies Is Venture's Goal," *Washington Post,* December 2, 1999, p. E1–6.

4. Dolan, "Abgenix and the XenoMouse."

5. Ibid.

6. B. Doherty, "Of Mice and Men: CEO Adds Chapter at Abgenix," *San Francisco Business Times,* January 25, 2002, p. 18.

7. C. W. L. Hill, "Monsanto: Building a Life Sciences Company," in *Cases in Strategic Management,* eds. C. W. L. Hill and G. Jones (Boston: Houghton Mifflin, 2004); and S. Brooks, M. A. Schilling, and J. Scrofani, "Monsanto: Better Living through Genetic Engineering?" in *Strategic Management, Competitiveness and Globalization,* 5th ed., eds. M. Hitt, R. Hoskisson, and R. D. Ireland (Minneapolis/St. Paul: West Publishing, 2002).

8. R. T. Fraley, S. B. Rogers, and R. B. Horsch, "Use of a Chimeric Gene to Confer Antibiotic Resistance to Plant Cells. Advances in Gene Technology: Molecular Genetics of Plants and Animals," *Miami Winter Symposia* 20 (1983a), pp. 211–21.

9. R. Melcer, "Monsanto Wants to Sow a Genetically Modified Future," *St. Louis Post Dispatch,* February 24, 2003.

10. M. Takanashi, J. Sul, J. Johng, Y. Kang, and M. A. Schilling, "Honda Insight: Personal Hybrid," New York University teaching case, 2003; and "Toyota, Honda Forge Ahead in Hybrid Vehicle Development," AP Newswire, March 13, 2002.

11. L. Gunter, 2002, "The Need for Speed," *Boeing Frontiers.* Retrieved November 20, 2002, from www.boeing.com/news/frontiers/archive/2002/july/i_ca2.html.

12. Su Han Chan, W. John Kensinger, J. Arthur Keown, and D. John Martin, "Do Strategic Alliances Create Value?" *Journal of Financial Economics* 46 (1997), pp. 199–221.

13. G. Hamel, Y. L. Doz, and C. K. Prahalad, "Collaborate with Your Competitors—and Win," *Harvard Business Review,* January–February 1989, pp. 133–39; W. Shan, "An Empirical Analysis of Organizational Strategies by Entrepreneurial High-Technology," *Strategic Management Journal* 11 (1990), pp. 129–39; G. P. Pisano, "The R&D Boundaries of the Firm: An Empirical Analysis," *Administrative Science Quarterly* 35 (1990), pp. 153–76; and R. Venkatesan, "Strategic Sourcing: To Make or Not to Make," *Harvard Business Review* 70, no. 6 (1992), pp. 98–107.

14. D. Teece, "Profiting from Technological Innovation: Implications for Integration, Collaboration, Licensing and Public Policy," *Research Policy* 15 (1986), pp. 285–305.

15. D. C. Mowery, J. E. Oxley, and B. S. Silverman, "Technological Overlap and Interfirm Cooperation: Implications for the Resource-Based View of the Firm," *Research Policy* 27 (1998), pp. 507–24; J. A. C. Baum, T. Calabrese, and B. S. Silverman, "Don't Go It Alone: Alliance Network Composition and Startups' Performance in Canadian Biotechnology," *Strategic Management Journal* 21 (2000), p. 267; J. P. Liebeskind, A. L. Oliver, L. Zucker, and M. Brewer, "Social Networks, Learning, and Flexibility: Sourcing Scientific Knowledge in New Biotechnology Firms," *Organization Science* 7 (1996), pp. 428–44; and L. Rosenkopf and P. Almeida, "Overcoming Local Search through Alliances and Mobility," *Management Science* 49 (2003), p. 751.

16. J. Hagerdoon, A. N. Link, and N. S. Vonortas, "Research Partnerships," *Research Policy* 29 (2000), pp. 567–86.

17. "More Cohesive Industry Standards Ahead?" *Frontline Solutions* 3, no. 9 (2002), p. 58; and B. Smith, "OMA Starts Ringing in the Future," *Wireless Week* 8, no. 42 (2002), pp. 1, 46.

18. N. S. Vonortas, National Cooperative Research Act–Research Joint Ventures (NCRA–RJV) database, unpublished tabulations, Center for International Science and Technology Policy, Elliott School of International Affairs, George Washington University, Washington, DC, 2001.

19. J. Hagerdoon, Maastricht Economic Research Institute on Innovation and Technology (MERIT), Cooperative Agreements and Technology Indicators (CATI) database, unpublished tabulations, Maastricht, Netherlands, 2001.

20. Rosenkopf and Almeida, "Overcoming Local Search through Alliances and Mobility"; and Liebeskind, Oliver, Zucker, and Brewer, "Social Networks, Learning, and Flexibility."

21. G. Ahuja, "Collaboration Networks, Structural Holes, and Innovation: A Longitudinal Study," *Administrative Science Quarterly* 45 (2000), pp. 425–55.

22. N. H. Kang and K. Sakai, "International Strategic Alliances: Their Role in Industrial Globalisation," Paris, Organisation for Economic Co-operation and Development, Directorate for Science, Technology, and Industry, working paper 2000/5.

23. Teece, "Profiting from Technological Innovation."

24. M. A. Schilling and K. Steensma, "The Use of Modular Organizational Forms: An Industry Level Analysis," *Academy of Management Journal* 44 (2001), pp. 1149–69.

25. R. McGrath, "A Real Options Logic for Initiating Technology Positioning Investments," *Academy of Management Review* 22 (1997), pp. 974–96.

26. S. Ghoshal and P. Moran, "Bad for Practice: A Critique of the Transaction Cost Theory," *Academy of Management Review* 21 (1996), pp. 13–47.

27. C. K. Prahalad and G. Hamel, "The Core Competence of the Corporation," *Harvard Business Review,* May–June 1990, pp. 79–91; and Hamel, Doz, and Prahalad, "Collaborate with Your Competitors—and Win."

28. Y. Doz and G. Hamel, "The Use of Alliances in Implementing Technology Strategies," in *Managing Strategic Innovation and Change,* eds. M. L. Tushman and P. Anderson (Oxford: Oxford University Press, 1997).

29. G. W. Weiss, "The Jet Engine That Broke All the Records: The GE-SNECMA CFM-56," *Case Studies in Technology Transfer and National Security;* and P. Siekman, "GE Bets Big on Jet Engines," *Fortune,* December 19, 2002.

30. A. Nanda and C. A. Bartlett, "Corning Incorporated: A Network of Alliances," Harvard Business School case #9-391-102, 1990.

31. K. R. Harrigan, "Strategic Alliances: Their New Role in Global Competition," *Columbia Journal of World Business* 22, no. 2 (1987), pp. 67–70.

32. Hamel, Doz, and Prahalad, "Collaborate with Your Competitors—and Win."

33. Ibid.

34. J. R. Harbison and P. Pekar, *Smart Alliances: A Practical Guide to Repeatable Success* (San Francisco: Jossey Bass, 1998); and Accenture estimates, 2000.

35. Thomson Financial, SDC Platinum, 2003; and Associated Press, May 15, 2002.

36. P. E. Teague, "Other People's Breakthroughs," *Design News* 58, no. 2 (2003), pp. 55–56.

37. I. Dierickx and K. Cool, "Asset Stock Accumulation and Sustainability of Competitive Advantage," *Management Science* 35 (1989), pp. 1504–14; and C. W. L. Hill, "Strategies for Exploiting Technological Innovations: When and When Not to License," *Organization Science* 3 (1992), pp. 428–41.

38. E. Baatz, "Rapid Growth Changes Rules for Purchasing," *Purchasing* 126, no. 10 (1999), pp. 33–36.

39. "U.S. and Worldwide Outsourcing Markets and Trends, 1998–2003," International Data Corporation.

40. J. Holmes, "The Organization and Locational Structure of Production Subcontracting," in *Production, Work, Territory: The Geographical Anatomy of Industrial Capitalism,* eds. M. Storper and A. J. Scott (Boston: Allen and Unwin, 1986), pp. 80–106; and Teece, "Profiting from Technological Innovation."

41. Schilling and Steensma, "The Use of Modular Organizational Forms."

42. W. Royal, "Contract Manufacturing: Perils and Profits," *Industry Week,* November 11, 1999.

43. Nortel Networks, 10K, 2002.

44. M. Heinsl, "Buying into the New Economy," *The Wall Street Journal,* July 25, 2000, pp. B1–B4.

45. D. Lei and M. A. Hitt, "Strategic Restructuring and Outsourcing: The Effect of Mergers and Acquisitions and LBOs on Building Firm Skills and Capabilities," *Journal of Management* 21 (1995), pp. 835–60.

46. Prahalad and Hamel, "The Core Competence of the Corporation."

47. Ibid.

48. Pisano, "The R&D Boundaries of the Firm."

49. Schilling and Steensma, "The Use of Modular Organizational Forms."

50. V. K. Narayanan, *Managing Technology and Innovation for Competitive Advantage* (Upper Saddle River, NJ: Prentice Hall, 2001).

51. C. Pellerin, "Consortia: Free Enterprise Meets Cooperation and the Results Can Be Good for Robotics," *The Industrial Robot* 22, no. 1 (1995), p. 31.

52. Associated Press, July 11, 2002.

53. C. W. L. Hill, "Strategies for Exploiting Technological Innovations: When and When Not to License," *Organization Science* 3 (1992), pp. 428–41; W. Shan, "An Empirical Analysis of Organizational Strategies by Entrepreneurial High-Technology," *Strategic Management Journal* 11 (1990), pp. 129–39; and Teece, "Profiting from Technological Innovation."

54. M. A. Schilling and C. W. L. Hill, "Managing the New Product Development Process: Strategic Imperatives," *Academy of Management Executive* 12, no. 3 (1998), pp. 67–81.

55. O. E. Williamson, *The Economic Institutions of Capitalism* (New York: Free Press, 1985).

56. J. Bleeke and D. Ernst, "Is Your Strategic Alliance Really a Sale?" *Harvard Business Review* 73, no. 1 (1995), pp. 97–105; T. K. Das and B. Teng, "Between Trust and Control: Developing Confidence in Partner Cooperation in Alliances," *Academy of Management Review* 23 (1998b), pp. 491–512; R. M. Kanter, "Collaborative Advantage: The Art of Alliances," *Harvard Business Review* 72, no. 4 (1994), pp. 96–108; and B. Uzzi, "Social Structure and Competition in Interfirm Networks: The Paradox of Embeddedness," *Administrative Science Quarterly* 42 (1997), pp. 35–67.

57. T. K. Das and B. S. Teng, "Managing Risks in Strategic Alliances," *Academy of Management Executive* 13, no. 4 (1999), pp. 50–62.

58. Ibid.

59. J. G. Crump, "Strategic Alliances Fit Pattern of Industry Innovation," *Oil & Gas Journal,* March 31, 1997, p. 59; and Das and Teng, "Managing Risks in Strategic Alliances."

60. Das and Teng, "Managing Risks in Strategic Alliances."

61. T. Pietras and C. Stormer, "Making Strategic Alliances Work," *Business and Economic Review* 47, no. 4 (2001), pp. 9–12.

62. R. Gulati and H. Singh, "The Architecture of Cooperation: Managing Coordination Costs and Appropriation Concerns in Strategic Alliances," *Administrative Science Quarterly* 43 (1998), pp. 781–814.

63. L. Segil, "Strategic Alliances for the 21st Century," *Strategy & Leadership* 26, no. 4 (1998), pp. 12–16.

64. Pietras and Stormer, "Making Strategic Alliances Work."

Chapter **Nine**

Protecting Innovation

Sun Microsystems and Java[1]

Sun Microsystems was founded in 1982 in Mountain View, California, as a manufacturer of high-end computer workstations. Since its inception, Sun believed that the power of the computer was in the network, not the individual personal computer (PC). A PC-centered approach to computing constrained a user's processing power and software applications to that contained within a single PC, but a network-centered approach enabled users to share processing power and applications that were distributed across a network. Sun believed that a network-centered approach would become increasingly powerful as computers (and their users) became more and more interconnected via advances in information technologies. Sun's motto was "The network is the computer." Following this belief, Sun produced workstations and servers with the greatest amount of intercommunication ability technology allowed. Sun also preferred to use technology based on shared standards rather than proprietary standards to ensure compatibility between Sun's products and those of other producers. By 1995, Sun had earned $7 billion in revenues and had grown to 20,000 employees.

Introducing Java: A Universal Language

In May 1995, Sun developed a new Web-oriented software programming language called Java with the aim of revolutionizing the computing industry. Unlike other programs, Java-based software was capable of being run on any computer, using any operating system. A program created in the Java language could be "written once, and run anywhere." It could even work on small electronic devices such as personal digital assistants and cellular telephones.[2] Sun believed that the combination of Java and the rapidly growing Internet could shift the computer industry away from its "PC-centric" focus to a "network-centric" focus. Because Java enabled applications to run on any type of operating system, users would be able to share applications easily across different computing platforms. This would lessen the pressure to have a single operating system standard (and thus lessen the importance of Microsoft's Windows), while increasing the demand for products that encouraged interconnectivity (such as Sun's network-based products).

Liberal Licensing

Sun distributed Java through an extensive licensing agreement. Initially, Sun's licensing agreement allowed users to obtain and use Java for a small licensing fee. Sun required all licensees to submit their Java-based programs to Sun for compatibility tests, and limited the amount of changes licensees could make to the standard. Sun also retained control over all Java-related intellectual property, meaning that any changes, additions, or improvements that licensees made to Java were owned by Sun.

However, as the number of software engineers using Java grew to 900,000 by the end of 1998, many industry leaders thought that Java had outgrown Sun's control. Furthermore, some members of the computing industry resented Sun's restrictive licensing policy and argued that the policy contradicted Sun's open standards mantra. Even IBM, Sun's most loyal Java ally, believed Sun should have relinquished control of Java to independent standards bodies. Patricia Sueltz, then general manager for IBM's Java software, stated, "Java is bigger than any one company."[3]

Scott McNealy, chief executive officer, Sun Microsystems, however, feared that if Java were released to standards bodies, it would suffer the same fate as UNIX. In the early 1990s, the software community tried to standardize the UNIX operating language, but the effort failed. Though many companies adopted UNIX, each company customized the program to suit their purposes, causing fragmentation of the standard. Instead of a single unifying UNIX, many incompatible versions of UNIX emerged. "The problem with UNIX is that nobody protected the brand to mean something and the brand lost value," McNealy stated.[4]

A Change in Policy

Under heavy pressure from the computing industry, Sun gradually made Java more open. By 2003, Sun was freely distributing the Java source code under its "community source" program and had eliminated all royalty fees. However, Sun still required all Java-based software to be subjected to compatibility tests and retained all control over the intellectual property.[5] Sun also created its own standards body for Java, called the Java Community Process (JCP). This group consisted of leading Java programmers and, under the supervision of Sun, was in charge of managing Java. The JCP was responsible for all changes, updates, and regulations of the Java language. Sun believed that allowing companies to participate in the JCP would satisfy their demands for standardization, while at the same time retaining Sun's ultimate control over Java.

Discussion Questions

1. Why did Sun Microsystems freely distribute the Java source code even though the product could be protected through copyright?
2. How did Sun Microsystems expect to profit from Java if it gave the product away?

3. Why did other companies believe that Sun Microsystems was obligated to make Java even more open?

4. What were some reasons Sun Microsystems resisted giving away more control of Java?

OVERVIEW

A crucial element of formulating a firm's technological innovation strategy is determining whether and how to protect its technological innovation. Traditionally, economics and strategy have emphasized the importance of vigorously protecting an innovation in order to be the primary beneficiary of the innovation's rewards, but the decision about whether and to what degree to protect an innovation is actually complex. Sometimes *not* vigorously protecting a technology is to the firm's advantage—encouraging other producers (and complementary goods providers) to support the technology may increase its rate of diffusion and its likelihood of rising to the position of dominant design. In this chapter, we first will review the factors that shape the degree to which a firm is likely to appropriate the returns from its innovation, and the mechanisms available to the firm to protect its innovation. We then will consider the continuum between a wholly proprietary strategy and a wholly open strategy, examining the trade-offs inherent in decisions about whether (and to what degree) to protect or diffuse a technological innovation. The chapter concludes by listing factors the firm should consider in formulating its protection strategy.

APPROPRIABILITY

appropriability
The degree to which a firm is able to capture the rents from its innovation.

The degree to which a firm can capture the rents from its innovation is termed **appropriability.** In general, the appropriability of an innovation is determined by how easily or quickly competitors can imitate the innovation. The ease with which competitors can imitate the innovation is, in turn, a function of both the nature of the technology itself and the strength of the mechanisms used to protect the innovation.

tacit knowledge
Knowledge that cannot be readily codified or transferred in written form.

socially complex knowledge
Knowledge that arises from the interaction of multiple individuals.

Some technological innovations are inherently difficult for competitors to copy; the knowledge underlying the technology may be rare and difficult to replicate. A firm's unique prior experience or talent pool may give it a foundation of technical know-how that its competitors do not possess. If this knowledge base is **tacit** (i.e., it cannot be readily codified into documents or procedures) or **socially complex** (i.e., it arises through complex interactions between people), competitors will typically find it very difficult to duplicate.[6] For example, a firm that has a team of uniquely talented research scientists may have a rare and difficult-to-imitate knowledge base. While some of the skill of the research scientists may be due to imitable training procedures, *talent* typically implies that an individual (or group) has a natural endowment or ability that is very difficult, if not impossible, to replicate through training. Furthermore, if the unique capabilities of the research team arise in part from the nature of the interactions between the scientists, their performance will be socially complex. Interactions between individuals can significantly shape what each individual perceives, and thus what each individual—and the collective group—discovers or learns. The outcomes of these interactions are path dependent, and thus are idiosyncratic to the combination of individuals, the moment of the interaction, and the nature of the interaction. This means that knowledge can emerge from the interaction of a group that could not be replicated by any individual or any different group.

Many innovations, however, are relatively easy for competitors to imitate. Individuals and firms often employ legal mechanisms to attempt to protect their innovations. Most countries offer legal protection for intellectual property in the form of patent, trademark, copyright, and trade secret laws.

PATENTS, TRADEMARKS, AND COPYRIGHTS

patent
A property right protecting a process, machine, manufactured item (or design for manufactured item), or variety of plant.

trademark
An indicator used to distinguish the source of a good.

copyright
A property right protecting works of authorship.

While patents, copyrights, and trademarks are all ways of protecting intellectual property, they are each designed to protect different things. A **patent** protects an invention, and a **trademark** protects words or symbols intended to distinguish the source of a good. A **copyright** protects an original artistic or literary work. Thus, a typical computer might have components whose designs are protected by patents, logos such as "IBM Thinkpad" that are protected by trademark law, and software that is protected by copyright (though as discussed later in the section on patents, many types of software are now also eligible for patent protection).

Most sources attribute the origin of formalized protection of intellectual property to 15th century England, when the English monarchy began granting certain privileges to manufacturers and traders as signified by a "Letters Patent," which was marked with the king's Great Seal. The first known of these was granted by Henry VI to John of Utynam in 1449. This patent gave John a 20-year monopoly on a method of producing stained glass that had not been previously known in England.[7] Copyright protection did not arrive until 1710, when an Act of Parliament gave protection to books and other written works. While the use of trademarks (or more generally, marks of ownership) can be traced back as early as 3500 BC, trademark protection laws did not begin to emerge until the late 1700s. In 1791, Thomas Jefferson supported the requests of sailcloth makers by recommending the establishment of trademark protection based on the commerce clause of the constitution. Trademark laws were later enacted in France (1857) and the United Kingdom (1862).[8] The first international trademark agreement was reached in 1883 at the Paris Convention for the Protection of Industrial Property.

Patents

In many countries, inventors can apply for patent protection for their inventions. In the United States, a patent is a property right granted by the federal government that excludes others from producing, using, or selling the invention in the United States, or from importing the invention into the United States, for a limited time in exchange for public disclosure of the nature of the invention at the time the patent is granted.[9]

Patents are often categorized into different types. In the United States, a *utility* patent may be granted to an inventor who creates or discovers a new and useful process, machine, manufactured item, or combination of materials. A *design* patent may be granted to the inventor of an original and ornamental design for a manufactured item. A *plant* patent may be granted to an inventor who invents or discovers and asexually reproduces any distinct and new variety of plant. Under U.S. patent law, an invention must pass three tests to be patentable:

1. It must be *useful* (i.e., it must produce a desirable result, solve a problem, improve on or propose a new use for an existing development or show potential of doing so).
2. It must be *novel* (i.e., it must not already be patented or described in public literature, or be in public use for more than a year).
3. It must *not be obvious* (i.e., a person with experience or skill in the particular art of the patent would not be expected to achieve the same invention with a normal amount of effort).

Discovery of scientific principles that pertain to natural laws (e.g., gravity) cannot be patented because they are considered to have always existed. Specifically, the following are not typically patentable:

- Substituting one material for another (e.g., plastic for metal).
- Merely changing the size of an already existing device.
- Making something more portable.
- Substituting an element for an equivalent element.
- Altering an item's shape.

Printed materials are not typically patentable, but it may be possible to protect them by copyright, as discussed in the next section.

Before 1998, most software algorithms were not eligible for patent protection—they were eligible only for copyright protection. However, when a Supreme Court case in 1998 upheld a patent on a computerized method of managing mutual funds that relied on software algorithms, it unleashed a flood of patent applications for software algorithms. From 1997 to 2000, patent filings for software-enabled methods of doing business increased more than 700 percent.[10] For example, Amazon patented its "I-click" system that streamlines the process by which customers place orders.[11]

Patenting an invention is a serious undertaking. To apply for a patent, the inventor must explain how to make and use the invention, and make claims about what it does that makes it a new invention. Drawings of the new invention are also often required. In the United States, this application is reviewed by a patent examiner who may modify the scope of the claims made by the patent. The patent is then published for a time in which other inventors can challenge the patent grant (if, for example, they believe that the patent infringes on previously granted patents). If the standards for patentability are met, the patent is then granted. The entire process from application to granting of the patent can take between two and five years. A number of costs are also involved in filing and maintaining a patent. The U.S. Patent and Trademark Office has two fee schedules—one for "small entities" (independent inventors and companies with less than 500 employees) and one for larger entities (see Figure 9.1). The entire patenting process in the United States typically costs a small entity between $3,000 and $8,000.[12] Part of this cost is in the form of filing, issuance, and maintenance fees paid to the patent

FIGURE 9.1
U.S. Patent and
Trademark
Office Fee
Schedule as of
January 2003

Fee Types	Regular Fee	Small Entity Fee
Patent Filing Fees		
Basic patent filing fee—utility	$750	$375
Design patent filing fee	330	165
Plant patent filing fee	520	260
Provisional patent application filing fee	160	80
Patent Issuance Fees (paid after Patent Office approves patent)		
Utility patent issue fee	$1,300	$650
Design patent issue fee	470	235
Plant patent issue fee	630	315
Patent Maintenance Fees (to keep patent in force)		
Due at 3.5 years after issuance of patent	$ 890	$ 445
Due at 7.5 years after issuance of patent	2,050	1,025
Due at 11.5 years after issuance of patent	3,150	1,575

office. Most inventors will also require the assistance of a patent attorney or patent agent, which imposes an additional cost.

Utility patents are typically granted more protection than other types of patents. Before 1995, the United States granted patent owners a term of 17 years of protection; however, in 1995, that term was extended to 20 years. While patent law varies considerably by country (as discussed in more detail below), almost every country assigns a protection term of 20 years to utility patents.

Patent Law around the World

Almost every country has its own laws governing patent protection. A patent granted in one country does not provide protection in other countries. People or firms seeking patent protection in multiple countries must apply in each of the countries in accordance with those countries' requirements.

Significant differences exist in national patent laws, and U.S. patent law is one of the more unusual. For example, in most other countries, publication of information about the invention before applying for a patent will bar the right to a patent, but the United States allows a one-year grace period (that is, an inventor can publish an invention up to a year before applying for the patent). Thus, if international patent protection will eventually be sought, inventors must uphold the stricter standard of applying for patent before publishing information about the patent, even if they plan to first patent the invention in the United States. Many countries also require that the invention be manufactured in the country in which a patent was granted within a certain time frame (often three years) from the time the patent is granted. This is called the "working requirement," and it effectively prevents inventors from patenting inventions in countries in which they have no intention of setting up production.

Several international treaties seek to harmonize the patent laws around the world. Two of the most significant are the Paris Convention for the Protection of Industrial Property and the Patent Cooperation Treaty.

Paris Convention for the Protection of Industrial Property

The Paris Convention for the Protection of Industrial Property (also known as the Paris Convention Priority) is an international intellectual property treaty adhered to by 164 countries as of January 2003. Under the Paris Convention, a citizen of any member country may patent an invention in any of the member countries and enjoy the same benefits of patent protection as if the inventor were a citizen of those countries. That is, the Paris Convention eliminates (for its member countries) any differential patent rights afforded to citizens of the country versus foreign nationals. Furthermore, the treaty also provides the right of "priority" for patents and trademarks. Once an inventor has applied for patent protection in one of the member countries, the inventor may (within a certain time period) apply for protection in all the other member countries. The time period is 12 months for utility patents and 6 months for design patents and trademarks. Most important, the applications to these later countries will be treated as if they were made on the same date as the first application. This enables the inventor to establish priority over any other patents applied for in those countries after the inventor made the first application. For example, if an inventor applied for a utility patent for an invention in Madagascar in January 2003, and another inventor applied for a patent for a very similar invention in France in June 2003, the Madagascar inventor can apply for patent protection in France in December 2003 and claim priority over the French invention. The French inventor would have to prove that his or her invention was substantively different from the Madagascar invention or the French inventor's patent would be denied.

As mentioned previously, in many countries, public disclosure of an invention makes it impossible to subsequently patent that invention. However, with the priority rights established under the Paris Convention, an inventor who patents an invention in one of the member countries can then publicly disclose information about that invention without losing the right to patent the invention in the other countries—each patent application will be treated as if it were applied for at the same time as the first application, and thus as if it were applied for before public disclosure. Without this treaty, it would be nearly impossible for an inventor to patent an invention first in the United States and then in other countries because U.S. patent applications are made available to the public.

Patent Cooperation Treaty (PCT)

Another very significant international patent treaty is the Patent Cooperation Treaty, or PCT. This treaty facilitates the application for a patent in multiple countries. An inventor can apply for a patent to a single PCT governmental receiving office, and that application reserves the inventor's right to file for patent protection in more than 100 countries for up to 2 1/2 years. Once the inventor has filed the application, a PCT governmental searching office will perform the patent search for the application (this search verifies that the invention is not already subject to a prior claim). Once the search is completed, the inventor can choose to enter Chapter II of the process wherein the PCT governmental office assesses the patentability of the invention subject to the standards of the Patent Cooperation Treaty. Eventually, the inventor must have the PCT application filed in each of the national patent offices in which the inventor is seeking protection.

FIGURE 9.2
Global
Coverage of
the Patent
Cooperation
Treaty,
January 2003

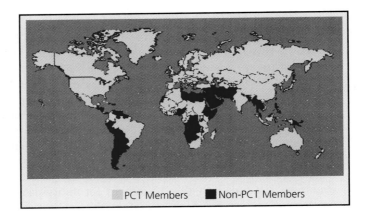

PCT Members ■ Non-PCT Members

Filing a single PCT application offers numerous advantages. First, applying for the PCT patent buys the inventor the option to apply to multiple nations later without committing the inventor to the expense of those multiple applications. With a PCT application, the inventor can establish a date of application in multiple countries (protecting the inventor's priority over later claims), while paying only the single PCT application fee rather than the numerous national application fees. Though the inventor will eventually have to pay for national applications in the countries in which protection is sought, the inventor can delay those costs. Thus, the inventor has time to assess the likelihood of the patent being granted and the potential profitability of the invention. If the PCT process suggests that the patent will not be granted or if it appears the invention has limited potential for earning returns, the inventor can forgo the expense of applying to the national offices.

Another advantage of the PCT process is that it helps make the results of patent applications more uniform. Though individual countries are not required to grant a patent to those inventions that are granted a patent by the PCT governing office, the granting of the patent by the PCT provides persuasive evidence in favor of granting the patent in the individual national offices. As of January 2003, there were 118 member states of the Patent Cooperation Treaty (see Figure 9.2).

Trademarks and Service Marks

A trademark is a word, phrase, symbol, design, or other indicator that is used to distinguish the source of goods from one party from the goods of others. The "Intel Inside" logo on many computers is one example of a trademark, as is the familiar Nike "swoosh" symbol. A service mark is basically the same as a trademark, but distinguishes the provider of a service rather than a product. Often the term *trademark* is used to refer to both trademarks and service marks.

Trademarks and service marks can be embodied in any indicator that can be perceived through one of the five senses. Most marks are embodied in visual indicators, such as words, pictures, and slogans. However, marks are also registered that use other senses such as sound (e.g., tones that are associated with a particular company or brand) or smells (as in fragrance). Trademark rights may be used to prevent others from using a mark that is similar enough to be confusing, but they may not be used to prevent others from producing or selling the same goods or services under a clearly different mark.

The rights to a trademark or service mark are established in the legitimate use of the mark and do not require registration; however, registration provides several advantages. First, registering the mark provides public notice of the registrant's claim of ownership over the mark. Second, marks must be registered before a suit can be brought in federal court against an infringement of the mark. Third, registration can be used to establish international rights over the trademark, as when the U.S. registration is used to establish registration in other countries, and to protect the mark against infringement from imported products. As of January 2003, the U.S. Patent and Trademark Office charged a $335 application fee and a $100 issuance fee for trademark registration. It normally takes from 10 to 16 months to receive certification from the U.S. Patent and Trademark Office, but the protection offered by the registration of the trademark begins from the date of filing. Unlike patents and copyrights, trademark protection can last as long as the trademark is in use, but the registration requires periodic renewal.

Trademark Protection around the World

Nearly all countries offer some form of trademark registration and protection. National or regional offices maintain a Register of Trademarks that contains information on all trademark registrations and renewals. To eliminate the need to register separately in each country (or region), the World Intellectual Property Organization administers a System of International Registration of Marks governed by two treaties: the Madrid Agreement Concerning the International Registration of Marks, and the Madrid Protocol. Countries that adhere to either (or both) the Madrid Agreement or Madrid Protocol are part of the Madrid Union. Any individual that lives in, is a citizen of, or maintains an establishment in a Madrid Union country can register with the trademark office of that country and obtain an international registration that provides protection in as many other Madrid Union countries as the applicant chooses. As of January 2003, there were 70 member countries of the Madrid Union.

Copyright

Copyright is a form of protection granted to works of authorship. In the United States, the authors of original literary, dramatic, musical, artistic, and certain other intellectual works can obtain copyright protection.[13] Like trademarks, the rights of copyright protection are established by legitimate use of the work. This protection is available whether or not the work is published and prevents others from producing or distributing that work. Under section 106 of the 1976 Copyright Act, the owner of the copyright has the exclusive right to do (or authorize others to do) the following:

- Reproduce the work in copies or phonorecords.
- Prepare derivative works based upon the work.
- Distribute copies or phonorecords of the work to the public by sale or other transfer of ownership, or by rental, lease, or lending.

- Perform the work publicly, in the case of literary, musical, dramatic, and choreographic works, pantomimes, and motion pictures and other audiovisual works.
- Display the copyrighted work publicly, in the case of literary, musical, dramatic, and choreographic works, pantomimes, and pictorial, graphic, or sculptural works, including the individual images of a motion picture or other audiovisual work.
- Perform the work publicly by means of a digital audio transmission (in the case of sound recordings).

There are, however, limitations to these rights. In particular, the doctrine of fair use stipulates that in most circumstances it is not a violation of copyright for others to use copyrighted material for purposes such as criticism, comment, news reporting, teaching, scholarship, or research. Furthermore, some types of work cannot be protected by copyright. For example, work that has not been fixed in a tangible form of expression (for example, a choreographed dance or improvisational speech that was not notated or recorded) is not eligible for copyright protection. Titles, names, short phrases, slogans, familiar symbols, and lists of ingredients also cannot be copyrighted.

Unlike patent protection, copyright protection is secured automatically when an eligible work is created and fixed in a copy or phonorecord for the first time. No publication or registration with the Copyright Office is necessary to establish this copyright, though registering the copyright is advantageous in that it establishes a public record of the copyright claim and is required before filing an infringement suit in court. As of February 2003, basic registration of copyright with the U.S. Copyright Office cost $30, and it took about four to six months to receive a certificate of registration.

Before 1978, copyright protection lasted only 28 years from the time it was secured (though during the last year the author could opt to renew the protection for an additional term). Revisions to U.S. copyright law, however, give copyright protection to works created after 1978 that lasts for the author's life plus an additional 70 years.

Copyright Protection around the World

As with patents and trademarks, no international copyright law automatically protects an author's work throughout the world. Copyright protection varies from country to country. However, most countries do offer copyright protection to both domestic and foreign works, and there are international copyright treaties for simplifying the process of securing such protection. One of the most significant is the Berne Union for the Protection of Literary and Artistic Property (known as the Berne Convention). The Berne Convention specifies a minimum level of copyright protection for all member countries, and it requires member countries to offer the same protection to both its own citizens and foreign nationals. Other treaties include the Universal Copyright Convention (UCC); the Rome Convention for the Protection of Performers, Producers of Phonograms and Broadcasting Organizations; the Brussels Convention Relating to the Distribution of Program-Carrying Signals Transmitted by Satellite; and the World Intellectual Property Organization Copyright Treaty.

TRADE SECRETS

trade secret
Information that
belongs to a
business that is
held private.

Rather than disclosing detailed information about a proprietary product or process in exchange for the grant of a patent, inventors or firms often will choose to protect their intellectual property by holding it as a **trade secret**. A trade secret is information that belongs to a business that is generally unknown to others. Trade secrets need not meet many of the stringent requirements of patent law, enabling a broader class of assets and activities to be protectable. For example, while the formula for a beverage is not patentable, it can be considered a trade secret. Trade secret law traces its history back to Roman law punishing individuals who induced someone to reveal the details of their employer's commercial affairs.[14]

Information is typically considered to be a trade secret only if it (*a*) offers a distinctive advantage to the company in the form of economic rents, and (*b*) remains valuable only as long as the information remains private. Examples of trade secrets might include information about a firm's customers, its marketing strategies, or its manufacturing processes. Trade secret law protects such information from being wrongfully taken by another party. In the United States, trade secret law is implemented at the state level, but the Uniform Trade Secret Act attempts to make these laws consistent from state to state.

For information to qualify as a trade secret under the Uniform Trade Secret Act, the information must meet the following three criteria:

- The information must not be generally known or readily ascertainable through legitimate means.
- The information must have economic importance that is contingent upon its secrecy.
- The trade secret holder must exercise reasonable measures to protect the secrecy of the information.

If information meets these criteria, the Uniform Trade Secret Act stipulates that its owner can prevent others from benefiting from this information without the owner's permission. In particular, the act states that no individual or group can copy, use, or otherwise benefit from a trade secret without the owner's authorization if they meet *any* of the following conditions:

1. They are bound by a duty of confidentiality (e.g., employees, lawyers).
2. They have signed a nondisclosure agreement.
3. They acquire the secret through improper means such as theft or bribery.
4. They acquire the information from someone who did not have the right to disclose it.
5. They learn about the secret by mistake but have reason to know that the information was a protected trade secret.

In most U.S. states, if owners of a trade secret believe that another party has stolen or improperly disclosed their trade secret, they can ask a court to issue an injunction against further use of the secrets, and they may also be able to collect damages for any economic harm suffered by the improper use of the trade secret. For example, in November 2002, Procter & Gamble sued Potlatch Corporation, claiming that Potlach had stolen trade secret methods used to produce Bounty paper towels and Charmin bath tissue by hiring away two of Procter & Gamble's paper manufacturing experts. Potlatch is a large, private-label tissue manufacturer that produces toilet paper, facial tissues, napkins, and paper towels for grocery store chains such as Albertsons and Safeway. By March 2003, the two companies had reached an agreement to settle out of court, keeping the terms of the settlement confidential.[15]

THE EFFECTIVENESS AND USE OF PROTECTION MECHANISMS

The methods—and their effectiveness—used to protect innovation vary significantly both within and across industries.[16] In some industries, such as pharmaceuticals, legal protection mechanisms such as patents are very effective. In other industries, such as electronics, patents and copyright provide relatively little protection because other firms can often invent around the patent without infringing on it (as IBM discovered with its personal computer design as described in the accompanying Theory in Action). It is also notoriously difficult to enforce patents protecting industrial processes such as manufacturing techniques. If patents provide little protection, the firm may rely more heavily on trade secrets; however, the ability to protect trade secrets also varies with the nature of the technology and the industry context. To protect a trade secret, a firm must be able to expose its product to the public without revealing the underlying technology, but in many cases, revealing the product reveals all.

For some competitive situations, protecting a technology may not be as desirable as liberally diffusing it. In industries characterized by increasing returns, firm sometimes choose to liberally diffuse their technologies to increase their likelihood of rising to the position of dominant design. As discussed in Chapter Four, learning curve effects and network externalities can cause some industries to demonstrate increasing returns to adoption: The more a technology is adopted, the more valuable it becomes.[17] This dynamic can lead to winner-take-all markets that create natural monopolies. A firm that controls the standard can reap monopoly rents and can exert significant architectural control over both its own industry and related industries.[18]

This enviable position can be so lucrative that firms may be willing to lose money in the short term to improve their technology's chance of rising to the position of dominant design. Thus, firms may liberally diffuse their technologies (through, for example, **open source software** or liberal licensing arrangements) to accelerate the technology's proliferation and thereby jump-start the self-reinforcing feedback effect that can lead to the technology's dominance. However, the firm often faces a dilemma: If it liberally diffuses the technology to would-be competitors, it relinquishes the opportunity to capture monopoly rents when and if the technology emerges as a dominant design. Furthermore, once control of a technology is relinquished, it can be very hard to regain; thus, such diffusion may result in the firm losing all hope of controlling the technology. Finally, liberal diffusion of the technology can result in the fragmentation of the technology platform: As different producers add improvements to the technology that make it better fit their needs, the "standard" may

open source software
Software whose code is made freely available to others for use, augmentation, and resale.

In 1980, IBM was in a hurry to introduce a personal computer. When personal computers first began to emerge at the end of the 1970s, most of the major computer manufacturers considered it no more than a peculiar product for a hobbyist market. The idea that individuals would want personal computers on their desks seemed ludicrous. However, as total U.S. personal computer sales reached $1 billion, IBM began to worry that the personal computer market could actually turn out to be a significant computer market in which IBM had no share. To bring a personal computer to market quickly, IBM decided to use many off-the-shelf components from other vendors, including Intel's 8088 microprocessor and Microsoft's software. However, IBM was not worried about imitators because IBM's proprietary basic input/output system (BIOS), the computer code that linked the computer's hardware to its software, was protected by copyright. While other firms could copy the BIOS code, doing so would violate IBM's copyright and incur the legendary wrath of IBM's legal team.

However, getting around IBM's copyright turned out to not be difficult. Copyright protected the written lines of code, but not the functions those codes produced. Compaq was able to reverse-engineer the BIOS in a matter of months without violating IBM's copyright. First, a team of Compaq programmers documented every function the IBM computer would perform in response to a given command, without recording the code that performed the function. This list of functions was then given to another team of "virgin" programmers (programmers who were able to prove that they had never been exposed to IBM's BIOS code).[19] These programmers went through the list of functions and wrote code to create identical functions. The result was a new BIOS that acted just like an IBM BIOS but did not violate its copyright. Compaq sold a record-breaking 47,000 IBM-compatible computers in its first year, and other clones were quick to follow.

be split into many nonstandardized versions (as with UNIX, as mentioned in the opening vignette, and described in more detail later in the chapter). To resolve these trade-offs, firms often adopt a strategy of partial protection for their innovations, falling somewhere on the continuum between wholly proprietary systems and wholly open systems.

Wholly Proprietary Systems versus Wholly Open Systems

wholly proprietary systems
Goods based on technology that is owned and vigorously protected through patents, copyrights, secrecy, or other mechanisms. Wholly proprietary technologies may be legally produced and augmented only by their developers.

Wholly proprietary systems are those based on technology that is company-owned and protected through patents, copyrights, secrecy, or other mechanisms. Such technologies may be legally produced or augmented only by their developers. Wholly proprietary systems are often not compatible with the products offered by other manufacturers. Because their operation is based on protected technology, other manufacturers are often unable to develop components that may interact with the proprietary system. Proprietary systems typically provide their developers with the opportunity to appropriate rents from the technology. However, they might also be less likely to be adopted readily by customers due to their higher costs and the inability to mix and match components.

wholly open systems
Goods based on technology that is not protected and that is freely available for production or augmentation by other producers.

In **wholly open systems,** the technology used in a product or process is not protected by secrecy or patents; it may be based on available standards or it may be new technology that is openly diffused to other producers. Wholly open technologies may be freely accessed, augmented, and distributed by anyone. Such technologies are usually quickly commoditized and provide little appropriability of rents to their developers.

Many technologies are neither wholly proprietary nor wholly open—they are partially open, utilizing varying degrees of control mechanisms to protect their technologies. It is useful to think of a control continuum that stretches from wholly proprietary to wholly open (see Figure 9.3). For instance, most of the major video game console producers (Nintendo, Sony, and Microsoft) utilize a wholly proprietary strategy for their consoles, but a limited licensing policy for their games. The licensing policies are designed to encourage developers to produce games for the systems, while simultaneously enabling the console producers to retain a great deal of control over the games produced. All games developed for the consoles must be approved by the console producer before they can be made commercially available. For example, in the case of Microsoft, would-be Xbox games developers must first apply to the Xbox Registered Developer Program (for established games developers) or the Xbox Incubator Program (for smaller or newer games developers). If accepted into one of these two programs, the developer will receive access to development tools, but this does not guarantee the approval of any resulting game titles. The games are subjected to a separate, rigorous approval process.

original equipment manufacturers (OEMs)
Firms that assemble goods using components made by other manufacturers, also called value-added resellers (VARs).

By contrast, the licensing policies for Microsoft's Windows are more open. Windows is protected by copyright, and Microsoft defends its exclusive right to augment the software; however, it also permits complementary goods providers to access portions of the source code to facilitate development of complementary goods, licenses the rights to such providers to produce complementary applications, and licenses **original equipment manufacturers (OEMs)** to distribute the software by bundling it with hardware. Those who purchase a license for the software can execute

FIGURE 9.3
Examples on the Continuum from Wholly Proprietary to Wholly Open

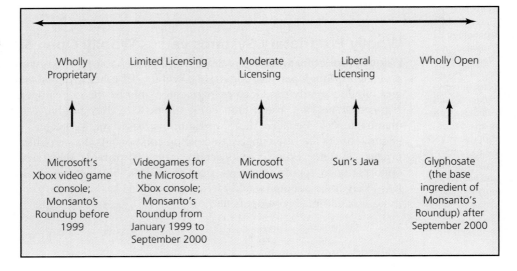

and bundle the software with other goods but may not augment the software. For example, software applications developers may produce and distribute value-added applications for use with Windows as long as those applications do not affect the functionality of the Windows program itself.

As described in the opening vignette, Sun's "community source" (as opposed to "open source") policy for Java is even more open. This policy grants anyone immediate access to the complete source code for Java and allows users to develop commercial applications based on the code, or to augment the code for their own implementations. These developers pay no license fee to Sun. However, any augmentation to the core structure of Java must be approved by the Java Community Process, which is managed by Sun. Sun's "community source" principle is meant to encourage the broader software community to improve Java and develop complementary applications, but it allows Sun to retain some control over the core platform to ensure that the platform does not become fragmented through unmanaged development by the software community.

Many technologies that were once wholly proprietary or partially open become wholly open once their patents or copyrights expire. For instance, Monsanto's highly profitable Roundup herbicide is based on a patented chemical ingredient called glyphosate. This extremely potent herbicide was adopted by farmers in more than 100 countries and accounted for a substantial portion of Monsanto's sales.[20] However, facing impending expiration of its patents, Monsanto began to license the rights to glyphosate production to a few other companies (including Dow Agrosciences, DuPont, and Novartis) in 1999. In September 2000, the U.S. patent on glyphosate expired, and any chemical company was free to produce and sell glyphosate-based herbicides in the United States, making glyphosate a wholly open technology.

Advantages of Protection

Because proprietary systems offer greater rent appropriability, their developers often have more money and incentive to invest in technological development, promotion, and distribution. If a single firm is the primary beneficiary of its technology's success, it has much greater incentive to invest in further developing the technology. The profits from the technology may be directly reinvested in further improvements in the technology. The sponsor of a proprietary technology might also adopt a penetration pricing strategy (that is, it may offer the technology at a low price or free) to rapidly build its installed base, it may spend aggressively on advertising to increase awareness of the technology, and it may even subsidize the production of complementary goods to increase the desirability of its technology to customers. A firm may be willing to lose money in the short term to secure the technology's position as the standard, because once the technology has emerged as a standard, the payoff can be substantial and enduring. By contrast, when multiple firms can produce a technology, losing money on the technology in the short term to promote it as a standard is highly risky because the long-term distribution of the payoffs is uncertain. While the technology's developer may have borne the bulk of the cost in developing the technology, multiple firms may vie for the profits to be made on the technology.

architectural control
The ability of a firm (or group of firms) to determine the structure, operation, compatibility, and development of a technology.

Protecting the technology also gives the developing firm architectural control over the technology. **Architectural control** refers to the firm's ability to determine the structure and operation of the technology, and its compatibility with other goods and services. It also refers to the firm's ability to direct the future development path of the technology. Architectural control can be very valuable, especially for technologies in which compatibility with other goods and services is important. By controlling the technology's architecture, the firm can ensure that the technology is compatible with its own complements, while also restricting its compatibility with the complements produced by others.[21] The firm can also control the rate at which the technology is upgraded or refined, the path it follows in its evolution, and its compatibility with previous generations. If the technology is chosen as a dominant design, the firm with architectural control over the technology can have great influence over the entire industry. Through selective compatibility, it can influence which other firms do well and which do not, and it can ensure that it has a number of different avenues from which to profit from the platform.

Microsoft's Windows is the quintessential embodiment of this strategy. Because Windows is the dominant operating system in the personal computing market and because it serves as the interface between a computer's hardware and software, Microsoft has considerable market power and architectural control over the evolution of the personal computer system. Among other things, Microsoft has been able to incorporate ever more utility programs into the core program, thereby expanding and taking over the roles of many other software components. Once a user purchased an operating system, uninstaller programs, disk-compression programs, and memory management programs separately, but Windows 95 and 98 integrated all these products and more into the operating system. This "feature creep" had a major impact on competition in the industry; many utility producers such as Qualitas, Stac Electronics, Microhelp, Quarterdeck, and others were forced to abandon their once-profitable products.

Advantages of Diffusion

The primary argument for diffusing a technology rather than protecting it is that open technologies may accrue more rapid adoptions. If multiple firms are producing, distributing, and promoting the technology, the technology's installed base may accumulate much more rapidly than if one firm alone is responsible for such activities. Competition among producers may drive the price of the technology down, making it more attractive to customers. Both customers and complementary goods providers may also perceive the technology as better (or its future more certain) if there are multiple companies backing the technology. This perception can lead to much more rapid adoption of the technology by customers and complementary goods providers, which further stimulates more companies to back the technology. Thus, a liberal diffusion strategy can stimulate the growth of the installed base and availability of complementary goods.[22]

Open technologies can also benefit from the collective development efforts of parties external to the sponsoring firm. For instance, Netscape Navigator, UNIX, and Linux are all technologies that have benefited significantly from external development. By making the source code freely available to the vast world of developers who could benefit from the technology, the technologies reaped the advantages of having a much larger pool of talent and resources directed at improving the technologies than could have been rallied by the original developers.

External development, however, poses some costs and risks. First, external development efforts typically lack the coordination of internal development. External developers may have very diverse objectives for the technology; rather than working together toward some unified vision of what the technology could achieve in the future, they might work in different, possibly even conflicting, directions.[23] Much of their effort may be redundant, as different external developers work on solving the same problems without communicating with each other. Finally, whether and how these improvements get incorporated into the technology and disseminated to other users of the technology can prove very problematic. UNIX provides a stark example of this.

UNIX was an operating system first developed by AT&T's Bell Laboratories in 1969. Though a Department of Justice injunction forbade AT&T from selling software commercially, it made the source code for the product available through licensing arrangements. Early licensees (notably, University of California—Berkeley) began using and adapting the software for their purposes, causing many incompatible versions of the software to emerge. Though the software community made several attempts to standardize the UNIX operating language, their efforts failed. AT&T also challenged the commercialization of several UNIX variants, but to no avail. Ultimately, AT&T sold the division responsible for UNIX to Novell, and Novell handed over the rights to the UNIX trademark to the X/Open standards setting body.[24]

Given the range of advantages (and risks) of protecting versus diffusing a technology, a firm must carefully consider the following factors in deciding whether, and to what degree, it should protect its innovation.

Production Capabilities, Marketing Capabilities, and Capital

If the firm is unable to produce the technology at sufficient volume or quality levels (or market the technology with sufficient intensity), then protecting the technology so that the firm is its sole provider may significantly hinder its adoption. For example, when JVC was promoting its VHS standard for video recorders, its management knew JVC was at a disadvantage in both manufacturing and marketing capabilities compared to Sony (which was promoting the Beta technology). JVC chose to vigorously pursue both licensing and OEM agreements, lining up Hitachi, Matsushita, Mitsubishi, and Sharp to boost the technology's production rate.[25]

Similarly, if complementary goods influence the value of the technology to users, then the firm must (*a*) be able to produce the complements in sufficient range and quantity, (*b*) sponsor their production by other firms, or (*c*) encourage collective production of the complements through a more open technology strategy. The only firms that have been successful in the U.S. video game industry were those that were able to produce games in-house (ensuring that a wide range of games would be available at the console's launch) and that encouraged third-party development of games (to ensure that the number of game titles grew quickly). Both Nintendo and Sega had previous arcade experience, and thus possessed considerable game development expertise. Microsoft had long been a producer of PC-based video games, so it had some game developing experience, and it also acquired a few small game developers (e.g., Bungie) to expand its expertise in developing console-type games.[26] Sony had no prior game experience, but aggressively acquired in-house developers, licensed external developers, and set up a program with Metrowerks to provide developer tools that would make it easier for external developers to produce PlayStation games. If a firm lacks the production capability or expertise to produce a sufficient range of complementary goods, or the capital to acquire such capabilities quickly, it should encourage collective production of complements through a more open technology strategy and utilize forms of sponsorship.

Industry Opposition against Sole Source Technology

Sometimes other industry members are able to exert strong pressure against the adoption of a technology that would give one (or a few) producer(s) undue control and power, causing a technology that is restricted to such production to be rejected or more hotly contested than a more open technology. This was the case with Sony and Philips' Super Audio CD (SACD) audio format. Sony and Philips had jointly created the original compact disc (CD) format and split the royalties on every CD player every sold, totaling hundreds of millions of dollars. The rest of the world's leading consumer electronics producers (including Hitachi, JVC, Matsushita, Mitsubishi, and Toshiba) and record producers (including Time Warner and Seagram's Universal Music group) banded together to form the Digital Video Disk (DVD) Audio consortium. This consortium's purpose is to promote the DVD Audio standard that is intended to displace the CD and enable royalties to be split among the 10 companies that control the patents.[27] Industry observers note that a driving force underlying the formation of the consortium was to prevent Sony and Philips from controlling yet another generation of audio formats. The degree of industry opposition to a sole-source technology needs to be considered when the firm formulates its technology strategy. If the industry is able to pose significant opposition, the firm may need to consider a more open technology strategy to improve the technology's likelihood of being chosen as a dominant design.

Resources for Internal Development

If a firm does not have significant resources (capital, technological expertise) to invest in the technology's functionality, it may have difficulty producing a technology that has an initial performance level, and rate of improvement, that the market finds attractive. In such instances, it can be valuable to tap the external development efforts of other firms (or individuals) through utilizing a more open technology strategy. For example, when Netscape found itself in a race to match browser capabilities with Microsoft, it was at a tremendous disadvantage in both human resources and capital. Microsoft had legions of internal developers and a lot of money to invest in Explorer; there was no way that Netscape could match those resources internally. Instead, Netscape tapped the external development community by giving them access to its source code and incorporating their improvements into the Navigator product.

Control over Fragmentation

For technologies in which standardization and compatibility are important, maintaining the integrity of the core product is extremely essential, and external development can put it at risk. As the UNIX example illustrates, if the developing firm relinquishes all control over the development of the technology, the technology will have no shepherd with the ability and authority to direct its trajectory and ensure that a single standard remains intact. This suggests that the developer of any technology that requires standardization and compatibility should retain some degree of control over the technology, or find/establish another governing body with the authority to do so.

Incentives for Architectural Control

Architectural control over the evolution of a technology is always valuable; however, it becomes particularly valuable if a firm is a significant producer of complements to the technology in question. A firm with architectural control can typically design the technology to be compatible with its own complements and incompatible with those of competitors. If the technology is chosen as the dominant design, this architectural control allows the firm to ensure that it reaps the lion's share of the rewards in complements production. Furthermore, by making the technology selectively compatible with some competitors and not others, the firm can exert great influence over the competitive field.

Architectural control can also enable the firm to direct the development efforts put into the technology so that it exploits the firm's core competencies. Technology trajectories are path dependent; minor events in their evolution can set them careening off into unexpected directions. A firm that has a significant stake in a particular evolution path (because, for example, it has technological competencies that are much more amenable to one path of evolution than other potential paths) may place a high value on architectural control, which can enable it to co-opt or destroy less favorable development paths by denying their progenitors access to the market.

Summary of Chapter

1. The degree to which a firm can capture the rents from its innovation efforts is largely determined by the degree to which competitors can quickly and easily imitate the innovation. Some innovations are inherently difficult to copy; others are difficult to copy due to the mechanisms the firm uses to protect its innovation.

2. The three primary legal mechanisms used to protect innovation in most countries are patents, trademarks, and copyrights. Each mechanism is designed to protect a different type of work or good.

3. International treaties have helped to harmonize patent, trademark, and copyright laws around the world. Most countries now have patent, trademark, and copyright laws of some form, and in some instances protection can be applied for in multiple countries simultaneously.

4. Trade secrets provide another mechanism of protecting innovation. Firms that protect their intellectual property as a trade secret often have legal recourse if another party wrongfully takes and uses such property.

5. Legal mechanisms for protecting innovation are more effective in some industries than others; in some industries, inventing around a patent or copyright is relatively easy. Similarly, in some industries it is nearly impossible to protect an innovation using trade secrets because commercializing the innovation reveals its underlying technologies.

6. Sometimes the choice between protecting versus diffusing a technology is not obvious. Both strategies offer potential advantages. Many firms use neither a wholly open nor wholly proprietary strategy, but rather a partially open strategy.

7. Protecting an innovation helps ensure that the firm earns the lion's share of the returns from the innovation. These returns can then be reinvested in further developing the technology, promoting the technology, and producing complementary goods.

8. Protecting an innovation also preserves the firm's architectural control, enabling it to direct the technology's development, determine its compatibility with other goods, and prevent multiple incompatible versions of the technology from being produced by other firms.

9. Diffusing a technological innovation can encourage multiple firms to produce, distribute, and promote the technology, possibly accelerating its development and diffusion. Diffusion can be particularly useful in industries that accrue increasing returns to adoption. It is also useful when the firm has inadequate resources to be the sole developer, producer, distributor, and marketer of a good.

Discussion Questions

1. What are the differences between patents, copyrights, and trademarks?

2. What factors should a firm considering marketing its innovation in multiple countries use formulating its protection strategy?

3. When are trade secrets more useful than patents, copyrights, or trademarks?

4. Identify a situation in which none of the legal protection mechanisms discussed (patents, copyrights, trademarks, trade secrets) will prove useful.

5. Describe a technological innovation not discussed in the chapter, and identify where you think it lies on the control continuum between wholly proprietary and wholly open.

6. What factors do you believe influenced the choice of protection strategy used for the innovation identified above? Do you think the strategy was a good choice?

Endnotes

1. D. Essner, P. Liao, and M. A. Schilling, "Sun Microsystems: Establishing the Java Standard," Boston University teaching case #2001–02, 2001.

2. www.java.sun.com.

3. Hof, D. Robert "Sun Power," *Business Week,* January 18, 1999, p. 78.

4. "Why Java Won't Repeat the Mistakes of UNIX," *Byte,* January 1997, p. 40.

5. Antone Gonsalves and Scot Petersen, "Sun Pulls Plug on Java Standardization Efforts," *PC Week,* December 12, 1999.

6. J. B. Barney, "Firm Resources and Sustained Competitive Advantage," *Journal of Management* 17 (1991), pp. 99–120.

7. U.K. Patent Office.

8. U.S. Trademark History Timeline at www.lib.utexas.edu/engin/trademark/timeline/tmindex.html.

9. Definition from the United States Patent and Trademark Office.

10. "Software Patent," *Bank Technology News* 14, no. 3 (2001), p. 25.

11. A. B. Silverman, "Software Patents for Methods of Doing Business—a Second Class Citizen No More," *JOM* 52, no. 19 (2000), p. 64.

12. www.patentcafe.com.

13. U.S. Copyright Office.

14. The Trade Secrets home page.

15. S. Decker, "Procter & Gamble, Potlatch Resolve Trade Secrets Suit," *Seattle Post Intelligencer,* March 14, 2003.

16. R. Levin, A. Klevorick, R. Nelson, and S. Winter, "Appropriating the Returns from Industrial Research and Development," *Brookings Papers on Economic Activity, Microeconomics* 3 (1987), pp. 783–820; and J. Bound, C. Cummins, Z. Griliches, B. H. Hall, and A. Jaffe, "Who Does R&D and Who Patents?" in *R&D Patents, and Productivity* ed. Z. Griliches (Chicago: University of Chicago Press for the National Bureau of Economic Research, 1984).

17. W. B. Arthur, *Increasing Returns and Path Dependency in the Economy* (Ann Arbor: The University of Michigan Press, 1994).

18. C. H. Ferguson and C. R. Morris, *Computer Wars* (New York: Random House, 1993); and R. Henderson and K. Clark, "Architectural Innovation: The Reconfiguration of Existing Product Technologies and the Failure of Established Firms," *Administrative Science Quarterly* 35 (1990), pp. 9–30.

19. R. Cringely, *Accidental Empires* (New York: HarperCollins, 1992).

20. S. Brooks, M. A. Schilling, and J. Scrofani, "Monsanto: Better Living through Genetic Engineering?" in *Strategic Management, Competitiveness and Globalization,* 5th ed., eds. M. Hitt, R. Hoskisson, and R. D. Ireland (Minneapolis/St. Paul: West Publishing, 2001).

21. M. A. Schilling, "Toward a General Modular Systems Theory and Its Application to Interfirm Product Modularity," *Academy of Management Review* 25 (2000), pp. 312–34.

22. C. W. L. Hill, "Establishing a Standard: Competitive Strategy and Technological Standards in Winner-Take-All Industries," *Academy of Management Executive* 11, no. 2 (1997), pp. 7–25; and M. A. Schilling, "Winning the Standards Race: Building Installed Base and the Availability of Complementary Goods," *European Management Journal* 17 (1999), pp. 265–74.

23. R. Garud, S. Jain, and A. Kumaraswamy, "Institutional Entrepreneurship in the Sponsorship of Common Technological Standards: The Case of Sun Microsystems and Java," *Academy of Management Journal* 45 (2002), pp. 196–214.

24. D. Essner, P. Liao, and M. A. Schilling, "Sun Microsystems: Establishing the Java Standard," Boston University teaching case #2001-02, 2001.

25. M. Cusumano, Y. Mylonadis, and R. Rosenbloom, "Strategic Maneuvering and Mass Market Dynamics: VHS over Beta," *Business History Review,* Spring 1992.

26. J. Kittner, M. A. Schilling, and S. Karl, "Microsoft's Xbox," New York University teaching case, 2002.

27. J. Brinkley, "Disk versus Disk: The Fight for the Ears of America," *New York Times,* August 8, 1999.

Part **Three**

Implementing Technological Innovation Strategy

In this section, we will cover the key aspects of implementing a technological innovation strategy, including:

- Structuring the firm to improve its likelihood of innovating, its effectiveness at new product development, and its speed of new product development.
- Managing new product development processes to maximize fit with customer needs, while simultaneously minimizing development cycle time and controlling development costs.
- Composing, structuring, and managing new product development teams to maximize new product development effectiveness.
- Crafting a strategy for effectively deploying the innovation into the marketplace, including timing, licensing strategies, pricing strategies, distribution, and marketing.

Implementing Technological Innovation Strategy

Chapter **Ten**

Organizing for Innovation

Procter & Gamble's "Organization 2005"

In fiscal year 2003, Procter & Gamble (P&G) earned $43.4 billion in net revenues, making it the largest household and personal products company in the world. Its most well-known brands included Tide, Cheer, and Ariel in laundry detergents; Cover Girl, Clairol, Oil of Olay, and Pantene in beauty care; Pampers and Luvs in diapers; Crest, Vicks, Prilosec, and Scope in health care; Eukanuba and Iams in pet food; Charmin, Bounty, and Puffs in paper products; and Folgers coffee and Pringles potato chips in beverages and snacks.

The Importance of Innovation at P&G

To spur sales growth in the mature and competitive markets in which it competes, P&G focuses heavily on new product development. P&G invests 4 percent of its worldwide sales in R&D, amounting to about $1.7 billion in 2003. In 2003, the company had almost 7,500 scientists working in 20 technical centers on four continents. In fact, Procter & Gamble employed more scientists holding PhDs than the combined science faculties of Harvard University, Stanford University, and MIT. The company receives about 3,800 patents a year and holds more than 29,000 active patents, making it one of the world's largest patent holders. P&G has more than 200 proprietary technologies on the market, organized into a dozen areas of technological competence such as metal ions (important in detergents and toothpaste), fats and oils (enabling innovations such as Olean, a noncaloric fat substitute used in products such as the "Wow!" line of Frito-Lay products and fat-free Pringles), and absorbent structures and materials (crucial for P&G's diaper, feminine hygiene, and paper tissue/towel lines).

P&G's innovation efforts were focused on two dimensions: setting new performance standards in existing product categories, and creating new product categories. For example, P&G set new performance standards in laundry detergent by introducing versions of Tide that removed stains and sanitized laundry while protecting the original fabric colors. Another new product performance standard was set in diapers, when the company developed the only diaper designed to treat and prevent diaper rash (Pampers Rash Guard). Examples of the company's development of new product categories include Febreze, an odor-eliminating fabric spray, and Dryel, a home dry-cleaning product. P&G's management believed that three key abilities provided the foundation for its success in new product development:

1. A deep understanding of consumers, their habits and product needs.
2. The capability to acquire, develop, and apply technology across P&G's broad array of product categories.
3. The ability to make connections between consumer desires and what technology could deliver.[1]

Organization 2005

"Organization 2005 is focused on one thing: Leveraging P&G's innovative capability. Because the single best way to accelerate our growth—our sales, our volume, our earnings growth—is to innovate bigger and move faster consistently across the entire company,"

Durk I. Jager, CEO of Procter & Gamble.[2]

In 1999, P&G had embarked on one of its biggest reorganizations in history: Organization 2005. The Organization 2005 program was a far-reaching set of initiatives designed to accelerate innovation and growth at the company. The program involved comprehensive changes in the company's structure, work processes, and culture. It would also entail many plant closures, laying off about 15,000 employees, and taking a large restructuring charge. The restructuring was expected to cost $1.9 billion to implement, but was also expected to save approximately $900 million annually by 2004. The plan would take seven years and would be led by Durk I. Jager who took the helm as CEO of P&G in January 1998. The Dutch-born Jager was known as a hard-driving taskmaster with a tough, hands-on approach.[3] His abrasive style and the aggressive changes he initiated at P&G earned him the nickname "Crazy Man Durk."[4]

A major thrust of the reorganization was to eliminate many of the bureaucratic layers at the company's Cincinnati headquarters, which would help make the company more nimble and responsive. Rather than centralizing all decision-making authority at the Cincinnati headquarters, more decisions would be made in the field. Furthermore, instead of all new product development occuring at headquarters, products would be developed both in foreign markets and in the United States. They would then be tested in foreign markets and midsize U.S. cities simultaneously. P&G's managers hoped this strategy would enable P&G to learn more about foreign markets and develop and deploy products more quickly. At the same time, regional divisions in the company would be broken apart and reassembled into global product-line divisions.

From Geographic Business Units to Product-Line Business Units

Before the reorganization, Procter & Gamble had four business units based on geographic regions: North America; Asia; Latin America; and Europe, Middle East and Africa. Within these business units were country managers who marketed a variety of products to a region. After the restructuring, P&G would have seven global business units based on product lines: baby care; beauty care; fabric and home care; feminine protection; food and beverage; health care and corporate; tissues and towel. Several of these business units would be headquartered in foreign cities. This shift was expected to foster greater—and faster—innovation by focusing strategy and profit responsibility on brands rather than geographies. This program would also simplify and standardize P&G's manufacturing operations by reducing P&G's production lines to a smaller number of standardized manufacturing platforms. To ensure that the diverse needs of local markets were still met, the initiative established new "market development organizations" responsible for tailoring the market strategies for the global brands to local markets. This shift appeared to have significantly shortened new product rollout. For example, in the Pantene shampoo and Pampers diaper lines, rollouts had decreased from three or more years to 18 months.[5]

Centralizing Business Services

Activities such as accounting, human resources, order management, and information technology had been highly decentralized before Organization 2005. The reorganization would bring these activities together into four regionally based global business services centers that would provide these services to all P&G business units at "best-in-class quality, cost, and speed."[6] Increasing the centralization of service activities was expected to help standardize work processes, simplify transactions, and leverage economies of scale. It was hoped that these changes would both improve service and reduce costs.

Transforming the Culture

P&G had long been known as a company with a culture of obsessive perfectionism and risk aversion.[7] Jager would attempt to transform the company's culture into one that permitted—even encouraged—risk-taking. By tearing apart the old-fashioned network of 144 regional managers, Jager broke up decades-old fiefdoms. He encouraged new managers to abandon P&G's tradition of consensus management and to instead be more innovative.[8] To reorient managers to focus on bolder goals and bigger innovations, the program would establish a reward system that more closely tied executive compensation with aggressive "stretch" business goals and results. Jager himself had committed to double-digit earnings gains in less than a year.

The Market Gets Impatient

By 2000, however, stockholders were beginning to wonder if Jager had overpromised and underdelivered. Early 2000 earnings continued to drop. Sales had been slower than expected, in part due to a strong dollar that hurt P&G's revenue in Europe. When Jager announced the numbers would be flat in March 2000, an already edgy stock market responded by dropping P&G's stock price more than 30 percent in a single day. In July 2000, when the company posted flat earnings instead of the 15 to 17 percent growth Jager had promised, the board of directors pressured Jager to step down from his role as CEO. He had spent only 18 months in the position. Jager was replaced by company veteran Alan Lafley as CEO, and in a surprising move, the CEO Jager had originally replaced, "Gentleman John" E. Pepper, came out of retirement to take over as chairman of the board. The company announced it would continue aspects of Jager's plan but would return to more traditional, conservative ways of doing business. Lafley stated, "In hindsight, it's clear we changed too much, too fast." The press even mockingly referred to the Organization 2005 initiative as "Dis-Organization 2005." By 2001, Lafley was even vowing to slow down on new product initiatives and was focusing his efforts on cutting underperforming product lines.

Some analysts thought the market had not given the reorganization enough time to take effect. For example, Daniel Peris from Argus Research noted, "The market's just impatient. It's not allowing executives as much time as they used to have, and it's inappropriate because a company like P&G cannot be turned around very quickly."[9] Peris also noted that part of the market's impatience was likely due to the dazzling stock performances of the high-tech sectors during the late 1990s: Investors were unwilling to wait out a tough time on P&G stock when other stock prices were soaring. Some analysts even felt that the abrasive Jager had been P&G's best hope of breaking through the company's rigid bureaucracy. As noted by Tim Ghriskey, a senior portfolio manager at the Dreyfus Corporation (a big P&G shareholder), "This was historically the ultimate white-shoe firm … P&G has always tested everything to death before bringing something new to market, or trying a new commercial or anything, and he [Jager] has just cut through that bureaucracy and really invigorated the company and modernized it, and you have to applaud that."[10]

Discussion Questions

1. What are some of the advantages and disadvantages of replacing P&G's regional divisions with global product divisions? What impact was this likely to have on P&G's innovation processes?
2. What are some of the advantages and disadvantages of centralizing P&G's business services?
3. What are some of the challenges of changing the culture of a company as big as P&G?
4. Was Organization 2005 a good idea? Should P&G's board of directors have given Jager more time?

OVERVIEW

The structure of an organization and the degree to which it uses formalized and standardized procedures and controls can significantly influence its likelihood of innovating, the effectiveness of its innovation projects, and the speed of its new product development processes.[11] For example, it is often argued that, small, flexible organizations with a minimum of rules and procedures will encourage creativity and experimentation, leading to more innovative ideas. At the same time, it is also frequently pointed out that well-developed procedures and standards can ensure that the organization makes better development investment decisions and is able to implement projects quickly and efficiently. How then do managers decide what structure and controls would make the most sense for their firm? In this chapter, we will review the research on how firm size and structural dimensions such as formalization, standardization, and centralization affect a firm's innovativeness. By focusing on these underlying structural dimensions, we will elucidate why some structures may be better for encouraging the creativity that leads to idea generation, while other structures may be better suited for efficient production of new products. We will also explore structural forms that attempt to achieve the best of both worlds—the free-flowing organic and entrepreneurial structures and controls that foster innovation, plus the formalized and standardized forms that maximize efficiency while ensuring coherence across all of the corporation's development activities. The chapter then turns to the challenge of managing innovation across borders. Multinational firms face particularly difficult questions about where to locate—and how to manage—their development activities. We will review some of the work emerging on how multinational firms can balance the trade-offs inherent in these choices.

SIZE AND STRUCTURAL DIMENSIONS OF THE FIRM

Size: Is Bigger Better?

In the 1940s, Joseph Schumpeter challenged supporters of antitrust law by proposing that large firms would be more effective innovators.[12] Schumpeter pointed out that (1) capital markets are imperfect, and large firms are better able to obtain financing for R&D projects, and (2) firms with larger sales volume over which to spread the fixed costs of R&D would experience higher returns than firms with lower sales volume. Large firms are also likely to have better-developed complementary activities such as marketing or financial planning that enable them to be more effective innovators, and they are also likely to have greater global reach to obtain information or other resources.

Another advantage of size may arise in scale and learning effects. If large firms spend more on R&D in an absolute sense, they might also reap economies of scale and learning curve advantages in R&D—that is, they may get better and more efficient at it over time.[13] Through investing in R&D, the firm develops competencies in the new product development process and thus may improve its development process. It may accumulate better research equipment and personnel. Furthermore, as a large firm gains experience in choosing and developing innovation projects, it may learn to make better selections of projects that fit the firm's capabilities and have a higher likelihood of success.

Large firms are also in a better position to take on large or risky innovation projects than smaller firms.[14] For example, only a large company such as Boeing could develop and manufacture a 747, and only large pharmaceutical companies can plow millions of dollars into drug development in hopes that one or two drugs are successful.[15] This suggests that in industries that have large development scale (i.e., the average development project is very big and costly), large firms will tend to outperform small firms at innovation. In theory a coalition of small firms ought to achieve the same scale advantages, but in practice, coordinating a coalition of firms tends to be very difficult. While a single large firm can exert hierarchical authority over all of the development activities to ensure cooperation and coordination, coalitions often do not have such a well-defined system of authority and control.

On the other hand, as a firm grows, its R&D efficiency might decrease because of a loss of managerial control.[16] That is, the bigger a firm gets the more difficult it can become to effectively monitor and motivate employees. Furthermore, as a firm grows, it becomes increasingly difficult for individual scientists or entrepreneurs to appropriate the returns of their efforts, therefore their incentives diminish.[17] Thus, as the firm grows, the effectiveness of its governance systems may decrease.

Large firms may also be less innovative because their size can make them less nimble and responsive to change. Large firms typically have more bureaucratic inertia due to many layers of authority and well-developed policies and procedures.[18] For example in the early 1980s, Xerox discovered that the administrative layers it had added to prevent errors in new product development had the unintended effect of blocking a project's progress, making product development cycles unacceptably long and putting Xerox at a disadvantage to more nimble Japanese competitors.[19]

High numbers of employees, large fixed-asset bases, and a large base of existing customers or supplier contracts can also be sources of inertia, making it difficult for the firm to change course quickly. As the number of employees grows, communication and coordination may become more difficult and prone to decision-making delays. When large firms have large fixed-asset bases and/or significant fixed costs, they often prefer to stick with existing sources of cash flow rather than gambling on big changes. Strategic commitments to customers and suppliers can also tie the firm to its existing businesses and technologies, making it more difficult to respond to technological change. Strategic commitments can thus lead to an *Icarus Paradox*—a firm's prior success in the market can hinder its ability to respond to new technological generations (for more on the Icarus Paradox see the accompanying Theory in Action).

Small firms are often considered more flexible and entrepreneurial than large firms. They are unencumbered by multiple layers of administration, large fixed-asset bases, or strategic commitments to large numbers of employees, customers, and suppliers. Small firms may also find it much simpler to monitor employees and reward them for their effort or success at innovation.[21] Because resources are less abundant, small firms may also be more motivated to choose projects more carefully, leading to higher rates of new product success.

A number of empirical studies have attempted to test whether large size improves or hampers innovation productivity. Several studies of patent counts, new drug introductions, and technological innovations that improve product performance have indicated that small firms often outperform large firms in innovation.[22] For example, a few studies of patenting output have concluded that small firms appear to spend their R&D dollars more carefully and are more efficient, receiving a larger number of patents per R&D dollar.[23] One study of 116 firms developing new business-to-business products also found that small firms (those with annual sales less than $100 million) had

According to Greek mythology, when King Minos imprisoned the craftsman Daedalus and his son Icarus, Daedalus built wings of wax and feathers so that he and his son could fly to their escape. Icarus was so enthralled by his wings and drawn to the light of the sun that despite his father's warning, he flew too high. The sun melted his wings, crashing Icarus to his death in the sea.[23] This was the inspiration for the now well-known Icarus Paradox—that which you excel at can ultimately be your undoing. Success can engender overconfidence, carelessness, and an unquestioning adherence to one's way of doing things.

For example, in the 1960s and 1970s, Xerox had such a stranglehold on the photocopier market that it did not pay much attention when new Japanese competitors began to infiltrate the market for smaller, inexpensive copiers. Xerox management did not believe competitors would ever be able to produce machines comparable to Xerox's quality and cost. However, Xerox was dangerously wrong. By the mid-1970s, Xerox was losing market share to the Japanese at an alarming rate. When Canon introduced a copier that sold for less than Xerox's manufacturing costs, Xerox knew it was in trouble and had to engage in a major benchmarking and restructuring effort to turn the company around.

significantly shorter development cycles than large firms (those with $100 million and more in sales), even when considering the relative magnitude of the innovation.[24] However, a few studies have indicated that large firms may still outperform small firms in innovation in some industries.[25]

While the firm's overall size is not an easy-to-manipulate attribute of the firm, many firms have found ways of making even large firms feel small. One primary method is to break the overall firm into several smaller subunits, and then encourage an entrepreneurial culture within these subunits. Multiple studies have observed that in industries characterized by high-speed technological change, many large and hierarchical firms have been **disaggregated** (or "unbundled") into networks of smaller, often more specialized, autonomous divisions or independent firms.[26] In such industries, many firms have undergone large-scale downsizing, with many functions and layers of management eliminated. The giant multidivisional firms of the 20th century were replaced by leaner firms that were more focused and flexible, loosely coupled in a network of alliances, supplier relationships, and distribution agreements.[27] This phenomenon led to the rise of terms such as *virtual organization,*[28] *network organization,*[29] and *modular organization.*[30]

> **disaggregated**
> When something is separated into its constituent parts.

Since firms also use big company–small company hybrids to vary other structural dimensions of the firm (including formalization, standardization, and centralization), these ambidextrous approaches to organizing will be covered in more depth after reviewing the structural dimensions of the firm.

Structural Dimensions of the Firm

Structural dimensions of the firm that are most likely to influence both its propensity to innovate and its effectiveness at innovation include formalization, standardization, and centralization.

formalization
The degree to which the firm utilizes rules, procedures, and written documentation to structure the behavior of individuals or groups within the organization.

The **formalization** of the firm is the degree to which the firm utilizes rules, procedures, and written documentation to structure the behavior of individuals or groups within the organization. Such rules and procedures can facilitate the standardization of firm activities, and help to regulate employee behavior by providing clear expectations of behavior, and decision-making criteria. Formalization can substitute for some degree of managerial oversight, and thereby help large companies run smoothly with fewer managers. This is demonstrated in the accompanying Theory in Action about 3M, where both Lehr and Jacobson responded to the difficulty of managing the growing firm by imposing more discipline and rules. By creating formal processes for choosing and managing development projects, Lehr and Jacobsen hoped to improve the overall efficiency and coherence of the firm's many decentralized development activities. However, high degrees of formalization can also make a firm rigid.[31] If a firm codifies all of its activities with detailed procedures, it may stifle employee creativity. Employees may not feel empowered or motivated to implement new solutions. This is also noted in the 3M example, when employee resentment of the new planning methods led to morale and motivation problems.

standardization
The degree to which activities are performed in a uniform manner.

Similarly, while **standardization** can ensure that activities within the firm run smoothly and yield predictable outcomes, standardization can also stifle innovation. Standardization is the degree to which activities in a firm are performed in a uniform manner. Standardization may be used to ensure quality levels are met and that customers and suppliers are responded to consistently and equitably. However, by minimizing variation, standardization can limit the creativity and experimentation that leads to innovative ideas.

centralization/ decentralization
Centralization is the degree to which decision-making authority is kept at top levels of management. Decentralization is the degree to which decision-making authority is pushed down to lower levels of the firm.

Centralization is the degree to which decision-making authority is kept at top levels of the firm, while **decentralization** is the degree to which decision-making authority is pushed down to lower levels of the firm. Centralization can refer both to the geographical location of activities (that is, the degree to which activities are performed in a central location for the firm) and to where power and authority over activities are located. That is, activities might occur in locations far from the corporate headquarters, but the authority and decision making over those activities may be retained at headquarters—leading to greater centralization than their physical location would suggest.

For firms that have multiple R&D projects ongoing, whether to centralize or decentralize R&D activities is a complex issue. Decentralizing R&D activities to the divisions of the firm enables those divisions to develop new products or processes that closely meet their particular division's needs (see Figure 10.1). The solutions they develop are likely to fit well within the operating structure of the division, and be closely matched to the requirements of the customers served by that division. The development projects also take advantage of the diversity of knowledge and market contacts that may exist in different divisions. But there is much risk of reinventing the wheel when R&D activities are decentralized. Many redundant R&D activities may be performed in multiple divisions, and the full potential of the technology to create value in other parts of the firm may not be realized. Furthermore, having multiple R&D departments may cause each to forgo economies of scale and learning curve effects.

FIGURE 10.1
Centralized and Decentralized R&D Activities

By contrast, if the firm centralizes R&D in a single department, it may maximize economies of scale in R&D, enabling greater division of labor among the R&D specialists and maximizing the potential for learning curve effects through the development of multiple projects. It also enables the central R&D department to manage the deployment of new technologies throughout the firm, improving the coherence of the firm's new product development efforts and avoiding the possibility that valuable new technologies are underutilized throughout the organization. Consistent with this, a study by Laura Cardinal and Tim Opler found that research-intensive firms that were highly diversified were more likely to establish separate research and development centers to facilitate communication and transfer of innovation across divisions.[32] Industry plays a role here too; for example, consumer products companies tend to utilize more decentralized R&D, tailoring projects to local markets, while firms in electronics industries tend to centralize R&D in centers of excellence that are devoted to leveraging particular competencies.[33]

There is some disagreement about whether centralization enhances or impedes a firm's flexibility and responsiveness to technological change (or other environmental shifts). A highly centralized firm may be better able to make a bold change in its overall direction because its tight command-and-control structure enables it to impose such change on lower levels of the firm in a decisive manner. Decentralized firms may struggle to get the cooperation from all the divisions necessary to undergo a significant change. But decentralized firms may be better able to respond to some types of technological or environmental change because not all decisions need to be passed up the hierarchy to top management; employees at lower levels are empowered to make decisions and changes independently and thus may be able to act more quickly.

In 1916, William McKnight, then general manager of sales and production for 3M, authorized the creation of the company's first research laboratory to improve 3M's sandpaper. McKnight had a strong belief in the power of individual entrepreneurship and innovation. He encouraged innovation through a combination of setting ambitious goals for new product development and giving individuals considerable freedom in how they pursued those goals. For example, McKnight established a companywide objective that 25 percent of sales should come from products created in the past five years. He also endorsed a "bootlegging" program whereby researchers could spend up to 15 percent of their time on whatever projects they were interested in pursuing.

As the firm grew, McKnight continued to support a centralized R&D lab while also encouraging divisions to pursue their own development initiatives in response to market needs they encountered. However, as 3M's product portfolio grew, it became increasingly difficult for 3M to manage functions such as production and sales. In 1944, McKnight began to experiment with an even more decentralized organizational form wherein divisions would not only have their own R&D labs, but also their own production operations and sales force. McKnight believed that small independent businesses would grow faster than a large company, leading to his "grow and divide" philosophy: Each division would be independent, and as its development projects grew into successful departments, they too would be spun off into new divisions.

By 1980, when Lou Lehr took the helm, 3M had grown to have 85 basic technologies and competed in about 40 major product markets. Lehr feared that 3M's greatest strength had become its weakness—the proliferation of independent businesses had led to a fragmentation of effort. Lehr worried that divisions might be wasting too much time on redundant activities and not taking advantage of the opportunity to leverage technologies across multiple divisions where they might be valuable. He wanted to ensure that divisions with related technologies would cooperate on development projects, and that new technologies would be diffused across the

company. So he consolidated the company's 42 divisions and 10 groups into four business sectors based on their relatedness of technology. He also created a three-tiered R&D system: central research laboratories that concentrated on basic research with long-term potential, sector labs that would serve groups of related divisions and develop core technologies to drive medium-term (5 to 10 years) growth, and division labs that would continue to work on projects with immediate applications. Lehr also imposed much more formal planning on the development process—some of 3M's managers began to refer to it as "planning by the pound." He also eliminated many projects that had been struggling for years.

The arrival of "Jake" Jacobson in 1986 as the new CEO led 3M into an era of even greater discipline. Jacobson increased the target of sales from products developed within the past five years to 35 percent. He increased the R&D funding rate to about twice that of other U.S. companies, but also directed the company to become more focused in its project selection and to shorten development cycle times. He also implemented a companywide move toward using teams for development rather than encouraging individual entrepreneurs. Though Jacobson's initiatives improved efficiency, many researchers began to resent some of the changes. They believed that the move to manage all development projects with teams was destroying the individualistic culture of entrepreneurship at 3M and that the focus on discipline came at the expense of creativity and excitement. Motivation and morale problems began to emerge.

Thus, when "Desi" Desimone became the CEO in 1991, he eased the company back toward a slightly looser, more entrepreneurial focus. He believed his predecessors had established a good architecture for ensuring that innovation did not run away in an uncontrolled fashion, but he also believed the company needed more balance between freedom and control, as reflected in the following quote:

Senior management's role is to create an internal environment in which people understand and value 3M's way of operating. It's a culture in which innovation and respect for the individual are still

continued

central. If you have senior management who have internalized the principles, you create a trust relationship in the company. The top knows it should trust the process of bottom-up innovation by leaving a crack open when someone is insistent that a blocked project has potential. And the lower levels have to trust the top when we intervene or control their activities.

Source: Adapted from C. Bartlett and A. Mohammed, "3M: Profile of an Innovating Company," Harvard Business School case #9-395-016, 1995.

Mechanistic versus Organic Structures

mechanistic
An organization structure characterized by a high degree of formalization and standardization, causing operations to be almost automatic or mechanical.

The combination of formalization and standardization results in what is often termed a **mechanistic** structure. Mechanistic structures are often associated with greater operational efficiency, particularly in large-volume production settings. The careful adherence to policies and procedures combined with standardization of most activities results in a well-oiled machine that operates with great consistency and reliability.[34] For example, Dell Computer achieves its operational excellence, delivering products cost effectively and with minimal convenience, by being highly centralized, disciplined, and streamlined.[35]

While mechanistic structures are often associated with high centralization, it is also possible to have a highly decentralized mechanistic structure by using formalization as a substitute for direct oversight. By establishing detailed rules, procedures, and standards, top management can push decision-making authority to lower levels of the firm while still ensuring that decisions are consistent with top management's objectives.

organic
An organization structure characterized by a low degree of formalization and standardization. Employees may not have well-defined job responsibilities and operations may be characterized by a high degree of variation.

Mechanistic structures, however, are often deemed unsuitable for fostering innovation. Mechanistic structures achieve efficiency by ensuring rigid adherence to standards and minimizing variation, potentially stifling creativity within the firm. **Organic** structures that are more free-flowing, and characterized by low levels of formalization and standardization, are often considered better for innovation and dynamic environments.[36] In the organic structure, employees are given far more latitude in their job responsibilities and operating procedures. Because much innovation arises from experimentation and improvisation, organic structures are often though to be better for innovation despite their possible detriment to efficiency.[37]

Size versus Structure

Many of the advantages and disadvantages of firm size that were discussed at the beginning of the chapter are related to the structural dimensions of formalization, standardization, and centralization. Large firms often make greater use of formalization and standardization because as the firm grows it becomes more difficult to exercise direct managerial oversight. Formalization and standardization ease coordination costs, at the expense of making the firm more mechanistic. Many large firms attempt to overcome some of this rigidity and inertia by decentralizing authority, enabling divisions of the firm to behave more like small companies. For example, firms such as General Electric, Hewlett-Packard, Johnson and Johnson, and General Motors have attempted to take advantage of both bigness and smallness by organizing their companies into groups of small companies that can access the large corporation's resources and reach while retaining a small company's simplicity and flexibility.[38] The next section examines several methods by which firms can achieve some of the advantages of large size, and the efficiency and speed of implementation afforded by mechanistic structures, while simultaneously harnessing the creativity and entrepreneurial spirit of small firms and organic structures.

The Ambidextrous Organization: The Best of Both Worlds?

ambidextrous organization
The ability of an organization to behave almost as two different kinds of companies at once. Different divisions of the firm may have different structures and control systems, enabling them to have different cultures and patterns of operations.

Most firms must simultaneously manage their existing product lines with efficiency, consistency, and incremental innovation, while still encouraging the development of new product lines and responding to technological change through more radical innovation. Tushman and O'Reilly argue that the solution is to create an ambidextrous organization.[39] An **ambidextrous organization** is a firm with a complex organizational form that is composed of multiple internally inconsistent architectures that can collectively achieve both short-term efficiency and long-term innovation.[40] Such firms might utilize mechanistic structures in some portions of the firm and organic structures in others. This is one of the rationales for setting up an R&D division that is highly distinct (either geographically or structurally) from the rest of the organization; a firm can use high levels of formalization and standardization in its manufacturing and distribution divisions, while using almost no formalization or standardization in its R&D division. Incentives in each of the divisions can be designed around different objectives, encouraging very different sets of behavior from employees. A firm can also centralize and tightly coordinate activities in divisions that reap great economies of scale such as manufacturing, while decentralizing activities such as R&D into many small units so that they behave like small, independent ventures.

Similarly, firms that have multiple product divisions might find that one or more divisions need a more organic structure to encourage creativity and fluid responses to environmental change, while other divisions benefit from a more structured and standardized approach. For example, when *USA Today* decided to establish an online version of the popular newspaper, management discovered it would need more flexible procedures to respond to both rapid technological change and the real-time information updating requirements of the online paper. The paper would also require different incentive schemes to attract and retain technologically savvy employees. The company established the online paper as a separate division with a different reporting structure, less formalization, a different pay structure, and even different cultural norms about appropriate work attire and working hours.

Apple provides another example. In 1980, Apple was churning out Apple II personal computers at a fast clip. However, Steve Jobs was not content with the product design; he wanted a product that would revolutionize the world by dramatically changing the way people interact with computers. He wanted to develop a computer so user-friendly and self-contained that it would appeal even to people who had no interest in the technological features of computers—it would become an extension of their everyday lives. Jobs began working with a team of engineers on a new project called Macintosh (originally developed by another Apple engineer, Jef Raskin). Jobs did not believe that the growing corporate environment at Apple was conducive to nurturing a revolution, so he created a separate division for the Macintosh that would have its own unique culture. He tried to instill a free-spirited entrepreneurial atmosphere reminiscent of the company's early beginnings in a garage, where individualistic and often eccentric software developers would flourish. The small group of team members was handpicked and sheltered from normal corporate commitments and distractions. He encouraged the Macintosh team members to consider themselves renegades, and even hung a pirate's skull-and-crossbones flag over their building. Jobs would also take the team on regular retreats to isolated resorts and reaffirm the renegade culture with quotes like "It's more fun to be a pirate than to join the Navy."[41]

If big firms can have internal structures with the incentives and behavior of small firms, then much of the logic of the impact of firm size on technological innovation rates becomes moot. A single organization may have multiple cultures, structures, and processes within it; large firms may have entrepreneurial divisions that can tap the greater resources of the larger corporation, yet have the incentive structures of small firms that foster the more careful choice of projects or enhance the motivation of R&D scientists. Such entrepreneurial units may be capable of developing discontinuous innovations within the large, efficiency-driven organizations that tend to foster incremental innovations.

Firms can also achieve some of the advantages of mechanistic and organic structures by alternating through different structures over time.[42] Schoonhoven and Jelinek studied Intel, Hewlett-Packard, Motorola, Texas Instruments, and National Semiconductor and found that these firms maintained a "dynamic tension" between formal reporting structures, quasiformal structures, and informal structures.[43] While the organizations had very explicit reporting structures and formalized development processes, the organizations were also reorganized frequently to modify reporting relationships and responsibilities in response to a changing environment. Thus, while the organizations used seemingly mechanistic structures to ensure systematic and efficient production, frequent reorganizing enabled the firms to be flexible.

These firms also used what Schoonhoven and Jelinek term *quasiformal structures* in the form of teams, task forces, and dotted-line relationships (that is, reporting relationships that were not formally indicated on the organizational chart). These quasiformal structures were more problem-focused and could change faster than the rest of the company. They also provided a forum for interaction across divisions and thus played an important boundary-spanning role. One advantage of quasiformal structures is that they fostered interactions based on interests rather than on hierarchy. This can foster more employee motivation and cross-fertilization of ideas. As noted by one employee: "Sometimes [innovation] happens in the men's room. One guy's talking to another guy, and another guy's standing, eavesdropping on the conversation, scribbling on a napkin."[44] Some of the downsides to such quasiformal structures were that they required time to manage, and they could be hard to kill. Since the quasi-structures were not part of the formal reporting structure, it could sometimes be difficult to establish who had the authority to disband them.

MODULARITY AND "LOOSELY COUPLED" ORGANIZATIONS

Another method firms use to strike a balance between efficiency and flexibility is through the adoption of standardized manufacturing platforms or components that can then be mixed and matched in a modular production system. This enables them to achieve standardization advantages (such as efficiency and reliability) at the component level, while achieving variety and flexibility at the end product level.

Modular Products

Modularity refers to the degree to which a system's components may be separated and recombined.[45] Making products modular can exponentially increase the number of possible configurations achievable from a given set of inputs.[46] For example, many of IKEA's shelving systems are designed so that users can mix and match a number of components to meet their needs. The shelves and supports come in a range of standardized sizes, and they can all be easily attached with standardized connectors. Similarly, some stoves now offer customers the ability to expand the range of the stove's functionality by removing the burners and plugging in other cooking devices such as barbecue grills and pancake griddles. Publishers have even embraced modularity by utilizing recent information technology advances to enable instructors to assemble their own textbooks from book chapters, articles, cases, or their own materials.

Many other products are produced in a modular way, even though the customer does not perceive the modularity. For example, Sony uses a modular production design for products such as the Walkman, even though the end product does not typically enable the customer to mix and match any of the product components. By standardizing a number of common components and using flexible manufacturing technologies that can quickly shift from one assembly configuration to another, Sony can produce a wide variety of product models just by changing which components are combined. Thus, Sony is able to offer more than 75 models of its Walkman portable stereo that differ in size, color, music format (e.g., MP3, minidisk, CD, cassette, radio signal), while still achieving economies of scale and efficiency in the individual components. Similarly, Chrysler achieves one of the fastest new product development cycles in the automobile industry while also keeping new product development costs low through its practice of using a few standard platforms upon which all of its new car models are built.

Modularity is achieved in product design through the specification of standard interfaces. For example, by designing all of its shelving components to work with its standardized connectors, IKEA ensures that components can be freely mixed and matched. Individual components can be changed without requiring any design changes in the other components. Because modularity enables a wider range of end configurations to be achieved from a given set of inputs, it provides a relatively cost-effective way for firms to meet heterogeneous customer demands. Furthermore, since modularity can enable one component to be upgraded without changing other components, modularity can enable firms and customers to upgrade their products without replacing their entire system. The personal computer is an excellent example of a modular system that enables upgrading. For example, if users want their personal computer to have more memory or a better monitor, they do not need to replace their entire computer system—they can simply purchase and install additional memory or a new monitor.

Loosely Coupled Organizational Structures

Modularity in products can also enable modularity in organizational forms,[47] or what is often termed *loosely coupled* organizational structures. In a loosely coupled structure, development and production activities are not tightly integrated but rather achieve coordination through their adherence to shared objectives and common standards. If, for example, each development group agrees to a development plan and standardized interfaces that enable the components they develop to connect and interact effectively, there may be little need for close coordination between the groups. The standard interface provides "embedded coordination" among all the development and production participants.[48] This can enable components of a product to be produced by highly autonomous divisions of the firm, or even by multiple independent firms.

Advances in information technology have also enabled loosely coupled organizational structures to become more common.[49] Information technology can enable a firm to access and process more information at a lower cost, vastly increasing the firm's options for development configurations.[50] For example, information technology lowers a firm's search costs for locating suitable development partners, as well as the costs of monitoring the partner's performance. This was clearly demonstrated in a study by Nick Argyres of the development of the B-2 "Stealth" bomber, a highly advanced military aircraft, developed jointly by Northrop, Boeing, Vaught, and General Electric.[51] Argyres found that enhanced information technology limited the need for coordination of activities through hierarchical control. By using information technology and developing a standard interface—a shared "technical grammar" that facilitated communication across firms—the firms involved in the development of the bomber could work autonomously, yet cooperatively.

Less need for integration frees firms to pursue more flexible research and development and production configurations. For instance, firms can become more specialized by focusing on a few key aspects of technological innovation that relate closely to the firm's core competencies, while obtaining other activities through outsourcing or alliances. By focusing on those activities in which the firm has a competitive advantage, the firm can improve its chance of developing a product that has a price-to-value ratio that attracts customers while reducing the overhead and administrative complexity of maintaining a wide scope of activities.

There are, however, disadvantages of loose coupling. Many activities reap significant synergies by being integrated.[52] In particular, activities that require the frequent exchange of complex or tacit knowledge are likely to need closer integration than a loosely coupled development configuration can offer. For example, suppose the design of a delivery mechanism for a drug will require intensive coordination with the design of the drug itself. It may be that the strength and dosage of the drug must be carefully calibrated and adjusted in accordance to the speed at which the delivery mechanism releases the drug. Alternative materials considered for the delivery mechanism may also have to be evaluated for their risk of potential interaction with chemicals used in the drug solution. If ongoing intensive coordination is required, the development activities might be better carried out through close integration of all parties.

An integrated firm also has mechanisms for resolving conflict that may be more effective or less expensive than those available in the market.[53] For example, if a dispute should arise over the development of a new product among development groups that are within the same firm, top managers can decide what action to take and exercise their authority over the development groups. But if the development groups are in separate companies, developing a new product in a collaboration agreement, neither firm may possess the authority to resolve the dispute and enforce a particular outcome. If the firms are unable to resolve the dispute themselves, they may face going to court or arbitration to resolve the dispute, an expensive and time-consuming option.

MANAGING INNOVATION ACROSS BORDERS

The 1990s saw a dramatic expansion in the international R&D activities of many firms.[54] By the late 1990s, firms in countries such as the Netherlands and Switzerland were conducting more than 50 percent of their R&D activities in divisions located in other countries, while the average for Western Europe reached 30 percent and 5 percent for U.S. firms.[55] The organization of innovation activities becomes particularly interesting for multinational firms. Many of the same issues that shape the centralization-versus-decentralization decision discussed earlier become highly amplified in the multinational firm. Foreign markets offer highly diverse sources of information and other resources. They may also have highly diverse product needs and different operating norms. This prompts many firms to consider decentralizing R&D to take advantage of local information and tailor innovation activities to the local market. However, innovations developed in this decentralized manner might never be diffused to the other divisions. The customization of products and processes to the local markets makes them particularly difficult to transfer to divisions serving different markets. Divisions that are accustomed to developing their own innovations may be reluctant to share them with others for fear of giving away their proprietary knowledge. They may also be reluctant to adopt other divisions' innovations because of the belief that innovations that are not developed locally will not suit their local market needs (a phenomenon known as *not-invented-here syndrome*). However, much of the value creation potential of a multinational is the opportunity to leverage technological innovation (and other core competencies) into multiple markets. Allowing innovation activities to become completely autonomous and disconnected risks forfeiting this opportunity. How does the multinational resolve this dilemma? A series of studies by Christopher Bartlett and Sumantra Ghoshal highlight some advantages and disadvantages of various approaches to the management of multinational innovation. They identify four primary strategies used by firms: center-for-global, local-for-local, locally leveraged, and globally linked.[56]

center-for-global strategy
When all innovation activities are conducted at a central hub and innovations are then diffused throughout the company.

The **center-for-global strategy** entails conducting all innovation activities at a centralized hub. These innovations are then deployed globally throughout the company. The centralization of innovation activities enables management to:

- Tightly coordinate all R&D activities (both across functions and projects).
- Achieve greater specialization and economies of scale in R&D activities while avoiding duplication of activities in multiple divisions.
- Develop and protect core competencies.
- Ensure that innovations are standardized and implemented throughout the company.

Managers are likely to choose a center-for-global approach to innovation when they have a strong desire to control the evolution of a technology, when they have strong concerns about the protection of proprietary technologies, when development activities require close coordination, or when there is a need to respond quickly to technological change and dispersed efforts are likely to create inefficiencies.[57] However, a center-for-global approach tends to not be very responsive to the diverse demands of different markets. Furthermore, the divisions that serve these markets might resist adopting or promoting centrally developed innovations. As a result, innovations developed centrally may not closely fit the needs of foreign markets and may also not be deployed quickly or effectively. The opening vignette demonstrated that P&G recognized this possibility. Part of the Organization 2005 restructuring was to shift from an almost exclusive reliance on centralized R&D to having both centralized and decentralized R&D. Developing products simultaneously in the United States, and in foreign markets was expected to speed up innovation and new product rollouts.

local-for-local strategy
When each division or subsidiary of the firm conducts its own R&D activities, tailored for the needs of the local market.

A **local-for-local strategy** is the opposite of the center-for-global strategy. Each national subsidiary uses its own resources to create innovations that respond to the needs of its local market. A local-for-local strategy takes advantage of access to diverse information and resources, and it customizes innovation for the needs and tastes of the local market. Managers are likely to choose a local-for-local strategy when divisions are very autonomous and when markets are highly differentiated.

There are several downsides to the local-for-local strategy, however. It can result in significant redundancy in activities as each division reinvents the wheel. Furthermore, each division may suffer from a lack of scale in R&D activities, and there is a risk that valuable innovations will not be diffused across the firm.

locally leveraged strategy
When each division or subsidiary of the firm conducts its own R&D activities, but the firm attempts to leverage resulting innovations throughout the company.

Over time, firms have developed variants of these strategies that attempt to reap advantages of both the center-for-global and local-for-local strategies. Bartlett and Ghoshal identify one such strategy as the **locally leveraged strategy.** A firm implementing a locally leveraged strategy attempts to take the most creative resources and innovative developments from the divisions and deploy them across the company. This strategy enables the firm to take advantage of the diverse ideas and resources created in local markets, while leveraging these innovations across the company. One way this strategy is employed in consumer markets is to assign an individual the role of international brand custodian. This person is responsible for ensuring that a successful brand is deployed into the firm's multiple markets while also maintaining consistency in the product's image and positioning.[58] Such a strategy can be very effective if different markets the company serves have similar needs.

globally linked strategy
Innovation activities are decentralized, but also centrally coordinated for the global needs of the corporation.

Another approach, the **globally linked strategy,** entails creating a system of decentralized R&D divisions that are connected to each other. Each geographically decentralized division might be charged with a different innovation task that serves the global company's needs. For example, a multinational auto manufacturer may empower one of its European divisions with the responsibility for developing new subcompact models that most closely fit the European markets but that may ultimately also be sold in the United States, Canada, and South America. In the meantime, its American division might bear the bulk of the responsibility for collaborating with other manufacturers to develop more efficient manufacturing processes that will ultimately be deployed corporatewide. Thus, while innovation is decentralized to take advantage of resources and talent pools offered in different geographic markets, it is also globally coordinated to meet companywide objectives. This approach also attempts to enable the learning accrued through innovation activities to be diffused throughout the firm. This strategy can be quite powerful in its ability to tap and integrate global resources, but it is also expensive in both time and money as it requires intensive coordination.

In both the locally leveraged and globally linked strategies, R&D divisions are decentralized and linked to each other. The difference lies in the missions of the R&D divisions. In the locally leveraged strategy, the decentralized R&D divisions are largely independent of each other and work on the full scope of development activities relevant to the regional business unit in which they operate. This means, for example, that if their regional business unit produces and sells health care items, beauty care products, and paper products, the R&D division is likely to work on development projects related to all of these products. However, to ensure that the best innovations are leveraged across the company, the company sets up integrating mechanisms (such as holding regular cross-regional meetings, or establishing a liaison such as an international brand custodian) to encourage the divisions to share their best developments with each other. By contrast, in the globally linked strategy, the R&D divisions are decentralized, but they each play a different role in the global R&D strategy. Rather than working on all development activities relevant to the region in which they operate, they specialize in a particular development activity. For example, an R&D division may be in a regional business unit that produces and sells health care, beauty care, and paper products, but its role may be to focus on developing paper innovations, while other R&D divisions in the firm work on health care items or beauty care products. Or it might focus on basic chemistry applications relevant to all of the products, while another division explores packaging innovations, and so on. The role of the division should exploit some local market resource advantage (such as abundant timber or a cluster of chemical technology firms). This strategy attempts to take advantage of the diversity of resources and knowledge in foreign markets, while still linking each division through well-defined roles in the company's overall R&D strategy.

Bartlett and Ghoshal argue that overall the multinational firm's objective is to make centralized innovation activities more effective (that is, better able to serve the various local markets) while making decentralized innovation activities more efficient (that is, eliminating redundancies and exploiting synergies across divisions). Bartlett and Ghoshal propose that firms should take a *transnational* approach wherein resources and capabilities that exist anywhere within the firm can be leveraged and deployed to exploit an opportunity that arises in any geographic market. They argue that this can be achieved by:

1. Encouraging reciprocal interdependence among the divisions of the firm (that is, each division must recognize its dependency on the other divisions of the firm).
2. Utilizing integration mechanisms across the divisions, such as division-spanning teams, rotating personnel across divisions, and so on.
3. Balancing the organization's identity between its national brands and its global image.

Ericsson provides an excellent example of this approach. Rather than using a strictly centralized or decentralized structure for its innovation activities, Ericsson's structure ebbs and flows between centralization and decentralization. Sometimes Ericsson increases levels of centralization and global integration for particular projects, while other times it decentralizes much more authority over innovation activities to its geographically dispersed divisions. Similar to the dynamic tension approach described by Jelinek and Schoonhoven, Ericsson regularly modifies its structure to adjust the balance between integration and autonomy. To encourage interunit integration, Ericsson also sends teams of 50 to 100 engineers to a different subsidiary for a year or two. Such member rotation programs facilitate the diffusion of knowledge throughout the firm.[59] Furthermore, encouraging engineers to become integrated into multiple areas of the company helped the engineers identify with both the global company and particular divisions.

Summary of Chapter

1. The impact of firm size on innovation has been debated for more than 50 years. Size is thought to confer advantages such as economies of scale in R&D, greater access to complementary resources (like capital and market access), and learning benefits. However, size may also associated with disadvantages such as inertia and governance problems.

2. Many firms attempt to make big companies feel small by breaking them into networks of more specialized divisions. These divisions can behave like smaller, more entrepreneurial firms.

3. Structural dimensions of the firm, including formalization, standardization, and centralization, also affect the firm's propensity to innovate and its effectiveness at innovation. Formalization and standardization tend to improve efficiency, but can stifle experimentation and creativity. Centralization has a more ambiguous effect on innovation; in some cases, centralization can enable significant innovation to occur more rapidly, and in other situations, decentralization fosters more innovation by enabling managers to respond quickly to local needs.

4. Traditionally, scholars have divided organization structures into two major types: mechanistic structures, which are highly formalized and standardized, and are good for efficient production, and organic structures, which are loose and free flowing and are good for creativity and experimentation.

5. Ambidextrous organizations attempt to achieve both the efficiency advantages of large mechanistic firms and the creativity and entrepreneurial spirit of small organic firms. These firms may have divisions with different structures and control schemes, or they may alternate between different structures.

6. Recently many firms have begun forming loosely coupled networks both within and between firms to conduct development activities. Part of this transition is attributed to the rise in information technology and the resultant decrease in coordination costs.

7. Multinational firms face significant challenges in determining where and how to conduct their R&D activities. One primary challenge is to balance the need to tap the knowledge and resources of local markets while also achieving coherence

across the corporation and ensure that technological innovations are diffused and leveraged throughout the organization.

Discussion Questions

1. Are there particular types of innovation activities for which large firms are likely to outperform small firms? Are there types for which small firms are likely to outperform large firms?
2. What are some advantages and disadvantages of having formalized procedures for improving the effectiveness or efficiency of innovation?
3. What factors should a firm consider when deciding how centralized its R&D activities should be? Should firms employ both centralized and decentralized R&D activities?
4. Why is the tension between centralization and decentralization of R&D activities likely to be even greater for multinational firms than firms that compete in one national market?
5. What are some of the advantages and disadvantages of the transnational approach advocated by Bartlett and Ghoshal?

Endnotes

1. "Product Innovation at P&G," Procter & Gamble press release, June 9, 1999.
2. "Organization 2005 Drive for Accelerated Growth Enters Next Phase," Procter & Gamble press release, June 9, 1999.
3. P. Galuszka and J. Ott, "P&G: How New and Improved? Investors Aren't Exactly Swooning over Its Reorganization Plan," *Business Week,* June 21, 1999, p. 36.
4. E. Neuborne and R. Berner, "Warm and Fuzzy Won't Save Procter & Gamble," *Business Week,* June 26, 2000, p. 48.
5. Procter & Gamble Annual Report, 2003.
6. "Organization 2005 Drive for Accelerated Growth Enters Next Phase."
7. Galuszka and Ott, "P&G: How New and Improved?"
8. Neuborne and Berner "Warm and Fuzzy Won't Save Procter & Gamble."
9. G. Schneider, "Procter & Gamble CEO to Step Down; Jager's Short Term Latest in Trend," *Washington Post,* June 9, 2000, p. E-1.
10. D. Canedy, "A Consumer Products Giant Will Most Likely Stay with What It Knows," *New York Times,* January 25, 2000, p. C-10.
11. D. Dougherty, "Reimagining the Differentiation and Integration of Work for Sustained Product Innovation," *Organization Science* 12 (2001), p. 612–31; A. Griffin, "The Effect of Project and Process Characteristics on Product Development Cycle Time," *Journal of Marketing Research* 34 (1997), pp. 24–35; E. H. Kessler and A. K. Chakrabarti, "Innovation Speed: A Conceptual Model of Context, Antecedents, and Outcomes," *Academy of Management Review* 21 (1996), pp. 1143–91; and A. Menon, J. Chowdhury, and B. Lukas, "Antecedents and Outcomes of New Product Development Speed: An Interdisciplinary Conceptual Framework," *Industrial Marketing Management* 31 (2002), pp. 317–28.
12. J. A. Schumpeter, *Capitalism, Socialism and Democracy* (New York: Harper & Brothers Publishers, 1942).

13. W. M. Cohen and D. A. Levinthal, "Absorptive Capacity: A New Perspective on Learning and Innovation," *Administrative Science Quarterly* 35 (1990), pp. 128–52; and M. I. Kamien and N. L. Schwartz, "Market Structure and Innovation—a Survey," *Journal of Economic Literature* 13 (1975), pp. 1–37.

14. F. Damanpour, "Organizational Size and Innovation," *Organization Studies* 13 (1992) pp. 375–402.

15. R. L. Daft, *Organization Theory and Design* (Minneapolis: West Publishing Company, 1995).

16. W. Cohen and R. Levin, "Empirical Studies of Innovation and Market Structure," in *Handbook of Industrial Organization,* vol. II, eds. R. Schmalensee and R. D. Willig (Amsterdam: Elsevier Science Publishers B.V., 1989).

17. Ibid; and J. Rotemberg and G. Saloner, "Benefits of Narrow Business Strategies," *American Economic Review* 84, no. 5 (1994), pp. 1330–49.

18. G. Gilder, "The Revitalization of Everything: The Law of the Microcosm," *Harvard Business Review* 66, no. 2 (1988), pp. 49–61.

19. M. Kharbanda "Xerox Corporation: A Case Study in Revitalizing Product Development," in *Time-Based Competition: The Next Battleground in American Manufacturing,* ed. J. D. Blackburn (Homewood, IL: Business One Irwin, 1991), pp. 177–90.

20. Rotemberg and Saloner, "Benefits of Narrow Business Strategies."

21. J. Bound, C. Cummins, Z. Griliches, B. H. Hall, and A. Jaffe, "Who Does R&D and Who Patents?" in *R&D, Patents, and Productivity,* ed. Z. Griliches (Chicago: University of Chicago, 1984); A. K. Chakrabarti and M. R. Halperin, "Technical Performance and Firm Size: Analysis of Patents and Publications of U.S. Firms," in *Innovation and Technological Change: An International Comparison,* eds. A. J. Acs and D. B. Audretsch (Ann Arbor, MI: University of Michigan Press, 1991); S. B. Graves and N. S. Langowitz, "Innovative Productivity and Returns to Scale in the Pharmaceutical Industry," *Strategic Management Journal* 14 (1993), pp. 593–605; and G. N. Stock, N. P. Greis, and W. A. Fischer, "Firm Size and Dynamic Technological Innovation," *Technovation* 22 (2002), pp. 537–49.

22. Z. Griliches, "Patent Statistics as Economic Indicators: A Survey," *Journal of Economics Literature* 28 (1990), pp. 1661–707; and F. M. Scherer, "The Propensity to Patent," *International Journal of Industrial Organization* 1 (1983), pp. 107–28.

23. A. Cotterel, *The Encyclopedia of Mythology* (London: Smithmark, 1996).

24. A. Griffing, "Product Development Cycle Time for Business-to-Business Products," *Industrial Marketing Management* 31 (2002), pp. 291–304.

25. W. M. Cohen and S. Klepper, "A Reprise of Firm Size and R&D," *Economic Journal* 106 (1996), pp. 925–51; and R. Henderson and I. Cockburn, "Scale, Scope and Spillovers: The Determinants of Research Productivity in Drug Discovery," *Rand Journal of Economics* 27 (1996), pp. 32–59.

26. R. Ashkenas, D. Ulrich, T. Jick, and S. Kerr, *The Boundaryless Organization: Breaking the Chains of Organizational Structure* (San Francisco: Jossey-Bass Publishers, 1995); J. Hagel and M. Singer, "Unbundling the Corporation," *Harvard Business Review,* March–April 1999, pp. 133–41; M. A. Schilling and K. Steensma, "The Use of Modular Organizational Forms: An Industry Level Analysis," *Academy of Management Journal* 44 (2001), pp. 1149–69; C. Snow, R. Miles, and H. J. Coleman, "Managing 21st Century Network Organizations," *Organizational Dynamics* 20, no. 3 (1992), pp. 5–20; and T. R. Zenger and W. S. Hesterly, "The Disaggregation of Corporations: Selective Intervention, High-Powered Incentives, and Molecular Units," *Organization Science* 8 (1997), pp. 209–23.

27. R. S. Achrol "Changes in the Theory of Interorganizational Relations in Marketing: Toward a Network Paradigm," *Academy of Marketing Science* 25 (1997), pp. 56–71.

28. H. Chesbrough and D. Teece, "When Is Virtual Virtuous? Organizing for Innovation," *Harvard Business Review,* January–February 1996, pp. 65–73; and D. Churbuck and J. S. Young, "The Virtual Workplace," *Forbes* 150, no. 12 (1992), pp. 184–90.

29. C. Jones, W. Hesterly, and S. Borgatti, "A General Theory of Network Governance: Exchange Conditions and Social Mechanisms," *Academy of Management Review* 22 (1997), pp. 911–45; R. E. Miles and C. C. Snow, "Organizations: New Concepts for New Forms," *California Management Review* 28, no. 3 (1986), pp. 62–73; and R. E. Miles and C. C. Snow, "Causes of Failures in Network Organizations," *California Management Review* 34, no. 4 (1992), pp. 53–72.

30. D. Lei, M. A. Hitt, and J. D. Goldhar, "Advanced Manufacturing Technology: Organizational Design and Strategic Flexibility," *Organization Studies* 17 (1996), pp. 501–24; R. Sanchez, "Strategic Flexibility in Product Competition," *Strategic Management Journal* 16 (1995), pp. 135–60; R. Sanchez and J. Mahoney, "Modularity, Flexibility, and Knowledge Management in Product and Organization Design," *Strategic Management Journal* 17 (1996), pp. 63–76; and Schilling and Steensma, "The Use of Modular Organizational Forms: An Industry Level Analysis."

31. Menon, Chowdhury, and Lukas, "Antecedents and Outcomes of New Product Development Speed."

32. L. Cardinal and T. Opler, "Corporate Diversification and Innovative Efficiency: An Empirical Study," *Journal of Accounting & Economics* 19 (1995), pp. 365–82.

33. P. N. Golder, "Insights from Senior Executives about Innovation in International Markets," *Journal of Product Innovation Management* 17 (2000), pp. 326–40.

34. P. S. Adler, "Building Better Bureaucracies," *Academy of Management Executive* 13, no. 4 (1999), pp. 36–50.

35. M. Treacy and F. Wiersema, "Customer Intimacy and Other Value Disciplines," *Harvard Business Review* 71, no. 1 (1993), pp. 84–94.

36. M. P. Miles, J. G. Covin, and M. B. Heeley, "The Relationship between Environmental Dynamism and Small Firm Structure, Strategy, and Performance," *Journal of Marketing Theory and Practice* 8, no. 2 (2000), pp. 63–75.

37. D. Leonard, *Well-Springs of Knowledge: Building and Sustaining the Sources of Innovation* (Boston: Harvard Business School Press, 1996); C. Moorman and A. Miner, "Organizational Improvisation and Organizational Memory," *Academy of Management Review* 23, no. 4 (1998), pp. 698–723; and D. Dougherty, "Reimagining the Differentiation and Integration of Work for Sustained Product Innovation," *Organization Science* 12 (2001), pp. 612–31.

38. Daft, *Organization Theory and Design;* and Menon, Chowdhury, and Lukas, "Antecedents and Outcomes of New Product Development Speed."

39. M. L. Tushman and C. A. O'Reilly III, "Ambidextrous Organizations: Managing Evolutionary and Revolutionary Change," *California Management Review* 38, no. 4 (1996), pp. 8–31.

40. M. L. Tushman and C. A. O'Reilly, *Winning through Innovation: A Practical Guide to Leading Organizational Change and Renewal* (Boston: Harvard Business School, 1997); and M. L. Tushman and W. Smith, "Organizational Technology: Technological Change, Ambidextrous Organizations and Organizational Evolution," in

Companion to Organizations, ed. J. A. Baum (New York: Blackwell Publishers, 2002), pp. 386–414.

41. M. Rogers, "It's the Apple of His Eye," *Newsweek,* March 1, 2003.

42. N. Siggelkow and D. Levinthal, "Temporarily Divide to Conquer: Centralized, Decentralized, and Reintegrated Organizational Approaches to Exploration and Adaptation," *Organization Science* 14 (2003), pp. 650–69.

43. M. Jelinek and C. Schoonhoven, *The Innovation Marathon: Lessons from High Technology Firms* (Oxford, UK: Basil Blackwell, 1990); and C. B. Schoonhoven and M. Jelinek, "Dynamic Tension in Innovative, High Technology Firms: Managing Rapid Technological Change through Organizational Structure," in *Managing Strategic Innovation and Change,* eds. M. L. Tushman and P. Anderson (Oxford: Oxford University Press, 1996).

44. Schoonhoven and Jelinek, "Dynamic Tension in Innovative, High Technology Firms."

45. M. A. Schilling, "Toward a General Modular Systems Theory and Its Application to Interfirm Product Modularity," *Academy of Management Review* 25 (2000), pp. 312–34.

46. C. Y. Baldwin and K. B. Clark, *Design Rules, Volume 1: The Power of Modularity* (Cambridge, MA: MIT Press, 2000); R. Garud and A. Kumaraswamy, "Technological and Organizational Designs for Realizing Economies of Substitution," *Strategic Management Journal* 16 (1995), pp. 93–109; and Sanchez, "Strategic Flexibility in Product Competition."

47. Sanchez and Mahoney, "Modularity, Flexibility, and Knowledge Management in Product and Organization Design."

48. Schilling and Steensma, "The Use of Modular Organizational Forms"; and Sanchez and Mahoney, "Modularity, Flexibility, and Knowledge Management in Product and Organization Design."

49. E. Brynjolfsson, T. W. Malone, V. Gurbaxani, and A. Kambil, "Does Information Technology Lead to Smaller Firms?" *Management Science* 40 (1994), pp. 1628–45; and T. R. Zenger and W. S. Hesterly, "The Disaggregation of Corporations: Selective Intervention, High-Powered Incentives, and Molecular Units," *Organization Science* 8 (1997), pp. 209–23.

50. E. Brynjolfsson, "Information Assets, Technology, and Organization," *Management Science* 40 (1994), pp. 1645–63; and L. M. Hitt, "Information Technology and Firm Boundaries: Evidence from Panel Data," *Information Systems Research* 10, no. 2 (1999) pp. 134–50.

51. N. S. Argyres, "The Impact of Information Technology on Coordination: Evidence from the B-2 'Stealth' Bomber," *Organization Science* 10 (1999), pp. 162–81.

52. Chesbrough and Teece, "When Is Virtual Virtuous?" and Schilling and Steensma, "The Use of Modular Organizational Forms."

53. Chesbrough and Teece, "When Is Virtual Virtuous?"

54. R. D. Pearce and M. Papanastassiou, *The Technological Competitiveness of Japanese multinationals* (Ann Arbor: University of Michigan Press, 1996); and R. D. Pearce and M. Papanastassiou, "R&D Networks and Innovation: Decentralized Product Development in Multinational Enterprises," *R&D Management* 26 (1996), pp. 315–33.

55. O. Gassman and M. von Zedtwitz, "Trends and Determinants of Managing Virtual R&D Teams," *R&D Management* 33, no. 3 (2003), pp. 243–62; J. Dunning, "Multinational Enterprises and the Globalization of Innovatory Capacity," *Research Policy* 23 (1994),

pp. 67–88; and P. Patel, "Localised Production of Technology in Global Markets," *Cambridge Journal of Economy* 19 (1995), pp. 141–53.

56. C. A. Bartlett and S. Ghoshal, "Managing Innovation in the Transnational Corporation," in *Managing the Global Firm,* eds. C. A. Bartlett, Y. Doz, and G. Hedlund (London, NY: Routledge, 1990).

57. Ibid; and A. M. Rugman, "Research and Development by Multinational and Domestic Firms in Canada," *Canadian Public Policy* 7 (1981), pp. 604–16.

58. Golder, "Insights from Senior Executives about Innovation in International Markets."

59. T. Madsen, E. Mosakowski, and S. Zaheer, "The Dynamics of Knowledge Flows: Human Capital Mobility, Knowledge Retention and Change," *Journal of Knowledge Management* 6, no. 2 (2002), pp. 164–77.

Chapter Eleven

Managing the New Product Development Process

Product Development at Ideo

IDEO is a leading product design firm that grosses between $50 million and $60 million annually, and whose client list includes heavy hitters such as Apple Computer, AT&T, BMW, Nike, Pepsi, Canon, and GM/Hughes.[1] Headquartered in California's Silicon Valley, the company achieved national prominence when ABC shot a 30-minute segment of the company redesigning a shopping cart. By 2001, the company employed more than 300 people (despite founder David Kelley's assertion in 1990 that the company would never employ more than 40 people).

Despite its size, IDEO held vigorously to its informal culture that encouraged playfulness, experimentation, and unfettered creativity. The company's motto was "fail often to succeed sooner," encouraging employees to use brainstorming to rapidly generate ideas. The IDEO management believed in a funnel approach whereby a project would start with many ideas that would gradually be filtered down to a single product design. Management also encouraged rapid and frequent prototyping, believing that visual aids greatly enhanced the creativity process and facilitated the transmission of ideas. Typical prototypes were not carefully crafted, functional devices, but instead were rough models quickly put together with such materials as cardboard and foam that could be revised or scrapped as new ideas emerged.

Though the company emphasized a free-flowing approach to the innovation process, IDEO also utilized a five-phase system to provide structure to the development process.[2]

Phase 0—Understand/Observe

In this phase, the project team attempted to understand the new client and its business. The team would research everything it could about previous product models, including cost structure and how the product was used. By the end of this phase, the project team would have constructed a "feasibility record" as well as recorded its insights about the users and market.

Phase I—Visualize/Realize

In this phase, the team would create prototypes to visualize the direction a product solution was heading. This phase involved close coordination with the client to ensure timely feedback. By the end of this phase, the team would have three-dimensional models of the product and would have outlined the manufacturing strategy.

Phase II—Evaluate/Refine

In this phase, fully functional prototypes were built so that the team could identify and resolve technical problems and issues in the ways users interacted with the product. By this phase, the emphasis had shifted from human factors to engineering, and the phase would culminate in the delivery of a complete product design with technical specifications.

Phase III—Implement (Detailed Engineering)

The team would verify the manufacturability and performance of the completed product in this phase. Though the emphasis was on engineering, engineers stayed in close contact with design team members to ensure that the product was evolving in a way that met both manufacturability and usage goals. At the end of this phase, the team would begin selecting vendors.

Phase IV—Implement (Manufacturing Liaison)

In this phase, the team coordinated the release of the product design to the manufacturer. The team would supervise production of tooling, regulatory testing and approvals, and pilot runs of the manufacturing process. At the end of this phase, the team officially would turn the product over to the client.

Discussion Questions

1. What are the strengths and weaknesses of IDEO's approach to product development?
2. To what degree do you think IDEO's success is based on its size, culture, or development process?
3. Do you think IDEO's success is sustainable? Why or why not?
4. Would IDEO's development process be effective in a firm that manufactured, marketed, and distributed its own products?

OVERVIEW

In many industries, the ability to develop new products quickly, effectively, and efficiently is now the single most important factor driving firm success. In industries such as computer hardware and software, telecommunications, automobiles, and consumer electronics, firms often depend on products introduced within the past five years for more than 50 percent of their sales. Yet despite the avid attention paid to new product development, the failure rates for new product development projects are still agonizingly high. By many estimates, more than 95 percent of all new product development projects fail to result in an economic return.[3] Many projects are never completed, and of those that are, many flounder in the marketplace. Thus, a considerable amount of research has been focused on how to make the new product development process more effective and more efficient. This chapter discusses some strategic imperatives for new product development processes that have emerged from the study of best—and worst—practices in new product development.

We will begin by looking at the three key objectives of the new product development process: maximizing fit with customer requirements, minimizing cycle time, and controlling development costs. We then will turn to methods of achieving these objectives, including adopting parallel development processes, using project champions, and involving customers and suppliers in the development process. Next we will look at a number of tools firms can utilize to improve the effectiveness and efficiency of the development process, including creating go/kill decision points with stage-gate processes, defining design targets with quality function deployment, reducing costs and development time with design for manufacturing and CAD/CAM systems, and using metrics to assess the performance of the new product development process.

OBJECTIVES OF THE NEW PRODUCT DEVELOPMENT PROCESS

For new product development to be successful, it must simultaneously achieve three sometimes-conflicting goals: (1) maximizing the product's fit with customer requirements, (2) minimizing the development cycle time, and (3) controlling development costs.

Maximizing Fit with Customer Requirements

For a new product to be successful in the marketplace, it must offer more compelling features, greater quality, or more attractive pricing than competing products. Despite the obvious importance of this imperative, many new product development projects fail to achieve this. This may occur for a number of reasons. First, the firm may not have a clear sense of which features customers value the most, resulting in the firm overinvesting in some features at the expense of features the customer values more. Firms may also overestimate the customer's willingness to pay for particular features, leading them to produce feature-packed products that are too expensive to gain significant market penetration. Firms may also have difficulty resolving heterogeneity in customer demands; if some customer groups desire different features from other groups, the firm may end up producing a product that makes compromises between these conflicting demands, and the resulting product may fail to be attractive to any of the customer groups.

Numerous new products have offered technologically advanced features compared to existing products but have failed to match customer requirements and were subsequently rejected by the market. For example, consider Apple's Newton MessagePad, a relatively early entrant into the personal digital assistant market. The Newton was exceptional on many dimensions. It had a highly advanced ARM610 RISC chip for superior processing performance. Its operating system was object oriented (a feature that software programmers had been clamoring for), and Apple openly licensed the architecture to encourage rapid and widespread adoption by other vendors. Also, its weight, size, and battery life were better than many of the other early competitors. However, the Newton MessagePad was still much too large to be kept in a pocket, limiting its usefulness as a handheld device. Many corporate users thought the screen was too small to make the product useful for their applications. Finally, early problems with the handwriting recognition software caused many people to believe the product was fatally flawed.

Another example is Philips' attempt to enter the video game industry. In 1989, Philips introduced its Compact Disc Interactive (CD-i). The CD-i was a 32-bit system (introduced well before Sega's 32-bit Saturn or Sony's 32-bit PlayStation), and in addition to being a game player, it offered a number of educational programs and played audio CDs. However, Philips had overestimated how much customers would value (and be willing to pay for) these features. The CD-i was priced at $799, more than double the cost of Nintendo or Sega video game systems. Furthermore, the product was very complex, requiring a half-hour demonstration by a skilled sales representative. Ultimately, the product failed to attract many customers and Philips abandoned the product.

Minimizing Development Cycle Time

Even products that achieve a very close fit with customer requirements can fail if they take too long to bring to market. As discussed in Chapter Five, bringing a product to market early can help a firm build brand loyalty, preemptively capture scarce assets, and build customer switching costs. A firm that brings a new product to market late may find that customers are already committed to other products. Also, a company that is able to bring its product to market early has more time to develop (or encourage others to develop) complementary goods that enhance the value and attractiveness of the product.[4] Other things being equal, products that are introduced to the market earlier are likely to have an installed base and availability of complementary goods advantage over later offerings.

development cycle time
The time elapsed from project initiation to product launch, usually measured in months or years.

Another important consideration regarding **development cycle time** relates to the cost of development and the decreasing length of product life cycles. First, many development costs are directly related to time. Both the expense of paying employees involved in development and the firm's cost of capital increase as the development cycle lengthens. Second, a company that is slow to market with a particular generation of technology is unlikely to be able to fully amortize the fixed costs of development before that generation becomes obsolete. This phenomenon is particularly vivid in dynamic industries such as electronics where life cycles can be as short as 12 months (e.g., personal computers, semiconductors). Companies that are slow to market may find that by the time they have introduced their products, market demand has already shifted to the products of a subsequent technological generation.

Finally, a company with a short development cycle can quickly revise or upgrade its offering as design flaws are revealed or technology advances. A firm with a short development cycle can take advantage of both first-mover *and* second-mover advantages.

Some researchers have pointed out the costs of shortening the development cycle and rushing new products to market. For example, Dhebar points out that rapid product introductions may cause adverse consumer reactions; consumers may regret past purchases and be wary of new purchases for fear they should rapidly become obsolete.[5] Other researchers have suggested that speed of new product development may come at the expense of quality or result in sloppy market introductions.[6] Compressing development cycle time can result in overburdening the development team, leading to problems being overlooked in the product design or manufacturing process. Adequate product testing may also be sacrificed to meet development schedules.[7] However, despite these risks, most studies have found a strong positive relationship between speed and the commercial success of new products.[8]

Controlling Development Costs

Sometimes a firm engages in an intense effort to develop a product that exceeds customer expectations and brings it to market early, only to find that its development costs have ballooned so much that it is impossible to recoup the development expenses even if the product is enthusiastically received by the market. This highlights the fact that development efforts must be not only *effective,* but also *efficient.* Later in the chapter, ways to monitor and control development costs are discussed.

SEQUENTIAL VERSUS PARTLY PARALLEL DEVELOPMENT PROCESSES

Before the mid-1990s, most U.S. companies proceeded from one development stage to another in a sequential fashion (see Figure 11.1a). The process included a number of gates at which managers would decide whether to proceed to the next stage, send the project back to a previous stage for revision, or kill the project. Typically, R&D and marketing provided the bulk of the input in the opportunity identification and concept development stages, R&D took the lead in product design, and manufacturing took the lead in process design. According to critics, one problem with such a system emerges at the product design stage when R&D engineers fail to communicate directly with manufacturing engineers. As a result, product design proceeds without manufacturing requirements in mind. A sequential process has no early warning system to indicate that planned features are not manufacturable. Consequently, cycle time can

FIGURE 11.1
**Sequential
versus Partly
Parallel
Development
Processes**

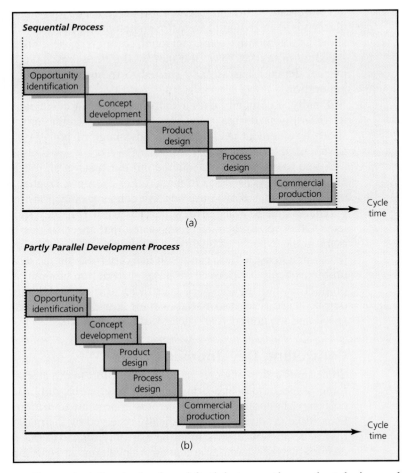

partly parallel
development
process
A development
process in which
some (or all) of
the development
activities at least
partially overlap.
That is, if activ-
ity A would pre-
cede activity B
in a partly paral-
lel development
process, activity
B might com-
mence before
activity A is
completed.

lengthen as the project iterates back and forth between the product design and process design stages.[9]

To shorten the development process and avoid time-consuming and costly iterations between stages of the development cycle, many firms have adopted a **partly parallel development process** (also sometimes called simultaneous engineering), as
shown in Figure 11.1b.[10] Product design is initiated before concept development is
complete, and process design is begun long before product design is finalized,
enabling much closer coordination between the different stages and minimizing the
chance that R&D will design products that are difficult or costly to manufacture. This
should eliminate the need for time-consuming iterations between design stages and
shorten overall cycle time.

Parallel development processes are not universally endorsed, however. In some situations, using a parallel development process can substantially increase the risks or
costs of the development process. If, for example, variations in product design require
significant changes to the process design, beginning process design before product
design is finalized can result in costly rework of the production process. Such risks are

especially high in markets characterized by rapid change and uncertainty.[11] Furthermore, once process design has commenced, managers may be reluctant to alter the product design even if market testing reveals that the product design is suboptimal. It is precisely these risks that the stage-gate process (discussed later in the chapter) attempts to minimize.

PROJECT CHAMPIONS

A number of studies on new product development have suggested that firms should assign (or encourage) a senior member of the company to champion a new product development project.[12] Senior executives have the power and authority to support and fight for a project. They can facilitate the allocation of human and capital resources to the development effort, ensuring that cycle time is not extended by resource constraints, and help ensure that the project can sustain the necessary momentum to surmount the hurdles that inevitably will arise. A senior project champion also can stimulate communication and cooperation between the different functional groups involved in the development process. Given that interfunctional communication and cooperation is necessary both to compress cycle time and to achieve a good fit between product attributes and customer requirements, the use of executive sponsors can improve the effectiveness of the development process. As of 2001, 68 percent of North American firms, 58 percent of European firms, and 48 percent of Japanese firms reported using senior managers to champion new product development projects.[13] An example of a successful use of project championing is described in the accompanying Theory in Action.

Risks of Championing

Vigorous project championing, however, also has its risks. A manager's role as champion may cloud judgment about the true value of the project. Optimism is the norm in product development—surveys indicate a systematic upward bias in estimates of future cash flows from a project.[14] In the role of champion, this optimism is often taken to extreme levels. Managers may fall victim to escalating commitment and be unable (or unwilling) to admit that a project should be killed even when it is clear to many others in the organization that the project has gone sour, or the factors driving the project's original value are no longer relevant. While it is common to read stories about projects that succeed against all odds due to the almost fanatical zeal and persistence of their champions, bankruptcy courts are full of companies that should have been less zealous in pursuing some projects. Managers who have invested their reputations and years of their lives in development projects may find it very difficult to cut their losses, in much the same way that individuals tend to hold losing stocks much longer than they should due to the temptation to try to recoup what they have lost. Though the champion's seniority is an asset in gaining access to resources and facilitating coordination, this same seniority may also make others in the firm unwilling to challenge the project champion even if it has become apparent that the project's expected value has turned negative.[15]

Theory in Action   The Development of Zantac

In the 1970s, Glaxo Holdings PLC of Great Britain was one of the larger health care conglomerates in the world, known principally for its baby food, but it needed a new hit product to stimulate sales. While contemplating research possibilities, the head of Glaxo's research laboratory, David Jack, attended a lecture by James Black, a Nobel Prize-winning scientist and researcher for U.S.-based SmithKline Beecham. During the lecture, Black described a new possibility for treating ulcers that involved compounds called H_2 blockers that would inhibit gastrointestinal cells from secreting acid. Jack was intrigued. Ulcers were a common problem, and thus represented a large market opportunity for an effective solution. Jack began experimenting with different compounds in pursuit of a formula that would be safe and effective. Unfortunately, researchers at SmithKline Beecham beat Glaxo to the finish line, introducing Tagamet in 1977. Tagamet revolutionized ulcer treatment, and sales grew phenomenally.[16]

Discouraged but not thwarted, Jack's team kept working. Other companies (including Merck and Eli Lilly) were also developing their own ulcer treatments, and Jack believed that beating them to market might still give the company a shot at a significant share. In that same year, the team came up with a compound based on ranitidine (Tagamet was based on a compound called cimetedine) that achieved the desired objectives. However, Jack realized that if Glaxo was going to beat Merck and Eli Lilly to market, it would need to radically shorten the typical 10-year testing period required to secure regulatory approval and bring the product to market. To achieve this, Jack proposed the first parallel development process used in the pharmaceutical industry. Instead of following the typical sequence of testing (e.g., from rats to monkeys, and from short-term toxicity to long-term toxicity), Jack proposed doing all of the tests concurrently.[17] This intensified development process could potentially cut the cycle time in half—to five years—however, it would also be expensive and risky. If the development efforts increased the research costs substantially, it would be much harder to recoup those expenses through sales of the drug.

Fortunately for Jack's team, Paul Girolami, Glaxo's director of finance, chose to champion the project. Girolami argued that the company should be willing to risk its range of decently profitable products for one potentially sensational drug, stating, "Having all your eggs in one basket concentrates the mind because you had better make sure it is a good basket."[18] Not only was he able to convince the company that it was worth investing in the shortened development process, but he also insisted that the product be modified so that it could be taken once a day (Tagamet required twice-a-day use) and so that the product would have fewer side effects than Tagamet. These features would help differentiate Zantac as a superior product, and it was hoped they would enable Glaxo to take share away from SmithKline Beecham. The development process was successful, and the product was ready for launch in 1982. To recoup its development costs, Girolami chose a premium pricing strategy for the product (one-third higher than Tagamet), arguing that its advantages would warrant its additional cost. He also insisted that the product be launched globally in all major markets, and he set up a distribution alliance with Hoffman-LaRoche to speed up the product's penetration of the U.S. market.

Girolami's strategies were successful, and by the end of the year, Zantac was stealing about 100,000 patients a month from Tagamet. By 1987, Zantac sales had exceeded Tagamet's, and by 1991 Zantac became the world's No. 1 selling prescription drug and the first drug ever to achieve $1 billion in U.S. sales.[19] Both David Jack and Paul Girolami were knighted, and Sir Paul Girolami was appointed chairman of Glaxo.[20]

Research Brief   Five Myths about Product Champions

Stephen Markham and Lynda Aiman-Smith argue that a number of myths have become widely accepted about new product champions. While Markham and Aiman-Smith believe that product champions are critical to new product development, they also argue that for product champions to be effective, their role in the development process must be completely understood. Markham and Aiman-Smith conducted a systematic review of the theoretical and empirical literature on product champions and identified five popular myths:

1. *Projects with champions are more likely to be successful in the market.* Markham and Aiman-Smith's review of the empirical data on use of project champions found that projects with champions were just as likely to be market failures as market successes. Markham and Aiman-Smith point out that while champions may improve the likelihood of a project being completed, the factors determining its market success are often beyond the champion's control.[21]

2. *Champions get involved because they are excited about the project, rather than from self-interest.* Markham and Aiman-Smith report that empirical evidence suggests champions are more likely to support projects that will benefit the champion's own department.[22]

3. *Champions are more likely to be involved with radical innovation projects.* Empirical evidence from multiple large sample studies indicates that champions were equally likely to be involved with radical versus incremental innovation projects.

4. *Champions are more likely to be from high (or low) levels in the organization.* Markham and Aiman-Smith argue that there are myths about both high-level and low-level managers being more likely to be product champions. Though stories abound featuring prominent senior managers supporting projects, as do stories featuring low-level champions fighting vigorously for a project's success, empirical evidence suggests that champions may arise from any level in the organization. (Note that this research does not indicate champions from all levels of the firm are equally effective.)

5. *Champions are more likely to be from marketing.* Markham and Aiman-Smith argue that while anecdotal evidence may more often emphasize champions that have marketing backgrounds, an empirical study of 190 champions found that champions arose from many functions of the firm. Specifically, the study found that 15 percent of champions were from R&D, 14 percent were from marketing, 7 percent were from production and operations, and 6 percent were general managers. Interestingly, 8 percent of champions were potential users of the innovations.[23]

Firms may benefit from also developing "antichampions" who can play the role of devil's advocate. Firms should also encourage a corporate culture open to the expression of dissenting opinion, and champions should be encouraged to justify their projects on the basis of objective criteria, without resorting to force of personality.[24] The accompanying Research Brief describes five myths that have become widely accepted about project champions.

INVOLVING CUSTOMERS AND SUPPLIERS IN THE DEVELOPMENT PROCESS

As mentioned previously, many products fail to produce an economic return because they do not fulfill customer requirements for performance and price, or because they take too long to bring to market. Both of these problems can be reduced by involving customers and suppliers in the development process.

Involving Customers

Firms often make decisions about projects based on financial considerations and level of production and technical synergy achieved by the new product proposal rather than on marketing criteria. This can lead to an overemphasis on incremental product updates that closely fit existing business activities.[25] The screening decision should focus instead on the new product's advantage and superiority to the consumer, and the growth of its target market.[26] The customer is often the one most able to identify the maximum performance capabilities and minimum service requirements of a new product. Including the customer in the actual development team or designing initial product versions and encouraging user extensions can help the firm focus its development efforts on projects that better fit customer needs.[27]

Many firms use *beta testing* to get customer input early in the development process. Beta versions also enable a firm to signal the market about its product features before the product reaches the commercial production stage. For a firm developing a product with very attractive features, this can persuade customers to forestall purchases of competing products until the firm can introduce its own product. Netscape and NetDynamics both make extensive use of beta testing. Netscape's beta testing enables it to take advantage of lead users as product testers and debuggers. When developing its versions of Navigator, Netscape was at a significant size disadvantage compared to Microsoft. Its beta programs, however, enabled it to partially level the playing field by tapping external developers. NetDynamics, which produces development tools for designing Web pages, uses betas and brings customers into the company early in the development process to rank the priorities of the development process.

Some studies suggest that firms should focus on the input of lead users in their development efforts rather than a large sample of customers. **Lead users** are those who face the same needs of the general marketplace but face them months or years earlier than the bulk of the market, and expect to benefit significantly from a solution to those needs.[28] More detail on how firms use lead users is provided in the accompanying Theory in Action section.

lead users
Customers who face the same general needs of the marketplace but are likely to experience them months or years earlier than the rest of the market and stand to benefit disproportionately from solutions to those needs.

Involving Suppliers

Much of the same logic behind involving customers in the new product development process also applies to involving suppliers. By tapping into the knowledge base of its suppliers, a firm expands its information resources. Suppliers may be actual

Hilti AG, a European manufacturer of construction components and equipment, turned to the lead user method in its development of a pipe hanger (a steel support that fastens pipes to walls or ceilings of buildings). The firm first used telephone interviews to identify customers who had lead user characteristics (were ahead of market trends and stood to benefit disproportionately from the new solution). The lead users were invited to participate in a three-day product concept generation workshop to develop a pipe hanging system that would meet their needs. At the end of the workshop, a single pipe hanger design was selected as the one that best met all the lead users' objectives. The company then presented this design to 12 routine users (customers who were not lead users but who had a long, close relation-

ship with Hilti). Ten of the 12 routine users preferred the new design to previously available solutions, and all but one of the 10 indicated they would be willing to pay a 20 percent higher price for the product. Not only was the project successful, but the lead user method was also faster and cheaper than the conventional market research methods the firm had used in the past to develop its product concepts. Hilti's typical process took 16 months and cost $100,000, but the lead user method took 9 months and cost $51,000.

Source: C. Herstatt and E. von Hippel, "Developing New Product Concepts via the Lead User Method: A Case Study in a Low-Tech Field," *Journal of Product Innovation Management* 9 (1992), pp. 213–21.

members of the product team or consulted as an alliance partner. In either case, they can contribute ideas for product improvement or increased development efficiency. For instance, a supplier may be able to suggest an alternative input (or configuration of inputs) that would achieve the same functionality but at a lower cost. Additionally, by coordinating with suppliers, managers can help to ensure that inputs arrive on time and that necessary changes can be made quickly to minimize development time.[29] Consistent with this argument, research has shown that many firms produce new products in less time, at a lower cost, and with higher quality by incorporating suppliers in integrated product development efforts.[30] For example, consider Chrysler. Beginning in 1989, Chrysler reduced its supplier base from 2,500 to 1,140, offering the remaining suppliers long-term contracts and making them integrally involved in the process of designing new cars. Chrysler also introduced an initiative called SCORE (Supplier Cost Reduction Effort) that encouraged suppliers to make cost-saving suggestions in the development process. The net result was $2.5 billion in savings by 1998.

Boeing's development of the 777 involved both customers and suppliers on the new product development team; United employees (including engineers, pilots, and flight attendants) worked closely with Boeing's engineers to ensure that the airplane was designed for maximum functionality and comfort. Boeing also included General Electric and other parts suppliers on the project team, so that the engines and the body of the airplane could be simultaneously designed for maximum compatibility.

TOOLS FOR IMPROVING THE NEW PRODUCT DEVELOPMENT PROCESS

Some of the most prominent tools used to improve the development process include stage-gate processes, quality function deployment—house of quality, design for manufacturing, and computer-aided design/computer-aided manufacturing. Using the available tools can greatly expedite the new product development process and maximize the product's fit with customer requirements.

Stage-Gate Processes

go/kill decision points
Gates established in the development process where managers must evaluate whether or not to kill the project or allow it to proceed.

As discussed in a previous section, escalating commitment can lead managers to support projects long after their expected value has turned negative, and the cost of pushing bad projects forward can be very high. To help avoid this, many managers and researchers suggest implementing tough **go/kill decision points** in the product development process. The most widely known development model incorporating such go/kill points is the stage-gate process developed by Robert G. Cooper.[31] The stage-gate process provides a blueprint for moving projects through different stages of development. Figure 11.2 shows a typical stage-gate process.

At each stage, a cross-functional team of people (led by a project team leader) undertakes parallel activities designed to drive down the risk of a development project. At each stage of the process, the team is required to gather vital technical, market, and financial information to use in the decision to move the project forward (go), abandon the project (kill), hold, or recycle the project.

In Stage 1, the team does a quick investigation and conceptualization of the project. In Stage 2, the team builds a business case that includes a defined product, its business justification, and a detailed plan of action for the next stages. In Stage 3, the team begins the actual design and development of the product, including mapping out the manufacturing process, the market launch, and operating plans. In this stage, the team also defines the test plans utilized in the next stage. In Stage 4, the team conducts the verification and validation process for the proposed new product, and its marketing and production. At Stage 5, the product is ready for launch, and full commercial production and selling commence.[32]

Preceding each stage is a go/kill gate. These gates are designed to control the quality of the project and to ensure that the project is being executed in an effective and efficient manner. Gates act as the funnels that cull mediocre projects. Each gate has three components: *deliverables* (these are the results of the previous stage and are the inputs for the gate review), *criteria* (these are the questions or metrics used to make the go/kill decision), and *outputs* (these are the results of the gate review process and may include a decision such as go, kill, hold, or recycle; outputs should also include an action plan for the dates and deliverables of the next gate).

Because each stage of a development project typically costs more than the stage preceding it, breaking down the process into stages deconstructs the development investment into a series of incremental commitments. Expenditures increase only as uncertainty decreases. Figure 11.3 shows the escalation costs and cycle time for each stage of a typical development process in a manufacturing industry.

FIGURE 11.2
Typical Stage-Gate Process, from Idea to Launch

Source: Adapted from R. G. Cooper, "Doing It Right," *Ivey Business Journal* 64, no. 6 (2000), pp. 54–60.

	GATE 1	GATE 2	GATE 3	GATE 4	GATE 5	
	Idea Screen	Second Screen	Decision to Develop	Decision to Test	Decision to Launch	
	Does the idea merit any work?	Does the idea justify extensive investigation?	Is the business case sound?	Should the project be moved to external testing?	Is the product ready for commercial launch?	
IDEA	**SCOPING**	**BUILDING BUSINESS CASE**	**DEVELOPMENT**	**TESTING & VALIDATION**	**LAUNCH**	**POST-LAUNCH REVIEW**
	STAGE 1	STAGE 2	STAGE 3	STAGE 4	STAGE 5	
	• Preliminary market assessment • Preliminary technical assessment • Preliminary financial and business assessment • Action plan for Stage 2	• User needs and wants study • Competitive analysis • Value proposition defined • Technical feasibility assessment • Operations assessment • Product definition • Financial analysis	• Technical development work • Rapid prototypes • Initial customer feedback • Prototype development • In-house product testing • Operations process development • Full launch and operations plans	• Extended in-house testing • Customer field trials • Acquisition of production equipment • Production trials • Test market/trial sell • Finalized launch and operations plans • Post launch and life cycle plans	• Market launch and rollout • Full production • Selling begun • Results monitoring • Post launch and life cycle plans under way	How did we do vs. projections? What did we learn?

FIGURE 11.3
Escalation of Development Time and Costs by Stage

Source: Adapted from F. Buggie, "Set the 'Fuzzy Front End' in Concrete," *Research Technology Management* 45, no. 4 (2002), pp. 11–14.

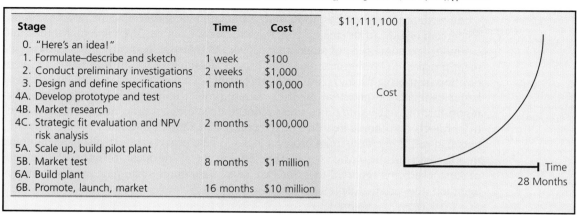

Stage	Time	Cost
0. "Here's an idea!"		
1. Formulate–describe and sketch	1 week	$100
2. Conduct preliminary investigations	2 weeks	$1,000
3. Design and define specifications	1 month	$10,000
4A. Develop prototype and test		
4B. Market research		
4C. Strategic fit evaluation and NPV risk analysis	2 months	$100,000
5A. Scale up, build pilot plant		
5B. Market test	8 months	$1 million
6A. Build plant		
6B. Promote, launch, market	16 months	$10 million

$11,111,100

Cost

Time

28 Months

FIGURE 11.4
Exxon Research and Engineering's Stage-Gate System

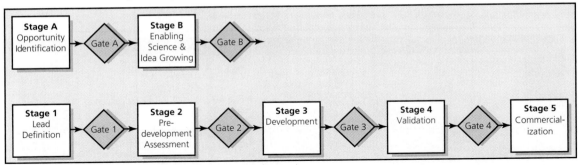

Many companies have adapted the stage-gate process to more specifically meet the needs of their firm or industry. For example, while managers at Exxon were strong advocates of using a stage-gate process to track and manage development projects, they also felt that the standard five-stage system did not adequately address the needs of a company in which basic research was a primary component in generating innovations. Exxon managers created their own extended stage-gate system to include directed basic research. The resulting stage-gate system included two basic research stages (Stages A and B in Figure 11.4) and five applied research and development stages. In Stage A, the company identifies the potential business incentives and competitive advantages of an envisioned technology. The company then develops a basic research plan that establishes specific scientific deliverables, the methods of achieving these deliverables, and the required resources. In Stage B, Exxon's research division begins to execute the plan developed in Stage A, using scientific methods to generate leads for addressing the business opportunity. Stage 1 then identifies the best leads, using "proof-of-principle" assessments to establish whether the leads are feasible.[33] Stages 2 through 5 proceed according to a typical stage-gate process.

According to a study by the Product Development and Management Association, 68 percent of U.S. firms (including IBM, Procter & Gamble, 3M, General Motors, and Corning) use some type of stage-gate process to manage their new product development process.[34] Corning has made the process mandatory for all information system development projects, and Corning managers believe that the process enables them to better estimate the potential payback of any project under consideration. They also report that the stage-gate process has reduced development time, allows them to identify projects that should be killed, and increases the ratio of internally developed products that result in commercial projects.[35] Stage-gate processes have also been adopted in other parts of the world. As of 2001, 56 percent of European firms and 59 percent of Japanese firms reported that they use some version of stage-gate process to manage their new product development.[36]

Quality Function Deployment (QFD)—The House of Quality

QFD was developed in Japan as a comprehensive process for improving the communication and coordination among engineering, marketing, and manufacturing personnel.[37] It achieves this by taking managers through a problem-solving process in a very structured fashion. The organizing framework for QFD is the "house of quality" (see Figure 11.5). The house of quality is a matrix that maps customer requirements against product attributes. This matrix is completed in a series of steps.

1. The team must first identify customer requirements. In Figure 11.5, market research has identified five attributes that customers value most in a car door: it is easy to open and close, it stays open on a hill, it does not leak in the rain, it isolates the occupant from road noise, and it protects the passengers in the event of crashes.

2. The team weights the customer requirements in terms of their relative importance from a customer's perspective. This information might be obtained from focus group sessions or direct interaction with the customers. The weights are typically entered as percentages, so that the complete list totals 100 percent.

3. The team identifies the engineering attributes that drive the performance of the product—in this case the car door. In Figure 11.5, four attributes are highlighted: the weight of the door, the stiffness of the door hinge (a stiff hinge helps the door stay open on a hill), the tightness of the door seal, and the tightness of the window seal.

FIGURE 11.5
Quality Function Deployment House of Quality for a Car Door

Customer Requirements	Engineering Attributes	Importance	Weight of Door	Stiffness of Hinge	Tightness of Door and Seal	Tightness of Window Seal	Competitor A	Competitor B	Evaluation of New Design
	Easy to Open	15	9	3			7	4	
	Stays Open on Hill	10	3	9			6	7	
	Does Not Leak	35			9	9	7	6	
	Isolates Occupant from Road Noise	20	1		9	9	4	7	
	Crash Protection	20	9				4	7	
Relative Importance of Each Engineering Attribute			365	135	495	495			
Design Targets									

4. The team enters the correlations between the different engineering attributes to assess the degree to which one characteristic may positively or negatively affect another. The correlations are entered into the matrix that creates the peaked roof of the house. In this case, the negative sign between door weight and hinge stiffness indicates that a heavy door reduces the stiffness of the hinge.

5. The team fills in the body of the central matrix. Each cell in the matrix indicates the relationship between an engineering attribute and a customer requirement. A number (in this example, one, three, or nine) is placed in the cell located at the intersection of each row (customer requirements) with each column (engineering attributes), which represents the strength of relationship between them. A value of one indicates a weak relationship, a three indicates a moderate relationship and a nine indicates a strong relationship. The cell is left blank if there is no relationship.

6. The team multiplies the customer importance rating of a feature by its relationship to an engineering attribute (one, three, or nine). These numbers are then summed for each column, yielding a total for the relative importance of each engineering attribute.

7. The team evaluates the competition. A scale of one to seven is used (one indicating a requirement is not addressed, and seven indicating a requirement is completely satisfied) to evaluate the competing products (in this case A and B) on each of the customer requirements. These scores go in the righthand "room" of the house of quality.

8. Using the relative importance ratings established for each engineering attribute and the scores for competing products (from Step 7), the team determines target values for each of the design requirements.

9. The team evaluates the new design that was created based on the design targets from Step 8. The team assesses the degree to which each of the customer requirements has been met, entering a one to seven in the far right column of the house of quality, permitting it to compare the new design with the scores of the competing products.

The great strength of the house of quality is that it provides a common language and framework within which the members of a project team may interact. The house of quality makes the relationship between product attributes and customer requirements very clear, it focuses on design trade-offs, it highlights the competitive shortcomings of the company's existing products, and it helps identify what steps need to be taken to improve them. The house of quality is used in settings as diverse as manufacturing, construction, police service, and educational curriculum design.[38] Advocates of QFD maintain that one of its most valuable characteristics is its positive effect upon cross-functional communication and, through that, upon cycle time and the product/customer fit.[39]

Design for Manufacturing

Another method of facilitating integration between engineering and manufacturing, and of bringing issues of manufacturability into the design process as early as possible, is the use of design for manufacturing methods (DFM). Like QFD, DFM is

FIGURE 11.6
Design Rules for Fabricated Assembly Products

Source: Adapted from M. A. Schilling and C. W. L. Hill, "Managing the New Product Development Process," *Academy of Management Executive* 12, no. 3 (1998), pp. 67–81.

Design Rule	Impact on Performance
Minimize the number of parts	Simplifies assembly; reduces direct labor; reduces material handling and inventory costs; boosts product quality
Minimize the number of part numbers (use common parts across product family)	Reduces material handling and inventory costs; improves economies of scale (increases volume through commonalty)
Eliminate adjustments	Reduces assembly errors (increases quality); allows for automation; increases capacity and throughput
Eliminate fasteners	Simplifies assembly (increases quality); reduces direct labor costs; reduces squeaks and rattles; improves durability; allows for automation
Eliminate jigs and fixtures	Reduces line changeover costs; lowers required investment

simply a way of structuring the new product development process. Often this involves articulating a series of design rules. Figure 11.6 summarizes a set of commonly used design rules, along with their expected impact on performance.

As shown in Figure 11.6, the purpose of such design rules is typically to reduce costs and boost product quality by ensuring that product designs are easy to manufacture. The easier products are to manufacture, the fewer the assembly steps required, the higher labor productivity will be, resulting in lower unit costs. DEKA Research makes a point of bringing manufacturing into the design process early, because as founder Dean Kamen points out, "It doesn't make sense to invent things that ultimately are made of unobtanium or expensium."[40] In addition, designing products to be easy to manufacture decreases the likelihood of making mistakes in the assembly process, resulting in higher product quality.

The benefits of adopting DFM rules can be dramatic. Considering manufacturing at an early stage of the design process can shorten development cycle time. In addition, by lowering costs and increasing product quality, DFM can increase the product's fit with customer requirements. For example, when NCR used DFM techniques to redesign one of its electronic cash registers, it reduced assembly time by 75 percent, reduced the parts required by 85 percent, utilized 65 percent fewer suppliers, and reduced direct labor time by 75 percent.[41]

Computer-Aided Design/Computer-Aided Manufacturing

Computer-aided design (CAD) is the use of computers to build and test product designs. Rapid advances in computer technology have enabled the development of low-priced and high-powered graphics-based workstations. Using these workstations, it is now possible to achieve what could previously be done only on a supercomputer: construct a three-dimensional "working" image of a product or subassembly. This enables product prototypes to be developed and tested in virtual reality. Engineers can quickly adjust prototype attributes by manipulating the three-dimensional model, allowing them to compare the characteristics of different product designs. Eliminating the need to build physical prototypes can reduce cycle time and lower costs as illustrated in the accompanying Theory in Action. Visualization tools and 3-D software are even being used to allow nonengineering customers to see and make minor alterations to the design and materials.

Computer-aided manufacturing (CAM) is the implementation of machine-controlled processes in manufacturing. CAM is faster and more flexible than traditional manufacturing.[42] Computers can automate the change between different product variations and allow for more variety and customization in the manufacturing process.

TOOLS FOR MEASURING NEW PRODUCT DEVELOPMENT PERFORMANCE

Many companies use a variety of metrics to measure the performance of their new product development process. In addition to providing feedback about a particular new product, such performance assessments help the company improve its innovation strategy and development processes. For example, evaluating the performance of its new product development process may provide insight into which core competencies the firm should focus on, how projects should be selected, whether or not it should seek collaboration partners, how it should manage its development teams, and so on.

At Microsoft, almost all projects receive either a postmortem discussion or a written postmortem report to ensure that the company learns from each of its development experiences. These postmortems tend to be extremely candid and can be quite critical. As noted by one Microsoft manager, "The purpose of the document is to beat yourself up." Another Microsoft manager notes that part of the Microsoft culture is to be very self-critical and never be satisfied at getting things "halfway right." A team will spend three to six months putting together a postmortem document that may number anywhere from less than 10 pages to more than 100. These postmortem reports describe the development activities and team, provide data on the product size (e.g., lines of code) and quality (e.g., number of bugs), and an evaluation of what worked well, what did not work well, and what the group should do to improve on the next project. These reports are then distributed to the team members and to senior executives throughout the organization.

Source: M. A. Cusumano and R. W. Selby, *Microsoft Secrets* (New York: Free Press, 1995).

Both the metrics used by firms and the timing of their use vary substantially across firms. In a survey by Goldense and Gilmore, 45 percent of companies reported using periodic reviews at calendar periods (e.g., monthly or weekly) and at predetermined milestones (e.g., after product definition, after process design, post launch, etc.).[43] Microsoft, for example, uses postmortems to measure new product development performance, as described in the accompanying Theory in Action. Measures of the success of the new product development process can help management to:

- Identify which projects met their goals and why.
- Benchmark the organization's performance compared to that of competitors or to the organization's own prior performance.
- Improve resource allocation and employee compensation.
- Refine future innovation strategies.[44]

Multiple measures are important because any measure used singly may not give a fair representation of the effectiveness of the firm's development process or its overall innovation performance. Also, the firm's development strategy, industry, and other environmental circumstances must be considered when formulating measures and interpreting results. For example, a firm whose capabilities or objectives favor development of breakthrough projects may experience long intervals between product introductions and receive a low score on measures such as cycle time or percent of sales earned on projects launched within the past five years, despite its success at its strategy. Conversely, a firm that rapidly produces new generations of products may receive a high score on such measures even if it finds its resources are overtaxed and its projects are overbudget. Additionally, the success rate of new product development can vary significantly by industry and project type. Some authors argue that even firms with excellent new product development processes should not expect to have a greater than 65 percent success rate for all new products launched.[45]

New Product Development Process Metrics

Many firms use a number of methods to gauge the effectiveness and efficiency of the development process. These measures capture different dimensions of the firm's ability to successfully shepherd projects through the development process. To use such methods it is important to first define a finite period in which the measure is to be applied in order to get an accurate view of the company's current performance; this also makes it easier for the manager to calculate a response. The following questions can then be asked:

1. What was the average cycle time (time to market) for development projects? How did this cycle time vary for projects characterized as breakthrough, platform, or derivative?
2. What percentage of development projects undertaken within the past five years met all or most of the deadlines set for the project?
3. What percentage of development projects undertaken within the past five years stayed within budget?
4. What percentage of development projects undertaken within the past five years resulted in a completed product?

Overall Innovation Performance

Firms also use a variety of methods to assess their overall performance at innovation. These measures give an overall view of the bang for the buck the organization is achieving with its new product development processes. Such measures include:

1. What is the firm's return on innovation? (This measure assesses the ratio of the firm's total profits from new products to its total expeditures, including research and development costs, the costs of retooling and staffing production facilities, and initial commercialization and marketing costs.)
2. What percentage of projects achieve their sales goals?
3. What percentage of revenues are generated by products developed within the past five years?
4. What is the firm's ratio of successful projects to its total project portfolio?

Summary of Chapter

1. Successful new product development requires achieving three simultaneous objectives: maximizing fit with customer requirements, minimizing time to market, and controlling development costs.
2. Many firms have adopted parallel development processes to shorten the development cycle time and to increase coordination among functions such as R&D, marketing, and manufacturing.
3. Many firms have also begun using project champions to help ensure a project's momentum and improve its access to key resources. Use of champions also has its risks, however, including escalating commitment and unwillingness of others in the organization to challenge the project.

4. Involving customers in the development process can help a firm ensure that its new products match customer expectations. In particular, research indicates that involving lead users can help the firm understand what needs are most important to customers, helping the firm to identify its development priorities. Involving lead users in the development process can also be faster and cheaper than involving a random sample of customers in the development process.

5. Many firms use beta testing to get customer feedback, exploit external development of the product, and signal the market about the firm's upcoming products.

6. Firms can also involve suppliers in the development process, helping to minimize the input cost of a new product design and improving the likelihood that inputs are of appropriate quality and arrive on time.

7. Stage-gate processes offer a blueprint for guiding firms through the new product development process, providing a series of go/kill gates where the firm must decide if the project should be continued and how its activities should be prioritized.

8. Quality function deployment can be used to improve the development team's understanding of the relationship between customer requirements and engineering attributes. It can also be a tool for improving communication between the various functions involved in the development process.

9. Design for manufacturing and CAD/CAM are additional tools development teams can use to reduce cycle time, improve product quality, and control development costs.

10. Firms should use a variety of measures of their new product development effectiveness and overall innovation performance to identify opportunities for improving the new product development process and improving the allocation of resources.

Discussion Questions

1. What are some of the advantages and disadvantages of a parallel development process? What obstacles might a firm face in attempting to adopt a parallel process?

2. Consider a group project you have worked on at work or school. Did your group use mostly sequential or parallel processes?

3. Name some industries in which a parallel process would not be possible or effective.

4. What kinds of people make good project champions? How can a firm ensure that it gets the benefits of championing while minimizing the risks?

5. Is the stage-gate process consistent with suggestions that firms adopt parallel processes? What impact do you think using stage-gate processes would have on development cycle time and development costs?

6. What are the benefits and costs of involving customers and suppliers in the development process?

Endnotes

1. M. Byars, "IDEO: Masters of Innovation," *Graphis* 58, no. 335 (2001), pp. 103–5.

2. S. Thomke and A. Nimgade, "IDEO Product Development." Harvard Business School case #9-600-143, 2000.

3. E. Berggren and T. Nacher, "Introducing New Products Can Be Hazardous to Your Company: Use the Right New-Solutions Delivery Tools," *Academy of Management Executive* 15, no. 3 (2001), pp. 92–101.

4. M. A. Schilling, "Technological Lockout: An Integrative Model of the Economic and Strategic Factors Driving Success and Failure," *Academy of Management Review* 23 (1998), pp. 267–84; and W. B. Arthur, *Increasing Returns and Path Dependence in the Economy* (Ann Arbor: University of Michigan Press, 1994).

5. A. Dhebar, "Speeding High-Tech Producer, Meet Balking Consumer," *Sloan Management Review,* Winter 1996, pp. 37–49.

6. M. C. Crawford, "The Hidden Costs of Accelerated Product Development," *Journal of Product Innovation Management* 9, no. 3 (1992), pp. 188–200.

7. G. Pacheco-de-Almeida and P. Zemsky, "The Creation and Sustainability of Competitive Advantage: Resource Accumulation with Time Compression Diseconomies," mimeo, Stern School of Business, 2003.

8. E. J. Nijssen, A. R. Arbouw, and H. R. Commandeur, "Accelerating New Product Development: A Preliminary Empirical Test of a Hierarchy of Implementation," *Journal of Product Innovation Management* 12 (1995), pp. 99–104; R. W. Schmenner, "The Merits of Making Things Fast," *Sloan Management Review,* Fall 1988, pp. 11–17; A. Ali, R. Krapfel, and D. LaBahn, "Product Innovativeness and Entry Strategy: Impact on Cycle Time and Break-Even Time," *Journal of Product Innovation Management* 12 (1995), pp. 54–69; and R. Rothwell, "Successful Industrial Innovation: Critical Factors for the 1990s," *R&D Management* 22, no. 3 (1992), pp. 221–39.

9. A. Griffin, "Evaluating QFD's Use in US Firms as a Process for Developing Products," *Journal of Product Innovation Management* 9 (1992), pp. 171–87; and C. H. Kimzey, *Summary of the Task Force Workshop on Industrial-Based Initiatives* (Washington, DC: Office of the Assistant Secretary of Defense, Production and Logistics, 1987).

10. A. De Meyer and B. Van Hooland, "The Contribution of Manufacturing to Shortening Design Cycle Times," *R&D Management* 20, no. 3 (1990), pp. 229–39; R. Hayes, S. G. Wheelwright, and K. B. Clark, *Dynamic Manufacturing* (New York: Free Press, 1988); R. G. Cooper, "The New Product Process: A Decision Guide for Managers," *Journal Marketing Management* 3 (1988), pp. 238–55; and H. Takeuchi and I. Nonaka, "The New Product Development Game," *Harvard Business Review,* January–February, 64, no. 1 (1986), pp. 137–46.

11. K. Eisenhardt and B. N. Tabrizi, "Accelerating Adaptive Processes: Product Innovation in the Global Computer Industry," *Administrative Science Quarterly* 40 (1995), pp. 84–110; and C. Terwiesch and C. H. Loch, "Measuring the Effectiveness of Overlapping Development Activities," *Management Science* 45 (1999), pp. 455–65.

12. B. J. Zirger and M. A. Maidique, "A Model of New Product Development: An Empirical Test," *Management Science* 36 (1990), pp. 867–83; R. Rothwell, C. Freeman, A. Horley, P. Jervis, A. B. Robertson, and J. Townsend, "SAPPHO Updates—Project SAPPHO, PHASE II," *Research Policy* 3 (1974), pp. 258–91; A. H. Rubenstein, A. K. Chakrabarti, R. D. O'Keffe, W. E. Souder, and H. C. Young, "Factors Influencing Innovation Success at the Project Level," *Research Management,* May 1976, pp. 15–20; F. A. Johne and P. A. Snelson, "Product Development Approaches in Established Firms," *Industrial Marketing Management* 18 (1989), pp. 113–24; and Y. Wind and V. Mahajan, "New Product Development Process: A Perspective for Reexamination," *Journal of Product Innovation Management* 5 (1988), pp. 304–10.

13. E. Roberts, "Benchmarking Global Strategic Management of Technology," *Research Technology Management,* March–April 2001, pp. 25–36.

14. E. Rudden, "The Misuse of a Sound Investment Tool," *The Wall Street Journal,* November 1, 1982.

15. M. Devaney, "Risk, Commitment, and Project Abandonment," *Journal of Business Ethics* 10, no. 2 (1991), pp. 157–60.

16. A. Corsig, T. Soloway, and R. Stanaro, "Glaxo Holdings PLC: Zantac," in *New Product Success Stories,* ed. R. Thomas (New York: John Wiley & Sons, Inc., 1995), pp. 242–52.

17. Ibid.

18. C. Kennedy, "Medicine Man to the World," *Director* 46, no. 4 (1992), pp. 106–10.

19. "Anti-Ulcer Drugs: Too Much Acid," *The Economist* 318, no. 7700 (1991), pp. 82–84.

20. Corsig, Soloway, and Stanaro, "Glaxo Holdings PLC: Zantac."

21. S. Markham, S. Green, and R. Basu, "Champions and Antagonists: Relationships with R&D Project Characteristics and Management," *Journal of Engineering and Technology Management* 8 (1991), pp. 217–42; S. Markham and A. Griffin, "The Breakfast of Champions: Associations between Champions and Product Development Environments, Practices, and Performance," *The Journal of Product Innovation Management* 15 (1998), pp. 436–54; and S. Markham, "Corporate Championing and Antagonism as Forms of Political Behavior: An R&D Perspective," *Organization Science* 11 (2000), pp. 429–47.

22. Markham, "Corporate Championing and Antagonism as Forms of Political Behavior."

23. D. Day, "Raising Radicals: Different Processes for Championing Innovative Corporate Ventures," *Organization Science* 5 (1994), pp. 148–72.

24. Devaney, "Risk, Commitment, and Project Abandonment."

25. F. A. Johne and P. A. Snelson, "Success Factors in Product Innovation," *Journal of Product Innovation Management* 5 (1988), pp. 114–28; and F. W. Gluck and R. N. Foster, "Managing Technological Change: A Box of Cigars for Brad," *Harvard Business Review* 53 (1975), pp. 139–50.

26. R. G. Cooper, "Selecting Winning New Product Projects: Using the NewProd System," *Journal of Product Innovation Management* 2 (1985), pp. 34–44.

27. J. E. Butler, "Theories of Technological Innovation as Useful Tools for Corporate Strategy," *Strategic Management Journal* 9 (1988), pp. 15–29.

28. C. Herstatt and E. von Hippel, "Developing New Product Concepts via the Lead User Method: A Case Study in a Low-Tech Field," *Journal of Product Innovation Management* 9 (1992), pp. 213–21.

29. Asmus and Griffin found that firms that integrate their suppliers with engineering, manufacturing, and purchasing gain cost reductions, shortened lead times, lowered development risks, and tightened development cycles. D. Asmus and J. Griffin, "Harnessing the Power of Your Suppliers," *McKinsey Quarterly,* no. 3 (1993), pp. 63–79. Additionally, Bonaccorsi and Lipparini found that strategic alliances with suppliers lead to shorter product development cycles and better products, particularly in rapidly changing markets. A. Bonaccorsi and A. Lipparini, "Strategic Partnership in New Product Development: An Italian Case Study," *Journal of Product Innovation Management* 11, no. 2 (1994), pp. 134–46.

30. L. Birou and S. Fawcett, "Supplier Involvement in New Product Development: A Comparison of US and European Practices," *Journal of Physical Distribution and*

Logistics Management 24, no. 5 (1994), pp. 4–15; and A. Ansari and B. Modarress, "Quality Function Deployment: The Role of Suppliers," *International Journal of Purchasing and Materials Management* 30, no. 4 (1994), pp. 28–36.

31. R. Cooper and E. J. Kleinschmidt, "New Product Processes at Leading Industrial Firms," *Industrial-Marketing-Management* 20, no. 2 (1991), pp. 137–48; and R. G. Cooper, "Doing It Right," *Ivey Business Journal* 64, no. 6 (2000), pp. 54–61.

32. Cooper, "Doing It Right."

33. L. Y. Coyeh, P. W. Kamienski, and R. L. Espino, "Gate System Focuses on Industrial Basic Research," *Research Technology Management* 41, no. 4 (1998), pp. 34–37.

34. A. Griffin, 1997. "Drivers of NPD Success: The 1997 PDMA Report."

35. A. LaPlante and A. E. Alter, "Corning, Inc: The Stage-Gate Innovation Process," *Computerworld* 28, no. 44 (1994), p. 81.

36. E. Roberts, "Benchmarking Global Strategic Management of Technology," *Research Technology Management,* March–April 2001, pp. 25–36.

37. J. J. Cristiano, J. K. Liker, and C. C. White, "Key Factors in the Successful Application of Quality Function Deployment (QFD)," *IEEE Transactions on Engineering Management* 48, no. 1 (2001), p. 81.

38. I. Bier, "Using QFD to Construct a Higher Education Curriculum," *Quality Progress* 34, no. 4 (2001), pp. 64–69; N. Eldin, "A Promising Planning Tool: Quality Function Deployment," *Cost Engineering* 44, no. 3 (2002), pp. 28–38; and W. J. Selen and J. Schepers, "Design of Quality Service Systems in the Public Sector: Use of Quality Function Deployment in Police Services," *Total Quality Management* 12, no. 5 (2001), pp. 677–87.

39. K. B. Clark and S. C. Wheelwright, *Managing New Product and Process Development* (New York: Free Press, 1993); J. R. Hauser and D. Clausing, "The House of Quality," *Harvard Business Review,* May–June 1988, pp. 63–73; A. Griffin, "Evaluating QFD's Use in US Firms as a Process for Developing Products," *Journal of Product Innovation Management* 9 (1992), pp. 171–87; and A. Griffin and J. R. Hauser, "Patterns of Communication among Marketing, Engineering and Manufacturing," *Management Science* 38 (1992), pp. 360–73.

40. E. I. Schwartz, "The Inventor's Play-Ground," *Technology Review* 105, no. 8 (2002), pp. 68–73.

41. Clark and Wheelwright, *Managing New Product and Process Development.*

42. M. R. Millson, S. P. Raj, and D. Wilemon, "A Survey of Major Approaches for Accelerating New Product Development," *Journal of Product Innovation Management* 9 (1992), pp. 53–69.

43. B. L. Goldense and J. Gilmore, "Measuring Product Design," *Machine Design* 73, no. 14 (2001), pp. 63–67.

44. T. D. Kuczmarski, "Measuring Your Return on Innovation," *Marketing Management* 9, no. 1 (2000), pp. 24–32.

45. Ibid.

Chapter **Twelve**

Managing New Product Development Teams

New Product Development at Dell Computer

In 1993, after years of rapid growth, Dell Computer Corporation faced a cash flow crunch. Increasing competition and price wars caused Dell to experience its first year of losses, and Dell's stock price began to plummet. Dell's first line of notebook computers, introduced in 1992, had technical problems that led to a callback of 17,000 units. Notebook computers were the fastest-growing category of personal computer sales, and Dell's management thought the company's lack of a notebook computer left a gaping hole in its product line.[1] Development of a new notebook had to proceed carefully, however, since the investment community would be carefully watching Dell's next moves.

Dell had traditionally used a small research and development budget and an informal development process. In the early 1990s, Dell's new product development was carried out by autonomous teams that consisted primarily of experienced developers. The informal approach had often been successful, but its outcomes were inconsistent. Project leaders implemented their own execution process, and team members did not always share common objectives for the project. Often product design would be completed and then "thrown over the wall" to manufacturing. This meant that design problems were often not discovered until late in the development process. Dell's senior management concluded that a more structured approach to new product development was necessary.

In early 1993, Dell began to organize product development teams that consisted of a core team of development professionals from multiple functions within the company. These teams would nominate their own project leader and would be committed to the new development project from start to finish. By having design and manufacturing engineers interact daily on the development team, Dell hoped to identify problems in new product designs earlier in the development cycle. Dell also structured its development process around a serious of phases:

1. *Profile phase*—the product development team would define the product and market.

2. *Planning phase*—the product team would develop a complete business case for the development project, which would be scrutinized by senior management.
3. *Implementation phase*—the development team would design, produce, and test a functional prototype. The team also would begin making commitments to suppliers.
4. *Qualification phase*—Production prototypes would be evaluated by customers to obtain their input on potential improvements.
5. *Launch phase*—The development team would ramp up production and begin shipping completed products to customers.
6. *Acceptance phase*—Customer feedback would be compared to the development project's objectives.

The cross-functional teams would direct each phase of the development process, and would review and be held accountable for the outcome of each phase.

By the fall of 1994, Dell had introduced five new notebook models, and by 1995 Dell was selling $700 million worth of notebooks a year. Dell was a leader in notebook sales by 1998, and analysts attributed its success to its technical consistency.[2]

Discussion Questions

1. What are some advantages of Dell's adoption of a more structured new product development process? Are there risks in abandoning its previous informal approach?
2. How does including engineers from different functions affect Dell's development process?
3. What are the benefits and costs of keeping the same team members on the development project for its duration?
4. If you were a senior manager at Dell, what recommendations would you make for further improving the development process?

OVERVIEW

New product development often requires activities that are the responsibility of different departments within the organization. To facilitate coordination and cooperation across division boundaries, many organizations create cross-functional new product development teams to lead and manage the development process for the project. There is considerable variation, however, in how teams are formed and managed. In this chapter, we will look at several factors that affect the new product development team's performance, including its size, composition, structure, administration, and leadership.

CONSTRUCTING NEW PRODUCT DEVELOPMENT TEAMS

In constructing new product development teams, the organization must consider how the team's size and composition will affect its mix of skills, its access to resources, and its effectiveness in providing communication and coordination across the divisions.

Team Size

New product development teams may range from a few members to hundreds of members. For example, the development team that created the IBM personal computer had 19 members, but the average team size for development projects at IBM is close to 200.[3] The Yahoo! Internet portal was developed by 13 software developers, split into several small teams of one to three members.[4] By combining the efforts and expertise of multiple individuals, groups can often outperform individuals on many problem-solving tasks, implying that the size of the development team might be related to its potential for success.[5]

Bigger, however, is not always better. Large teams can create more administrative costs and communication problems, leading to costly delays. Additionally, the larger the team, the harder it can be to foster a shared sense of identity among team members. Further, as the size of the team increases, the potential for **social loafing** also increases. Social loafing occurs when, as the size of the team increases, individuals perceive that they will not receive full credit (or blame) for their contribution to the group effort and so their effort and commitment decreases.[6] The average team size used by U.S. organizations is 11 members,[7] but there is considerable variance in the size of teams used by organizations, and each team may vary in size over the course of a new product development project.

social loafing
When an individual in a team does not exert the expected amount of effort and relies instead on the work of other team members.

Team Composition

A lack of communication among the marketing, R&D, and manufacturing functions of a company can be extremely detrimental to new product development. A lack of cross-functional communication can lead to a poor fit between product attributes and customer requirements. R&D cannot design products that fit customer requirements unless it receives *and* attends to input from marketing regarding those requirements. The manufacturing/R&D interface is also of critical importance because of manufacturing's role in determining two key attributes of a product—*quality* and *price*. By working closely with R&D, manufacturing can ensure that R&D designs products that are relatively easy to manufacture. Designing for ease of manufacturing can lower both unit costs and product defects, which translates into a lower final price and higher quality. Similarly, a lack of cross-functional communication between functions can lead to longer cycle times as a product iterates back and forth between different stages in the process.

Firms can rectify this problem by building cross-functional product development teams.[8] **Cross-functional teams** include members drawn from more than one functional area, such as engineering, manufacturing, or marketing.[9] For instance, in Chrysler's "vehicle deployment platform teams," team members are drawn from

cross-functional teams
Teams whose members are drawn from multiple functional areas in the firm such as R&D, marketing, manufacturing, distribution, and so on.

design, engineering, purchasing, manufacturing, product planning, finance, and marketing. Firms around the world rely heavily on cross-functional teams for their new product development efforts. In 2000, 77 percent of U.S. firms, 67 percent of European firms, and 54 percent of Japanese firms reported using cross-functional teams.[10]

Teams that are composed of people from diverse backgrounds have several advantages over teams that are drawn from only one or a few functional areas.[11] A greater variety of specialists provides a broader knowledge base and increases the cross-fertilization of ideas.[12] Having specialists from different areas also allows the project to draw on a wider mix of information sources in the environment through scanning activities (for richer detail on this, see the accompanying Research Brief on boundary spanning activities).[13] Functional experts often actively read journals and are involved in associations that directly affect their trade. These activities can lead to the creation and improvement of innovative ideas, as well as provide solutions to product development problems.[14] By combining members of different functional areas into one project team, a wide variety of information sources can be ensured.

A number of arguments also support other types of diversity. Individuals who enter the organization at different times (organizational tenure diversity) are likely to have different contacts outside of the team, enabling the team to draw from a wider mix of resources. Teams that incorporate cultural diversity should show better problem solving by incorporating multiple viewpoints, and teams composed of members who are diverse in terms of gender or age will also ensure a variety of viewpoints are considered and external resources are tapped.[15] Studies have demonstrated that demographic diversity in teams can increase innovative outcomes and overall performance.[16]

Diversity of team members, however, can also raise coordination and communication costs. Individuals tend to interact more frequently and more intensely with other individuals who they perceive as being similar to them on one or more dimensions.[17] This phenomenon is known as **homophily.** Research on homophily suggests that individuals prefer to communicate with others they perceive as similar to them because it is easier and more comfortable to communicate with those who have similar dialects, mental models, and belief systems.[18] The perception of similarity can also be self-reinforcing—as individuals interact with frequency and intensity, they can develop a common dialect, greater trust, and greater familiarity with the knowledge each possesses. The common dialect, trust, and familiarity, in turn, make the individuals both more willing and more able to exchange information effectively in future interactions. When individuals perceive others as being very different from them, they may be less willing to interact frequently or intensely, and it may be more difficult for them to develop a shared understanding. Heterogeneous team often have greater difficulty integrating objectives and views, leading to conflict and lower group cohesion.[19] Research has also indicated, however, that the communication and coordination differences between heterogeneous or homogeneous teams diminishes if the groups maintain long-term contact. Presumably, through extensive interaction, heterogeneous teams learn to manage their group processes better.[20]

In sum, heterogeneous teams should possess more information, on average, than homogeneous groups. The heterogeneity of a team can also increase the creativity and

homophily
The tendency for individuals to like other people whom they perceive as being similar to themselves.

Research Brief Boundary-Spanning Activities in New Product Development Teams

To be successful, new product development teams must be able to manage relationships with groups that are beyond the team's boundaries. Teams need to be able to collect information and resources both within and outside of their organizations, and they also need to represent the team to other groups in the organization to ensure that the team continues to receive support and that team members are not overloaded with non-team-related activities.[21] The most successful new product development teams have gatekeepers who provide important links to the environment.[22]

Deborah Ancona and David Caldwell conducted a study to explore the full range of boundary-spanning activities in which teams engage and to identify which of these activities enhanced team performance. They interviewed 38 experienced product development team managers and collected data from 45 product development teams in five high-technology companies in the computer, analytic instruments, and photographic equipment industries. Ancona and Caldwell found that teams engaged in three primary types of boundary-spanning activity:

Ambassador activities—These activities were directed at representing the team to others and protecting the team from interference.

For example, an ambassador might convince other individuals in the organization that the team's activities are important.

Task coordination activities—These activities emphasized coordinating and negotiating the team's activities with other groups. For instance, task coordination activities might include negotiating delivery deadlines with other divisions of the firm or obtaining feedback about the team's performance.

Scouting activities—These activities were directed at scanning for ideas and information that might be useful to the team, enhancing its knowledge base. For example, scouting activities could include collecting data about what competitors were doing on similar projects or finding technical information that might be useful in the development project.

Ancona and Caldwell found that boundary-spanning activities affected the performance of the new product development team, and their impact depended on the timing of the activities. In particular, they found that scouting and ambassador activities were more beneficial if conducted early in the development project cycle, while task coordination activities were beneficial throughout the life of the team.[23]

variance in decision making, leading to more innovative outcomes and higher overall performance.[24] However, to realize this potential performance advantage, heterogeneous teams may require long-term contact and incentives to foster communication and cooperation.

The ability of team members to communicate and cooperate effectively is also a function of the personalities of the individuals on the team. A study by Susan Kichuk and Willi Wiesner explored whether five personality factors (conscientiousness, extroversion, neuroticism, agreeableness, and openness to experience) influenced the likelihood of success in new product development teams. Kichuk and Wiesner found that the personality characteristics that enhanced the success of a new product development team were high extroversion, high agreeableness, and low neuroticism.[25]

THE STRUCTURE OF NEW PRODUCT DEVELOPMENT TEAMS

Teams can be structured in a number of ways. One well-known typology classifies teams into four types: functional, lightweight, heavyweight, and autonomous.[26] Figure 12.1 depicts each of these types graphically.

Functional Teams

In functional teams, members remain in their functional departments (e.g., R&D, marketing, manufacturing, etc.), and report to their regular functional manager (see Figure 12.1, panel A); however, they may meet periodically to discuss the project. Such teams are usually temporary, and individuals may spend less than 10 percent of their time working on team-related activities. Functional teams also typically do not have a project manager or dedicated liaison personnel. While this team structure is

FIGURE 12.1

Types of Development Teams

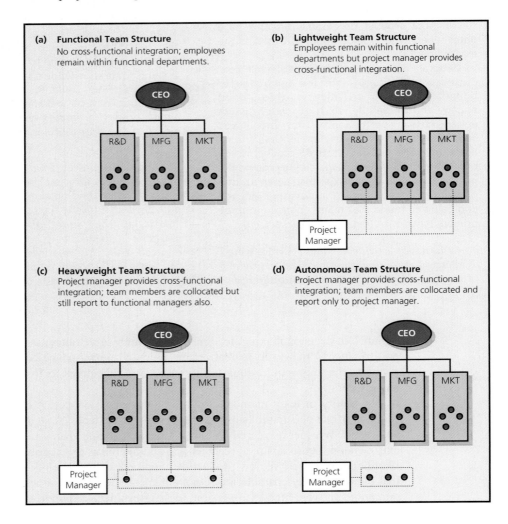

straightforward to implement because it requires little (if any) deviation from the firm's normal operations, this structure provides little opportunity for cross-functional coordination.[27] Further, since individuals are still evaluated and rewarded almost exclusively based on their functional performance, the team members may have little commitment to the development project. Functional teams are more likely to be appropriate for derivative projects that primarily affect only a single function of the firm.

Lightweight Teams

In lightweight teams, members still reside in their functional departments, and functional supervisors retain authority over evaluation and rewards (see Figure 12.1, panel B). Like functional teams, lightweight teams are typically temporary, and members spend the majority of their time on their normal functional responsibilities (up to 25 percent of their time might be spent on team-related activities). However, lightweight teams have a project manager and dedicated liaison personnel who facilitate communication and coordination among functions. Managers of lightweight teams are normally junior or middle management employees, who are not able to exert significant influence or authority over team members. As a result of these factors, lightweight teams offer a small improvement in team coordination and likelihood of success over functional teams. Such a team structure might be appropriate for derivative projects where high levels of coordination and communication are not required.

Heavyweight Teams

In heavyweight teams, members are removed from their functional departments so that they may be *collocated* with the project manager (see Figure 12.1, panel C). Project managers of heavyweight teams are typically senior managers who outrank functional managers, and have significant authority to command resources, and evaluate and reward team members.[28] The core group of team members in the heavyweight team is often dedicated full-time to the project. This combination of factors helps ensure that the team has strong cross-functional coordination and communication, and that team members are significantly committed to the development project. However, heavyweight teams are still often temporary; thus, the long-term career development of individual members continues to rest with their functional managers rather than the project manager. This type of team structure offers a significant improvement in communication and coordination over functional teams, and it is typically considered appropriate for platform projects.

Autonomous Teams

In autonomous teams, members are removed from their functional departments and dedicated full-time (and often permanently) to the development team (see Figure 12.1, panel D). Team members are collocated with the project manager, who is a very senior person in the organization. The project manager of an autonomous team is given full control over resources contributed from different functional departments, and the project manager has exclusive authority over the evaluation and reward of team members. Autonomous teams often do not conform to the operating procedures of the rest of the organization; instead they are permitted to create their own policies, procedures, and reward systems.[29] Autonomous teams are also held fully accountable for the success of the project; in many ways, autonomous teams act like independent divisions of the firm. Autonomous teams typically excel at rapid and efficient new product development, particularly when such development requires breaking away from the organization's existing technologies and routines. Thus, autonomous teams are typically considered to be appropriate for breakthrough projects and some major platform projects. They can be the birthplace of new business units.[30] However, the independence of the autonomous teams can cause them to underutilize the resources of the parent organization. Furthermore, autonomous teams are often hard to fold back into the organization if the project is completed or terminated. For an example of the use of autonomous teams, see the accompanying Theory in Action on Chrysler's "platform teams."

Figure 12.2 summarizes key dimensions across which the four teams vary, including a number of points that have not yet been dealt with in the text. The potential for

FIGURE 12.2
Summary of Characteristics of Team Types

Characteristics	Functional Team	Lightweight Team	Heavyweight Team	Autonomous Team
Project manager	None	Junior or middle manager	Senior manager	Senior manager
Power of project manager	NA	Low	High	Very high
Time spent on team activities	Up to 10%	Up to 25%	100%	100%
Location of team members	Functions	Functions	Collocated with project manager	Collocated with project manager
Length of commitment to team	Temporary	Temporary	Long-term but ultimately temporary	Permanent
Evaluation of team members	Functional heads	Functional heads	Project manager and functional heads	Project manager
Potential for conflict between team and functions	Low	Low	Moderate	High
Degree of cross-functional integration	Low	Moderate	High	High
Degree of fit with existing organizational practices	High	High	Moderate	Moderate-low
Appropriate for:	Some derivative projects	Derivative projects	Platform projects/ breakthrough projects	Platform projects/ breakthrough projects

Chrysler reduced its concept-to-market cycle for developing new cars from 60 months in 1988 to 24 months in 1996. It also kept its development costs remarkably low—roughly $550 in R&D costs per car (compared to more than $2,000 per car for Mercedes). The primary mechanism Chrysler used to achieve such development efficiency was the adoption of autonomous teams (called "platform teams" at Chrysler). All of the engineers and designers required to design a new car were collocated on a single floor, along with functional experts from marketing, finance, and purchasing, and outside suppliers. These groups were given target prices to achieve and considerable autonomy to achieve them. Close contact between the team members kept them fast, efficient, and flexible, enabling teams to consistently outperform their time and budget goals. By 1998, Chrysler's vehicle lineup was considered to be one of the most innovative in the industry.

Source: R. Bruner, P. Christmann, R. Spekman, B. Kannry, and M. Davies, "Daimler-Benz A.G.: Negotiations between Daimler and Chrylser," Darden teaching case #UVA-F-1241, 1998.

conflict between the functions and the team, particularly the project manager, rises with the move from functional teams to autonomous teams. The independence of heavyweight and autonomous teams may prompt them to pursue goals that run counter to the interests of the functions. Senior managers should keep such conflict in check.

THE MANAGEMENT OF NEW PRODUCT DEVELOPMENT TEAMS

For a new product development team to be effective, its leadership and administrative policies should be matched to the team's structure and needs.

Team Leadership

The team leader is responsible for directing the team's activities, maintaining the team's alignment with project goals, and serving as a communicator between the team and senior management. In heavyweight and autonomous teams, the team leader may also be the person who is primarily responsible for the evaluation, compensation, and promotion of individual team members. Effective team leaders are often much more directly related to the team's success than senior management or project champions. This may be because team leaders interact much more frequently with the team and more directly influence the team's behavior.[31]

As described in the team type and structure section above, different types of teams have different leadership needs. For instance, while lightweight teams might have a junior or middle-management leader who provides basic coordination between the functional groups, heavyweight and autonomous teams require senior managers with significant experience and organizational influence. In heavyweight and autonomous teams, the project manager must be someone who can lead and evaluate the team members, champion the development project both within the team and to the wider organization, and act as a translator between the various functions.[32] In particular, project managers in heavyweight and autonomous teams must have high status within the organization, act as a concept champion for the team within the organization, be good at conflict resolution, have multilingual skills (i.e., they must be able to talk the language of marketing, engineering, and manufacturing), and be able to exert influence upon the engineering, manufacturing, and marketing functions.[33] Other things being equal, teams whose project managers are deficient on one or more of these dimensions will have a lower probability of success.[34]

Team Administration

To ensure that members have a clear focus and commitment to the development project, many organizations now have heavyweight and autonomous teams develop a project charter and contract book. The *project charter* encapsulates the project's mission and articulates exact and measurable goals for the project. It might include a vision statement for the project (e.g., "Dell laptops will be the market standard for performance and value") and a background statement for why this project is important for the organization. The charter may describe who is on the team, the length of time members will spend on the team, and the percentage of their time that will be spent on team activities.[35] It may also stipulate the team's budget, its reporting timeline, and the key success criteria of the project (e.g., meeting a particular time-to-market goal, exceeding customer satisfaction criteria established for the project, capturing a target amount of market share within a defined period of time, etc.). Establishing an explicit set of goals for the project helps ensure that the team members have a common understanding of the project's overall purpose and priorities. Goals also help to structure the new product development process and can facilitate cooperation by keeping team members oriented toward a common outcome.[36]

Once the team charter is established, core team members and senior managers must negotiate a *contract book*. The contract book defines in detail the basic plan to achieve the goal laid out in the project charter. Typically, the contract book will estimate the resources required, the development time schedule, and the results that will be achieved. The contract book provides a tool for monitoring and evaluating the team's performance in meeting objectives by providing a set of performance benchmarks and deadlines to which the team's performance can be compared. More important, however, the contract book is an important mechanism for establishing team commitment to the project and a sense of ownership over the project. After negotiation and acceptance of this contract, all parties often sign the contract book as an indication of their intention to honor the plan and achieve the results. Team members who sign the contract book typically feel a greater sense of duty to work toward the project's goals. Furthermore, signing the contract book can give team members a sense of ownership over the project and empowerment to make decisions about the project. This ownership and empowerment can help team members identify with a project's outcome and can encourage them to exert extra effort to ensure its success.[37]

Managing Virtual Teams

virtual teams
Teams in which members may be a great distance from each other, but are still able to collaborate intensively via advanced information technologies such as videoconferencing, groupware, and e-mail or Internet chat programs.

Recent advances in information technology have enabled companies to make greater use of virtual teams. **Virtual teams** are teams in which members may be a great distance from each other, but are still able to collaborate intensively via advanced information technologies such as videoconferencing, groupware, and e-mail or Internet chat programs. Virtual teaming can enable individuals with unique skills to work on a project, regardless of their location. By meeting virtually, individuals who live at great distances can collaborate without incurring travel costs or disruption to their lives.[38] This is especially valuable for a company whose operations are highly global. For example, when IBM began deploying more its products globally, it increased its use of virtual teams. About one-third of IBM's employees will participate in virtual teams at some point in their career. When IBM needs to staff a project, it gives a list of the needed skills to the human resource division, which identifies an appropriate pool of people. If the skills and talent of the people are more important than their ability to meet face-to-face, a virtual team is formed.[39]

Virtual teams pose a distinct set of management challenges, however. As described earlier in the chapter, much of the work on the structure of new product development teams has emphasized the importance of collocation. Collocation facilitates communication and collaboration by giving team members opportunities for rich face-to-face communication and informal interaction. Proximity and frequent interaction help teams to develop shared norms and a dialect for communicating about the project. Virtual teams, by contrast, must often rely on communication channels that are much less rich than face-to-face contact and face significant hurdles in establishing norms and dialects.

In forming virtual teams, it is important to select personnel who are both comfortable with the technologies being used to facilitate collaboration and who have strong interpersonal skills.[40] Team members must be able to work independently and have a strong work ethic. Since distance makes it easy for team members to deflect opportunities for interaction, it is important to choose individuals who tend to seek interaction rather than avoid it. Furthermore, because many of the opportunities for informal interaction may be lost in a virtual environment, more types of interaction may have to be incorporated into the ground rules of the team. For example, the team leader might schedule daily or weekly unstructured "chat" times where team members are required to participate in a group conference call or online conference to share ideas that may not be uncovered in the team's more formal interactions.

Virtual teams also face challenges in developing trust, resolving conflict, and exchanging tacit knowledge, as discussed in the accompanying Research Brief about virtual international R&D teams.

Research Brief   Virtual International R&D Teams

Gassman and von Zedtwitz build on the transnational corporation model discussed in Chapter 10 by examining how such firms coordinate their international innovation efforts via virtual teams. Similar to some of the arguments made in Chapter 10 about loosely coupled R&D activities, virtual international R&D teams may jointly work on a single development project, utilizing information technologies (rather than geographical proximity) to achieve coordination. However, while information technology decreases the need to collocate R&D activities, it does not readily solve problems related to building trust and transferring tacit knowledge. The type of innovation project being undertaken and the type of knowledge that must be shared should influence the degree to which firms rely on decentralized, virtual coordination processes.

Gassman and von Zedtwitz studied 37 technology-intensive multinationals and identified four patterns of teams: (1) decentralized self-coordination, (2) system integrator as coordinator, (3) core team as system architect, and (4) centralized venture team. In the *decentralized self-coordinating* teams, there was no single source of power or authority over the teams. Teams communicated primarily through telephone, the Internet, shared databases, and groupware. Coordination was relatively weak and relied largely on a strong corporate culture. Decentralized self-coordination was more likely to arise if there were well-developed standard interfaces between components being developed in different locales; thus, it tended to be suited to modular innovation as opposed to architectural innovation (see Chapter Three).

In teams with a *system integrator as R&D coordinator,* a single individual or office takes responsibility for helping different divisions coordinate. The system integrator helps to build a common understanding of the project among each of the divisions, translates knowledge from one division to another, and tracks progress and contributions. While the overall project is decentralized, the system integrator enables some centralized coordination.

In the *core team as system architect* model, a core team of key decision makers from all of the decentralized R&D groups meets regularly to coordinate the otherwise decentralized groups. The core team often includes a strong project manager, leaders from each of the decentralized groups, and occasionally external customers or consultants. The core team constructs the overall architecture of the development project and maintains its coherence throughout its development. Because the core team has more direct authority over the individual divisions than the system integrator described above, the core team is better able to resolve conflict and enforce standards across the divisions. Because core teams can provide a significant level of integration across the divisions, core teams are often able to conduct architectural innovation.

In the *centralized venture team,* R&D personnel and resources are relocated to one central location to enable maximum integration and coordination. The team is likely to have a very powerful senior project manager with significant authority to allocate resources and define the responsibilities of individual team members. Gassman and Von Zedtwitz describe two examples of centralized venture teams—Asea Brown's "High Impact Projects" and Sharp's "Golden Badge" projects. Because of their high expense, such teams are likely to be used only for strategic innovations of the utmost importance.

Gassman and Von Zedtwitz's model is summarized in Figure 12.3. Overall, Gassman and von Zedtwitz argue that innovations that are radical, architectural, or require the intensive transfer of complex or tacit knowledge will require greater centralization. Innovations that are incremental, modular, and do not require the frequent transfer of complex or tacit knowledge can be more decentralized.

continued

concluded

FIGURE 12.3
Gassman and von Zedtwitz's Typology of International Virtual Teams

Decentralization ⟷ Centralization

Decentralized Self-Coordination	**System Integrator as Coordinator**	**Core Team as System Architect**	**Centralized Venture Team**
All R&D conducted by decentralized divisions that coordinate loosely with each other.	Most R&D activity conducted by decentralized divisions, but each coordinates with central integrator.	Core team takes lead role in R&D activities while also coordinating the R&D activities of the decentralized divisions.	R&D resources transferred to centralized venture team, which then conducts all R&D activities.

Source: Adapted from O. Gassman and M. von Zedtwitz, "Trends and Determinants of Managing Virtual R&D Teams," *R&D Management* 33, no. 3 (2003), pp. 243–62.

Summary of Chapter

1. Bringing multiple people together into a team enables multiple bases of expertise to be collectively directed toward problem solving; thus, teams are powerful mechanisms for problem solving. However, if teams become too big, administrative costs and communication problems can become significant.

2. Diversity of team members ensures that the team can draw on different perspectives and bases of expertise. In particular, functional diversity is often sought in new product development teams. Cross-functional teams enable design, manufacturing, and marketing objectives to be integrated in the new product development process.

3. Diversity of team members not only ensures that the individuals in the team possess different knowledge or viewpoints, but also have different sources of extra-team resources upon which to draw through boundary-spanning activities.

4. Diversity can also make it more difficult for teams to develop a common understanding of the new product development project and can result in lower group cohesion. Teams may need long-term contact and incentives for cooperation to overcome these challenges.

5. The way in which a team is structured (collocation, permanence, supervisory relationships, etc.) significantly influences how team members interact and the likely outcomes of a development project. Different types of teams are appropriate for different types of development projects.

6. Attributes of the team leader (seniority, authority, multilingual skills) must match the team type for teams to be most effective.

7. Many firms have teams develop and sign a project charter and contract book to ensure that all team members have a common understanding of the project's goals and possess a sense of ownership and commitment to the project's success.

8. When a company wishes to form a team with individuals who have unique skills but live great distances from each other, it might opt to form a virtual team. Virtual teams use information technologies to achieve communication and coordination. Virtual teams face a distinct set of challenges in promoting participation, cooperation, and trust. As a result, they require special consideration of the selection of team members and the team administration processes.

Discussion Questions

1. What are the trade-offs in choosing a team's size and level of diversity?
2. How can managers ensure that a team reaps the advantages of diversity while not being thwarted by some of the challenges team diversity raises?
3. Identify an example of a development project, and what type of team you believed they used. Do you think this was the appropriate type of team given the nature of the project?
4. What are some advantages and disadvantages of collocation? For what types of projects are virtual teams inappropriate?

Endnotes

1. S. Thomke and A. Nimgade, "Product Development at Dell Computer Corporation," Harvard Business School case #5-699-134, 1990.
2. J. Connolly, K. Burden, and A. Malloy, "Direct Hit," *Computerworld* 32, no. 46 (1998), pp. 81–88.
3. M. A. Cohen, J. Eliashberg, and T. Ho, "New Product Development: The Performance and Time-to-Market Trade-off," *Management Science* 42 (1996), pp. 173–86.
4. M. Iansiti and A. MacCormack, "Living on Internet Time: Product Development at Netscape, Yahoo!, NetDynamics, and Microsoft." Harvard Business School case #9-697-052, 1996.
5. B. E. Collins and H. Guetzkow, *A Social Psychology of Group Processes for Decision Making* (New York: Wiley, 1964); V. B. Hinsz, "Cognitive and Consensus Processes in Group Recognition Memory Performance," *Journal of Personality and Social Psychology* 59 (1990), pp. 705–18; and M. E. Shaw, "Comparison of Individuals and Small Groups in the Rational Solution of Complex Problems," *American Journal of Psychology* 41 (1932), pp. 491–504.
6. S. J. Karau and K. D. Williams, "Social Loafing: A Meta-Analytic Review and Theoretical Integration," *Journal of Personality and Social Psychology* 65 (1993), pp. 681–706.
7. D. J. Devine, L. D. Clayton, J. L. Philips, B. B. Dunford, and S. B. Melner, "Teams in Organizations: Prevalence, Characteristics, and Effectiveness," *Small Group Research* 30 (1999), pp. 678–711.
8. S. Brown and K. Eisenhardt, "Product Development: Past Research, Present Findings, and Future Directions," *Academy of Management Review* 20, no. 2 (1995), pp. 343–78.
9. Ibid.

10. E. Roberts, "Benchmarking Global Strategic Management of Technology," *Research Technology Management,* March–April 2001, pp. 25–36.

11. L. Rochford and W. Rudelius, "How Involving More Functional Areas within a Firm Affects the New Product Process," *Journal of Product Innovation Management* 9 (1992), pp. 287–99.

12. J. R. Kimberly and M. Evanisko, "Organizational Innovation: The Influence of Individual, Organizational, and Contextual Factors on Hospital Adoption of Technological and Administrative Innovations," *Academy of Management Journal* 24 (1981), pp. 689–713; F. Damanpour, "Organization Innovation: A Meta-Analysis of Effects of Determinants and Moderators," *Academy of Management Journal* 34, no. 3 (1991), pp. 555–90; and M. Aiken and J. Hage, "The Organic Organization and Innovation," *Sociology* 5 (1971), pp. 63–82.

13. T. J. Allen, *Managing the Flow of Technology: Technology Transfer and the Dissemination of Technological Information within the R&D Organization* (Cambridge, MA: MIT Press, 1977); D. G. Ancona and D. F. Caldwell, "Demography and Design: Predictors of New Product Team Performance," *Organization Science* 3 (1992), pp. 321–41; and D. G. Ancona, and D. F. Caldwell, "Bridging the Boundary: External Activity and Performance in Organizational Teams," *Administrative Science Quarterly* 37 (1992), pp. 634–65.

14. P. Jervis, "Innovation and Technology Transfer—the Roles and Characteristics of Individuals," *IEEE Transaction on Engineering Management* 22 (1975), pp. 19–27; and D. Miller and P. H. Friesen, "Innovation in Conservative and Entrepreneurial Firms: Two Models of Strategic Momentum," *Strategic Management Journal* 3 (1982), pp. 1–25.

15. I. L. Janis, *Victims of Groupthink* (Boston: Houghton Mifflin, 1972).

16. S. E. Jackson, K. E. May, and K. Whitney, "Understanding the Diversity of Dynamics in Decision Making Teams," in *Team Effectiveness and Decision Making in Organizations,* eds. R. A. Guzzo, E. Salas, and Associates (San Francisco: Jossey-Bass, 1995), pp. 204–61; and R. L. Priem, D. A. Harrison, and N. K. Muir, "Structured Conflict and Consensus Outcomes in Group Decision Making," *Journal of Management* 21 (1995), pp. 691–710.

17. P. F. Lazarsfeld and R. K. Merton "Friendship as a Social Process: A Substantive and Methodological Analysis," in *Freedom and Control in Modern Society,* ed. M. Berger (New York: Van Nostrand, 1954), pp. 8–66.

18. B. Uzzi, "Social Structure and Competition in Interfirm Networks: The Paradox of Embeddedness," *Administrative Science Quarterly* 42 (1997), pp. 35–67.

19. K. L. Bettenhausen, "Five Years of Groups Research: What We Have Learned and What Needs to Be Addressed," *Journal of Management* 17 (1991), pp. 345–81; and K. Williams and C. A. O'Reilly, "Demography and Diversity in Organizations: A Review of 40 Years of Research," *Research in Organizational Behavior* 20 (1998), pp. 77–140.

20. W. Watson, K. Kumar, and L. K. Michaelsen, "Cultural Diversity's Impact on Interaction Process and Performance: Comparing Homogeneous and Diverse Task Groups," *Academy of Management Journal* 36 (1993), pp. 590–602.

21. D. B. Ancona and D. F. Caldwell, "Making Teamwork Work: Boundary Management in Product Development Teams," in *Managing Strategic Innovation and Change,* eds. M. L. Tushman and P. Anderson (New York: Oxford University Press, 1997), pp. 433–42.

22. M. L. Tushman, "Special Boundary Roles in the Innovation Process," *Administrative Science Quarterly* 22 (1977), pp. 587–605; and E. B. Roberts and A. R. Fusfeld, "Staffing the Innovative Technology-Base Organization," *Sloan Management Review* 22, no. 3 (1981), pp. 19–34.

23. Ancona and Caldwell, "Bridging the Boundary."

24. Jackson, May, and Whitney, "Understanding the Diversity of Dynamics in Decision Making Teams."

25. S. L. Kichuk and W. H. Wiesner, "The Big Five Personality Factors and Team Performance: Implications for Selecting Successful Product Design Teams," *Journal of Engineering and Technology Management* 14, nos. 3–4 (1997), pp. 195–222.

26. S. C. Wheelwright and K. B. Clark, *Revolutionizing Product Development: Quantum Leaps in Speed, Efficiency and Quality* (New York: Free Press, 1992).

27. K. B. Clark and S. C. Wheelwright, "Organizing and Leading 'Heavyweight' Development Teams," *California Management Review* 34, no. 3 (1992), pp. 9–29.

28. Ibid.

29. Damanpour, "Organization Innovation."

30. Clark and Wheelwright, "Organizing and Leading 'Heavyweight' Development Teams."

31. E. F. McDonough, "Investigation of Factors Contributing to the Success of Cross-functional Teams. *Journal of Product Innovation Management* 17 (2000), pp. 221–35.

32. K. B. Clark and S. C. Wheelwright, *Managing New Product and Process Development* (New York: Free Press, 1993); E. F. McDonough and G. Barczak, "Speeding Up New Product Development: The Effects of Leadership Style and Source of Technology," *Journal of Product Innovation Management* 8 (1991), pp. 203–11; and G. Barczak and D. Wilemon, "Leadership Differences in New Product Development Teams," *Journal of Production and Innovation Management* 6 (1989), pp. 259–67.

33. Brown and Eisenhardt, "Product Development."

34. M. A. Schilling and C. W. L. Hill, "Managing the New Product Development Process: Strategic Imperatives," *Academy of Management Executive* 12, no. 3 (1998), pp. 67–81.

35. C. W. Miller, "Hunting for Hunting Grounds: Forecasting the Fuzzy Front End," in *The PDMA Toolbook for New Product Development,* eds. P. Belliveau, A. Griffin, and S. Sommermeyer (New York: John Wiley & Sons, 2002).

36. McDonough, "Investigation of Factors Contributing to the Success of Cross-functional Teams."

37. Ibid.

38. C. Joinson, "Managing Virtual Teams: Keeping Members on the Same Page without Being in the Same Place Poses Challenges for Managers," *Human Resource Magazine,* June 2002.

39. Ibid.

40. B. L. Kirkman, B. Rosen, C. B. Gibson, P. E. Tesluk, and S. O. McPherson, "Five Challenges to Virtual Team Success: Lessons from Sabre, Inc." *Academy of Management Executive* 16, no. 3 (2002), p. 67.

Chapter **Thirteen**

Crafting a Deployment Strategy

Deployment Tactics in the U.S. Video Game Industry

In the U.S. video game industry, the introduction of each generation of console has ushered in new battle for market dominance. New entrants have made startling entrances and toppled seemingly invincible incumbents. Games developers, distributors, and customers have had to watch the battle closely in order to place their bets about which console would emerge as the generation's victor. Each generation has also revealed which deployment strategies have paid off—or proven fatal—for the contenders.[1]

Pong: The Beginning of an Era

In 1972, Nolan Bushnell founded a company called Atari and introduced Pong, a ping-pong-like game that was played on a user's television set with the aid of the Atari console. In its first year, Pong earned more than $1 million in revenues. Pong and over 60 similar knockoffs soon flooded the market. In these early years of the video game industry, swift advances in integrated circuits enabled a rapid proliferation of new consoles and games. By 1984, video game console and games sales had reached $3 billion in the United States alone. However, console makers in this era did not utilize strict security measures to ensure that only authorized games could be played on their consoles, leading to explosive growth in the production of unauthorized games (games produced for a console without authorization of that console's producer). As a result, the market was soon saturated with games of dubious quality, and many unhappy retailers were stuck with video game inventories they were unable to move. Profits began to spiral, and by 1985, many industry observers were declaring the video game industry dead.

The Emergence of 8-Bit Systems

Much to everyone's surprise, however, two new companies from Japan entered the U.S. video game market: Nintendo, with its 8-bit Nintendo Entertainment System (NES) introduced in 1985, and Sega, which launched its 8-bit Master

System in the United States in 1986. Unlike Atari, which had spent only a few hundred thousand dollars on advertising, Sega and Nintendo spent $15 million promoting their systems. Both systems offered technological advantages over the previous generation of video game consoles. Sega's Master System appeared to be slightly superior to Nintendo's, but Nintendo spent much more on the development of quality games and characters and had more game titles available than Sega. The NES sold over 1 million units in the first year, sold 19 million units by 1990, and could be found in more than a third of the households in America and Japan.[2]

From 1985 to 1989, Nintendo held a near monopoly of the U.S. video game industry. The company sold its consoles for a price very close to production costs, while earning the bulk of its profits from games. Nintendo both made games for its system in-house and licensed third-party developers to produce games through very strict licensing policies that (*a*) limited the number of titles a developer could produce each year, (*b*) required the developer to preorder a minimum number of cartridges from Nintendo (which had its own contract manufacturers produce the games), and (*c*) restricted the developers from making similar games for other consoles. Nintendo also restricted the volume and pricing of consoles sold through distributors, ensuring that no single distributor acquired significant bargaining power.[3] Nintendo's restrictive policies were very profitable; however, they also caused the company to be sanctioned by the Federal Trade Commission, and they alienated distributors and developers, potentially leaving the company more vulnerable to a competitor.

The 16-Bit Video Game Systems

In September 1989, Sega introduced the 16-bit Genesis to the U.S. video game market. The Genesis offered dramatic performance enhancement over 8-bit systems. Further, Sega leveraged its popular arcade games to the Genesis and made it backward compatible with its 8-bit Master System games. There were 20 Genesis game titles available by December 1989. NEC also introduced a 16-bit system, the TurboGrafx-16, in the fall of 1989 and had 12 game titles by December 1989. Though Nintendo had its own 16-bit system in the works, it delayed introducing it to the United States for fear of cannibalizing its 8-bit system sales.

By the end of 1989, Sega had already sold 600,000 consoles in the United States, and NEC had sold 200,000. In 1990 and 1991, both Sega and NEC added game titles to their lists, bringing their totals to 130 and 80, respectively. By the end of 1991, Sega had sold 2 million consoles in the United States, and NEC had sold 1 million. Unlike Sega, which produced a major portion of its games in-house, NEC relied completely on external games developers, who found the system to have only a small technological advantage over 8-bit systems.[4] Developers began to abandon the NEC platform, and NEC exited the market in 1991. Nintendo finally introduced its own 16-bit Super Nintendo Entertainment System (SNES) in 1991, but it was too late to quell Sega's momentum. In 1992 Nintendo, controlled 80 percent of the video game market (based on combined 8-bit and 16-bit sales), but by 1994, Sega was the market leader.

Like Nintendo, Sega made little profit on the consoles and focused instead on increasing unit sales to drive game sales and software developer royalties. Sega, however, used less restrictive licensing arrangements than Nintendo and rapidly lured a large number of developers to make Sega game titles. Further, though Nintendo could have made its 16-bit system backward compatible, thus linkng the value consumers possessed in their 8-bit game libraries to the new system, Nintendo chose to make the system incompatible with the 8-bit games. By the end of 1991, the SNES had 25 game titles compared to the 130 available for Genesis. Nintendo had given Sega two years of installed base lead on a system that offered a significant technological advantage, and then entered the market at a ground-zero position with respect to the availability of complementary goods. The consequence of Nintendo's late move is aptly captured in a review of video game players published in *Fortune:* "To tell the truth, Nintendo just isn't cool anymore. This one is 16 bits, so it's better than the original Nintendo. But the company only made it to compete with Sega, and most kids already have that. So they don't need Super Nintendo, unless they're jerks and have to have everything. That's just idiotic."[5] Over time, sales of the Nintendo SNES accelerated, and it would ultimately prove to be one of the more successful game systems ever introduced, but Nintendo's near monopoly position had been broken; Sega had successfully leapfrogged Nintendo.

32/64-Bit Systems

The late 1980s and early 1990s also attracted other competitors to the video game market. In 1989, Philips announced its 32-bit Compact Disc Interactive (CD-i), an interactive multimedia compact disc system that would serve as a game player, teaching tool, and music system. However, the CD-i was very complex, requiring a 30-minute demonstration. Furthermore, it was expensive—introduced at $799 and later reduced to a below-cost $500 (more than twice the cost of Nintendo or Sega systems).[6] While the product was actually much more than a video game console, customers compared it to the popular Nintendo and Sega systems and were dismayed by its price and complexity. Making matters worse, Philips was reluctant to disclose the technical specifications, greatly limiting the software development for the system. The Philips CD-i never attained more than a 2 percent market share.[7] Other companies also introduced 32-bit systems, including Turbo Technologies' Duo and 3DO's Interactive Multiplayer, but the cost of the systems ($600 to $700) was prohibitive. Turbo Tech's Duo was very short-lived and received little attention. But 3DO's system received considerable attention. The company was founded in October 1993 by Trip Hawkins, formerly of video games developer Electronic Arts. However, 3DO's unique strategy of licensing out all game and hardware production made it impossible to achieve the low console prices of Sega and Nintendo by subsidizing console production with game royalties. The hardware producers (Matsushita and Panasonic) for 3DO did not sell games and were unwilling to sell the consoles without a margin. Sales of the machine never took off, and 3DO exited the market. Atari also made a surprising return to the video game market in 1993 with the technologically advanced Jaguar. However, Atari's long struggle had not inspired great confidence in either developers or distributors, and several of the large retail chains chose not to carry the product.[8]

In 1995, two 32-bit systems arrived on the scene that would survive: Sega's Saturn and Sony's PlayStation. Both systems were introduced with great fanfare and considerable developer support. Although only Sega had experience and brand image in the video game market, Sony entered with tremendous brand image in consumer electronics and access to (and leverage in) extensive distribution channels in electronics and media. To rapidly gain insight into the toy industry, Sony hired experienced toy industry veteran Bruce Stein to head the video game unit. Sony's size and previous success in several electronics markets (including the development and control of the compact disc format) also enabled it to persuade several games developers (including Electronic Arts, the largest game developer in the United States at that time) to produce only PlayStation titles for the first six months after its introduction. There were 50 PlayStation titles by the end of 1995, and this number had grown to 800 by the end of 2000.

Though Sega's Saturn had beaten Sony's PlayStation to market by several months, it was shipped to only four retailers due to limited supply: Toys "R" Us, Babbage's, Software Etc., and Electronics Boutique. This aggravated retailers such as Best Buy and Wal-Mart, which had long supported Sega.[9] Developers also felt that it was easier to program for the PlayStation than the Saturn, causing it to lose crucial developer support.[10] By the end of 1996, the installed base of Sony PlayStation in the United States (2.9 million units) was more than double that of the Sega Saturn (1.2 million units).

In 1996, after more than two years of announcements, Nintendo finally introduced its 64-bit game system called Nintendo 64. Though only two software titles were available at the console's release (one being Super Mario), the game units were sold out within weeks of their release. Though Nintendo's 64-bit system gained rapid consumer acceptance, neither Nintendo nor Sega were able to reclaim dominance over the video game industry. Though several new entrants (and one returning entrant, Atari) had tried to break into the video game industry through technological leapfrogging, only Sony had the successful combination of a product with a technological advantage, strategies and resources that enabled it to rapidly build installed base and availability of complementary goods, and a reputation that signaled the market that this was a fight it could win.

An Unfolding Battle: 128-Bit Systems

In September 1999, Sega launched its 128-bit Dreamcast console, a $199 gaming system that enabled access to the Internet. Before the Dreamcast release, Sega was suffering from its lowest market share in years at 12 percent. The Dreamcast was the first 128-bit system to market, and 514,000 units were sold in the first two weeks. An installed base of 5 million was achieved by October 2000. Sega's success turned out to be short-lived, however. In March 2000, Sony launched its 128-bit PlayStation2 (PS2) in Japan and introduced the system to the

United States in October. Despite price cuts on the Dreamcast and a promotion rebate that would make the console essentially free (in exchange for a two-year contract for Sega's SegaNet Internet service), the Dreamcast was crushed in the holiday sales season. In early 2001, Sega announced it would cease making consoles and transform itself into a third-party developer of games for other consoles.

Sony's PS2 was an unprecedented success. Not only did it offer a significant technological advantage over the 32-bit systems, but it was also backward compatible, enabling gamers to play their PlayStation games on the console until they amassed new game libraries.[11] During the opening sales weekend of March 4, 2000, PlayStation2 sales reached about 1 million units, a figure that eclipsed by 10 times the amount of original PlayStation units sold during the three-day release period in 1994. Demand for the new unit was so high that on the opening day of pre-orders on Sony's website, more than 100,000 hits in one minute were received, and Sony was forced to briefly shut down the website.

At the time of the PlayStation2 release, Nintendo had just postponed the launch of its new 128-bit system, the GameCube, to a release date in the first half of 2001. Unlike the PS2, the GameCube did not offer backward compatibility with Nintendo 64 games. The GameCube was also targeted toward a younger market (8- to 18-year-olds) than Sony's 16- to 24-year-old demographic. The real threat to Sony's PlayStation2 came in the form of a new entrant to the video console industry: Microsoft's Xbox. The Xbox, launched in November 2001, was targeted at the 18- to 34-year-old male, positioning it directly against the PS2.

Microsoft had previously produced PC-based computer games (such as Flight Simulator and the Age of Empires series) and operated an online gaming service (Microsoft Gaming Zone), and thus had some familiarity with the industry. However, it did not have either the arcade experience of Sega or Nintendo or the consumer electronics experience of Sony. By the time the Xbox hit the market, PlayStation2 already had a significant lead in installed base and availability of games (more than 300 PS2 game titles were available at the end of 2001), but Microsoft was counting on the technological advantages offered by the Xbox to tip consumer preferences. The Xbox offered a faster processor and more memory than the PlayStation2. Furthermore, customers did not have to trade off technological advantages against price: The Xbox launched at a retail price of $299, significantly less than its production costs (it is estimated that Microsoft lost between $100 and $125 per unit).[12]

To rapidly deploy the console and build installed base, Microsoft leveraged its existing relationships with distributors that carried its software, though it was now forced to seek much greater penetration into distributors such as Toys "R" Us, Babbages, and Circuit City. Microsoft also faced the challenge of cultivating a radically different brand image in the game console market than the one that it had achieved in the software market, and to make much greater use of marketing channels such as television advertising and gaming magazines. To that end, Microsoft budgeted $500 million to be spent over 18 months to market the Xbox—more than any other marketing campaign in the company's history.[13]

Microsoft planned to produce 30 to 40 percent of its games in-house and gave away $10,000 game development kits to attract third-party games developers.

Both the Xbox and Nintendo's GameCube were launched just in time for the extremely important 2001 Christmas season and sold briskly. By the year's end, it was estimated that 1.3 million GameCube units had been sold, and 1.5 million Xbox units had been sold.[14] However, both of the new consoles were outrun by PS2, which sold 2 million units in the month of December alone. By September 30, 2002, estimates put both Xbox and GameCube sales at just under 7 million units worldwide and PlayStation2 unit sales at over 40 million worldwide.[15]

Discussion Questions

1. What factors do you think enabled Sega to break Nintendo's near monopoly of the U.S. video game console market in the late 1980s?
2. Why did Nintendo choose to not make its video game consoles backward compatible? What were the advantages and disadvantages of this strategy?
3. What strengths and weaknesses did Sony have when it entered the video game market in 1995?
4. What strengths and weaknesses did Microsoft have when it entered the video game market in 2001?
5. Comparing the deployment strategies used by the firms in each of the generations, can you identify any timing, licensing, pricing, marketing, or distribution strategies that appear to have influenced firms' success and failure in the video game industry?

OVERVIEW

The value of any technological innovation is only partly determined by what the technology can *do*. A large part of the value of an innovation is determined by the degree to which people can understand it, access it, and integrate it within their lives. Deployment is not just a way for the firm to earn revenues from its innovations; deployment is a core part of the innovation process itself.

Deployment strategies can influence the receptivity of customers, distributors, and complementary goods providers. Effective deployment strategies can reduce uncertainty about the product, lower resistance to switching from competing or substitute goods, and accelerate adoption. Ineffective deployment strategies can cause even brilliant technological innovations to fail. As shown in the opening vignette, 3DO's Interactive Multiplayer and Philips' Compact Disk Interactive were two of the first 32-bit video game systems introduced to the market and offered significant technological advantages over previous generations of consoles. However, both were priced so high and introduced with so few games that neither was able to attract a significant share of the market. When Sega introduced its 32-bit system to the market—beating Sony's PlayStation by several months—the price was low and some popular games were available, but weak distribution ultimately hobbled the console's deployment. On the other hand, despite being a newcomer to the video game industry, Sony's exceptionally executed deployment strategies for the PlayStation made the console a nearly overnight success. Sony used a combination of intense marketing, low prices, strong games availability, and aggressive distribution to ensure that the product launched with unmistakable impact.

We will cover five key elements of the deployment process in this chapter: timing, licensing and compatibility, pricing, distribution, and marketing. Several of these topics warrant entire courses and textbooks in their own right; only an introduction to the issues most central to the deployment of a new technological innovation will be covered here.

TIMING

As illustrated by the video game industry, timing can be a significant part of a company's deployment strategy. For example, even though Nintendo had a 16-bit video game system in development when Sega's 16-bit Genesis was introduced, Nintendo delayed introducing a 16-bit system for fear of cannibalizing its 8-bit system sales. The advantages and disadvantages of being a first, early-but-not-first, or late mover were discussed in Chapter Five; the focus here is on how a firm can use timing as a deployment strategy.

Strategic Timing of Entry

Generally, firms try to decrease their development cycles in order to decrease their costs and to increase their timing of entry options, but this does not imply that firms should always be racing to introduce their products as early as possible. A firm can strategically use entry timing to take advantage of business cycle or seasonal effects, to position its product with respect to previous generations of related technologies, and to ensure that production capacity and complementary goods or services are in place. The role of each of these tactics is illustrated in the video game industry.

Nintendo, Sony, and Microsoft all took advantage of seasonal effects by introducing their consoles shortly before Christmas so that the hype of the consoles' launch would coincide with the Christmas buying season. The majority of video game consoles are sold in December. By launching their consoles close to December, firms could target their advertising for this time and leverage the free publicity that surrounded a console's launch such as press releases announcing the introduction and external product reviews.

Because the video game industry is characterized by distinct generations of technology, the timing of a console's launch also plays a key role in its positioning within a technological generation and with respect to competing consoles. If a console is introduced too early, it is likely to receive a tepid welcome because customers who recently purchased the previous-generation console are reluctant to spend money on a new console so soon. For example, though the Xbox offered a processor that was double the speed of the PlayStation2, its introductory timing positioned it as being in the same generation as the PlayStation2. Many customers saw it as a competitor to a product they already had, rather than as a next-generation technology. If the console is introduced too late, the company can lose its image as a technological leader and may have already conceded a considerable installed base lead to earlier entrants. This is aptly illustrated in the quote about Nintendo's late introduction of the SNES in the opening vignette: "To tell the truth, Nintendo just isn't cool anymore. This one is 16 bits, so it's better than the original Nintendo. But the company only made it to compete with Sega, and most kids already have that. So they don't need Super Nintendo...."

Finally, timing the introduction of a console to coincide with production capacity and games availability has proven very important in the video game console industry. For example, in Sega's rush to ensure that the Saturn beat Sony's PlayStation to market, it introduced the product before it had built adequate production capacity. Sega was subsequently unable to stock many important distributors, and it alienated companies that had supported Sega in previous generations. Similarly, the importance of having games available at the time of launch is also clearly demonstrated: Every video game console producer that has been successful in at least one generation (e.g., Atari, Nintendo, Sega, Sony, Microsoft) has ensured that games would be available at the console's launch, even if that meant buying games development companies to force them to produce compatible games! Games availability was also encouraged through licensing strategies, as discussed later in the chapter.

Optimizing Cash Flow versus Embracing Cannibalization

A second key point about timing of entry is also illustrated in the video game industry. For firms introducing a next-generation technology into a market in which they already compete, entry timing can become a decision about whether and to what degree to embrace **cannibalization.** Traditionally, research on product life cycles has emphasized the importance of timing new product introduction so as to optimize cash flows or profits from each generation and minimize cannibalization. If a firm's current product is very profitable, the firm will often delay introduction of a next-generation product until profits have begun to significantly decrease for the current product. This strategy is intended to maximize the firm's return on investment in developing each generation of the product. However, in industries driven by technological innovation, delaying the introduction of a next-generation product can enable competitors to achieve a significant technological gap. If competitors introduce products that have a large technological advantage over the firm's current products, customers might begin abandoning the firm's technology.

Instead, if the firm invests in continuous innovation and willingly cannibalizes its existing products with more advanced products, the firm can make it very difficult for other firms to achieve a technological lead large enough to prove persuasive to customers. By providing incentives for existing customers to upgrade to its newest models, the firm can further remove any incentive customers have to switch to another company's products when they purchase next-generation technology. Many would argue that this is where Nintendo made a key mistake. In the late 1980s, Nintendo was deriving significant profits from its 8-bit system and thus was reluctant to cannibalize those sales with a 16-bit system. However, by not embracing cannibalization,

cannibalization
When a firm's sales of one product (or at one location) diminish its sales of another of its products (or at another of its locations).

Nintendo enabled Sega to steal customers away by offering a product with a significant technological advantage.

LICENSING AND COMPATIBILITY

Chapter Nine revealed how making a technology more open (i.e., not protecting it vigorously or partially opening the technology through licensing) could speed its adoption by enabling more producers to improve and promote the technology and allowing complementary goods developers to more easily support the technology. However, the chapter also pointed out that making a technology completely open poses several risks. First, if a firm completely opens its technology, other producers may drive the price of the technology down to a point at which the firm is unable to recoup its development expense. If competition drives the price down so no producer earns significant margins on the technology, no producer will have much incentive to further develop the technology. Finally, opening a technology completely may cause its underlying platform to become fragmented as different producers alter it to their needs, resulting in loss of compatibility across producers and the possible erosion of product quality.

Each of these effects was demonstrated in the opening vignette. By not protecting their technologies enough, video game console producers in the first generation relinquished their ability to control game production quantity and quality. The resulting market glut of poor-quality games decimated the video game industry. But Nintendo's highly restrictive licensing policies for its 8-bit system made games developers eager to give their support to the first rival that appeared viable. In the 16-bit, 32/64-bit, and 128-bit generations, the console makers sought to achieve a delicate balance of making licensing open enough to attract developer support while making licensing strict enough to control game quantities and quality.

In deploying a technological innovation, often a firm must decide how compatible (or incompatible) to make its technology with that provided by others or with previous generations of its own technology. If there is an existing technology with a large installed base or availability of complementary goods, the firm can sometimes leverage the value of that installed base and complementary goods by making its technology compatible with current products. For instance, producers of IBM-compatible computers (as detailed in Chapter Nine) were able to tap IBM's installed base and complementary goods advantages by offering computers that operated identically to those made by IBM. Users of IBM compatibles reaped the same installed base advantages and had access to all the same software as they would have with an IBM computer.

If the firm wishes to avoid giving away its own installed base or complementary goods advantages to others, it may protect them by ensuring its products are incompatible with those of future entrants. Most competitors in the U.S. video game industry (with the exception of Atari) have been fairly successful at this strategy. Nintendo, for example, uses a security chip to ensure that only licensed Nintendo games may be played in its consoles, and only Nintendo consoles may be used to play Nintendo games.

backward compatible
When products of a technological generation can work with products of a previous generation. For example, a computer is backward compatible if it can run the same software as a previous generation of the computer.

Firms must also decide whether or not to make their products **backward compatible** with their own previous generations of technology. Nintendo repeatedly opted not to make its consoles backward compatible, believing it would be more profitable to require customers to purchase new games. This is understandable given that the consoles were sold at cost and profits were made through game sales; however, it also meant that Nintendo forfeited a significant potential source of advantage over Sega. In contrast, Sega made its 16-bit Genesis compatible with its 8-bit Master System games—though this may not have proven terribly persuasive to customers given the limited success of the Master System. More significantly, Sony made its PlayStation2 console backward compatible with PlayStation games, thereby not only ensuring a tremendous existing library of compatible games at its launch but also providing a significant incentive to PlayStation owners who were considering upgrading to a 128-bit system to choose the PlayStation2 as opposed to Sega's Dreamcast, or waiting for the Xbox or GameCube.

Some firms use a particularly powerful strategy that combines continuous innovation with backward compatibility. A firm that both innovates to prevent a competitor from creating a technological gap and utilizes backward compatibility so that its new platform or models are compatible with previous generations of complementary goods can leverage the existing value yielded by a large range of complementary goods to its new platforms. While such a strategy may cause the firm to forfeit some sales of complementary goods for the new platform (at least initially), it can also effectively link the generations through time and can successfully transition customers through product generations while preventing competitors from having a window to enter the market. Microsoft has utilized this strategy deftly with Windows—though the operating system is regularly updated, each successive generation provides backward compatibility with most of the major software applications developed for previous generations. Thus, customers can upgrade without having to replace their entire libraries of software applications.

PRICING

Pricing is a crucial element in the firm's deployment strategy. Price simultaneously influences the product's positioning in the marketplace, its rate of adoption, and the firm's cash flow. Before a firm can determine its pricing strategy, it must determine the objectives it has for its pricing model. For example, if a firm is in an industry plagued with overcapacity or intense price competition, the firm's objective may be simply *survival*. A survival price strategy prices goods to cover variable costs and some fixed costs. It is a short-run strategy, however; in the long run, the firm will want to find a way to create additional value. One common pricing objective is to *maximize current profits*. Under this pricing strategy, the firm first estimates costs and demand and then sets the price to maximize cash flow or rate of return on investment. This strategy emphasizes current performance, but may sacrifice long-term performance.

For new technological innovations, firms often emphasize either a *maximum market skimming* objective or a *maximum market share* objective. To skim the market, firms will initially set prices high on new products. The high price may signal the market that the new product is a significant innovation that offers a substantial performance improvement over previously available products. The high price can also help the firm recoup initial development expenses, assuming there is also high initial demand. However, high initial prices may also attract competitors to the market and can slow adoption of the product. If costs are expected to decline rapidly with the volume of units produced, a skimming strategy can actually prove less profitable than a pricing strategy that stimulates more rapid customer adoption.

penetration pricing
When the price of a good is set very low (or free) to maximize the good's market share.

When achieving high volume is important, firms will often emphasize a maximum market share objective. To maximize market share, firms often use **penetration pricing.** The firm will set the lowest price possible hoping to rapidly attract customers, driving volume up and production costs down. Effective utilization of penetration pricing often requires that the firm builds large production capacity in advance of demand. In the short run, the firm may bear significant risk from this capital investment, and it may lose money on each unit if the price is less than its initial variable costs. However, if its volume increases and drives its production costs down, the firm can achieve a very powerful position: It can have a low-cost position that enables it to earn profits despite a low price, and it can have a substantial share of the market.

Firms in industries characterized by increasing returns (strong learning curve effects and/or network externalities) will often use the objective of maximizing market share and a penetration pricing strategy. In such industries, there is strong pressure for the industry to adopt a single dominant design (as discussed in Chapter Four). It is in the firm's best interest to accelerate adoption of its technology, building its installed base, attracting developers of complementary goods, and riding down the learning curve for its production costs.

For example, Honda's hybrid electric vehicle the Insight was introduced at a price ($20,000) that actually caused Honda to lose money on each Insight it sold. However, Honda believed the hybrid technology would become profitable in the long term, and that the experience it would gain by working with hybrid technology and the continuance of its "green" car company image were strong enough motivations to sell the Insight at a loss for the first few years.[16]

Sometimes firms price below cost because the losses are expected to be recouped through profits on complementary goods or services. In the video game industry, this has proven to be a very important strategy. Nintendo, Sega, Sony, and Microsoft have each sold their video game consoles at a price very close to (or below) production costs while profiting from subsequent game sales and licensing royalties. Similarly, when Microsoft launched its Internet Explorer Web browser, it gave the product away so it could quickly catch up to Netscape's Web browser, which had been introduced to the market almost a year earlier. Though consumers paid nothing for the Internet Explorer browser, Microsoft earned profits selling other compatible software products to businesses.

Firms can also influence cash flow and the customers' perception of costs through manipulating the timing of when the price of a good is paid. For instance, while the most typical pricing model requires the customer to pay the full price before taking ownership, other pricing models enable the customer to delay paying the purchase price by offering a free trial for a fixed time. This permits the customer to become familiar with the benefits of the product before paying the price, and it can be very useful when customers face great uncertainty about a new product or service. Another pricing model enables customers to pay as they go, such as through leasing programs, or a pricing model whereby the initial product is free (or available at a low price) but the customer pays for service. For example, when cable television subscribers order cable service, they typically pay little or no fee for the equipment and instead pay a significant amount (often between $20 and $90 depending on the package) for monthly service that may include some portion for the equipment expense. By contrast, when users subscribe to XM Radio's satellite radio service, they must buy the equipment from one of the many manufacturers (e.g., Sony, Pioneer) for a price that might range from $150 to $1,000 and then pay a very low monthly fee (about $10) for the service.

When it is unclear how customers will respond to a particular price point, firms often use introductory pricing that indicates the pricing is for a stipulated time. This allows the company to test the market's response to a product without committing to a long-term pricing structure.

DISTRIBUTION

Selling Direct versus Using Intermediaries

manufacturers' representatives
Independent agents that promote and sell the product lines of one or a few manufacturers. They are often used when direct selling is appropriate but the manufacturer does not have a sufficiently large direct sales force to reach all appropriate market segments.

wholesalers
Companies that buy manufacturer's products in bulk, and then resell them (often in smaller or more diverse bundles) to other supply channel members such as retailers.

retailers
Companies that sell goods to the public.

Firms can sell their products directly to users through their direct sales force or an online ordering system or mail-order catalog. Alternatively, firms can use intermediaries such as **manufacturers' representatives, wholesalers,** and **retailers**. Selling direct gives the firm more control over the selling process, pricing, and service. It also can enable the firm to capture more information about customers and can facilitate the customization of products for customers. However, in many situations selling direct can be impractical or overly expensive. Intermediaries provide a number of important services that can make distribution more efficient. First, wholesalers and retailers *break bulk*. In general, manufacturers prefer to sell large quantities of a limited number of items, while customers prefer to buy limited quantities of a large number of items. Wholesalers and retailers can pool large orders from a large number of manufacturers and sell a wider range of goods in small quantities to customers.

For example, a typical book publisher produces a limited range of book titles, but desires to sell them in high volume. The average final consumer may wish to purchase only one copy of a particular book title, but often wants a wide range of book titles to choose from. Both wholesalers and retailers provide valuable bulk-breaking services in this channel. A wholesaler such as Ingram will purchase pallets of books from many different publishers such as McGraw-Hill, Simon & Schuster, or Prentice Hall. It then breaks apart the pallets and reassembles bundles of books that include titles from multiple publishers but have fewer copies of any particular book title. These bundles are then sold to retailers such as Barnes & Noble or Borders, which offer a wide range of titles sold on an individual basis. Though publishers could sell directly to final consumers using the Internet or a mail-order catalog, customers would have to examine the offerings of many different publishers to be able to consider the same range of books offered by a retailer.

Intermediaries also provide a number of other services such as transporting goods, carrying inventory, providing selling services, and handling transactions with customers. Many intermediaries also offer greater convenience for customers by offering geographically dispersed retail sites. Location convenience can be particularly important if customers are geographically dispersed and they are likely to want to examine or try different product options or to need on-site service. By contrast, if the product is primarily sold to a few industrial customers or if the product can be routinely ordered without close examination, trial, or service, geographic dispersion may be less important.

original equipment manufacturers (or value-added resellers)

A company that buys products (or components of products) from other manufacturers and assembles them or customizes them into a product that is then sold under the OEM's own name.

Original equipment manufacturers (OEMs) (also called **value-added resellers,** or VARs) provide an even more crucial role in the distribution process. An OEM buys products (or components of products) from other manufacturers and assembles them into a product that is customized to meet user needs. The OEM then sells this customized product under its own name and often provides marketing and service support for the product. OEMs are very common in the computer and electronics industries where manufacturers are often specialized in the production of individual components but users prefer to purchase whole, assembled products. Dell Computer, for example, is a very successful OEM in the computer industry. OEMs can provide a very valuable coordinating function in an industry by aggregating components and providing a single contact point for the customer.

disintermediation

When the number of intermediaries in a supply channel is reduced; for example, when manufacturers bypass wholesalers and/or retailers to sell directly to end users.

In some industries, advances in information technology (such as the Internet) have enabled **disintermediation** or a reconfiguration in the types of intermediaries used. For example, online investing services such as E-trade or Ameritrade caused some disintermediation in the investment market by enabling customers to bypass brokers and place their own stock or bond orders online. In industries where the product is information that can be conveyed digitally, such as newspapers, software, and music, the Internet can deliver the product from the manufacturer straight to the consumer. In most industries, however, information technology has simply shifted the roles of intermediaries or expanded the services they provide. For example, online stores such as Dell.com or Amazon.com enable customers to bypass traditional retail outlets such as computer stores or bookstores. However, in most cases this has not shortened the supply chain by which goods are delivered to customers—it has just rerouted it. In other instances, moving commerce online has required creating additional intermediaries (such as companies specialized in delivering the goods of others) or enhanced the services that intermediaries provide. For example, while grocers traditionally required customers to provide their own distribution for "the last mile" (the distance between the store and the customer's home), online grocery shopping shifts the responsibility of moving goods "the last mile" to the stores, requiring them to either develop their own delivery services or to purchase delivery services from other providers. Barnes & Noble uses online sales to complement its bricks-and-mortar retail outlets: Customers can come into the stores to see and physically handle books (an option many book shoppers express a strong preference for), but they can also order books online—from home or from within a Barnes & Noble store—if they are looking for a book that is not stocked at a convenient location.

To determine whether to use intermediaries and what type of intermediaries would be appropriate, the firm should answer the following questions:

1. *How does the new product fit with the distribution requirements of the firm's existing product lines?* Whether the firm already has an existing sales channel

that would suit the product will be a primary consideration in how the product should be distributed. For example, if the firm already has a large direct sales force and the new product would fit well with this direct sales system, there may be no need to consider other distribution options. On the other hand, if the firm does not have an existing direct sales force, it will have to determine whether the new product warrants the cost and time of building a direct sales force.

2. *How numerous and dispersed are customers, and how much product education or service will customers require? Is prepurchase trial necessary or desirable? Is installation or customization required?* If customers are dispersed but require little product education or service, mail order or online ordering may suffice. On the other hand, if customers are dispersed and require moderate amounts of education, service, or prepurchase trial, using intermediaries is often a good option because they can provide some on-site education and service and/or trial. If customers are not dispersed, or will require *extensive* education and service, it may be necessary for the firm to provide the education and service directly. Furthermore, if the product will require installation or customization, the firm will often need to employ either a direct sales force or an intermediary capable of providing extensive service.

3. *How are competing products or substitutes sold?* The firm must consider how competing or substitute products are sold, because this both determines the nature of the existing distribution channel options and shapes customer expectations about how products will be purchased. For example, if customers are used to purchasing the product in a retail environment where the product can be viewed and handled and where customers can receive personal sales assistance, they may be reluctant to switch to a sales channel with less contact, such as online purchasing or mail order. How the product is sold may also affect the product's positioning from the perspective of the customer. For example, if competing products are primarily sold in a high-contact mode such as specialty stores or via a direct sales force, selling the new product in a lower-contact channel such as mass discounters or through mail order might cause the customer to perceive the product as being of lower quality or more economical. Market research can assess how the sales channel influences the customer's perception of the product.

Strategies for Accelerating Distribution

When the industry is likely to select a single technology as the dominant design, it can be very important to deploy the technology rapidly. Rapid deployment enables the technology to build a large installed base and encourages the developers of complementary goods to support the technology platform. As the technology is adopted, producer and user experience can be used to improve the technology, and producer costs should also decrease due to learning effects and economies of scale. The firm can use a variety of strategies to accelerate distribution, such as forging alliances with distributors, creating bundling relationships, sponsoring or contracting with large customer groups, and providing sales guarantees.[17]

Alliances with Distributors

Firms introducing a technological innovation can use strategic alliances or exclusivity contracts to encourage distributors to carry and promote their goods. By providing a distributor a stake in the success of the new technology, the firm may be able to persuade the distributor to carry and promote the new technology aggressively. Firms that already have relationships with distributors for other goods are at an advantage in pursuing this strategy; firms without such relationships may need to cultivate them, or even consider forward vertical integration to ensure that their product is widely available.

Lack of distribution may have contributed significantly to the failure of the Sega Saturn to gain installed base. Sega had very limited distribution for its Saturn launch, which may have slowed the building of its installed base both directly (because customers had limited access to the product) and indirectly (because distributors that were initially denied product may have been reluctant to promote the product after the limitations were lifted). Nintendo, by contrast, had unlimited distribution for its Nintendo 64 launch, and Sony not only had unlimited distribution, but also had extensive experience negotiating with retailing giants such as Wal-Mart for its consumer electronics products. Consequently, Sony PlayStation had better distribution on its first day of business than the Sega Saturn, despite Sega's decade of experience in the market.[18]

Bundling Relationships

Firms can also accelerate distribution of a new technology by bundling it with another product that is already in wide use. Bundling enables the new technology to piggyback on the success of another product that already has a large installed base. Once customers acquire the new product in tandem with something else that they already use, switching costs may prevent customers from changing to a different product, even if the different product might have initially been preferred. As customers become familiar with the product, their ties to the technology (for instance, through the cost of training) increase and their likelihood of choosing this technology in future purchase decisions may also increase. Bundling arrangements have proven to be a very successful way for firms to build their installed base and ensure provision of complementary goods. Consider, for example, Conner Peripherals (whose disk drives were bundled with Compaq's personal computers), Microsoft's MS-DOS (whose initial bundling with IBM led to bundling arrangements with almost all PC clone makers and also facilitated the later bundling of Windows with PCs), and Microsoft's Internet Explorer (which gained a larger installed base through a bundling arrangement with America Online, one of the largest Internet providers in the United States).

Contracts and Sponsorship

Firms can also set up contractual arrangements with distributors, complementary goods providers, and even large end users (such as universities or government agencies) to ensure that the technology is used in exchange for price discounts, special service contracts, advertising assistance, or other inducements. For example, when medical equipment manufacturers introduce significantly new medical devices such as new ultrasound equipment or magnetic resonance imaging machines, they will often donate or lend a number of these machines to large teaching hospitals. As the new equipment's benefits become clear to the doctors and hospital administration, their likelihood of purchasing additional machines increases. Because large teaching hospitals train medical staff that may ultimately work for other hospitals and are often influential leaders in the medical community, providing these hospitals with free equipment can be an effective way of encouraging the rest of the medical community to adopt the product.

Guarantees and Consignment

If there is considerable market uncertainty about the new product or service, the firm can encourage distributors to carry the product by offering them guarantees (such as promising to take back unsold stock) or agreeing to sell the product on consignment. For example, when Nintendo introduced the Nintendo Entertainment System to the U.S. market, distributors were reluctant to carry the console or games because many had been stuck with worthless inventory after the crash of the video game market in the mid-1980s. Nintendo agreed to sell the Nintendo Entertainment System to distributors on consignment: Nintendo would be paid only for consoles that were sold, rather than requiring distributors to buy consoles up front. Retailers bore little risk in distributing the good because unsold units could be returned to Nintendo, and the video game industry was reborn.

A similar argument can be made for offering guarantees to complementary goods producers. If complementary goods producers are reluctant to support the technology, the firm can guarantee particular quantities of complementary goods will be purchased, or it can provide the capital for production, thus bearing the bulk of the risk of producing complementary goods for the technology. The complementary goods producer may still have forfeited time or effort in producing goods that may not have a long-term market, but its direct costs will be less at risk.

MARKETING

The marketing strategy for a technological innovation must consider both the nature of the target market and the nature of the innovation. For example, is the target market composed primarily of large industrial users or individual consumers? Is the innovation likely to appeal only to technophiles or to the mass market? Are the benefits of the technology readily apparent, or will they require considerable customer education? Will customers respond more to detailed technical content or eye-catching brand images? Can the marketer alleviate customer uncertainty about the innovation? Major marketing methods are briefly reviewed next, along with how marketing can be tailored to particular adopter categories. Also explored is how marketing can shape perceptions and expectations about the innovation's installed base and availability of complementary goods.

Major Marketing Methods

The three most commonly used marketing methods include advertising, promotions, and publicity/public relations.

Advertising

Many firms use advertising to build public awareness of their technological innovation. Doing so requires that the firm crafts an effective advertising message and chooses advertising media that can convey this message to the appropriate target market.

In crafting an advertising message, firms often attempt to strike a balance between achieving an entertaining and memorable message versus providing a significant quantity of informative content. Too much focus on one or the other can result in advertisements that are memorable but convey little about the product, or advertisements that are informative but quickly lose the audience's attention. Many firms hire an advertising agency to develop and test an advertising message.

The media used are generally chosen based on their match to the target audience, the richness of information or sensory detail they can convey, their reach (the number of people exposed), and their cost per exposure. Some of the advantages and disadvantages of various advertising media are provided in Figure 13.1.

FIGURE 13.1

Advantages and Disadvantages of Major Advertising Media

Source: Adapted from P. Kotler, *Marketing Management* (Upper Saddle River, NJ: Prentice Hall, 2003).

Medium	Advantages	Disadvantages
Newspapers	Timeliness; good local market coverage; broad acceptance; high believability	Short life; poor reproduction quality; small "pass-along" audience
Television	High sensory richness that combines sight, sound and motion; high attention; wide reach	High absolute cost; fleeting exposure; less audience selectivity
Direct mail	High audience selectivity; no ad competition within the same medium; personalization; enables communication of significant technical content; may be passed along to others	Relatively high cost; "junk mail" image
Radio	High geographic and demographic selectivity; medium reach; low cost	Audio presentation only; nonstandardized rate structures; fleeting exposure
Magazines	High geographic and demographic selectivity; high-quality reproduction; long life; can enable significant technical content; good pass-along readership	Long ad purchase lead time; some waste circulation
Outdoor (e.g., billboards)	High repeat exposure; low cost; low competition	Limited audience selectivity; creative limitations
Yellow Pages	Excellent local coverage; high believability; wide reach; low cost	High competition; long ad purchase lead time; creative limitations
Newsletters	Very high selectivity; full control; enables communication of significant technical content; interactive opportunities	Narrow reach; potential for high costs
Telephone	Interactive; can give personalized message	Relative high cost; can be perceived as annoyance
Internet	High selectivity; interactive possibilities; relatively low cost	Relatively new medium with low number of users in some countries; high clutter

Promotions

Firms can also use promotions at the distributor or customer level to stimulate purchase or trial. Promotions are usually temporary selling tactics that might include:

- Offering samples or free trial.
- Offering cash rebates after purchase.
- Including an additional product (a "premium") with purchase.
- Offering incentives for repeat purchase.
- Offering sales bonuses to distributor or retailer sales representatives.
- Using cross-promotions between two or more noncompeting products to increase pulling power.
- Using point-of-purchase displays to demonstrate the product's features.

Publicity and Public Relations

Many firms use free publicity (such as articles that appear in a newspaper or magazine about the company or its product) to effectively generate word of mouth. For example, Pfizer's drug Viagra got an enormous amount of free exposure from unofficial celebrity endorsements and humorous coverage on TV shows such as *The Tonight Show* and *Late Show with David Letterman*. Other firms rely on internally generated publications (e.g., annual reports, press releases, articles written by employees for trade magazines or other media) to reach and influence target markets. Firms may also sponsor special events (e.g., sporting events, competitions, conferences), contribute to good causes (e.g., charities), or exhibit at trade associations to generate public awareness and goodwill.[19] Farmos even involved potential customers in the testing process of its drug Domosedan to generate awareness, as described in the accompanying Theory in Action.

Tailoring the Marketing Plan to Intended Adopters

As described in Chapter Three, innovations tend to diffuse through the population in an s-shape pattern whereby adoption is initially slow because the technology is unfamiliar, it then accelerates as the technology becomes better understood and utilized by the mass market, and eventually the market is saturated so the rate of new adoptions declines. These stages of adoption have been related to the adopter categories of *innovators* (in the very early stages); followed by *early adopters,* which cause adoption to accelerate; then the *early majority* and *late majority* as the innovation penetrates the mass market; and finally the *laggards* as the innovation approaches saturation.[20] The characteristics of these groups make them responsive to different marketing strategies.

Innovators and early adopters are typically looking for very advanced technologies that offer a significant advantage over previous generations. They are willing to take risks and to pay high prices, and they will accept some incompleteness in the product, but they may also demand considerable customization and technical support.[21] They are more likely to respond to marketing that offers a significant amount of technical content and that emphasizes the leading-edge nature of the innovation. Marketing channels that enable high content and selective reach are appropriate for this market.

When the Finnish company Farmos Group Limited introduced its veterinary drug Domosedan, executives knew that building awareness of the drug among known opinion leaders would be crucial. Domosedan represented a disruptive innovation in painkillers for horses and cattle; it would significantly alter the way veterinarians performed their examinations and treatments. Unlike previous sedatives and painkillers used in the treatment of large animals, Domosedan enabled veterinarians to conduct clinical and surgical examinations without tying up or anesthetizing their patients. Animals could be treated while standing, and in most instances they would not have to be transported to the veterinarian's clinic.

Farmos knew that university professors and advanced practitioners were important opinion leaders in veterinary medicine. To educate this group and encourage them to support the product, Farmos asked them to help with the testing process required for the drug's approval and sales permit. University professors were involved in the preclinical testing, and visionary practitioners were utilized for clinical testing. By proactively involving these influential potential adopters, the testing simultaneously acted as a premarketing tool while establishing the drug's efficacy and safety. This enabled opinion leaders to acquire advanced knowledge of and experience with the product before it was released. By the time the drug was launched, many of these influential users were already enthusiastic supporters of the product.

Because the drug represented a scientific breakthrough, it was featured in presentations at scientific conferences and was investigated in numerous dissertations, generating further awareness and excitement about the drug. When it was launched in Finland, the company hosted a large dinner party for all practicing veterinarians to attend, creating a celebratory atmosphere for the drug's introduction. Farmos' tactics were successful—Domosedan was adopted rapidly, spreading quickly around the world, and became a significant commercial success.

Source: Adapted from Birgitta Sandberg, "Creating the Market for Disruptive Innovation: Market Proactiveness at the Launch Stage," *Journal of Targeting, Measurement and Analysis for Marketing* 11, no. 2 (2002), pp. 184–96.

To market to the early majority, on the other hand, requires that the company communicate the product's completeness, its ease of use, its consistency with the customer's way of life, and its legitimacy. For this market segment, detailed technical information is not as important as using market channels with high reach and high credibility.

Firms often find it is difficult to make the transition between successfully selling to early adopters versus the early majority. While early adopters may be enthusiastic about the innovation's technological features, the early majority may find the product too complex, expensive, or uncertain. This can result in a chasm in the product's diffusion curve: Sales drop off because the early adopter market is saturated and the early majority market is not yet ready to buy (see Figure 13.2).[22] The company must simultaneously weather a period of diminished sales while scaling up its production capacity and improving efficiency to target the mass market.

To target the late majority and laggards, firms will often use similar channels as those used to target the early majority, although emphasizing reducing the cost per exposure. The marketing message at this stage must stress reliability, simplicity, and cost-effectiveness. The marketing channel need not enable high content, but it must have high credibility and not be so expensive as to drive product costs up significantly.

FIGURE 13.2
**The Chasm
between Early
Adopters and
Early Majority
Customers**

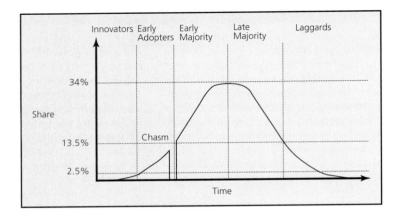

Recently, marketers have begun to tap the contagion-like spread of information by targeting individuals most likely to rapidly spread information. This is described in detail in the accompanying Research Brief.

Using Marketing to Shape Perceptions and Expectations

As described in Chapter Four, when distributors and customers are assessing the value of a technological innovation, they are swayed not only by evidence of the innovation's actual value, but also by their perception of the innovation's value and their expectations for its value in the future. Advertising, promotions, and publicity can play a key role in influencing the market's perceptions and expectations about the size of the installed base and the availability of complementary goods. Preannouncements can generate excitement about a product before its release, while press releases extolling forecasted sales can convince customers and distributors that the product's installed base will increase rapidly. The firm can also shape expectations about the future of the technology by signaling the market (including distributors, end users, manufacturers of complementary goods, and perhaps even other potential contenders for the new standard) that this is a battle it intends to win and is capable of winning. The firm's reputation may create a signal about its likelihood of success. Firms may also use credible commitments such as major fixed capital investments and guarantees to convince stakeholders that the firm has what it takes to challenge the incumbents.

Preannouncements and Press Releases

A firm that aggressively promotes its products can increase both its actual installed base and its perceived installed base. Even products that have relatively small installed bases can obtain relatively large mind-shares through heavy advertising. Since perceived installed base may drive subsequent adoptions, a large perceived installed base can lead to a large actual installed base. Such a tactic underlies the use of "vaporware"—preadvertised products that are not actually on the market yet and may not even exist—by many software vendors. By building the impression among customers that a product is ubiquitous, firms can prompt rapid adoption of the product when it actually is available. Vaporware may also buy a firm valuable time in bringing its product to market. If other vendors beat the firm to market and the firm fears that

Research Brief Creating an Information Epidemic

Some individuals, by virtue of their natural proclivities and talents, can initiate a cascade of information that travels with startling momentum through a population. Such individuals can have a remarkable affect on marketplace behavior. Gladwell identifies three distinct types of individuals who have such a disproportionate amount of influence: connectors, mavens, and salespersons.[23]

Connectors are individuals who tend to form an exceptionally large circle of acquaintances. Sociologists have found that if a random sample of people is asked to identify the individuals they know on a first-name basis, connectors will identify many times the number of people an average person identifies.[24] These people may have an exceptionally high social drive; they also tend to have a knack for remembering people's names and keeping track of social details such as birthdays. However, it is not just the quantity of acquaintances that distinguishes connectors. Connectors also tend to have a diverse array of affiliations. They may belong to a number of different kinds of clubs, associations, or other social institutions. They belong to multiple social worlds. Thus, connectors can bring together people who would otherwise be unlikely to meet.

Mavens are individuals who are driven to obtain and disseminate knowledge about one or more of their interests. Economists have widely studied "market mavens," otherwise known as "price vigilantes." These individuals will closely track the prices charged by various retailers (or other market outlets) and will vociferously

complain if they find something inappropriate, such as a promotion that is misleading.[25] Other mavens may take great pride in always knowing the best restaurants or hotels, or they may be avid readers of *Consumer Reports*. Mavens not only collect information, but they are also keenly interested in educating others. They will frequently volunteer information and derive great pleasure out of helping other consumers.

Finally, *salespersons* are those individuals who are naturally talented persuaders. Such individuals are gifted at providing verbal responses that their listener is likely to find compelling. They may also have an acute ability to send and respond to nonverbal cues, enabling them to influence other people's emotional response to something. These individuals can infect others with their mood![26]

Any of these individuals is capable of sparking an information epidemic. While a connector with a valuable piece of information is likely to expose a great number and diversity of people, the maven is likely to convey the information to fewer people but in more detail, making it more convincing. The salesperson may not expose as many people as the connector and may not be driven to acquire and disseminate the volumes of information that the maven transmits, but the people the salesperson does transmit information to are likely to find it irresistible. Some individuals possess more than one of these traits simultaneously, making them a veritable typhoon of influence in the marketplace.

customers may select a dominant design before its offering is introduced, it can use vaporware to attempt to persuade customers to delay purchase until the firm's product is available.

The Nintendo 64 provides an excellent example. In an effort to forestall consumer purchases of 32-bit systems, Nintendo began aggressively promoting its development of a 64-bit system (originally named Project Reality) in 1994, though the product would not actually reach the market until September 1996. The project underwent so many delays that some industry observers dubbed it "Project Unreality." Another interesting vaporware example was Nintendo's rewritable 64M disk drive. Though the product was much hyped, it was never introduced.

Major video game producers also go to great lengths to manage impressions of their installed base and market share, often to the point of exaggeration or deception. For example, at the end of 1991, Nintendo claimed it had sold 2 million units of the SNES to the U.S. market, while Sega disagreed, arguing that Nintendo had sold 1 million units at most. Nintendo also forecast that it would sell an additional 6 million units by the end of 1992 (actual installed base of Super Nintendo systems in the United States reached just over 4 million units in 1992). By May 1992, Nintendo was claiming a 60 percent share of the 16-bit market, and Sega was claiming a 63 percent share. Similar tactics were deployed in the battle for the 32/64-bit market. For example, in October 1995, Sony announced to the press that it had presold 100,000 consoles in the United States, to which Mike Ribero, Sega's executive vice president for marketing and sales, countered that Sony's figures were deceptive, arguing that many preorders would never materialize into actual purchases.[27]

Reputation

When a firm is poised to introduce a new technological innovation, its reputation for both technological and commercial competence will critically influence the market's expectation about its likelihood of success.[28] Customers, distributors, and complementary goods producers will use the firm's track record for technological innovation as an indicator of the new product's functionality and value. The firm's prior commercial success acts as an indicator of the firm's ability to build and manage the necessary support network around the new technology (distribution, advertising, alliances) to create the necessary momentum in the installed base-complementary goods cycle.

When Sega entered the video game market, it had the benefit of having several highly successful arcade games to its credit (both Atari and Nintendo had also been arcade game producers before developing home video games). The company had a reputation for developing exciting games, and this reputation may have facilitated customer acceptance of its 16-bit challenge to Nintendo's 8-bit dominance. By contrast, when Sony entered the video game market, it did not have the arcade background that underscored the other primary competitors. However, it did have a wealth of technological expertise as a consumer electronics manufacturer and exceptional brand equity in electronic products. Furthermore, Sony had demonstrated its ability to win a format war through its successful introduction of the CD format (with Philips) that supplanted vinyl records and analog cassettes.

Similarly, reputation is probably Microsoft's greatest strength in the battle for dominance over 128-bit video game systems. Microsoft's near monopoly in the personal computer operating system market was achieved through its unrivaled skill in using network externalities to its advantage. Microsoft had skillfully leveraged its controlling share in PC operating systems into domination over many categories of the software market, obliterating many would-be competitors. Microsoft's reputation sent a strong signal to distributors, developers, and customers that would shape their expectations for its future installed base and availability of complementary goods. Microsoft's success was not assured, but it was a powerful force to be reckoned with.

Credible Commitments

A firm can also signal its commitment to an industry by making substantial investments that would be difficult to reverse. For example, it was well-publicized that Sony spent more than $500 million developing the PlayStation, in addition to manufacturing the system and establishing an in-house games development unit. By contrast, 3DO's cumulative research and development costs at the launch of its multiplayer were less than $37 million, and the company utilized a strategy whereby all console and game production was performed by third parties. Thus, 3DO may not have signaled the market that it had enough confidence in the platform to bear the brunt of the capital risk.

Summary of Chapter

1. A firm can use its timing of entry strategy to take advantage of business cycle or seasonal effects, to influence its positioning vis-à-vis competitors, and to ensure that production capacity and complementary goods are sufficiently available at time of launch.

2. The timing of entry decision must also consider the need to harvest cash flows from existing product generations versus the advantages of willingly cannibalizing existing products to preempt competitors.

3. Successful deployment requires striking a careful balance between making a system open enough to attract complementary goods providers (and/or other producers if that is desirable) and protected enough to ensure that product quality, margins, and compatibility can be sustained.

4. Common pricing strategies for technological innovations include market skimming and penetration pricing. While the first attempts to maximize margins earned on early sales of the product, the second attempts to maximize market share. Pricing strategies should consider the firm's ability to earn profits from sales of complementary goods or services—if profits from complements are expected to be high, lower prices on the platform technology may be warranted.

5. Firms can manipulate the customer's perception of the product's price (and the timing of cash flows) through the timing of when the price is paid.

6. Intermediaries provide a number of valuable roles in the supply chain, including breaking bulk, transporting, carrying inventory, providing selling services, and managing customer transactions.

7. Sometimes a firm can accelerate distribution of its innovation by forging relationships with distributors, bundling the good with others that have a wider installed base, sponsoring large customer groups, or providing sales guarantees to distributors or complements producers.

8. Marketing methods vary in attributes such as cost, reach, information content, duration of exposure, flexibility of message, and ability to target particular segments of the market. When designing the marketing plan, the firm must take into account both the nature of the innovation (e.g., Is it complex? Are benefits easy to observe?) and the nature of the customer (e.g., Does the customer require in-depth technical detail? Is the customer likely to be influenced

by brand images and/or reputation? How much uncertainty is the customer likely to tolerate?)

9. Marketing strategies can influence the market's perception of how widely used the product is or will be, and thus can influence the behavior of customers, distributors, and complementary goods producers. Preannouncements, the firm's reputation, and credible commitments can all influence the market's assessment of the product's likelihood of success.

Discussion Questions

1. Identify one or more circumstances when a company might wish to delay introducing its product.

2. What factors will (or should) influence a firm's pricing strategy?

3. Pick a product you know well. What intermediaries do you think are used in bringing this product to market? What valuable services do you think these intermediaries provide?

4. What marketing strategies are used by the producers of the product you identified for Question 3? What are the advantages and disadvantages of these marketing strategies?

Endnotes

1. Adapted from M. A. Schilling, "Technological Leapfrogging: Lessons from the U.S. Videogame Industry," *California Management Review* 45, no. 3 (2003), pp. 6–32.

2. D. Sheff, *Game Over: How Nintendo Zapped an American Industry, Captured Your Dollars and Enslaved Your Children* (New York: Random House, 1993).

3. A. Brandenberger, "Power Play (A): Nintendo in 8-Bit Video Games," Harvard Business School case #9-795-167, 1995.

4. A. Brandenberger, "Power Play (B): Sega in 16-Bit Video Games," Harvard Business School case #9-795-103, 1995.

5. J. Hadju, "Rating the Hot Boxes," *Fortune* 128, no. 16 (1993), pp. 112–13.

6. N. Turner, "For Giants of Video Games It's an All-New Competition," *Investor's Business Daily,* January 24, 1996, p. A6.

7. J. Trachtenberg, "Short Circuit: How Philips Flubbed Its U.S. Introduction of Electronic Product," *The Wall Street Journal,* June 28, 1996, p. A1.

8. Y. D. Sinakin, "Players Take Bold Step to Keep up with New Rules," *Electronic Buyers' News,* February 19, 1996, p. 50.

9. P. Hisey, "Saturn Lands First at Toys 'R' Us," *Discount Store News* 34, no. 11 (1995), pp. 6–8.

10. T. Lefton, "Looking for a Sonic Boom," *Brandweek* 39, no. 9 (1998), pp. 26–30.

11. M. A. Schilling, R. Chiu, and C. Chou, "Sony PlayStation2: Just Another Competitor?" in *Strategic Management: Competitiveness and Globalization,* 5th ed., eds. M. Hitt, D. Ireland, and B. Hoskisson (St. Paul, MN: West Publishing, 2003).

12. D. Becker and J. Wilcox, "Will Xbox Drain Microsoft?" *CNET News.com,* March 6, 2001; L. P. Norton, "Toy Soldiers," *Barrons* 81, no. 20 (2001), pp. 25–30; and S. H. Wildstrom, "It's All about the Games," *Business Week* 37, no. 63 (2001), p. 22.

13. T. Elkin, "Gearing up for Xbox Launch," *Advertising Age* 71, no. 48 (2000), p. 16.

14. D. Frankel, "Video Game Business Boffo on Big Launches," *Video Business,* December 31, 2001, p. 38.

15. A. Pham, "Nintendo's First-Half Profit Drops by 45%," *Los Angeles Times,* November 22, 2002, p. C3.

16. J. Johng, Y. Kang, M. A. Schilling, J. Sul, and M. Takanashi, "Honda Insight: Personal Hybrid," New York University teaching case, 2003.

17. Schilling, "Technological Leapfrogging"; and M. A. Schilling, "Winning the Standards Race: Building Installed Base and the Availability of Complementary Goods," *European Management Journal* 17 (1999), pp. 265–74.

18. D. Machan, "Great Job-You're Fired," *Forbes* 158, no. 7 (1996), pp. 145–46.

19. P. Kotler, *Marketing Management* (Upper Saddle River, NJ: Prentice Hall, 2003).

20. E. M. Rogers, *Diffusion of Innovations,* 3rd ed. (New York: Free Press, 1983).

21. J. Mohr, *Marketing of High-Technology Products and Innovations* (Upper Saddle River, NJ: Prentice Hall, 2001).

22. G. Moore, *Inside the Tornado* (New York: Harper Business, 1995).

23. Adapted from M. Gladwell, *The Tipping Point* (Boston: Little, Brown and Company, 2000).

24. A. L. Barabasi, *Linked: The New Science of Networks* (Cambridge, MA: Perseus Books, 2002).

25. L. F. Feick and L. L. Price, "The Market Maven: A Diffuser of Marketplace Information," *Journal of Marketing* 51 (1987), pp. 83–97.

26. E. Hatfield, J. T. Cacioppo, and R. L. Rapson, *Emotional Contagion* (Cambridge: Cambridge University Press, 1994); and H. Friedman et al. "Understanding and Assessing Nonverbal Expressiveness: The Affective Communication Test," *Journal of Personality and Social Psychology* 39, no. 2 (1980), pp. 333–51.

27. M. E. McGann, "Crossing Swords," *Dealerscope Consumer Electronics Marketplace* 37, no. 10 (1995), pp. 63–65; and Schilling, "Technological Leapfrogging."

28. R. K. Chandy and G. Tellis, "The Incumbent's Curse? Incumbency, Size, and Radical Product Innovation," *Journal of Marketing* 64, no. 3 (2000), pp. 1–18.

Index

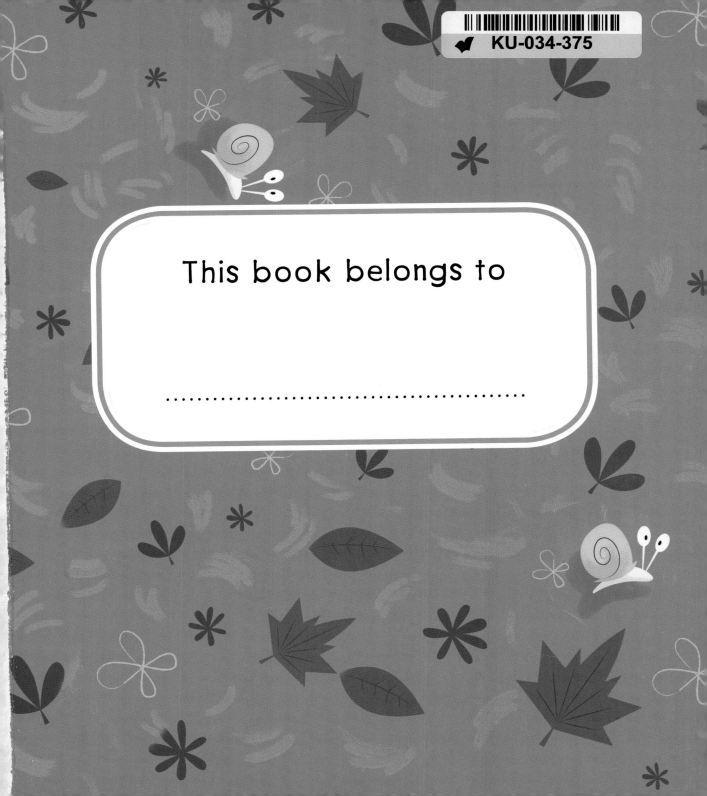

This book belongs to

....

OXFORD
UNIVERSITY PRESS

Great Clarendon Street, Oxford, OX2 6DP, United Kingdom

Oxford University Press is a department of the University
of Oxford. It furthers the University's objective of excellence
in research, scholarship, and education by publishing worldwide.
Oxford is a registered trade mark of Oxford University Press
in the UK and in certain other countries

The Bucket Rocket
Text © Catherine Baker 2017
Illustrations © Leo Antolini 2017

Can You Do This?
Text © Liz Miles 2017
Illustrations © Aleksei Bitskoff 2017

The Ant and the Carrot
Text © Narinder Dhami 2017
Illustrations © Tomislav Zlatic 2017

Thing
Text © Paeony Lewis 2017
Illustrations © Jonny Lambert 2017

Sam's Big Dinner
Text © Teresa Heapy 2017
Illustrations © Sarah Horne 217

Fang and the Dentist
Text © Kate Scott 2017
Illustrations © Ivana G. Kuman 2017

British Library Cataloguing in Publication Data
Data available

ISBN: 978-0-19-277379-1

10 9 8 7 6 5 4 3 2 1

Paper used in the production of this book is a natural, recyclable product made
from wood grown in sustainable forests. The manufacturing process conforms
to the environmental regulations of the country of origin.

Printed in China

Acknowledgements

Series Editor: Nikki Gamble

Thanks to Nadine Dillon

How this collection works

This collection offers six funny, action-packed, heart-warming and thought-provoking stories to engage your child and encourage reading progression. The stories are specially written to support and develop your child's early reading skills as they start to use letters and sounds to read simple words, and are fully in line with the phonics your child is learning at school.

How to use this book

Reading should be a shared and enjoyable experience for both you and your child. Pick a time when your child is not distracted by other things, and when they are happy to concentrate for about 10 minutes. Let them choose one or two of the stories for each reading session, so that they don't get too tired.

Read the tips on the next page, as they offer ideas and suggestions for getting the most out of this collection.

Tips for reading the stories together

Step 1 – Look together at the title page for each story before your child starts to read. What does your child think the story will be about? Use clues from the title and picture and talk about what might happen.

Step 2 — Ask your child to read the story out loud. Encourage them to stop and look at the pictures, and talk about what they are reading — either during the reading session, or afterwards. Your child will be able to read most of the words in the story, but if they struggle with a word, remind them to say the sounds in the word from left to right and then blend the sounds together to read the word, e.g. *r-o-ck-e-t, rocket*. If they come across a tricky word that they cannot sound out, simply read the word to your child, e.g. *I, the, no*.

Step 3 — When your child has finished reading the story, discuss it together. Then turn to the fun activities at the end. These will help your child think and talk about what they have read.

Contents

OXFORD
UNIVERSITY PRESS

The Bucket Rocket

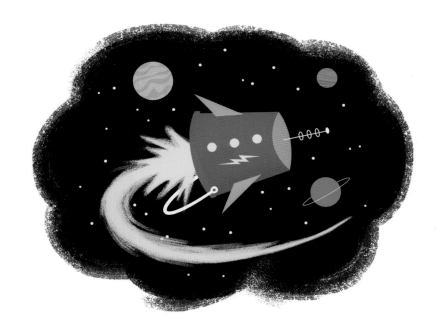

Written by Catherine Baker

Illustrated by Leo Antolini

Buzz spots Tim in a bucket.

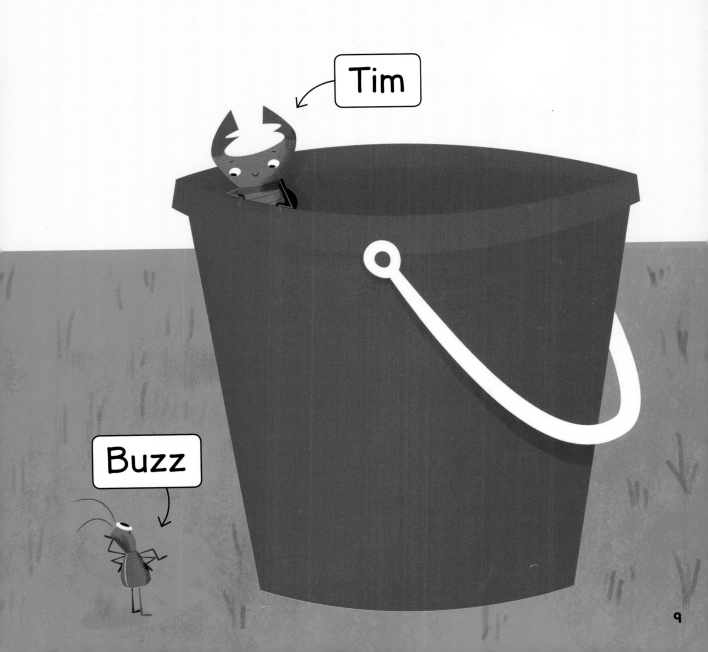

The bucket is **big**
and **red** and **cool!**

13

Tim and Buzz sit in the bucket rocket.

We will set off soon.

15

They sit and sit.

17

Buzz is fed up.

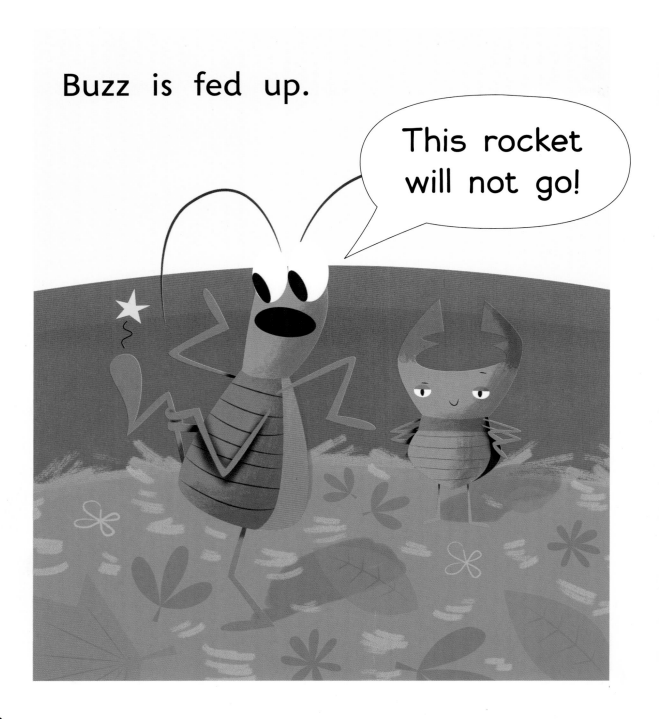

This rocket will not go!

But then the
bucket rocket tips!

21

Talk about it!

What did I say the bucket was really?

How did Buzz try to make the bucket go?

If you had a rocket, where would you go in it?

23

Rocket race

Trace a line with your finger to help the bucket rocket get to the planet!

Can You Do This?

Written by Liz Miles

Illustrated by Aleksei Bitskoff

27

28

29

30

31

No, Zac. You are the best!

32

39

Yes, Zac. I *can* catch!

Talk about it!

Why couldn't Dad swing on the climbing frame?

What happened when Dad tried to get into the cardboard castle?

How do you think Dad felt at the end of the story?

41

Odd one out

Which picture shows something Dad *can* do? Draw a circle round it.

The Ant
and the
Carrot

Written by Narinder Dhami

Illustrated by Tomislav Zlatic

The ant had a carrot.

But the carrot was big and long.

Then a rabbit got the carrot.

He bit off the top.

Yum!

That is *my* carrot!

Then the rabbit met a fox.

The rabbit ran into the forest.

Then the fox had the carrot.

She bit off the end.

Yuck!

That is *my* carrot!

The farmer was in the shed.

She saw the fox.

The fox ran into her den.

All the ants had the carrot!

Talk about it!

How did I feel when the rabbit got my carrot?

Who got the carrot after the rabbit?

Who helped me get the carrot in the end?

Spot the difference

Can you find three differences between the pictures?

Answers: The farmer's knee patch, the carrot and a leaf from the middle plant are missing.

Missing letters

Add the missing letters to finish
the words.

fo__

__armer

ra____it

__ed

sh   f

x   bb

Thing

Written by **Paeony Lewis**

Illustrated by **Jonny Lambert**

The meerkats are in the desert.
They see a spotty thing.

Fee runs to the spotty thing.

Look, Gus!

67

But Fee hooks the thing in the tree.

70

Fee jumps in her nest.

Fee has hurt her tail.

Sit down, Fee.

The meerkats see lightning.

Quick, run!

76

Soon the sun is back. The desert is hot again.

Talk about it!

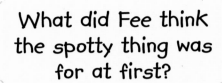

What did Fee think the spotty thing was for at first?

What happened when I jumped into the nest?

What did we use the thing for in the end?

Unjumble the letters

Unjumble the letters to make words from the story. Then match the words to the pictures.

r ee m t a k

r ee t

l ai t

n ai r

ng n igh i t l

Who has the thing?

Untangle the strings to find out which meerkat has the thing.

Gus

Fee

Sam's Big Dinner

Written by **Teresa Heapy**

Illustrated by **Sarah Horne**

85

Sam got a big pot and
a long spoon.

He put in a bit of butter.

He put in a tin of fish.

He put in a can of corn.

He put in a pot of pepper.

He put in a jug of milk.

Mum will love this!

He put in a jar of jam.

He put in a cup of coffee.

He put in a pack of mints.

He put in lots of fizzy drink.

The dinner was fizzing!

pop

fizz

It was a big mess.

Talk about it!

What did I put in first?

Why was the dinner fizzy?

What did Mum think of the dinner?

Odd one out

Draw a circle round the thing that Sam didn't put in the dinner.

Think of one more thing Sam could put in the dinner. Draw it and write its name.

_____

Fang and the Dentist

Written by **Kate Scott**

Illustrated by **Ivana G. Kuman**

Fang **moans** and **moans**.

Fang **yells** and **yells**.

Ouch, ouch! Stop that, Frog!

106

107

Otter hears Fang.

You must go to the dentist.

114

Fang sighs. Ant hops in to look.

Talk about it!

Why do you think Fang didn't want to go to the dentist at first?

How did the other animals get Fang to the dentist?

Did Fang feel better about going to the dentist by the end? Why?

Dentist dash

Draw a line to help get Fang to the dentist.

Finish the words

Choose the correct letters to finish the words from the story.

ur   oo   ee

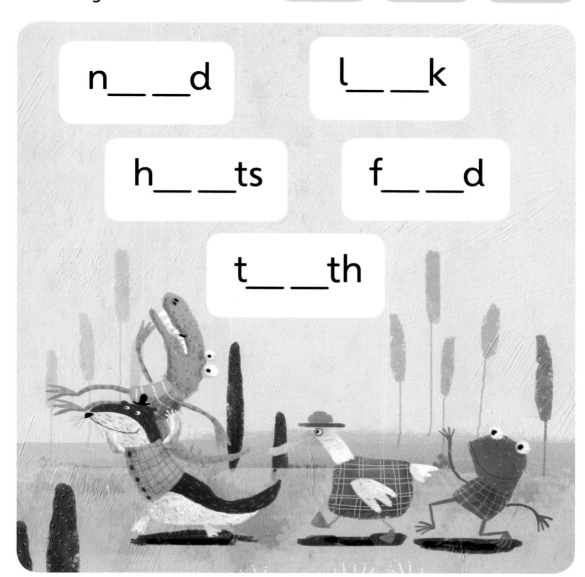

n__ __d

l__ __k

h__ __ts

f__ __d

t__ __th